RES PUBLICA

Roman Politics and Society according to Cicero

Selected and Translated by
W.K. Lacey
Sometime Scholar and Fellow of St Catherine's College, Cambridge
Professor of Classics, University of Auckland, New Zealand

and

B.W.J.G. Wilson
Sometime Scholar of Christ's College, Cambridge
Classics Master at King's School, Canterbury

PUBLISHED BY BRISTOL CLASSICAL PRESS
GENERAL EDITOR: JOHN H. BETTS

First published by Oxford University Press, 1970

Reprinted, with permission, 1978, 1990, 1994, 2001 by
Bristol Classical Press
an imprint of
Gerald Duckworth & Co. Ltd
61 Frith Street
London W1D 3JL
e-mail: inquiries@duckworth-publishers.co.uk
Website: www.ducknet.co.uk

A catalogue record for this book is available
from the British Library

ISBN 0-906515-09-2

Preface

It has been usual in England to study Ancient History by taking some text-book containing a scholar's analysis of the principal trends and problems of a given period, and further boiling down in class-work the author's synthesis into a series of 'answers' to 'questions'. Whatever the merits of such a method, one grave disadvantage is that the students often show in their examination answers that they feel a lack of immediacy: historical persons tend to become cardboard figures moving on a stage, and their actions are all too easily attributed to motives for which there is no vestige of ancient evidence.

This book is primarily a contribution to the new approach to Ancient History being promoted in England by JACT, an approach which attempts to set out the ancient evidence for the student to make up his own mind about the society he is studying and the human issues at stake in it, and to set it out in English in the hope that some students will also want to read the extracts here provided, and more, in the original language.

Cicero is the real author of this book and the extracts from his works are therefore not prefaced by his name. He was an important figure in the society of his time, though his importance is usually overshadowed in text-books by the perpetrators of the military *coups d'état*, but his ideal of a *res publica*, a community in which those who qualified themselves for government could take an independent part in it, has long outlived him, and even received lip-service from many governments which have not in fact practised it. So far as possible, we have restricted our selection to Cicero's public pronouncements; we have curtailed his exposition where it seems unnecessarily prolix or overburdened with illustrative materials from earlier Roman History and elsewhere, and we have omitted much that is merely abusive, or consists of detail relevant only to the lawcourt case in question. A number of isolated extracts (not all from Cicero's works) have also been included because they have a bearing on the life and institutions of the *res publica* of the Senate and Roman people, or the few important moments of history in which Cicero played a leading part. There is practically no military history in this book, and no attempt at an overall assessment of any one character such as Caesar, Pompey, or even Cicero himself. We have provided at the end a list of topics to which we think that users of this book may like to direct their attention. We do not offer answers to all, or indeed to any, of the questions, but we believe that the materials for reasoned answers may be found here.

Except in the selections from the *Letters to Atticus*, the text from which we have translated is the Oxford Classical Text where that is available, otherwise the latest Teubner text; we have used Dr. Shackleton Bailey's text (but our own translations) for the *Letters to Atticus*. In our references we have used the section-numbers only, and omitted reference to the chapters, and have not noted the exact point in the Latin where our translation begins or ends when these are in the course of a section. We hope that readers who wish to look up passages will not find it unduly difficult to find the place.

In reading Cicero's works, students should remember that he was frequently guilty of misrepresentation, and sometimes also of the slogan-making which is the stock in trade of politicians, but they should also bear in mind that the surviving speeches were published by Cicero in his lifetime, and therefore cannot contain statements so manifestly untrue that contemporaries could dismiss their author as a mere liar. Thus, though we must not accept any of Cicero's views without reservation, what he published must have been expected to strike some response in the public for whose attention he published them.

This is a joint book; both authors have read and commented on the parts for which the other has taken prime responsibility. We wish to express our gratitude to Dr. M. I. Finley, of Jesus College, on whose instigation the book was begun, to Mr. J. A. Crook, of St. John's College, whose comments on the introduction much improved it, to Dr. David Keeble, of St. Catharine's College, and the Geography Department of the University of Cambridge, for the map, to the University Type-writing Office, Cambridge, Mrs. M. M. T. Barham of Canterbury, for her work on the index, and to the staff of the Clarendon Press, Oxford, whose assistance in the production and co-ordination of our efforts has been invaluable, and the more so because, though the early stages in the planning of this book were conducted by discussion, the last have had to be managed by correspondence at a range of 12,000 miles.

All dates (except that immediately below) are B.C.

B. W. J. G. W.   W. K. L.
CANTERBURY, ENGLAND   AUCKLAND,
   January, 1970   NEW ZEALAND

Table of Contents

INTRODUCTION
1. Cicero's Home   *De legibus*, II, 1–6 (abridged)   1

CHAPTER I SULLA'S *RES PUBLICA*
2. Roscius of Ameria   *Pro Roscio Amerino*, 1–14   17
3. The Politics of *Municipia*   *Pro Roscio Amerino*, 15–29   21
4. The Law in Sulla's *Res Publica*   *Pro Roscio Amerino*, 124–154   26

CHAPTER II THE CHANGING *RES PUBLICA*
5. Cicero and Sicily   *Pro Plancio*, 64–66   33
6. Verres   *In Verrem* I, 1–6   34
7. The Methods and Perils of a
   Prosecutor   *In Verrem* I, 15–32   37
8. Judicial Scandals   *In Verrem* I, 35–38, 40–49   42
9. A Provincial Governor as Com-
   mander and Judge   *In Verrem* II, V, 1–4, 26–30,
   39–42   47
10. Verres' Crimes against the
    Provincials   *In Verrem* II, V, 106–115,
    126–127   51
11. Verres' Crimes against Roman
    Citizens   *In Verrem* II, V, 139–144, 160–
    170 (abridged)   57
12. Cicero and the Nobles of Sulla's
    Party   *In Verrem* II, V, 171–183   63
13. Political Manipulation   Plutarch, *Life of Lucullus*, V–VI
    (abridged)   68
14. Spartacus, the Slaves Revolt   Plutarch, *Life of Crassus*, X–XI
    (abridged)   69
15. Piracy and Conditions in Asia   Plutarch, *Life of Lucullus*, XX
    (abridged)   71
16. Pompey and Mithridates   *Pro lege Manilia*, 4–8, 11–19   72
17. Pompey the General   *Pro lege Manilia*, 27–50
    (abridged)   76
18. Precedents   *Pro lege Manilia*, 60–68   83
19. The Civil Law and Society   *Pro Caecina*, 65–75   87
20. The Ranks of Society under the Laws   *Pro Cluentio*, 145–146, 150–159   90
21. The Emergence of Caesar   Suetonius, *Divus Julius*, XI   95

Table of Contents

CHAPTER III CICERO'S *RES PUBLICA*

22. *Consul Popularis* and Land-Reform	*De lege agraria*, I, 22–27, II, 1–16, 100–103	97
23. *Senatus Consultum Ultimum*	Sallust, *Catiline* XXIX, 3	107
	Pro Rabirio (perduellionis reo), 1–31 (abridged)	107
24. Catiline	*In Catilinam* I, 1–10, 13–21	115
25. Catiline's Defence	Sallust, *Catiline*, XXXIV–XXXV	122
26. Catiline's Supporters	*In Catilinam* II, 17–23	123
27. The Conspirators Betrayed	*In Catilinam* III, 3–15	126
28. The Punishment of the Conspirators	*In Catilinam* IV, 1–7	131
29. *Concordia Ordinum*	*In Catilinam* IV, 14–24 (abridged)	134
30. The End of Catiline's Revolt, and the Aftermath		
(a) The Military Victory	Sallust, *Catiline* LXI	138
(b) Clashes with the Nobles	—	139
(c) Defence Counsel Defends Himself	*Pro Sulla*, 1–2, 21–35	139
31. Political Relationships in Rome		
(a) *Amicitia* and *Inimicitia* in the Courts	*Pro Sulla*, 48–50	146
(b) The Influence of a *Patronus*	*Pro Sulla*, 60–62	148
(c) Convictions and Sentences	*Pro Sulla*, 62–65	149

CHAPTER IV THE *RES PUBLICA* OF THE NOBLE *POPULARES*

32. A Trial for Sacrilege, and Pompey's Return		
(a) The Scandal Breaks	*Ad Atticum* I, 13, 3	151
(b) Pompey's First Impact	*Ad Atticum* I, 14, 1–4	152
(c) A Rigged Vote	*Ad Atticum* I, 14, 5	153
(d) A Rigged Trial	*Ad Atticum* I, 16, 2–6	154
33. Pompey in Politics		
(a) Pompey, the Popular Hero	*Ad Atticum* I, 16, 11	155
(b) Afranius Elected Consul	*Ad Atticum* I, 16, 12	156
34. The End of *Concordia Ordinum*		
(a) Quarrels Between Senate and *Equites*	*Ad Atticum* I, 17, 8–9	157
(b) Cicero's Isolation, and Failure	*Ad Atticum* I, 18, 1–3	158
35. Deadlock in the Senate		
(a) A Senate without a Policy	*Ad Atticum* I, 18, 6–7	159
(b) The Agrarian Law of Flavius	*Ad Atticum* I, 19, 4	159
36. New Political Alliances		
(a) Cicero and Pompey in 60	*Ad Atticum* II, 1, 6–7	160
(b) Cato's Intransigence	*Ad Atticum* II, 1, 8	161
(c) The Scene is Set for 59	*Ad Atticum* II, 3, 3–4	162

Table of Contents

37. The Year 59
    (a) Caesar and Bibulus   *Ad Atticum* II, 18, 1   163
    (b) Cicero, Pompey and Caesar from   *Ad Atticum* II, 19, 20, 22 & 23   164
38. Catiline's Friends Seek Revenge   *Pro Flacco*, 1–5   165
39. Greek Communities' Decrees   *Pro Flacco*, 14–19   167
40. Racial Prejudices   *Pro Flacco*, 64–68   170
41. The Political Character of Trials   *Pro Flacco*, 94–103   172
42. Clodius, Cicero's Exile and Return   —   175
43. Rome in Cicero's Absence
    (a) Riots and Disorders   *Post reditum in senatu*, 3–7   178
    (b) Cicero's Recall   *Post reditum in senatu*, 24–28   180
44. The Pleasures of a Returned Exile   *Post reditum ad Quirites*, 2–5   182

CHAPTER V RELIGION, LAW, AND VIOLENCE IN THE
RES PUBLICA

45. The Roman State Religion: 1. The *Pontifices*
    (a) Their Social Standing   *De domo sua*, 1–2   185
    (b) Intimidation   *De domo sua*, 8   186
    (c) Adoptions   *De domo sua*, 34–37   187
    (d) Laws against Individuals   *De domo sua*, 44–47   189
    (e) A Family's Gods   *De domo sua*, 108–112   190
    (f) Experience in Religious Matters   *De domo sua*, 117–118   192
46. The Roman State Religion.   —   194
    2. The Sibylline Books
47. The Roman State Religion.   *De haruspicum responso*, 18–19   194
    3. The *Haruspices*
48. Riots   *Ad Quintum fratem* II, 3, 2   196
49. Old *Populares* and New Ones   *De haruspicum responso*, 40–41,   198
         43–46, 60–end
50. Sestius   *Pro Sestio*, 1–7   202
51. Violence as the Antithesis of   *Pro Sestio*, 91–92   206
    Civilization
52. Political Morality – Who were the   *Pro Sestio*, 96–102   207
    Optimates?
53. Real and False Popular Sentiments
    (a) The Support enjoyed by   *Pro Sestio*, 103–127   210
    Genuine *Populares*
    (b) The Popular View of Cicero's   *Pro Sestio*, 131–132   222
    Return
54. Principles for Political Life   *Pro Sestio*, 136–139   223
55. Realignments, Ravenna and Luca   —   225
56. *Inimicitia*, and the interests of the   *De provinciis consularibus*, 1–2,   227
    Res publica   18–20, 23–31, 38–40, 44–47
         (abridged) *Pro Balbo*, 57–62

Table of Contents

CHAPTER VI SOCIAL ASPECTS OF THE *RES PUBLICA*

57. The Intemperance of Youth	*Pro Caelio*, 18, 25, 28–30	239
58. Advice to a Noble Woman		
(a) An Ancestor Speaks	*Pro Caelio*, 30–34	241
(b) A Modern Philosophy for Girls	*Pro Caelio*, 36	244
59. An Old-fashioned Education, and a Modern One	*Pro Caelio*, 39–47 (abridged)	244
60. An Immodest Woman's Entourage		
(a) A Woman more Sinning than Sinned against	*Pro Caelio*, 48–50	247
(b) Like Mistress, Like Slaves	*Pro Caelio*, 57–58	248
61. A Plot at the Baths	*Pro Caelio*, 61–65	249
62. Politics After the Conference at Luca	*Pro Plancio*, 93–94	252
63. Roman Elections		253
(a) The Roman People's Right to Choose	*Pro Plancio*, 5–13	254
(b) Noble Birth, and Local Support	*Pro Plancio*, 14–24	258
(c) A Virtuous Youth, an Outspoken Father	*Pro Plancio*, 29–35	262
(d) Bribery and Popularity	*Pro Plancio*, 37–39, 43–45, 48	265
(e) Electroral Processes, Nobles and 'New Men'	*Pro Plancio*, 49–55, 59–62	268
64. Pompey and the Revival of the Nobles in Politics	—	273

CHAPTER VII THE PROVINCES IN THE *RES PUBLICA*

65. Advice to Quintus (In the Province of Asia, 60)	*Ad Quintum fratrem* I, 1 (abridged)	275
66. Moral Issues in Government	*De officiis* I, 72–89 (abridged) II, 72–77 (abridged)	279
67. Cicero as a Provincial Governor (Of Cilicia, 51–50)	*Ad familiares* XV, 1 & 2 (abridged) *Ad Atticum* V, 16–21, VI, 1–2 (abridged)	282

CHAPTER VIII THE END OF THE *RES PUBLICA*

68. Civil War and Reconstruction		290
(a) Conciliation and Compromise Can Save the *Res publica*	*Pro Marcello*, 13–18	291
(b) Caesar's Duty to the *Res publica*, and to Himself	*Pro Marcello*, 21–32	293
(c) Caesar's *Clementia*	*Ad familiares* VI, 6, 8–10	298
69. Caesar and the Lost *Res publica*		
(a) Changing Times	*Ad familiares* IX, 17 & 15, 2–4	299

Table of Contents

(b) A Woman's Place in the Free *Res publica*	*Ad familiares* IV, 5 & IV, 6 (abridged)	301
(c) Arbitrary Government	*Philippic* II, 78–84	303
70. Caesar's Murder and the Sequel		
(a) The Conspirators' Motives	*Philippic* II, 25–29	305
(b) After the Ides of March	*Philippic* II, 88–93	307
(c) The Assassins' Failure	from *Ad Atticum* XIV	310
(d) The View of a Friend of Caesar's	*Ad familiares* XI, 28, 2–5	311
71. Antony's *Res publica*		
(a) Brutus and Cassius Protest	*Ad familiares* XI, 3, 1 & 3–4	313
(b) Cicero's View	*Ad familiares* X, 1	314
72. Octavian, and Cicero's Attempt to Save the *Res publica*		315
(a) December, 44	*Ad familiares* XI, 5 & 6 (abridged)	316
	Philippic III, 1–9 (abridged)	319
(b) Octavian's Family	*Philippic* III, 15–17	
(c) The Last Hope of Saving the *Res publica*	*Philippic* III, 28–39	321
Postscript		326
Roman Money		328
Suggested topics for study		329
Index		331

Introduction

1. *Res Publica*

Res publica was the Romans' usual name for their state. *Res publica* literally means 'public business', and this, says Cicero, with his typical and matter-of-fact Roman bluntness, means *res populi* – 'the people's business'. And who are 'the people'? 'The people' is 'A union of a number of men, acknowledging each other's common rights, and pursuing in common their advantage or interest'. *Res publica* then is the community, and the business of such a union of men, no more, and no less.

An aggressive 'common pursuit of their advantage or interest' was, regrettably, almost the only imperial policy the Roman Republic knew; relations with foreign states, of whatever political organization, were subject to this principle. The Romans had a theory that only defensive war was admissible, but the modern world is sufficiently conscious of the meaninglessness of such a claim not to be deceived.

The pursuit of their own advantage was also their basic principle in the government of the provinces, though here too there was an important theoretical principle moderating practice; this was that the Romans should act with trustworthiness (*fides*). The Romans believed that *fides* was an important ingredient in a man's character, and that those who surrendered to the Romans surrendered to the *fides* of the general commanding, who would be responsible as *patronus* (see 8 below) for securing for them a square deal. This had worked well enough for the beginnings of empire, but the notion that the *res publica* collectively should take over the undertakings given by the individuals in command of Roman forces was slow to grow. In Cicero's day however there were some, and Cicero was amongst them, who had begun to understand that government involves collective concern by the governing classes for the welfare of the governed.

'Acknowledging the common rights of others' involved renouncing arbitrary or personal rule, or rule by a small group of men, what the Romans called a '*factio*'; for this they had a wide range of derogatory words – '*regnum*' or '*dominatio*' being two of the favourite. *Res publica* meant that all citizens had a right to participate in political life – not to participate equally, but to participate.

'Nothing is so unequal as complete equality' Cicero once remarked, and he is certainly not untypical in this attitude. In the *res publica*, a man's position was, and the Romans would certainly have added, 'should be', governed by his contributions to the state. In early times this meant contributions in money to the treasury and in personal service in the army, but in Cicero's day the Romans had not paid any tribute for three generations, and, though military service was the preliminary to a political career, it was often regarded as a tiresome obligation. It was one of the weaknesses of the *res publica* in fact that the class who claimed to govern ceased to share the sympathies of the troops, or to have their interests at heart.

2. The Nobility, Senators and *Equites*

Nominally a democracy in that 'what the people has commanded is to be valid at law', the *res publica* was in fact organized as an aristocracy – or oligarchy. It was governed by a small circle of noble families, perhaps fifty, called '*nobiles*'. They were extensively intermarried, and their ideals, as expressed by the poet Lucretius, were 'to compete alike with native talent and high birth, and to come out on top, striving by night and day with unremitting labour, in order to enjoy abundant wealth and control the business of the state'. This nobility virtually monopolized, either by tenure in person or by patronage, the highest offices of the *res publica*, military, political and religious. The lower aristocracy, that is those members of the Senate (about six hundred in total number in Cicero's day) who were not nobles, were drawn from a rather wider circle of men, and it was not too hard for men of ambition and sufficient wealth to be admitted to this circle. Sufficient wealth however was an essential prerequisite, and, in theory, senators who lacked the minimum wealth qualifications, or were in debt, were struck off. This however did not happen frequently, and there were often impoverished men in the Senate.

Wealthy men who were not in the Senate were known as *equites*, or knights, because at one time they had formed the state's cavalry, earning their privileged position by the service of maintaining a horse for the national army.

Many *equites* were businessmen, and government contracts were one of the chief fields for business-activity; a feature of the *res publica* was that the collection of most taxes was regarded as a contract, and these contracts were managed by business-syndicates who paid a lump sum to the Roman treasury for the privilege of collecting taxes, and recovered their outlay from the provincials from whom they collected. These tax-contractors and their agents were known as *publicani* (the publicans of the Bible). Other *equites* were bankers and money-lenders (indistinguishable professions) or landowners, including the governing classes of the municipalities of the Italian peninsula; an example of this latter class was Cicero's father (see 9 below). Many senators avoided, or flouted, the laws against taking part in business; they lent money either directly, or through an agent, and they took part in the tax-contracting syndicates by owning shares rather as a modern wealthy man may own shares in a variety of public companies.

Senators were landowners, and some also had an income from a legal profession, as Cicero did. Roman lawyers did not charge fees, but they could and did accept gifts. Their ownership of the land made the Roman nobles very anxious about its disposition; as it was one of their principal sources of income, and their field for investment, they were very unwilling to tolerate measures designed to distribute it to the poor, or to prevent wealthy men from acquiring large estates. Their other sources of income were the rewards of public life; to govern a province almost guaranteed a profit, and to command an army in a successful campaign was an even surer road to a fortune.

Public life however was expensive; candidates for office had to put on a show; a retinue was required, and largesse had to be distributed; (it was not bribery to distribute largesse to the members of your own constituency (or tribe)). Public men had also to contribute towards the expenses of their friends for them to reciprocate, and the consequence of the need for money was that the more ambitious (and the less scrupulous) borrowed large sums of money to secure election to a post which would enable them to recover their outlay, and distributed bribes on a large scale for this purpose.

3. Roman Criminal Courts (*Quaestiones Perpetuae*).

Bribery both of electors and of jurors was illegal, though it was widely practised. So was extortion in the provinces, and the frequency of the laws to check both offences shows their prevalence. Sulla reorganized (82–81) the Roman system of criminal jurisdiction by setting up a permanent court (though the jurors changed annually) to deal with each of the main criminal offences; praetors presided over six of these, the remaining one being delegated to a more junior magistrate. The principal courts in which Cicero appeared were those concerned with bribery (*de ambitu*), extortion in the provinces (*de rebus repetundis*), violence or rioting (*de vi*), and murder by assassination or poison (*inter sicarios et de veneficiis*). Other courts dealt with treason (*de maiestate*), peculation (*de peculatu*), and forgery (*de falso*); from time to time special courts were also set up to deal with other offences, such as sacrilege, for which there was no standing court.

As is evident from Cicero's speeches these *quaestiones* were not at all like modern British assizes. They were held in public in the forum and the audience were involved in the case, often favouring one side or the other; considerations other than the simple question whether the accused was or was not guilty of the offence alleged were normally adduced. We find orators raking up irrelevant scandals about the private life of the accused, or the accuser, or the witnesses, and their respective public services were also thought to be worth bringing into the issue. Prosecuting a prominent citizen was a young man's normal way of making an entrance into politics; the victim chosen for prosecution was an indication of the political line he intended to take, so was the zeal with which he pressed his case. There were quite frequently compromised cases in which the prosecutor made no serious attempt to win, and to act in this way was to offer political alliance to the nominal victim. The jury too could be bribed, and very often it was; the notorious Verres, prosecuted by Cicero for extortion, is said to have said that the largest part of his ill-gotten gains would be devoted to bribing the court who would try him.

Prosecution was part of the political game; the consequence of conviction was loss of status because the convicted man went into exile to avoid punishment, and thus relinquished all part in the *res publica*, the public business of Rome. There was thus every incentive to bribe jurors, and the expenses of public life, and its scanty rewards for those not fortunate or successful, made jurors venal, especially senatorial jurors. Being part of the political game, prosecutions were sometimes intended for purely political purposes, merely to show a flag perhaps, and were not seriously pressed for this reason; they were also sometimes launched merely to prevent a rival from being a candidate in an election, and were dropped when the election was over. But many were pressed seriously, and thus they reflect the fierce quality of Roman public life; the enmities engendered in criminal cases were sometimes of great bitterness, increased by the coarse personal abuse which appears to have been the stock in trade of ancient orators. In trials very often were made strong bonds of alliance (*amicitia*) and enmity (*inimicitia*) which governed a man's whole public career.

4. *Dignitas*, and Offices (*Honores*)

A man's position and rank or standing (*dignitas*) was measured by a combination of the offices he had held in the state, and the opinion other people, especially senators, had of him. The highest office, that of consul, made the holder and his descendants nobles (*nobiles*). Families however, to retain their full standing as nobles, had to renew their rank (*nobilitas*) each generation. In normal circumstances men were not eligible for the consulate until they were 40 or 42 years old, and had been praetor. As there were only 2 consuls and 8 praetors every year, it is obvious that not all praetors could hope to become consul. The praetorship conferred a lower nobility. The two praetorships regarded as senior (though the tasks of the respective praetors were determined by lot) were *praetor urbanus* and *praetor peregrinus*; between them, they presided over all cases brought under the civil law (*ius civile*), and all other non-criminal cases. The others presided over the *quaestiones perpetuae* (see 3 above). Ex-consuls and ex-praetors were the cadre from which the provincial governors were drawn. The only obligatory magistracy before the praetorship was that of quaestor, of whom there were 20 annually, but leading politicians aspired to be aedile, an office which allowed a man who

was ambitious to progress further to make a display by giving games
or plays or other spectacles; there were four aediles elected every
year. The minimum age for quaestorship was about 30, that is, in
theory, after about 10 years of military service. The quaestors
managed the finances of the higher magistrates both at home and
abroad, and could act as their deputies.

The consuls were in charge of the state for their year of office.
With the priests (*pontifices*) they were in charge of the state's religion;
they presided in the Senate, and at the principal elections, and had
the right to address the people and submit legislation for approval.
They also had the right to issue orders even to senators, and to
prohibit anyone from actions of which they disapproved. Their
powers were limited in fact only by the laws, and by the potential
vetoes of their exactly equal colleague, and of the ten tribunes of the
people.

The tribunes of the people (usually called tribunes for short) were
originally not magistrates, but had represented the common soldiers
before their commanders while on campaign. However, they had for
long successfully asserted the right to veto any act of the consuls or
of the Senate, and to prevent the Senate from meeting, and the
consuls from summoning a meeting. They could themselves summon
meetings, harangue the people, and put proposals to them which
had the force of law. Various attempts had been made by the nobles
to curb the tribunes' powers, but the simplest method had proved
to be for the plebeian nobles (who were numerous) to hold the
office themselves, and thus, by their own vetoes, to prevent their
colleagues from challenging the nobility when it was united. The
tribunate however was open only to plebeians, a rule which was one
of the last vestiges of the struggle between them and the patricians
for the full incorporation of the former into the political life of the
res publica. It was one of the slogans of Roman politics that the
Senate and magistrates maintained the standing (*dignitas*) of their
order, the tribunes upheld the freedom (*libertas*) of the people.

5. Freedom (*libertas*), the Tribal Assembly

The freedom of the Roman people was something less than
absolute. Individuals were free from arbitrary arrest, and could
claim protection, even in provinces, against arbitrary actions by

magistrates which affected their person, or their purse above a certain amount. They were also guaranteed their civic rights and personal freedom under the laws – what the Romans called their *caput* – and their possessions legally obtained and maintained, but in a political sense *libertas* meant no more than the freedom to vote, that is, to vote in person in their own constituency or tribe.

In Roman assemblies a decision was reached by the votes of a majority of tribes (or centuries, see 6 below): an individual citizen's vote helped to determine only the vote of his group (tribe or century), and these groups were so arranged that the city poor, or many of them, were virtually disfranchised by being enrolled in the four urban tribes. In these, the numbers of citizens available to vote was greater than in any of the thirty-one rural tribes, and the urban tribes appear never to have had the right of voting first. This was an important right, since the vote of the first group was announced before the others voted, and it carried very great weight in the ultimate result, especially in elections. The rural poor who lived at any distance from the city were also virtually disfranchised, since voting took place in Rome only, and there was no system of representation or proxy-voting.

The Roman citizen did not enjoy the freedom of public speech; no Roman could mount the rostrum in the forum and address a public meeting without the consent of the magistrates and tribunes, who alone enjoyed the right to summon a public meeting and debate (*ius agendi cum populo*). In consequence, a Roman assembly was not a deliberative body; it listened to speeches, it made policy in that it approved or rejected a policy already formulated elsewhere, or laws already drafted and scrutinized elsewhere, but it did not debate. The ordinary Roman citizen could express his views only by failing to turn up to listen to a speaker with whom he knew he would not agree, or by going off to listen to a rival speaker, or (certainly in Cicero's day) by shouting, barracking, jeering or applauding loudly.

Expressions of public opinion of this sort took place in the theatre, where they were rather expected, and individual politicians could find themselves being hissed or booed when they entered, or received in stony silence, or, if they were popular, they could be welcomed by shouts of applause and cheers. Such expressions of opinion could be spontaneous, but they could also be organized: we hear of rhythmical shouting and clapping of the sort organized by sections of the crowds at modern British football matches, or by American cheer-leaders; it was a practice on which Cicero passed some caustic remarks. This habit spread from the theatre, where it was relatively harmless, to the forum, and the voting-gangways in the *comitium* at the end of the forum, and to the *Campus Martius*, where the most important votes were taken, especially in elections. This resulted in rioting at public meetings and intimidation at elections and meetings to vote on laws, and, at times when passions were most strongly roused, even led to gang-warfare in the streets. Cicero rightly saw – and said – that **this** sort of thing in fact destroyed the freedom of the Roman people.

6. Elections, the Centuriate Assembly

Since all Roman magistrates served for one year, and were in-eligible for immediate re-election except to the tribunate, to which re-election had occurred two generations before Cicero's career began, (and in the crisis of the Germans' invasion of 105–100, and in this crisis only in the past 100 years, to the consulate) elections formed a very important part of the Romans' political calendar. For elections (as for all other votes) the Roman people was divided into constituencies, either into the 35 tribes (4 urban and 31 rural) which voted each as a single entity, of which 18 constituted a suffi-cient majority, or else into centuries. The exact arrangements for the assembly by centuries (centuriate assembly, *comitia centuriata*) are not known for certain, since Cicero and all his contemporaries knew so well how they worked that they never stopped to explain it to juries or to other people. It was, in theory, the Roman people under arms, and therefore met outside the sacred limits of the city, on the *Campus Martius* (Field of Mars), and was summoned by a bugle. On the Janiculum hill a red flag flew which was to be lowered in the event of an Etruscan raid; and citizens could appear at this assembly in armour (defensive armour), as Cicero did when presiding at the consular elections for 62, held under his presidency in 63. In this theoretically military assembly, those who were liable to bear the brunt of the fighting, the heavy infantry, had a preponderant influence. One of their centuries always voted first, and it is most likely that their centuries, with the 18 centuries of Knights, or cavalry, enjoyed 88 out of the 197 available votes. This meant that a candidate unanimously favoured by the rich needed to collect no more than 11 votes out of all the other centuries. The poorest citizens were all lumped together in a single century known contemptuously as *capite censi* (mere heads) and voted last, which meant, in effect, not at all, since voting stopped when a majority was achieved. Since this assembly, not that organized by tribes, elected the most important magistrates, it is obvious that the poor had very little chance to express themselves effectively in elections.

7. The Senate

Was the sole official deliberative body in Rome; it was '*publicum consilium*', the council of the *res publica*. It met under the consuls or, if they were not in Rome, under the praetors and/or tribunes. It discussed and formulated policy, especially foreign policy; it heard embassies, sent replies, accepted or rejected alliances, and made recommendations for war and peace to the people. At home, it called for legislation, criticized proposals by magistrates, and submitted legislation to detailed review, even claiming from time to time it could annul proposals which had been passed by the people because they were improperly passed, or illegal for some reason or other. The Senate had life-long membership, it included all men who had any political experience, and the members received no pay. Throughout Cicero's political career, admission was obtained by holding the quaestorship, and the senators were ranked in accordance with the highest office they had held.

The Senate debated freely, but in accordance with strict conventions which gave weight to the senior members. The presiding magistrate opened the debate either by making a speech, or by addressing the senior senator of his choice with the question 'What do you think'? (*quid censes*), and either prescribing the subject, or leaving it open by saying 'about the *res publica*' (*de re publica*). The senior senators were the ex-consuls (*consulares*), of whom the first was known as *princeps senatus* (Doyen of the Senate), but there was, in Cicero's heyday, a period in which there was no *princeps senatus* appointed. By convention, however, the consuls-elect, when they were known, were called first, but thereafter the order was chosen by the president, which meant that a man's standing (as reflected by the place he held in the order of speaking) was always liable to be the subject of comment. The place amongst his peers in which a man was called, and the attention with which he was heard, reflected his authority (*auctoritas*). Less senior members when called could either speak, or merely express agreement with an earlier speaker, or, especially if very junior, cross the floor of the House to sit beside the senior speaker with whom they agreed. Consequently it was thought a mark of disgrace to be sitting with only a few supporters, and when that was liable to happen men tended to stay away. A massive staying away in protest against a consul's administration is also recorded, especially in Caesar's consulship in 59, and under Antony's arbitrary rule in 44.

Debates could be very long when conducted in this way: we hear of several which lasted for days, and at times proposals could be frustrated by interminable debate; on one occasion Cicero remarks in a letter that on the first day he 'made a long speech' and the next day 'we agreed to make shorter ones'. On a number of others we hear of attempts to filibuster which sometimes succeeded, and a question was talked out; one such was Cato's filibuster in 60, which prevented Caesar from gaining the concession (*privilegium*) of being allowed to present his name by proxy as a consular candidate for the year 59. Senatorial speeches, it is also important to remember, were liable to interruption by other senators; we hear of several occasions on which Cicero had an altercation: one with P. Clodius is recorded in a letter of 60; another, with L. Piso, was written up into the speech *In Pisonem*: it arose when Piso complained of Cicero's conduct towards him when he returned from his province of Macedonia in 53.

But the Senate was an essential part of the *res publica*; the official designation of the Roman state was SPQR (*Senatus Populus Que Romanus*, the Senate and Roman People), and this reflects the true status of the Senate.

8. *Paterfamilias* and *Patronus*

Collectively, the senators were addressed as *Patres Conscripti* (usually translated literally as Conscript Fathers), but not even the Romans knew the exact meaning of *Conscripti*. *Patres* however reflects the idea that they were the heads of the families of which the state was composed. The Roman *paterfamilias* had enormously wide powers over his family; in early times he was the sole owner of property, even his wife's dowry passing into his possession, and she herself into his power (*manus*), like one of his children, over whom he had the power of life and death, not merely at birth (as in Greece) but at any time, by judicial sentence. This social pattern had been much modified by Cicero's day, especially in respect of the women's position. Women still had to have a guardian to enable them to perform legal acts, but they had, in theory as well as in practice, the ability to put pressure on their guardians to allow them considerable freedom of action in respect of their property. Adult sons too were often emancipated (freed, that is, from the power of their *pater-familias*). The extent to which this happened, however, should not be exaggerated; as Cicero's speeches show, even in the upper classes young men could count it a point in their favour in the eyes of a jury if they had remained in the power of their *paterfamilias*. Epigraphical evidence too shows several families in which the women came fully into the power of their husband, by the old custom of marriage *cum manu*.

The family (*familia*) of a Roman noble comprised much more than his immediate relatives; it included slaves, who were very numerous, and the slaves to whom he or his father had given freedom (freedmen, *liberti*). Though not strictly in the *familia*, he also had large numbers of humble retainers (*clientes*) to whom he was patron (*patronus*). The *patronus/cliens* relationship is one of the most important features of Roman society. It had derived from the time when only the rich and powerful had any knowledge of the civil law, and these men had acted as judges of the disputes between humble folk. In Cicero's day, all the non-criminal litigation of the Romans was sent by the praetor for trial before private individuals whose judgements were binding, without any right of appeal to the public courts. A *patronus* however spoke for his *clientes* if they had to appear in a court, and he would help to promote their economic interests. In return they helped to promote his, and his political interests as well. A large following of *clientes* (*clientela*) was therefore valuable to a political man, and in Cicero's day these *clientelae* might embrace whole provinces, and even client-kings and foreign rulers on the borders of the Roman world. One result of Pompey's settlement after the Mithridatic wars was that most of the Eastern Mediterranean world came into his *clientela*.

A *paterfamilias* always – by custom – acted in consultation with a *consilium*, a group of friends whom he summoned to advise him. In this, the private *consilium* mirrors the *publicum consilium* of the Senate advising the magistrates. A man's *consilium* met in his own house at his own invitation and advised him on the matters he put before them. They would influence his mind in giving his decisions, and would be expected to help him in his public life in formulating speeches on policy, or in drafting proposals or laws for presentation to the Senate and people. Such people were his friends (*amici*), and a man's standing (*dignitas*) might also be gauged from the number and quality of the *amici* on whom he could count.

A Roman noble's house thus resembled a baron's castle, or the Palace of a Bishop Palatine of Durham or Lancaster in that it would be full of retainers (though they would not sleep or feed there); there would also be humble folk with petitions for help in all manner of things, cases for judgement or adjudication, or for advice on the law. It would also be frequented by the ambitious, the seekers of place and promotion, or of position in the patronage of the noble; there would also be young men of lesser families gaining experience in public life and making useful contacts, and enlarging their knowledge and experience of the civil law by listening to judgements and their exposition. Around the noble *paterfamilias* himself there would be his *consilium*, advising him when asked, and influencing his mind. The early morning was the customary time for people to assemble in the houses of the great, and to have the house full of callers was a mark of standing (*dignitas*).

In a social structure of this sort inequality was obvious, and was fully accepted as normal by the Romans.

9. Italy, the *Municipia* and the *Res Publica*

The organization of Roman society and politics was reflected in the towns (*municipia*) of all Italy south of the Po. During Cicero's lifetime all the inhabitants of this area became Roman citizens, but, though this ended their former independent municipal governments, they still had some measure of local autonomy. Within their own towns there were local aristocracies holding the local magistracies and forming the local Senate (*decuriones*); these aristocracies were largely comprised of the local landowners, though there seems not to have been any objection to businessmen serving on local councils. Cicero's family were of this landowning class. His grandfather had been a prominent local councillor at Arpinum, a town lying in the foothills of the Apennines, occupying lands which had once belonged to the Volscians. Arpinum had been part of the Roman state since 188, when it was incorporated along with 2 other small towns of the neighbourhood.

Most of Italy, however, had been incorporated in 90, as a result of a rebellion known as the Social war. This incorporation had led to fierce political struggles, and a civil war, and there was undoubtedly some resentment felt by the Roman nobles against 'new men' from the *municipia*, which was aggravated by the fact that the influx of voters of equestrian standing undermined the control over the *comitia centuriata* (and hence over the consular elections) which the nobles had previously managed to retain.

10. The *Res Publica* in Cicero's Day

Res publica is therefore a complex fabric, and an almost untranslatable word. Sometimes it means the Roman state itself, sometimes the constitution of the state, or its organs, sometimes the underlying society, sometimes the freedom implicit in the exercise of free speech, and the free choice of *amici* and *inimici*, and of policy to be advocated.

In Cicero's day the *res publica* was failing to cope with its problems. Modern writers have provided a variety of explanations, but to Cicero, as a contemporary politician, the fault lay in the greed, ambition, corruption or folly of his opponents. He saw himself as trying to preserve its integrity, and to maintain the superiority of the civil authorities over the military – in his own words, 'cedant arma togae, concedat laurea linguae' ('let arms give place to civilians' gowns, and soldiers' victories to those of orators').

I. CICERO'S BIRTH AND HOME

Cicero, or to give his full Roman name, Marcus Tullius, son of Marcus, grandson of Marcus, Cicero, was born on the country estate of his parents, their first child, on 3 January, 106.

He described his childhood home in a dialogue with his school-friend T. Pomponius Atticus, a treatise on the laws for his ideal state, written between 51 and the death of Caesar.

De legibus II, 1–6 (abridged):

Atticus: We have walked long enough now, and you must start a new topic of discussion; would you like to leave here and sit down on the island which is in the River Fibrenus – that, I think, is the name of that other river there – and turn to the rest of our talk?

Marcus: Of course; I love that place whether I want to write or read, or think something over.

Atticus: For my part, I can't have too much of it, especially as I have come at this time of year; I've no use for these stately villas and marble floors and ornamental ceilings . . . I used to think that there was nothing in these districts but rocks and mountains, and indeed your speeches and poems encouraged me to do so, so I used to be surprised that you liked this place so much; but now it's the opposite. I'm surprised that there's anywhere you would rather be when you are out of Rome.

Marcus: Whenever I can get way for a few days, especially at this season, I make for this lovely, healthy spot; but I can't often do it. Then of course I have another purely personal reason . . . this is my native place, and my brother's too; we belong to one of the oldest families in the district. Here are our family shrines, our roots, many traces of our forefathers. This villa here, as you see it now, was of course reconstructed and extended by my father. As he was an invalid, he spent virtually his whole career here in literary pursuits. Anyway, in this very place, I tell you, I was born, in my grandfather's lifetime, when the house was still small, and much more traditional in appearance . . .

Atticus: But here we are now on the island; really, this is the loveliest place. See how the Fibrenus stream is split by this point – just like the prow of a ship – and how the two branches run along the sides, lapping all the way along it till the stream comes back again into one, very quickly too; there's only enough land enclosed to do for a small recreation-ground. Then – as if it had done the only thing it was meant to do, to provide us with a site here for our discussion – it makes a leap straight into the Liris; then, like a plebeian adopted by a patrician, it loses its own humble name, and it makes the Liris much cooler. I've never come across a colder stream, though I've come across a good many; I could hardly bear to put my foot in it.

Cicero's father moved his family to Rome while Cicero and his brother, Quintus, were boys, in the interests of their education. He established his home in the unfashionable district known as Carinae, on the Esquiline Hill. Pompey's father also established his family in this quarter, and at the foot of the hill, in the 'teeming Suburra', lived the family of Julius Caesar. Cicero later claimed that he had known Caesar as a young man, and they both attended the classes of the famous Molon of Rhodes during Sulla's reign in Rome. Cicero was called up for military service in the Social war, and served one campaign under Pompey's father, in his consulate in 89. Whether through ill-health, or merely through a dislike of the army, he resumed his studies as soon as he could, and chose the civil law, which he studied in the company of Atticus, who says (*De legibus* I, 13) 'I remember from the time you began to study as a boy, you took an interest in the civil law, when I too used to go regularly to Scaevola's house'. Scaevola was the greatest jurist of the day, who (*Brutus*, 306) 'although he did not offer to teach anyone, nevertheless, by the replies he gave to those who consulted him, used to teach those who took the trouble to listen'. This is an example of what the famous writer on architecture, Vitruvius, who wrote under Augustus, describes (VI, 5, 1–2): 'Ordinary men do not need entrance courts and so on for their houses, in the grand style, because such men go round to the houses of others, rather than having others visit them. Money-lenders, and those who take the tax-farming contracts (*publicani*) have houses that are comfortable and secure. Lawyers and orators require houses that are more handsome and spacious in order to accommodate their audiences'. Thus, to be part of the audience listening to the judgements of the learned was the normal way for a young man to learn both the law and the practice of oratory.

I. Sulla's *Res publica*

Rome however in this period was more concerned with civil war than with eloquence. The question of who was to command the armies against Mithridates, king of Pontus on the South coast of the Black Sea, brought Sulla to march on Rome in 88. This coup was followed by the counter-coup of Cinna in 87, 3 years free of armed conflict, then Sulla's second invasion, in 84, and the civil war which culminated in the bloody battle at the Colline Gate on November 1, 82.

Sulla's dictatorship then followed, with its policy of ruthless genocide against the Samnites of the southern Appennines, who had formed the mainstay of his opponents, and the proscription of his Roman enemies. The latter programme took the form of proclamations, merely verbal at first, but later codified into lists, of men whose life was forfeit, their property confiscated, and their children debarred from public life. There was no trial, no investigation. Whole cities were treated in the same way; their lands were confiscated, their people driven off their farms to starve, or to stay on to work their own ancestral farms as the tenant, or even the virtual serf, of the demobilized veteran to whom they had been given. In Rome, opposition was silenced; the dictatorship, unused for more than a century, was revived and used to sweep away the traditional rights and immunities of the tribunes; a new constitution was drawn up, with the Senate established as sole arbiter of law and justice, the sole source of legislation and policy. All opposition was cowed; Etruria and Campania were held down by colonies of veterans; clubs (*collegia*) of liberated slaves held the city populace in dread; even the upper classes had witnessed, and could scarcely have failed to note the lesson of, the example made of Q. Lucretius Ofella, a faithful lieutenant of the dictator, cut down at his orders openly in the forum because he insisted on standing for the consulship while still unqualified.

2. ROSCIUS OF AMERIA

In the year 81, Sulla was dictator and consul simultaneously. His settlement proceeded, and it was declared that no more proscription-lists would be issued after June 1st. Later that year, Sextus Roscius, a wealthy landowner of Ameria, was murdered in the streets of Rome. His name was then added to the proscription-lists; his lands were sold for a song; subsequently his son was accused of parricide lest he expose the plot. The authors of this were two of Roscius' relatives, who had employed – and rewarded – Sulla's favourite, Chrysogonus, a freed slave (freedman), as the means for getting Roscius' name added to the proscription-list. Roscius however had powerful friends, who invited Cicero to undertake the defence when his trial took place in 80. Sulla was still dictator, and this was the first case to be tried in the newly reconstituted criminal courts – the *quaestiones perpetuae*; the jurors were all senators. Cicero opened his speech by claiming that his youth enabled him to enjoy freedom of speech, and by making it clear that it was Chrysogonus who was the real villain. He also points out the uncertainty of justice in Sulla's *res publica*.

Pro Roscio Amerino, 1–14:

1   I can well imagine, gentlemen of the jury, that you are somewhat surprised that I, of all people, should be leading for the defence when there are so many eminent counsel and distinguished persons present here in court today. After all, I am a young man and lack both their abilities and their reputations. All of them believe, as I do, that an injustice has been done, an injustice that is the product of an unprecedented crime, and all of them believe that the victim should be defended. But in times like these they dare not defend him themselves. So loyalty demands their presence here but survival their
2 silence. This is not to arrogate to myself the name of hero nor to claim a monopoly of loyalty to a friend. Much as I should like to affect such virtues, it would be tantamount to denying them to others and that I cannot allow.

    Why then have I undertaken the defence of Sextus Roscius where others have refused? The answer is simply this. If any of the influential and distinguished men you see here had spoken on his behalf, and if they had made any allusion to the political situation – as they would have been bound to do – far more would have been
3 read into their words than they had actually said. But even if I say everything that needs saying with complete freedom, I shall receive nothing like the publicity that they would get. Then again, they are

so distinguished and influential that nothing they say can escape publicity, and too old and too experienced to be forgiven for any error of judgement by which their speech may give offence. But in my case, if I am somewhat rash in what I say, either no-one will notice, because I am a newcomer to the *res publica*, or else the Powers That Be can afford to forgive me on the grounds of my youth and inexperience. Mind you, there is little sign now that the authorities know how to forgive, or on the other hand that they show any concern for discovering facts on which to base their condemnations.

4   But there is an additional consideration: whereas, perhaps, the others were asked in such a way that they did not feel morally obliged to agree, I was asked by men whose friendship, kindness, and high standing laid strong claims upon me, since I could neither forget their generosity, nor ignore their influence, nor refuse their

5   wishes. And that is why I am leading for the defence today, not as the first choice for the brilliance of my talents but as the last resort, the man who risked least by consenting to speak, and whose advocacy ensured for Sextus Roscius not an adequate defence but merely the presence of at least one supporter.

What then is the source of all this fear, this terror which prevents so many outstanding advocates from defending the rights and property of an accused man in the usual way? You might well ask, and it is hardly surprising that you do not know, since the prosecution have deliberately omitted any mention of the real reason behind this

6   trial. Let me tell you what it is. The father of Sextus Roscius owned property worth six million sesterces. This same property was bought from Lucius Sulla, the hero of our state whose very name lends distinction to my lips, for a mere two thousand sesterces by a young man who is the most powerful citizen in Rome today, Lucius Cornelius Chrysogonus. At least that is his story, gentlemen, and now, since he has laid hands illegally on such a large and desirable estate and finds that the only obstacle to his enjoyment of it is the continued existence of Sextus Roscius, he expects your verdict to rid him of all his fears and apprehensions on this score. For Roscius is innocent, and as long as he is alive Chrysogonus cannot see any way of keeping hold of the splendid property which belongs to Roscius by inheritance. But once Roscius is condemned and exiled, he hopes that what his crime acquired his extravagant tastes will be well able to

dissipate. But that is the nagging doubt that goads him day and night: can he get rid of Roscius? This he now requires you to do and so earn the name of accomplices in his disgraceful act of plunder.

7 But perhaps you think his demands are reasonable, gentlemen. In that case let me make a demand too, smaller, perhaps, but more reasonable, I think. First, I demand that Chrysogonus be content to take our money and our property but at least leave us our lives. Secondly, I must point out that Roscius is being framed, and ask you, gentlemen, to do all you can to hinder such criminal activities, to champion the cause of innocent men, and in the case of Sextus Roscius to repel a danger which ultimately threatens us all. If, how-
8 ever, you can find any substance in the accusation, any suspicion of crime, or even the very smallest hint of evidence to justify the decision to prosecute other than the lust for plunder I have already mentioned, I am prepared to allow Roscius to forfeit his life to the rapacity of his accusers. But if you can find no motive save the wish to ensure that men whom nothing will satisfy should indeed lack for nothing, no reason for mounting the prosecution at this moment save to allow them to feast themselves on Roscius' considerable wealth with Roscius' own condemnation served up as a sort of *pièce de résistance*, then surely you must feel that the final outrage, the crowning insult, is that they should have regarded it as likely that they would secure by your verdicts, given under oath, what they have hitherto had to secure for themselves by robbery and murder. I would remind you, gentlemen, that you were elected to the Senate out of public respect; you were appointed to this jury for your integrity. But these murderous cut-throats are not just asking you to spare them the punishment they have every reason to fear for their crimes, but also to set them free by due process of law to deck themselves in their ill-gotten gains.

9 I have a tale to tell, gentlemen, of vast and terrible crimes. That my language is inadequate, my delivery unimpressive, and my whole speech somewhat inhibited I am very well aware. But I have neither the ability to do my subject justice, nor the seniority to lend weight to my words, nor a political climate which would allow me to tell the whole truth. I am awed by my surroundings, daunted by my army of opponents, and appalled by my client's danger – sentiments which are hardly likely to counteract my own natural lack of

confidence. So I beg you, gentlemen, most earnestly, to hear me with
10 all the attention and generosity at your command. I have a burden far
beyond my powers to sustain, and I have taken it up only in the sure
confidence that I can rely upon your sound judgement and sense of
fair play. If therefore you can help me even a little along my path, I
shall bear my burden with such small strength and skill as I possess.
But even if my worst fears are realized and you leave me on my own,
nevertheless I shall not despair, and what I have undertaken I shall
carry through to the bitter end. And if I am doomed to failure, I
would rather fail upon some high endeavour than play the traitor,
and for want of courage lay down the trust that has been placed
upon me.

11   For you, too, Marcus Fannius, I have a most earnest request. You
proved yourself to the Roman people a great judge long ago when
you presided over this same court. Prove yourself so again today, I
beg, for the sake of Rome and for my client here. You see these vast
crowds of spectators; you know what they and every man alive
expect and yearn for: a searching investigation, a severe sentence.
It is many years since last we had a murder trial here; yet since then
there have been some monstrous and shocking crimes. It is our most
earnest hope that under your presidency this court will prove itself
a potent weapon in the fight against the flagrant crimes and daily
murders which disgrace our city.

12   Now it is strange to find the defence resorting to the kind of pleas
which characterize a prosecution speech; but on this occasion I shall
do so. I must beg you, Marcus Fannius, and you too, gentlemen of
the jury, to show no mercy in this case. You must not hestitate to
crush these criminals. Furthermore you must make your attitude
absolutely clear. If you do not, you must realize that you are giving
carte blanche to the whole criminal fraternity. And the result will be
that, if Roscius is condemned, murder will have ceased to be a deed
of darkness; for it will have done in the broad light of day, in this
forum, at your judgement seat, Marcus Fannius, and with your
blessing in this court of law, gentlemen of the jury.

Now that is the only real issue here – are you going to let this
happen? Look at the prosecutors: they have seized everything
Roscius possesses; look at the defendant: he is the proud owner of
nothing but his own misfortunes. The prosecutors reaped the benefits of his father's death; the only thing Roscius got out of it was

bereavement and poverty. It was the prosecutors who really wanted his father's throat cut; it was Roscius who needed the armed guard to get him here, in case he was cut down in this law court before your eyes. In fact the prosecutors are the ones everyone wants to see prosecuted; the defendant is the only survivor from their murderous
14 activities. And just so that you can get it absolutely clear, gentlemen, that the situation is really far worse than I have described, I shall tell you the whole story right from the beginning – and at the end I hope you will appreciate more fully just how much a totally innocent man can suffer, the enormity of these men's crimes, and the full implications of what is now a disaster to the *res publica*.

3. THE POLITICS OF MUNICIPIA

The narrative of the murder follows; it illustrates well the internal politics of one of the *municipia* of Italy, and their relations with Roman magnates.

Pro Roscio Amerino, 15–29:

15   Sextus Roscius senior, the defendant's father, was a citizen of the free city of Ameria. He came from a long line of distinguished ancestors, and this fact, coupled with his considerable fortune, made him the most important citizen in the whole area, as well as in Ameria itself. He was also a close personal friend of a number of noble families and enjoyed their respect and affection. He had not only family ties but also a close personal friendship with the Metelli, the Servilii and the Scipios – if I may mention such honoured and distinguished names with the respect that is their due. Indeed, these influential connections are the only legacy he has actually managed to leave his son. There is a certain irony in the fact that the robbers who have forcibly seized and still keep possession of his estate are his own relations, while it is left to these same friends and associates of Roscius senior to do battle for the life and reputation of his son.

16   Roscius senior's politics were always right wing and certainly during the constitutional crises of recent times, when the position and lives of the nobles have been seriously threatened, he gave the lead to all the people of that area by devoting time, energy, and influence to the cause of the nobility. For, of course, he felt bound to try and

defend the position of the men to whom he owed his own high
position among his fellows. Victory was duly won and the fighting
stopped. Thereafter, although proscriptions were widespread, and
in every part of Italy suspected opponents were being rounded up,
Roscius was regularly to be seen at Rome and was a centre of attention in the forum. Would it not be reasonable to regard this as the
behaviour of a man enjoying the aftermath of the nobles' victory,
and not of one expecting at any moment to suffer some dire catastrophe
himself?

17   But he had a long-standing feud with two other Roscii from
Ameria. One of them I can see sitting there with the prosecution
witnesses, and they tell me that the other is now the proud owner of
three of the Roscius estates. And indeed, if Roscius had been able
to take the precautions against these enemies which his fears
warranted, he would still be alive today. He feared them, gentlemen, and how right he was. Let me introduce them to you; they are
both called Titus Roscius; Magnus is the one here in court and
Capito is the other. Capito is a thug of considerable reputation and
achievement; Magnus has recently apprenticed himself to him. Now
as far as I know, before their latest 'project' Magnus was a complete
novice; but he has already surpassed his instructor in every form of
18 villainy. At the time of the murder, Sextus Roscius junior, my client,
was in Ameria, but Magnus (the one sitting over there) was in
Rome. Sextus, being a loyal son, was working long hours on the
family estate, for he had sacrificed himself to the limitations of a
country life for the sake of the family fortunes. But Magnus was
regularly in Rome, and it was in Rome, near the baths of Pallacina,
that Sextus Roscius senior was murdered on the way home from
dinner. I hope I make myself clear, gentlemen, and that there is no
doubt where suspicion for this crime lies. But these are only suspicions; if the facts do not make this issue as plain as day, you are
welcome to assume that my client was also implicated in the
murder.

Sextus Roscius, then, was murdered. The first news was brought
to Ameria by a man called Mallius Glaucia, a dubious character, a
freed slave, and a hanger-on and associate of Titus Roscius Magnus.
Furthermore, he brought the news not to Sextus, the son, but to
Capito, Roscius' old enemy. The murder was committed soon
after dark; yet by early dawn this messenger had reached Ameria.

In ten hours, at night, he had raced fifty-six miles by cabriolet, not only so as to be the first to bring the great news, but also to show Capito the murder weapon, newly extracted from the corpse, and the blood of his enemy while it was still really fresh.

20 Four days later Chrysogonus got the news in Sulla's camp at Volaterra.

He was told of Roscius' great wealth; the estates were clearly 'desirable' since he left thirteen farms, almost all of them along the banks of the Tiber. It was explained to him that my client had few friends and lived an isolated life on his property. If Sextus Roscius senior could be killed so easily, for all his distinction and influential friends, it would be simple to eliminate an unsuspecting country bumpkin whom no-one at Rome had ever heard of. Chrysogonus promised to help.

21 To cut a long story short, they went into partnership and got Sextus Roscius' name put on the proscription lists. Yet he was a zealous supporter of the nobles' cause, gentlemen, and anyhow proscriptions were by this stage unheard of; indeed, those who had fled from Rome in terror were now coming back again, since they believed themselves to be out of danger. Chrysogonus acted as purchaser for the group. Capito's share of the spoils were the three best farms: he still has them. Magnus over there moved in on the rest of the estate, acting, so he says, on behalf of Chrysogonus. Needless to say, gentlemen, I am quite certain Sulla knew nothing of what

22 was going on. He was heavily engaged in restoring the damaged fabric of the *res publica* and preparing for future emergencies which seemed to threaten; he was solely responsible for establishing a peaceful settlement and running the army; everyone was looking to him for guidance, and he was in charge of every department of administration; in fact he had so many vast burdens upon his shoulders that he could not draw breath for an instant. So it is hardly surprising that he should miss something, especially when so many people knew of his preoccupations and were only waiting for their chance to try something like this the moment his attention was distracted. Furthermore, for all his proverbial good fortune, it is impossible for anyone to have such a vast staff and not have some unreliable slave or freedman on it.

23 But to continue my story: our hero, Titus Roscius Magnus, Chrysogonus' minion, came to Ameria and marched into the

Roscius estates. My poor client himself was still distraught with grief and had not even finished dealing with his father's funeral. But just as he was, with hardly a stitch of clothing on his back, he was hustled out of hearth, house and home, and Magnus became lord of his wide acres. As usual, the man who had no property he could call his own was quite prepared to play havoc with someone else's. He quite blatantly removed much of the furniture to his own home, and took away still more of it in secret, and made generous gifts of it, too, to his accomplices; the rest he sold by public auction.

24   All Ameria was appalled. The whole city was full of tears and lamentation. They had plenty to weep about. They had seen a leading citizen cruelly murdered, his son reduced by a travesty of justice to grinding poverty, and denied even free access to his father's grave by that abominable monster; they had seen his property bought up in a mockery of an auction; they had seen robbery, pillage and graft. They would all have rather seen the whole place go up in smoke than Magnus preening himself as he lorded it over
25 the property of such an honest citizen as Sextus Roscius. The local council (*decuriones*) immediately passed a resolution that a committee of ten should go to Sulla and tell him the kind of man Sextus Roscius was, denounce the criminal activities of those scoundrels, and beg him in his kindness to restore the dead man's reputation and his son's property. Here is the resolution.

(The resolution is read)

In due course, then, the deputation reached Sulla's camp. (And now you must realize, gentlemen, as I have already reminded you, that all these crimes had been committed without Sulla's knowledge.) Chrysogonus went into action at once. He met them in person and got some of his friends among the nobles to impress upon them the importance of not going to Sulla, and to promise that Chrysogonus
26 himself would see that they got what they wanted. He was, of course, convinced that it was as much as his life was worth to let Sulla hear about his activities. Well, he was dealing with men of old-fashioned views on integrity, men who would imagine that anybody was as trustworthy as themselves. Once he had promised to have Roscius' name erased from the proscription lists and his estates handed back to his son, they believed him, especially since they had in addition the assurances of Roscius Capito, who was himself a member of the

deputation. So they returned to Ameria without putting their request to Sulla.

The conspirators' immediate reaction was to put off doing anything and to institute delaying tactics, at first from day to day, and then over longer periods as they tried to bamboozle the deputation. Finally, as you might expect, they began to plot against my client's life, since they felt that they could not keep their hands on his pro-
27 perty much longer if he stayed alive. As soon as he realized what was up, Roscius fled to Rome on the advice of his friends and relations. He took refuge with Caecilia, the sister of Metellus Nepos, and daughter of Balearicus, a lady of considerable distinction and a very old friend of his father's. This lady is an example to us all in this day and age, gentlemen, as we have always known, of course. She can still show us how a true friend ought to behave. Sextus Roscius had not a penny; he was homeless and without possessions, a fugitive from the daggers and threats of a gang of criminals. But she took him into her home, and gave him every assistance, although he was a victim of persecution and no-one gave much for his chances of survival. Thanks to her courage, her loyalty, her devotion he is here today alive and defending a law-suit, and not dead and adorning a proscription list.

28   Now it was when they realized that Roscius' life was closely guarded, and they were not going to get a chance to do him in, that the gang made a new plan of diabolical ingenuity. They decided to arraign him for parricide and to find an accuser who was an old hand at the game and might be able to say something plausible even in a case where there was not a shred of suspicion. They also thought that, since no charge was likely to stick, the climate of opinion and the general sense of political unease might be useful weapons. Their reasoning seems to have been that since the law-courts had not been functioning for some time, the first person prosecuted was bound to be convicted. And anyhow no-one would defend Roscius for fear of Chrysogonus' influence, let alone stand up in the witness box and say a word about the sale of his property and the activities of the gang. Indeed, the very mention of a crime as shocking as parricide would easily ensure his death since he would be undefended anyhow.

29   That was their plan, gentlemen, and they were mad enough to think that, since they could not kill him when they wanted to, they could hand him over to you to do the job for them.

4. THE LAW IN SULLA'S *Res Publica*

After the bulk of the speech, which is spent in refuting the actual charges, Cicero returns to Chrysogonus and the *res publica* of Sulla, and stresses the need to return from arbitrary rule to legally-based government. The party of nobles who put Sulla into power are severely criticized.

Pro Roscio Amerino, 124–9, 136–142, 148–154:

124   Let us now examine Chrysogonus' role in this whole affair. Chrysogonus means in Greek 'the golden-born', and the fact that he was the golden boy of the régime has certainly given a mask of respectability to the conspiracy. Now here I find it very difficult to make up my mind whether to tell the truth or to say nothing. If I say nothing, I shall be leaving out the best part of my story; but if I tell the truth, I am afraid of offending others – the effect on Chrysogonus himself does not concern me in the slightest. But at least I do not feel compelled to say very much against dealers in confiscated property as a body; just against this one, Chrysogonus. His activities are rather different, indeed unique.

125   It was Chrysogonus, you see, gentlemen, who bought up Sextus Roscius' property. Now the immediate question that concerns us is this: what was the legal justification for the sale of Roscius' property; and then, could there have been any such justification? Please note, gentlemen, that I do not intend to discuss the iniquity of the sale of an innocent citizen's property. There is nothing unique about the case of Sextus Roscius in that respect, and if we are going to make free play of that particular issue, there is nothing to make us discuss this case rather than a thousand others. No, the question I want to ask is simply this: within the terms of that proscription law, Valerian or Cornelian – I don't know which, indeed I've never known – how

126 did Roscius' property come to be sold at all? Officially the law states that 'a man's property shall be sold if he has been proscribed' – which Roscius was not – 'or if he was killed within the enemy lines' – yet when there were any lines to be 'within', he was in Sulla's. Furthermore, it was when the fighting was over and peace fully established that he was killed, at Rome, on his way home from dinner. If, then, he was legally killed, his property was I agree legally sold. But if you accept that his death was in defiance of all law, whether ancient or modern, then I demand to know what

possible justification there can be in law or equity for the sale of his property.

127   Now I know, Erucius, that you would like to think that I am getting at Sulla in all this. But I am not. I made that quite clear at the beginning of my speech, and anyhow his exemplary character would acquit him of any suspicion. No, I say that everything I have described is the work of Chrysogonus; it was deliberate perjury designed to blacken the character of my client, to make it appear that he was killed fighting for Sulla's enemies, and to prevent Sulla from learning the truth from the deputation from Ameria. Indeed, I have a nasty feeling that the property was not sold at all and I shall

128   try to prove this to you, if I may, gentlemen, in due course. For the law laid down, if I remember rightly, a time limit for proscriptions and sales, and that was the first of June. Yet the murder took place months after that and so did the sale of the property. So, either there have been no official records kept of this sale and this scoundrel is making complete fools of us all, or else, if records have been kept, they have been tampered with, since it is at least quite clear that the property can not have been sold legally.

I am, of course, aware that I am perhaps raising this issue somewhat prematurely, gentlemen, and that it may even be a tactical error to pursue this particular red herring at this moment. After all, Sextus Roscius is not worried about the money – in fact he could not care less about it, since he thinks that he can put up with poverty easily enough if he can only clear his name of this frightful

129   slur. But I would ask you as a favour, gentlemen, to view what little I have left to say as a statement of my own personal feelings as well as a defence of Sextus Roscius. There are, you see, certain aspects of this case which I personally find deplorable. I think they will affect us all unless we are careful, and I should like to discuss them since I feel so strongly about them. . . . . .

136   All those who know me know that, once my own objective of an agreed settlement (sc. of the civil war) failed, I worked for the nobles' victory to the best of my limited abilities. After all, any-one could see that here was a challenge to the authority of our noblest citizens by some of the lowest elements in the state. It would have been an act of gross disloyalty for any citizen not to support the party on whose survival depended the moral stability of our country and its prestige abroad. I am delighted to say, gentlemen, that all

was well; the social order was preserved; the will of heaven and the vigorous efforts of the Roman people triumphed under the skilful
137 generalship of the ever-successful Lucius Sulla. That our most ruthless opponents were condemned naturally causes me no concern; that the brave men who contributed so magnificently to our victory were rewarded affords me satisfaction. After all, this is what we were fighting for and I admit that I was wholly on their side. But if the only result has been that the scum of Rome should grow rich at the expense of others, and play havoc with the property of everyone of us, protected by law from any kind of censure let alone physical restraint, then this war has not renewed the *res publica* nor has it restored it – it has suppressed it and ground it into the dust. But of
138 course this has not happened, gentlemen – far from it. And that is why, so far from damaging the position of the nobles' government if you resist these men, you will enhance its prestige. After all, its critics usually confine their complaints to the excessive powers of Chrysogonus – and this is the very thing which the government's supporters say he has not got.

In fact, gentlemen, there is nothing you can complain about in the present state of affairs. It is no use taking a fool's or a coward's way out and saying that there were measures you wanted and would have voted for or things you would have done if you could. You can – there is no-one stopping you; you have only to vote for any reasonable measures and everyone will applaud you; you have only to
139 produce a legal and honest verdict and everyone will cheer. There was a period, of course, when the situation demanded a Sulla in complete personal control. But he has now re-appointed magistrates and passed laws restoring to each their traditional tasks and powers. And if the men appointed want to keep these powers, they can, for ever – but not if they indulge or acquiesce in acts of robbery and murder, or in such lavish expenditures as I have described. I do not want to bring bad luck to anyone by saying anything too harshly critical, gentlemen, but I must insist that unless the nobles show themselves true guardians of the state, brave and merciful, they will have to surrender to men who have such virtues the very powers they
140 have so recently acquired. In fact, it is high time they stopped denouncing those who merely publish too many unpalatable truths; it is high time they stopped supporting Chrysogonus and regarding attacks upon him as a slur upon themselves. They must avoid the dis-

graceful charge that men who could not tolerate the power of the knights (*equites*) were quite prepared to be ruled by a slave and a criminal. So far, gentlemen, that slave has exercised his power else-where; but you can see now where his ambitions lie. He has designs upon your integrity, your oaths, your verdicts – almost the only things left in this state which no-one has yet managed to corrupt or

141 destroy. If Chrysogonus really thinks that he can achieve his own ends even here, the situation becomes totally intolerable. It is not that I am afraid he will actually get what he wants: but the fact that he had the nerve to try it, that he even dreamed he could use you to destroy an innocent man – that is what I find so deplorable.

The nobles have recovered control of the *res publica* by force of arms. They cannot allow their efforts, so long delayed, to end with freed-men and their own slaves abusing our property, our fortunes, our

142 very altars for their own evil ends. If they do, I confess that I was on the wrong side; I was mad to support them, though I did not actually fight for them, gentlemen. But if the victory of the nobles is supposed to contribute to the glory and welfare of the *res publica* and people of Rome, then surely my speech can only be welcomed by every true patriot among the nobles. And if there is any man here who feels himself or his party slighted by my attacks on Chrysogonus, he merely condemns himself, and shows that he does not know where his party's true interests lie. If we fight every criminal, if we destroy every villain who supports Chrysogonus or thinks his own interests coincide with his, if we refuse to allow such men to sully its noble ideals, then, gentlemen of the jury, we can only enhance the glory of our party and increase the honour in which it is held. . . .

148 Or perhaps you regard it as a crime that we should have gone to so much trouble to defend Sextus Roscius. Believe you me, if every-one who was indebted to Roscius' father for help or kindness was willing to attend this court or dared speak openly on his behalf, then his defence would indeed be adequate and eloquent. If all these men dared to stand up as champions of Sextus Roscius – and of the whole *res publica*, since its welfare is involved with his – I should certainly not be required to offer my feeble efforts here. For there is nothing in his present defence for his opponents to object to or to make them feel their arguments are being steam-rollered out of

149 existence. After all, Caecilia is merely looking after his general wel-fare while Marcus Messala is managing the legal side of his affairs,

as you know, gentlemen. If Messala was a bit older and stronger, he would himself be speaking on behalf of Sextus Roscius, but his youth and the modesty which is one of youth's most endearing characteristics, has led him to hand over the defence to me since he knows that it is a duty and a pleasure to me, and he feels unable to undertake it himself. But it is thanks to him alone and his determination, skill, influence and untiring efforts that Roscius has been saved from the clutches of the dealers in confiscated property and brought to judgement in a court of law. That, gentlemen, is exactly the kind of action for which a large part of the state fought to put the nobles back in power; they fought to restore men to do exactly what you see Messala doing: defend the innocent, resist wrong doing, and devote their powers to preserving life, not destroying it. If only all men of high birth like him would do that, they would be less trouble to the *res publica* and a good deal more popular into the bargain.

150   But if Chrysogonus cannot be persuaded to be content with our money and to leave us our lives, if he cannot be restrained from depriving us of the light of day which is the common property of all men, when he has already robbed us of all else that is ours, if it is not enough for him to glut his avarice on money but needs must have a blood sacrifice as well, then there is only one escape, one chance for Sextus Roscius and for the *res publica*: it lies, gentlemen, in your long tradition of mercifulness and integrity. If it is not lost, we can all survive even at this eleventh hour. But if the cruelty and the bloodshed which have been such a feature of the *res publica* recently has hardened even your hearts, gentlemen, (though I find it hard to believe) and blunted even your humanity, then we are all doomed, and a life among the beasts of the wild would be

151   preferable to life in such a vicious state as ours. We have not kept the rule of law and selected you as jury merely to provide executioners for anyone whom murderers and cut-throats could not butcher, like shrewd generals who position reserve troops on an enemy's expected line of retreat to ambush anyone who escapes. Yet it certainly looks as if our shrewd property dealers thought that that is just what you were here to do, to catch anyone who slips through their fingers. God forbid, gentlemen, that what our ancestors regarded as the council of the *res publica* should now be thought

152   of as a dealer's protection society. Do you not realize that their only objective is to eliminate the sons of proscribed citizens by hook or

by crook, starting with Sextus Roscius, and with yourselves, a sworn jury, as executioners. Can you seriously have any doubts about who are the real criminals when you see on one side, as accuser, a property dealer who is a known assassin and the sworn enemy of Sextus Roscius, and on the other side Roscius' son, reduced to poverty but respected by all his friends, a man of blameless life to whom not a shred of suspicion attaches? Can you not see that Roscius' only crime is to be the son of the man whose property was sold?

153   But if you become accomplices and offer your assistance to these men, if you show that your court exists to try the sons of those whose property has been sold, then, gentlemen, you are paving the way for a new and much bloodier series of proscriptions. Yet the Senate was reluctant to sanction even the first series, which was directed against those who actually fought, for fear of giving official approval to an act of unprecedented severity. But this next one is aimed at children and babes in swaddling clothes: and unless you reject and condemn it utterly, gentlemen, I swear by all the gods in heaven you are bringing to the *res publica* a menace such as you have never dreamed of.

154   It is now the duty of all wise men of authority and influence such as yours to seek to remedy the ills which encumber the *res publica*. Every single one of you knows full well that the Roman people, whose clemency towards their enemies was once proverbial, is now itself the victim of dire and self-inflicted cruelty. Blot out this cruelty, gentlemen, I beseech you; do not suffer it to endure a moment longer within the confines of the *res publica*; it is an evil and pernicious thing, so evil indeed, and so pernicious that it has horribly destroyed innumerable citizens, and by the custom of fell deeds has blocked our natural sympathies. Hour by hour, day by day, we see and hear of dreadful deeds; bloodshed and destruction have been so in use that, kind and gentle though we are, it is beginning to steal all pity from our hearts.

Rocius was acquitted.

ROME AFTER SULLA

Sulla died in 78; even before his death it was apparent that his party had no wide support, in that one of the consuls, M. Aemilius Lepidus, was an overt opponent. After Sulla's death he attempted to overturn Sulla's settlement, and was supported by an eruption, perhaps spontaneous, of the Etruscan peoples whose livelihood had been ruined by Sulla. The attempt failed, and Lepidus fled in 77 to Sardinia where he died. M. Brutus, a supporter of his, and the father of Caesar's assassin, was beseiged by Pompey in Mutina and put to death on his surrender.

This rising, and the elections for 77, which produced two consuls whose sympathies lay with the rebels, showed the difficulties which Sulla's party of nobles faced. It was their failure to meet them, and particularly to deal with the problem of how to secure just government for the provinces and strict and impartial justice in the lawcourts which caused them to lose men's respect, and this in turn led to irresistible demands that the senators should be deprived of their monopoly of power in the state.

II. The Changing *Res Publica*

Cicero served as quaestor at Lilybaeum, at the western end of Sicily, in 75. This was the first step in his public career. The only descriptions of his experiences there come from his own mouth, and therefore must be treated with some caution. The upshot, however, was two-fold; on the one hand Cicero decided that service in the provinces was not the way to rise to the top in the world of politics; on the other, the Sicilians regarded him as a friend in need when they received a governor of exceptional brutality and rapacity in C. Verres. Many years later, in 54, he recounted the experience which taught him his lesson.

Pro Plancio, 64–6:

I am not afraid of seeming to make extravagant claims for myself if I mention my quaetorship, gentlemen. It was, of course, a considerable success, but I have held such distinguished offices since then that I do not feel I can extract very much glory from that one. But I am quite certain, none the less, that no-one would seriously claim that there ever was a more successful or popular quaestorship in Sicily than mine. And I must confess, alas, that I imagined at the time that all Rome was talking about it. After all, I had sent vast quantities of corn to the city when there was a major shortage. Businessmen had found me approachable, merchants fair, contractors generous, and the allies reasonable in my demands; in fact everyone thought me immensely conscientious in performing all my duties, while the Sicilians themselves dreamed up unprecedented
65 honours for me. As a result I left there fondly expecting that when I got home the people of Rome would grant my every wish almost without my having to ask. How wrong I was! On my way home from my province at that time I happened to pay a visit to Puteoli at the height of the season, when most of the fashionable and wealthy people are there. You could have knocked me down with a feather, gentlemen, when someone asked me how long ago I had left Rome

and if there was any news from there. I retorted that I was on my way home from my province. 'Oh! Africa I suppose', he said. 'Sicily actually', I replied rather loftily, upon which one of those people who know all the answers piped up and said, 'What! Didn't you know he was quaestor at Syracuse?' Well, after that I gave up and lost myself among the crowd of holiday-makers there.

66   But I am rather inclined to think, gentlemen, that that little episode was more valuable to me than if I had been met with universal acclamation. For it brought home to me the lesson that the Roman people use their eyes, which are perceptive and alert, rather more than their ears. As a result, I gave up worrying about the effects of rumour on my reputation and saw to it that men should see me daily in the flesh instead. I was for ever in the public eye, became a permanent fixture in the forum, and kept open house day and night.

After 75, Cicero never voluntarily served in the provinces. His life was in the city, in the forum and in the Senate-house. He governed Cilicia in 51–50 only because a law of Pompey's, passed in 52, compelled him to do so; otherwise, he left Rome seldom, and only for holidays, or when he had no choice. Such occasions were his exile, in 58–57, the civil war, in 49–47, and other occasions when he could not endure the way the *res publica* was being mismanaged, as by Caesar in 59, the coalition of Pompey, Caesar and Crassus in 56–55, and the dictatorships and virtual dictatorships of Caesar and Antony in 46–44.

6. VERRES

The Sicilians' appeal to Cicero came in 70. C. Verres was their governor from 73–71. He had been a firm supporter of Sulla's party, by whose influence he rose to the praetorship in 74. His misgovernment of Sicily was so atrocious that it was noticed in Rome while he was still there, and when he left the province the Sicilians determined to prosecute him for his actions. They appealed to Cicero, whom they remembered for his justice. In taking up the case, Cicero took a firm political stand against Sulla's party, a stand that was made the clearer by the fact that the party rallied round Verres. Cicero first disposed of a rival prosecutor, whom he represents, probably rightly, as a man of straw, in the extant *Divinatio in Q. Caecilium*. He then spent 50 days in Sicily collecting documentary evidence and witnesses; he also secured for himself election as aedile for 69, an election his opponents tried to stop, and on 5 August, 70, began his opening speech, the *Actio prima in Verrem*.

Verres, Cicero says, is manifestly guilty, but has decided to rely on money to get himself off, and to fix the date of the trial so as to favour himself.

Actio prima in Verrem, 1–6:

A long awaited opportunity has arrived, gentlemen of the jury, indeed the only real opportunity you will get to redeem the good-will of the nation for your order and the good name of the courts which you control. It is an opportunity that seems to have been devised not by the wit of man but rather almost by the will of Heaven, and it has been vouchsafed to you at a critical time in the affairs of the *res publica.* For over the years it has come to be generally accepted that in these courts, as they are at present constituted, it is impossible for a rich man to be condemned, however guilty he may be. Such a reputation, widely published as it is not only in Rome but also abroad, does great disservice to the *res publica* and
2 menaces your own position, gentlemen. But now, at this critical moment for your order and the courts which you control, when there are enemies ready and waiting for a chance to make capital out of your unpopularity by fiery speeches and legislative proposals, you have assembled here to try the case of Gaius Verres, a man whose life and crimes have guaranteed his condemnation in all opinions but his own, but whose wealth is so enormous that he himself expects and has publicly forecast his acquittal. And in this prosecution, which has aroused the support and interest of the nation, I have agreed to play the leading part, not because I want to stir up further prejudice against you, gentlemen, but rather to help redeem a slur on your order. For I have brought to trial a man who will give you a splendid opportunity to restore the lost reputation of the courts, regain your own popularity among the Roman people, and make restitution to the nations abroad. For he has robbed the Treasury, wrought havoc in Asia and Pamphylia, made a fortune from his urban praetorship at Rome, and proved a pestilential ruin to his pro-
3 vince, Sicily. If you judge him strictly, as your oaths require, gentle-men, you will retain the honour which is yours by right; but if his vast wealth can destroy the sanctity and integrity of these courts, my only achievement will have been to show that it is the *res publica* which needs honest law courts, and not the juries who need criminals to try, nor the criminals who need men to bring them to justice.

Now, gentlemen, many are the plots that Gaius Verres has

hatched against me on land and sea. Some I have survived by my own efforts, others I have defeated thanks to the devoted loyalty of my friends. But I must confess that never have I felt myself in so much danger, never been so apprehensive as at this moment in this

4 court. It is not so much the interest aroused by my prosecution, nor yet the enormous crowds about us here that make me so afraid – alarming, indeed, though these things are – but rather the thought of the treacherous plots devised by this monster against us all at once – against myself, against you jurors, gentlemen, and against Manius Glabrio, the president of this court, against the Roman people, their allies and their foreign friends, even against the Senate and its reputation. For he has been saying repeatedly that the only men who have anything to fear are those who steal merely enough for themselves, whereas he has stolen enough to satisfy an army. For there is nothing, he says, so sacred that money cannot corrupt

5 it, nothing so strong that money cannot batter down its walls. And indeed, had he been as subtle in the execution of his crimes as he was bold in their conception, he might have managed to have concealed them from me, partly at least, for a time, but fortunately it transpires that his incredible audacity is allied to an inspired stupidity. He made no secret of his extortions, but positively advertised his schemes and plans for tampering with the jury at his trial. Just once in his life, he admits, he was afraid: the moment when I first instituted proceedings against him. At that time he was just back from his province, the hatred and loathing felt for him were no novelty but deeply ingrained and of long standing, and the

6 time itself was hardly ripe for bribing jurymen. But the moment I asked for just a little time to gather evidence in Sicily, he suborned someone to ask for two days less to do the same in Achaea. It was not that the man wanted to put detailed and careful finishing touches to a case which, like mine, was already the product of hours of toil and many a sleepless night – indeed, he never even got as far as Brundisium on the way to Achaea to get his evidence; whereas I travelled the length and breadth of Sicily in fifty days and compiled a complete dossier of verbal and written evidence on Verres' crimes against all the cities and individuals there. So it must be perfectly clear to anyone that this prosecutor was a fake, employed by Verres not to prosecute a criminal but to delay the start of these proceedings and deprive me of precious time.

7. METHODS AND PERILS OF A PROSECUTOR

Cicero then sketches Verres' career, and the charges (11–15), and explains how the *factio* of the Metelli tried to prejudice the trial and to attack Cicero himself. He well illustrates the complications of getting business done in the conditions dictated by the Roman calendar.

Actio prima in Verrem, 15–32:

15 And for these reasons, gentlemen, this criminal madman is fighting me by new methods. He has decided not to pit his counsel's eloquence against mine, nor to rely on any man's influence, prestige or power to help him in the struggle. Of course, he pretends to be dependent on such methods, but he cannot deceive me; his real intentions are all too transparent. He has paraded the empty titles of the nobles and flaunted before me in a meaningless charade the names of certain arrogant gentlemen who are his backers. But their nobility does far less to hinder my cause than their notoriety does to advance it. He pretends to be relying on their protection, but in

16 fact for some time now he has had another trick up his sleeve. What it is that he is really working at and plotting, gentlemen, I shall now explain to you briefly; but I must ask you to listen first while I sketch in the background to this case.

As soon as he returned from Sicily, Verres went to considerable expense to bribe the whole jury for his trial. He made a contract and agreement with a bribery agent, and until the challenging of jurors was completed, this arrangement held good. Fortunately for Rome, when the jurors were selected, the luck of the draw considerably dashed his hopes, and at the challenging of jurors my own meticulous investigations enabled me to put paid to their outrageous schemes. As a result, when the challenge was over, the agent threw up the whole contract. So everything now looked thoroughly

17 satisfactory. Everyone knew the list of your names as jurors for this trial. It looked as if there would be no chance to mark your votes with secret signs, smudges, or dabs of colour; and Verres himself, who had hitherto radiated confidence and vigour, suddenly looked so depressed and harassed that obviously his condemnation was a foregone conclusion not only to the Roman people but even to himself. And then suddenly, in the last few days since the finish of the consular elections, the same men have been back at the same

old tricks, plotting to destroy your reputations and the safety of the state by bigger and better bribes. I first got wind of this, gentlemen, thanks to a tiny shred of evidence that came my way. But once my suspicions were aroused, I have made my way remorselessly to the very heart of this new conspiracy.

18   It began like this. Hortensius had just been elected consul for next year, and was being escorted home by an enormous crowd of supporters, when, quite by chance, Gaius Curio met them. Now it is not my intention to bring Curio's good name into disrepute – indeed the reverse – but I shall repeat the remarks he made on that occasion, since obviously, if he had not wanted them to be generally known, he would not have made them so openly and publicly in front of that enormous gathering. But I want to make it clear that my affection for him is profound and my respect unbounded; so I

19 shall try to play the whole story down as best I can. Very near the Arch of Fabius Curio spotted Verres in the crowd. So he shouted out to him and offered his congratulations at the top of his voice – never a word to Hortensius the man who had just won the consulship, nor his relations and friends who were with him. No, it was Verres he stopped to talk to; he flung his arms around him, and told him there was nothing to worry about now, announcing with mock solemnity that 'I hereby declare that the result of the day's elections is that Verres is acquitted'. Now there was a large number of men of high principle in that crowd, and when they heard this little exchange they reported it to me at once; indeed it was the first thing anyone mentioned to me when he saw me. The reactions of these good people varied; some thought it scandalous, some merely ludicrous. The latter believed that the outcome of the trial would be decided by the integrity of the witnesses, the validity of the charges and the power vested in the jurors – not by the results of the consular elections; the more percipient were scandalized, since they regarded Curio's felicitations as evidence that the trial was already rigged. The former were inclined to dismiss the episode as a

20 joke, the latter regarded it as a disgrace. That, anyway, was the way these people looked at it, and, both in their private conversations and in their discussions with me, the general opinion of the best of our citizens was that the law courts were now manifestly a dead loss – as they deserved to be when a defendant who had written off his own chances the day before could bank on an acquit-

tal as soon as his counsel was elected consul. In other words, the fact that the whole of Sicily, all the provincials and Roman business-men alike, and a mass of documents both private and official, had been concentrated at Rome for the trial meant nothing, if the con-sul designate expressed his disapproval. The implications are absolutely monstrous: that the jury will pay no attention to the charges, the evidence, and their own standing with the Roman people, since the whole outcome is to depend on the power of one man's decision. I am not exaggerating, gentlemen. I found the whole prospect deeply depressing, not least because the men of standing in this city kept saying to me: 'Verres will slip through your clutches, but the senators will not keep control of these courts much longer, since no-one can hesitate to put them into different

21 hands, if they are capable of acquitting Verres'. It was a shocking business altogether, gentlemen, and what really irked these good men was not so much the sudden boost to the morale of a hardened criminal as the fact that a man of such high standing as Curio could offer such an unprecedented form of congratulation to a man like that. I apologize, gentlemen; I had hoped not to show how strongly I feel about this, but to conceal my distress behind a mask of silence.

But at about the same time there was another startling develop-ment. The praetors for the following year drew lots to decide their particular spheres of duty, and Marcus Metellus drew the presidency of the Extortion Court. This news, I gather, brought Verres such a flood of congratulations that he even sent slaves off home to take

22 the news to his wife. Certainly I myself was not exactly elated by the news, but I saw no particular reason to feel unduly despondent about the outcome of that ballot. But one thing I did discover from certain regular sources of information that I have, and that was that a number of money-bags containing Sicilian coin had found their way to a Roman banker from a certain member of the Senate; and that about ten of these money-bags had stayed with the senator for reasons connected with my forthcoming election for the aedileship. I also heard that the bribery-agents for all the tribes had been called

23 one night to a meeting at Verres' house. Now one of these agents, who felt it his duty to help me in every way he could, visited me that same night and reported what Verres had said. He had re-minded the agents, apparently, of his generous treatment of them in the past, both when he was standing for the praetorship himself

and at the recent consular and praetorian elections; he then went on to say forthwith that if they kept me out of office, they could name their price. At this, some said they would not dare, others that it could not be done; but one of his own relatives turned up trumps – Quintus Verres of the tribe Romilia, one of the old school of bribery-agents, who had been a pupil and friend to Verres' father. He said that he would do the job for 500,000 sesterces cash down, upon which some of the others jumped on the bandwaggon and said they would help too. In view of all this, my very good friend advised me to take all possible precautions.

24 And so, in that same small space of time I had a number of vital matters preying on my mind. The elections were hard upon me and in them I was up against a very large sum of money; the trial was approaching also, and here too I had those Sicilian money-bags to contend with. I could not give all my undivided attention to the trial because of my preoccupation with the elections, nor could I canvass whole-heartedly because I had to work at my brief for the trial; nor could I put pressure on the bribery-agents, since I knew that they knew that I was heavily tied down by my legal commit-

25 ments here. It was at that very moment I first got the news that Hortensius had summoned the Sicilians to meet him at his house; however, they were not going to be so easily brow-beaten, and, since they knew what they were being summoned for, they refused to go. Meanwhile the elections for the aediles got under way, with Verres assuming that he had them under control as he has had all the other elections this year. So he did his round of the tribes, accompanied by his charming and popular son, looking every inch the political boss, greeting and mustering the support of those old friends of the family money-bags, the bribery-agents. However, the Roman people soon got wind of what was up, and once the news got around, they demonstrated their goodwill towards me by ensuring that the wealth of the man who had failed to rob me of my honour should not deprive me of high office either.

26 Once that particular electoral problem was off my mind, I was free and had the time to give my undivided attention to preparing and planning for the trial. I discovered, gentlemen, that the defence had so planned and organized their campaign as to ensure that, by fair means or foul, the trial should be so protracted that it would take place before Marcus Metellus, the praetor for next year. This

would have certain advantages for them: first, the fact that Metellus himself was well disposed towards them. Then, Hortensius would be consul, and not only Hortensius but also Quintus Metellus, whose close friendship with the defendant you might note with interest, gentlemen, since the first indications of that friendship are so considerable that he might be said to have repaid already the debt which he owes Verres for securing for him the first votes at the

27 consular elections. (You cannot really expect me to keep silent about such vital matters, or to have any concern for anyone or anything except my duty and position, when the whole *res publica* and my own reputation are in danger.) Metellus, Hortensius' colleague as consul for next year, summoned the Sicilians. Some of them came because his brother Lucius Metellus was praetor in Sicily. What he said to them went something like this: 'I am to be consul; one of my brothers is governor of Sicily, the other is going to be in charge of the Extortion Court. Many precautions have been taken to see that

28 Verres comes to no harm.' I must say, I should like to know Metellus' definition of judicial corruption if it does not include intimidation of witnesses (particularly these nervous and downtrodden Sicilians) by misuse of personal prestige, a consul's authority, and the power of two praetors. What on earth would he do to help a kinsman who was also innocent, if he is prepared to ignore his duty and degrade his office for a man who is a master criminal and not even a distant relative, thereby confirming for all who do

29 not know him the truth of what Verres said about him? For he is supposed to have remarked that the rest of the Metellus family got the consulship by Destiny's hand, Quintus by Verres'.

So the defendant will have two consuls, gentlemen, and a court president to suit his taste. His line of reasoning must have gone something like this: 'I cannot possibly be acquitted under a president like Manius Glabrio, whose investigations are too rigorous and his concern for his own reputation too high. But there is more to it than that. One of the jurors is Marcus Caesonius, a colleague of the prosecutor, and a man with a proven reputation for honesty in court. I certainly can't afford to have him in a jury I am trying to tamper with at all. After all, he was a juror in the case which was tried before the praetor Junius, and not only was he scandalized by the corruption then, but even insisted on making the whole affair

30 public. But he will not be a juror after the 1st January; nor will

Quintus Manlius, nor Quintus Cornificius, both men as strict as they are impartial; they will both be tribunes of the people. Then there is Publius Sulpicius; he is a humourless fellow, and far too honest – but he will have to start his magistracy on the 5th December; there are also three others, all men with old-fashioned ideas, who will be military tribunes and therefore not available to be jurors after the 1st January: Marcus Crepereius, who comes from that very strict equestrian family, Lucius Cassius, whose family has a long tradition of being as strict as jurors as they are in everything else, and Gnaeus Tremellius, who is a man of high principle and painstakingly conscientious. We shall also have to have another ballot to replace Marcus Metellus, since he is going to preside over the actual trial. So after 1st January, with a new praetor and almost completely new jury, I shall be able to make a complete mockery, if I like, of the trial, and turn the alarming threats which the prosecution is making and the high hopes which are centred on this trial to suit my own low tastes!'

31   Today, gentlemen, is 5 August; this court convened at two o'clock; so, as far as the defence are concerned, today does not even count. There are ten days to go till the thanksgiving games, which Gnaeus Pompey will be celebrating. These games will deprive us of fifteen days. Immediately after that come the Roman Games. So it is only after about forty days that they reckon they will have to answer the charges that we shall make. And then, by filibuster and prevarication, they expect to last out easily till the Victory Games, and the Plebeian Games which follow them at once. Thereafter there are only at best a few days left for the trial. Since the whole case will be as dead as a doornail by then, it will obviously have to come up for
32   re-trial before Marcus Metellus, the new praetor. In fact, gentlemen, if I really distrusted Metellus' sense of honour, I would have rejected him as a juror for this trial. I do not; but nevertheless, in my present frame of mind, I would rather have the case tried before him as a juror than a praetor; I would rather trust him with his own voting-tablet under oath, than with everyone else's when he has not had to take an oath at all . . .

8. JUDICIAL SCANDALS

Cicero then attacks Q. Hortensius, leading counsel for Verres, and speaks of how the notorious judicial scandals had damaged the Senate's prestige,

(39–40) and were the basic reason for the political campaign then being waged against their monopoly of power. The court *de rebus repetundis* is seen, not as a protection for the allies, but as a device to make their lot even worse.

Actio prima in Verrem, 35–8, 40–9:

35   It certainly seemed to me at first, gentlemen, that in prosecuting a villain already condemned before the bar of public opinion, there was nothing to justify the care and attention which I have lavished on this case. But alas, Hortensius, you have chosen to put at the disposal of this desperate criminal the enormous and quite intolerable political power which you exert, and that same personal ambition which you have sought to gratify in a number of trials in recent years. In fact you obviously derive enormous satisfaction from lording it like a despot in our courts. And for that reason, and because there are a number of men in Rome whom neither shame nor disgust can turn from their licentious and disgraceful lives, who seem, indeed, to have flung down the gauntlet and deliberately courted the hatred and hostility of the Roman people, I hereby make public proclamation that I have decided to accept their challenge. For massive though the task may be, and dangerous to myself, it certainly deserves to have every ounce of energy and
36   strength at my command. Our whole order is being harassed by the criminal audacity of a tiny clique and oppressed by the corruption of our courts; and so, I repeat, I hereby make public proclamation that to men like these I shall prove a merciless prosecutor, a vindictive, remorseless, and cruel enemy. This is the course I have chosen to carve out for myself as the prime objective of my aedileship, this the task for that high office in which the Roman people have seen fit to place me from next January, bidding me work with them for the good of the *res publica* and the destruction of criminals; and I swear that this will be the finest and fairest gift my aedileship can bestow upon the Roman people. My enemies have been warned. This is my public proclamation, this is my declaration of war: whosoever makes it his business to give, take, or receive bribes, to promise them, to act as agent or go-between for those who corrupt our juries, whosoever aids or abets such criminals, whether by misuse of power or personality, let him beware, and in the trial of Verres let him keep his hands and thoughts from all such villainy.

37 For though Hortensius as consul will by then be supreme in power
and influence, and though I shall be only aedile, a minor official
little better than a private citizen compared with him, none the less,
the task which I am promising to perform is so welcome and so
pleasing to the Roman people, that in this affair at any rate compared with me he will seem of less account, if it were possible, than
even a private citizen.

I shall tell all, gentlemen; I shall produce irrefutable evidence
and lay before you all the crimes and villainies which have been
committed in these courts in the ten years since they were trans-

38 ferred to the Senate's control. The Roman people will hear from
me all the details of how, for the fifty consecutive years in which the
equites staffed the courts, not even the slightest vestige of suspicion
ever fell upon one of their jurors of accepting bribes to bring in a
corrupt verdict; of how, once the courts had been transferred to the
senatorial order and the Roman people had lost the power to control each single one of you, Quintus Calidius could remark, on being
found guilty, that it was an insult to a man of praetorian rank to be
convicted for less than 3 million sesterces; of how, when Quintus
Hortensius was presiding over the extortion court, the damages
awarded against Publius Septimius, the senator, took into con-

40 sideration the fact that he had received bribes as a juror . . . and
finally, of how, when the senatorial order formed the juries, the
voting-tablets of these men, who had each sworn to return an honest
verdict, were actually stained with different coloured marks. I
promise you, gentlemen, that with all this I shall deal thoroughly
and with strict regard for truth.

Imagine my feelings, too, gentlemen, if I discover that in this
trial also there has been the slightest sign of similar sharp practice
and corruption, especially since I can produce abundant evidence
to prove that in Sicily Verres was in the habit of saying, in front of
many witnesses, that he had a certain powerful friend whose
protection gave him *carte blanche* to ravage the province. He was not
collecting the money only for himself, he would explain; indeed, he
had carved up the anticipated profits of his three-year term as
governor in such a way that he would feel he had been generously
treated if he kept the proceeds of the first year for himself, those of
the second for the costs of his defence, while those of the third, the
most lucrative and profitable year of all, were earmarked exclusively

41 for distribution to the men who tried him. Indeed, I might repeat at this juncture a remark I made before Manius Glabrio recently, when I was rejecting some of the jurors appointed for this trial, and I know it horrified the Roman people at the time. 'I think', I said, 'that our foreign subjects will soon be sending deputations to the Roman people to ask them to repeal the extortion law and the extortion court. If there were no court, then each governor would only steal what he thought enough for himself and his children; but at present, with the courts as corrupt as they are, each governor takes enough to satisfy himself, his lawyers and defending counsel, the judge and the jury – and that amounts to millions. The provincials believe that they can find the cash to satisfy the most rapacious governor on earth, but not enough to guarantee the acquittal of the guiltiest.'

42 Altogether, it is a sad reflection on our courts and the good name of our order when the allies of the Roman people want the self-same extortion court abolished which was expressly established by our ancestors for their protection. After all, Verres would never have been so confident of acquittal had he not been brought up to believe the worst of you, gentlemen of the jury. It ought to make you hate him even more, if that were possible, than the Roman people do, that he can imagine you to be a match for himself in rapacity,

43 villainy, and perjury. So here we have a situation, gentlemen, which requires all your gifts of wisdom and foresight. And I most earnestly advise you to realize what is all too apparent to myself, that here you have a heaven-sent opportunity to free your whole order from the hatred, the loathing, the obloquy, and disgrace which now encumbers you. For the general public believes that the courts are so totally ineffective and corrupt that they might just as well not exist at all. We are despised and rejected by the Roman people; we have been far too long a flagrant and dreadful example of corrup-

44 tion. And this is the real reason why the people fought so hard for the restoration of the tribunes' powers. What was ostensibly a demand for the tribunate was in fact a plea for honest law courts. Quintus Catulus, whose ability is as remarkable as his intelligence, showed that he realized this all too well when Gnaeus Pompey, our most distinguished and courageous general, was bringing his proposal for the restoration of the tribunes' powers before the Senate. He was called upon to give his views, and opened his speech

with a crushing indictment. 'The management of the courts by the Senate', he said 'has been corrupt and dishonest; if the senators had only done their duty and fulfilled the hopes of the Roman people in their courts, the Roman people would not have felt such a crying

45 need for the restoration of the tribunate.' So too when Pompey himself first addressed the people as consul-elect and, predictably, declared that he would restore the tribunes' powers, he was greeted with applause and expressions of delight. But when he went on to say that the provinces had been harassed and cruelly devastated, that the law courts were a sink of iniquity, and that he intended to do something about it, the Roman people registered its joy not with

46 polite applause but with a tremendous roar of acclamation. But now the whole wide world is watching you, to see what steps each one of you will take to honour your oaths and guard the constitution. They know that, since the passage of the tribunician bill, only one impoverished senator has been condemned so far; and though there is nothing reprehensible in that, it is certainly nothing to write home about. After all, there is nothing particularly creditable in being honest when the defendant has neither the means nor inclination to

47 offer bribes. But now we have a case in which you yourselves, gentlemen, stand trial before the bar of public opinion no less than Verres before you; your verdicts here will settle the question once and for all whether a senatorial jury will ever convict a man whose load of guilt is as enormous as his bank-balance. Here you have a defendant who never does things by halves – his crimes are stupendous; so is his fortune. As a result, if he is acquitted, men will reach only one conclusion, and that the worst of all. For neither goodwill, nor family connections, neither compensating achievements, nor any evidence of moderation in villainy could ever mitigate by one degree the vast and countless crimes of Verres.

48 In short, gentlemen, in my conduct of this case I shall lay before you facts so notorious, so fully documented, so dreadful, so utterly irrefutable that no-one will dare to use their influence to get you to acquit. Furthermore, I have a completely reliable method of observing my opponents' activities and finding out exactly what they are up to; I shall see to it that all their deliberations will be made as public as if the Roman people were there themselves to see

49 as well as hear their secret plans. The whole reputation of the Senate has been in shreds for years. Now, gentlemen, you can remove, you

can eliminate the shame and the disgrace of it all. Opinion is
unanimous that never in the history of our courts, as we know them
now, has there been a jury to match this one for honour and distinction. But if there is one breath of scandal in this case, men will
assume that the Senate has no better representatives to form a jury;
and from this they will conclude that they must look to some other
order altogether to find the men to run the courts hereafter.

The speech ends with an appeal to the president of the court, and to the
jury, and a sketch of the line that his prosecution will take. Verres did not
await the verdict. He went into exile. At this period, exile was not a
statutory punishment; it was a voluntary act, undertaken to avoid punishment. Its effect, however, was that the exile was debarred from all part in
public life, in the *res publica* of Rome.
   Later in the year 70, a *lex Aurelia* ended the Senate's monopoly of control
of the lawcourts, and despite his success in his election, and in the prosecution, Cicero published his full indictment of Verres, the *Actio secunda in
Verrem*, in 5 books.

9. A PROVINCIAL GOVERNOR AS COMMANDER AND JUDGE

(*i*)

In the fifth and final book Cicero starts by outlining the duties of a provincial governor.

Actio secunda in Verrem, v, 1–4, 26–30:

1   I take it then, gentlemen, as proven that in Sicily Verres blatantly
     despoiled all property sacred and secular, private and public, and
     that in the course of every form of robbery and plunder he displayed
     a total contempt for all religious feeling and such a blind disregard
     for public opinion that he made no attempt to conceal his activities.
     But I gather he has another defence, most impressive and really so
     remarkable that I must give very considerable thought to the question
     of how to reply to it. It goes like this: that thanks to his courage and
     supreme vigilance at a time of dire emergency he saved the province
     of Sicily from the dangerous war that threatened it when the
2   survivors of Spartacus's revolt escaped. (See p. 69 below). What
     can I do gentlemen? It makes an accusation almost impossible and

I am lost. Whatever I say, the defence can stonewall by pointing to Verres' virtues, his bravery as a general who gallantly defended his province. This is hackneyed stuff, but I can see Hortensius will have a field-day dilating upon the dangers of war, the dark days we live in, and our shortage of really good commanders. He will start by appealing to your sympathies but will then assert his authority as a consul-elect and insist that you do not rob Rome of the services of a first-class general on the evidence of mere natives, and certainly not show any willingness to detract from his achievements because of trivial accusations of avarice.

3   Let me be quite frank with you, gentlemen. I am very much afraid that, thanks to the remarkable courage he apparently showed as a general, Verres will escape the penalty he deserves for his crimes. I cannot help remembering the trial of Manius Aquilius and the remarkable effect of the speech Marcus Antonius made on his behalf (in 98 or 97). Antonius was a skilful and passionate orator and at the end of his speech he suddenly seized hold of Aquilius, stood him up in the middle of the court and tore his tunic from him so that everyone, people and jury alike, could see the scars on his chest – none of course on his back. He then waxed eloquent about the head-wound inflicted on Aquilius by the enemy commander and in fact made the jury frightened to death to condemn him in case it looked as if they were flouting the wishes of Providence which had saved him from the weapons of Rome's enemies, and people would say that the man who should have been given a hero's welcome had been

4   saved up as a sacrifice to the jury's own more vicious instincts. The defence is now using the same technique and with the same objectives. It does not matter to them that he is guilty of theft, sacrilege and every crime in the calendar; he is a good general and a lucky one: 'Just the man for a crisis', they say; 'We can't afford to lose him'. But, gentlemen, I don't want a military testimonial; I want proof that he kept his hands off other people's property. All the same, I am not going to stand upon my rights and demand the defence which I am entitled to expect, though the law is quite specific on this point. No! Let us fight on ground of Verres' own choosing and take a closer look at his military record.

26   Let us examine some of his qualities for a start. Now on active service mobility is one of a soldier's most irksome but essential requirements – and in Sicily it is absolutely vital. Verres displayed

considerable resource in making a virtue of necessity. Winter poses
the problem of ice, storm and flood, but he overcame it brilliantly by
basing himself on Syracuse whose geographical position and climate
are reputedly so admirable that, however wild and stormy a day
may be, the sun will always shine for some of it. Here our brilliant
general spent the winter months so comfortably that one rarely saw
him out of bed let alone out of doors, since he devoted the few daylight hours to feasting and the long nights to fornication.

27   But once spring began he became a man of action. (Incidently it
was not the West winds or constellations that told him spring had
arrived but the first May roses in his bedroom). Now he really
showed his mettle – he was tough, vigorous, enthusiastic. No-one
ever saw him on horseback (while the men walked). No indeed!
Like any Bithynian king he rode in an eight-man litter with a
shimmering Maltese cushion stuffed with rose petals at his back,
with garlands on his head and round his neck, and a rose-filled
reticule of the finest linen crochet-work held daintily to his nostrils.
And when they reached some city and the long day's march was
done, in this same litter he was carried all the way to his bedroom,
and there the Sicilian magistrates and Roman knights flocked to pay
court to him, as you have heard on oath from many witnesses. Here
too disputes were brought to him – privately; the matter was
'arranged' and his verdict duly made public moments later. Having
dallied thus for a while settling legal cases on a strictly cash basis, he
closed his court with the final verdict that he had a debt to settle

28   with Venus and Bacchus which required his attention. Here too I
must pay tribute to the remarkable thoroughness and attention to
detail of our illustrious general. In every city in Sicily where the
praetor stops to hold assizes he had a woman of high birth specially
selected to serve his lust. Some were 'invited' openly to dinner. The
more virtuous came at an appointed hour, thereby avoiding attention and publicity. And these were no quiet parties worthy of a
praetor and general of Rome, graced with the decorum which befits
an official banquet; there were scenes of wild tumult and disorder
which sometimes degenerated into regular pitched battles. For our
stern and dedicated praetor, who never obeyed the laws of Rome,
always bowed to the law of the bottle. As a result the dining room
usually ended up like a battlefield with some, the walking wounded,
being helped away and others left there dead to the world and most

of them lying about totally incapable, the whole scene looking not so much like the Governor's dinner party as the massacre of Cannae.

29   Now in Sicily high summer is a busy time for praetors. They are for ever on the move making a special effort to inspect their whole province at threshing time – for a number of reasons: it is when the labour force is concentrated and they can check up on the number of slaves at a time when hot weather and hard work are most likely to breed discontent; it is the obvious time for travel too because of the abundance of food and the good weather conditions. But of course Verres was a general with a difference and was not disposed

30   to follow his predecessors' example. When summer came he set up a permanent camp, elaborately equipped with fine linen marquees, in the most delightful quarter of Syracuse at the very mouth of the harbour where the bay sweeps up from the open sea towards the city. He did the job thoroughly too. He left Hiero's palace, which was now the Governor's residence, and settled down in his new camp and was not seen again that summer. The only people who had access to him were those who organized or assisted at his sexual orgies.

(ii)

Even on the way to his province, a governor was expected to take action to deal with the problems of local communities.

Chapters 39–42 (abridged):

Of course you might also care to mention the little local difficulty at Tempsa right at the end of the Italian slave revolt. By a great stroke of good fortune you happened to be there, Verres, just after it happened. But your behaviour was absolutely typical: you showed not an ounce of guts or determination and you refused to help.

40   Yet the men of Valentia had come to you and begged you to do so through their eloquent and distinguished spokesman Marcus Marius. As he said, you held the powers and position of praetor, so he asked you to take control of the operation to eliminate that tiny band of insurgents. But you refused, and just stood there, inactive, on the sea-shore, flaunting that woman of yours, Tertia, full in the public eye. Yet Valentia was an important allied town with a fine record of

loyalty and this was an important matter to its citizens; but that was
the answer given them by a praetor of Rome receiving a formal
deputation in his dirty smock and gaudy Greek cloak. You can
imagine, therefore, gentlemen, what he did in his province and on
his way there, if on his way home he was prepared to behave like
that – without even getting his normal pleasures to alleviate the
41 disgrace either. That was the day the Senate packed the temple of
Bellona to debate the news from Tempsa. If you remember, gentlemen, evening was falling and the news of our little setback had just
come in, and no-one was available to take over. Some-one pointed
out that Verres was not far from Tempsa and could take control.
There was a general chorus of 'no' from all sides and the senior
senators spoke quite openly against the suggestion. How well they
knew their Verres! How well he vindicated their judgement! Is it
not then remarkable that, after being convicted on so many counts
and by the testimony of so many witnesses, he should still hope for
acquittal from the very men who openly condemned him before his
case was even heard, especially now that they are protected by the
jury's right of secret ballot.

42   So much for that then. He clearly gets no credit from the slave war
nor the threat of such a war, since in Sicily at least it did not exist
and he certainly took no precautions against it. But it may be
argued that he maintained a first-class fleet against the pirates and
showed exemplary efficiency in so doing and, as a result, provided a
really sound defence for his province.

Cicero then describes how Verres took bribes not to demand their quota
of ships or corn from those communities who were due to supply them, and
demanded a quota from those not so due; he also demanded money instead
of supplies in kind for the fleet and its crews, which he then pocketed. In
consequence he had no serviceable fleet, and, since he released the sailors
who paid for the privilege, no effective crews. The result was that a pirate
fleet occupied Syracuse harbour.

10. VERRES' CRIMES AGAINST THE PROVINCIALS

(i)

The description of Verres' cruelty to the Sicilians begins with his punishment of the captains of the ships, whom he blamed for the disaster (see 9

above). Cleomenes, however, a Sicilian nobleman whom Verres had put in charge of the fleet was spared; his wife was one of Verres' mistresses.

Actio secunda in Verrem v, 106–115, 126–7:

Verres suddenly stormed out of his headquarters in a blazing fury bent on murder, marched into the forum and ordered the ships' captains to be summoned. They came at once since they had no reason to fear or suspect anything. He ordered these poor, innocent wretches to be thrown into prison, and when they appealed to him as governor, and therefore champion of their rights, and asked what they had done wrong, he accused them of betraying the fleet to the pirates. There was a gasp of sheer astonishment from the bystanders that any man could have the sheer, brazen audacity to attribute to others a disaster which was entirely the result of his own avarice, and to accuse others of betraying Sicily to the pirates when everyone had assumed that he himself had been aiding and abetting them all along, especially since it was already two weeks since the fleet had been lost. Meanwhile people began to wonder where Cleomenes had gone. It was not that anyone thought that even he deserved punishment for the defeat, scoundrel though he may have been; after all, what could he have done? Not even Cleomenes could work miracles with ships that had been denuded of their crews by Verres' avarice, and I would be the last to try and blame an innocent man. But the picture rather changed when he was spotted sitting as usual up beside the praetor whispering asides to him and obviously on the best of terms. This was the thing that really riled them, to see honest citizens, the elected leaders of their cities, chained and bound while Cleomenes was rewarded with the praetor's friendship for conniving at his vices and crimes. Nevertheless a prosecutor was organized, one Naevius Turpio, who was well qualified for the job since he had himself had a conviction for assault under Gaius Sacerdos, and had been Verres' agent in fiddling tax returns, making false prosecutions for capital offences, and rigging the whole judicial machinery of Sicily.

The parents and relations of these wretched youngsters were shattered by the news of this unexpected disaster. They hurried to Syracuse to see their sons loaded with irons and carrying on their necks and shoulders the rewards for Verres' avarice. They appeared in court, defended their sons, and uttered impassioned appeals to your sense of justice, Verres, though of course there has never been such a thing. One of your own most distinguished friends, Dexo of Tyndaris, appeared for his son. You had enjoyed his hospitality and called him your friend and yet, for all his distinction and desperate as he was, neither his tears nor his old age nor your obligations to him for his kindness could conjure up in you the least vestige of your

109 long-forgotten humanity. But of course it is absurd for me, gentlemen, to talk about the laws of friendship to a monster like him. After all, he had enjoyed boundless hospitality from his friend Sthenius of Thermae and used it to drain him of every penny he possessed, then indicted him in his absence and condemned him to death without a hearing. What is the point of talking to him about duties or obligations to one's friends? Indeed, it is hard to tell if we are dealing merely with a savage or rather with a wild animal of unparalleled ferocity. You, Verres, could not be moved by a father weeping for his son in the hour of his danger, although you had a father of your own at home and a son with you in your entourage. But neither the presence of your own son nor a father far away could resurrect in you the least recollection of how dear children are or

110 what a father's love means. Dexo's son, Aristeus, your own personal friend, you heaped with chains. 'So what?' you say, 'He betrayed the fleet.' Oh? How big was the bribe? 'Well he deserted it anyhow.' Didn't Cleomenes too, then? 'Yes, but Aristeus showed cowardice in the face of the enemy.' But once before you decorated him for valour. 'But on this occasion he got rid of his crews.' Only because you had exempted them from service for a fee.

Another father, gentlemen, a nobleman from an equally distinguished household, tried another approach and in the course of his defence of his son denounced Cleomenes. He was almost literally torn to pieces. What was anyone allowed to say for the defence? However relevant it was to the case, Verres allowed no mention of Cleomenes to be made on pain of death – he was never one to mince his words. He construed a complaint about a shortage of oarsmen as a personal attack upon the praetor and threatened to break the speaker's neck. When the whole case rests on the inadequacies of the praetor and his minions, such behaviour makes it rather difficult to conduct a defence at all.

111 Yet another local dignitary, Heracleus of Segesta, was actually

one of the accused. In the name of our common humanity, gentlemen, listen to his tale for it is typical of the miseries and misfortunes our allies suffered at Verres' hands. Heracleus' problem was that he had serious eye trouble and did not join the fleet, but stayed on leave in Syracuse, having been given permission to do so by the appropriate authority. Whatever else he did, he neither betrayed the fleet, nor lost his nerve and fled, nor deserted his post. And if he had, he should have been brought to book much sooner, at the time when the fleet was actually leaving Syracuse. Nevertheless he was treated exactly like a criminal caught red-handed, although they could not get a conviction against him even on a false charge.

112   Then there was another captain, Furius of Heraclea – some of them had Latin names like that – a man who all his life and even after his death had had considerable fame and distinction all over Sicily as well as in his own home town. He was brave enough to make a stinging attack on Verres at the trial, having decided he might as well be hung for a sheep as a lamb; and then, when he was condemned to death, he managed to put his defence on record in written form, composing it against a background of lamentation from his mother who sat weeping beside him day and night. As a result everyone in Sicily has a copy of his speech and reads it regularly and learns from it the whole grim tale of that man's enormities. In it he documents precisely the number of sailors provided by his city, the number he had to exempt on Verres' orders and the price he was paid, together with the number retained for service – and likewise with all the other ships. When he stated this in court, you, Verres, had him lashed across the eyes with rods. Since he was bound to die he bore the pain easily enough, but protested vigorously to the end, as he had already done in his written testimonial, that it was a disgrace that the pleas of a promiscuous woman had persuaded you to spare Cleomenes while the tears of his own mother, a virtuous woman, had weighed so much less with you that they had failed even

113   to save her son's life. In that same document, gentlemen of the jury, he makes a prophecy, a prophecy which will be proved true if you do not break faith with the Roman people. For he proclaims that Verres could destroy the witnesses but not the evidence; as for himself, his own evidence would carry far more weight in the law courts of eternity than in any mortal tribunal; if he lived he could bear witness only to Verres' avarice, but by his death he would be a

witness to the viciousness and cruelty of his crimes. He finished, gentlemen, with these memorable words: 'One day you will come to judgement, Verres, and on that day there will flock to your trial more than a host of mortal witnesses – for up from the dread kingdom of the underworld shall come the avenging spirits of all innocent men and the grim furies that are the bane of criminals. For me my death is but a light matter, for far worse things have I already seen: with my own eyes I have watched two Roman citizens in an assembly of their peers struck down by your orders and your whetted axes, and I have looked upon the face and hands of Sextius your executioner and blood-letter.' In short, gentlemen, you gave

114 free speech to men who were your allies. This Furius used in full measure though the cruel manner of his death was worthy rather of your most abject slaves.

So his advisers (*consilium*) found them guilty and Verres condemned them all. It seems remarkable that in such an important case, involving so many men, he did not call in his quaestor and close adviser Titus Vettius to help him, nor the excellent Publius Cervius whom he even refused to have on the jury because he had been his chief lieutenant in Sicily. No, the jury that condemned

115 these men whole-sale were his own cronies, a veritable gang of robbers. This was a sign for all Sicilians, our oldest and most loyal allies, a people for long the recipients of our ancestors' generosity, to tremble and fear for their property and their very lives. They were appalled to see the mercy and kindness which had been so characteristic of our empire corrupted to a bestial inhumanity, to see so many men condemned simultaneously on an empty accusation and their villainous praetor seeking to cover his crimes by butchering innocent men.

You may well feel, gentlemen, that I can add no more to this horrific tale of perverted and lunatic cruelty. But you would be wrong.

(ii)

Cicero then elaborates: with diabolical ingenuity Verres and his henchmen proceeded to extract money from the realtives of the condemned men by offering alleviations of their fate for a fee, alleviations such as food and clothing while in prison, one clean stroke of the axe instead of a messy execution, and finally the head and body back for decent burial. It is redress for such treatment which is behind the following passage; strictly the *quaestio de rebus repetundis* was a court for recovery of stolen property, but it was also the only source of redress provincials had against their governor.

126   Where then can the allies turn to beg for help? What can they hope for in life if you, gentlemen, desert them now? They cannot ask the Senate to punish Verres: such a move is unprecedented and unconstitutional. If they appeal to the people there is an easy answer; the people have passed a law protecting allied interests and devised the appropriate machinery to give it effect. This court, then, is the only place for them to appeal to; it is, as it were, the harbour, sanctuary, and citadel of their rights. But they come to it now in a very different spirit from our allies in the past; they are not seeking restitution of their silver, gold, furnishings, slaves or the adornments of their cities and shrines; for these poor unsophisticated souls suspect that Rome permits and approves the plunder of such things. After all, we have watched in silence for many years now while the wealth of the world has poured into the hands of a few powerful men. And our tacit consent and total unconcern has seemed all the more self-evident because none of these men has made the least attempt to

127   conceal his avarice. In the fair city of Rome, with its wealth of art treasures, there is not a statue or painting that was not fairly captured from our enemies in war. But the country houses of these dreaded few are stuffed full of masterpieces looted from the cities of our most loyal allies. What do you think has happened to the wealth of the penniless nations of today, Athens, Pergamum, Cyzicus, Miletus, Chios, Samos – all Asia Minor in fact – Achaea, Greece, Sicily? You will find it all hoarded in the homes of these same few men. But, as I say, gentlemen, the allies are prepared to accept this with equanimity. By their devoted loyalty they have hitherto protected themselves from devastation by decree, and have managed somehow to satisfy though not resist the appetites of the individual predators who came their way. But now resistance is impossible and the supplies have all run out. They have said goodbye to their property and are not even concerned to recover it, though that is strictly the function of this court. Rather, as their appearance suggests, their appeal is for something far more urgent,

and if you want to know what it is, gentlemen, take a long, hard look now at these, your rag-bag, tatterdemalion allies here in court today.

II. VERRES' CRIMES AGAINST ROMAN CITIZENS

After further examples, Cicero turns to the wrongs inflicted on Roman citizens. The power and emotional force of his vindication of the citizens' rights shows how important they were held to be.

Actio secunda in Verrem v, 139–44, 160–4, 166–70:

139 So much for the grievances of the Sicilians. I have said enough, I think, to honour my obligations to men with whom I have established close ties of friendship, and to satisfy the undertakings and promises I made to them. There remains, however, gentlemen, another side to this case, not strictly part of my brief but inseparable from it and derived from my own personal feelings in a matter for which I care very deeply. It concerns the safety, the lives, the survival not just of allies but of citizens of Rome, and that means every one of us here in court today.

Now, for what I have to say, gentlemen, you need not expect me to advance specific proofs, as though the facts were open to dispute. They are not, since I could produce the whole of Sicily as evidence for them if necessary. For by this stage a kind of madness had possessed Verres, which, allied to his habitual audacity and criminal activities, so bewitched his crazed mind and brutal character that he never even hesitated to inflict publicly on Roman citizens in their local assemblies the very punishments that are reserved by law for

140 convicted slaves. I could not begin to tell you, gentlemen, how many citizens he had flogged; suffice to say that, as far as Verres the praetor was concerned, it made no difference whether you were a Roman citizen or not. And so, by sheer force of habit lictors came to do violence to citizens without even waiting for his command.

You cannot deny, Verres, that in the forum at Lilybaeum, where a large body of citizens had gathered for the assizes, Gaius Servilius, a senior member of the Roman business community at Panhormus, was flogged to his knees before your very feet. Deny that for one, if

you dare; everyone in Lilybaeum saw it happen and everyone in
Sicily heard about it. Yes, he was flogged by your lictors till he
collapsed exhausted before your eyes: a Roman citizen, Verres!

141 And what was the reason? It is, of course, a denial of the rights and
privileges of citizenship even to suggest that there ever could have
been a legal reason for such treatment of a Roman citizen, but I
must ask you, gentlemen, to allow me to discuss that reason just this
once and I shall not do so again in any detail. Servilius had made
some rather outspoken remarks about the dishonesty and crimes of
the praetor. As soon as this was reported to Verres he ordered him to
produce guarantees for his appearance at Lilybaeum to answer a
charge laid against him by a slave from the temple of Venus Erycina.
This Servilius did, and reported to Lilybaeum; but no-one produced
either a civil or a criminal charge against him. So Verres tried to
pressurize him into accepting a challenge from one of his lictors for a
thousand sesterces to prove that he was not a professional thief. When
Verres undertook to appoint the assessors for this challenge from his
own retinue, Servilius naturally refused, protesting that no prosecutor had emerged for the original summons, and that he should
not be required to face what was in effect a capital charge before a

142 rigged jury. While he was actually making this protest the six burly
lictors, all of them experts in brutality, surrounded him and began
to beat him up savagely with their rods; in the end the senior lictor,
Sextius – whom I have already mentioned to you – reversed his
cudgel and proceeded to clout the wretched man about the eyes. He
finally collapsed with blood pouring from his face and eyes, but they
went on kicking him in the back to try to force him to accept the
challenge in the end. However, he was finally taken for dead and
carted out and did in fact die soon afterwards. And then Verres, the
champion of Venus, in more senses than one, looking as though
butter wouldn't melt in his mouth, went off and dedicated a silver
Cupid in her temple from the now confiscated estate of Servilius.
This is a fine example of his misuse of other men's property to pay
off the vows he made for the success of his own nocturnal adventures.

143 It would probably be better, gentlemen, if I did not deal individually with all the other punishments he inflicted on our citizens
but confined myself to generalities. Dionysius, the cruellest of the
Syracusan tyrants, had built a prison there, nicknamed the Quarry,
and under Verres it became a sort of home-from-home for Roman

citizens. Anyone whose attitude or appearance he did not like was immediately consigned to the Quarry. I can see you are appalled by this, gentlemen, as indeed you made it clear you were in the first part of the trial when evidence was being given on this subject. For I know you believe that the rights of the free citizens of Rome should be defended all over the world whenever they are infringed and not just here in Rome, where they are so jealously guarded by the tribunes of the people, the magistrates, the law-courts of the forum, the majesty of the Senate and the massive pressure of public opinion; for you all realize full well that only thus can we defend that freedom

144 and our own self-respect. It staggers belief that you can have dared, Verres, to incarcerate so many citizens in a prison designed for the scum of the foreign criminal fraternity, for brigands and the public enemies of Rome. Did it never cross your mind that one day you might face trial in a law-court, or impeachment before the people, or have to endure the loathing and hatred in the eyes of all the crowds who see you here? Did you never picture to yourself the awe-inspiring spectacle of this vast assembly of the Roman people? Did you really think that you would never have to face them, never return to the forum at Rome and fall before the full majesty and

160 rigour of the law? . . . I must now deal with the case of Gavius of Consa. He was one of the Roman citizens imprisoned by Verres, but somehow he managed to escape from the Quarry unnoticed. He reached Messana and could already see Italy and the walls of the Roman city of Rhegium. But his escape from the valley of the shadow of death to a city where he could now breathe the clear air of freedom and justice from across the sea seems to have revived him; he became a different man and began to let his grievances be known in Messana. He explained that he was a Roman citizen who had been flung into prison; that he was going straight to Rome and would be there at the gates to greet Verres on his return. The poor man did not realize that he might just as well have said all this in Verres' own palace since, as I have already explained, Verres had specially selected this city as a partner in crime, the repository of the proceeds of his robberies, and the accomplice in all his misdeeds. Gavius was immediately taken to the chief magistrate and, as chance would have it, Verres visited Messana that day. He was told that there was a Roman citizen who had been complaining that he had been in the Quarry at Syracuse and had been dragged ashore as he

was embarking for the mainland uttering all manner of dire threats against him. This man was now under arrest waiting for Verres to
161 decide what to do with him. He thanked them profusely and commended their loyalty and goodwill, and then entered the forum with murder in his heart. His eyes blazed; his whole face was contorted with cruelty, and everyone was agog to see how far he would go and what he would do. He suddenly ordered Gavius to be thrown down, stripped naked in the middle of the forum and tied up, and the rods to be unfastened from the axes. The poor man cried out that he was a Roman citizen, a burgher of Consa, had served in the army with the noble knight Lucius Raecius, who was now in business at Panhormus and would confirm all this if asked. Verres replied that it had come to his knowledge that Gavius was a spy, sent to Sicily by the leaders of the slave revolt, though he had neither information, evidence nor any grounds for even suspecting such a thing. 'Flog him', he said to his lictors, 'all of you, as hard as you can.' And
162 flogged he was, gentlemen, in the middle of the forum at Messana – a Roman citizen. And amid the groans, the howls, the crack of the blows, that was the only thing the poor man could say, as he did again and again: 'I am a Roman citizen'. He thought, alas, that the rights of citizenship would protect him from flogging and torture. Well, they certainly gave him no protection from the flogging, and when he went on and on clamouring for those rights, of all unbelievable cruelties a cross was set up for this poor, hapless creature who had never even set eyes on such a bestial form of punishment
163 before. So much for the name of the Romans' liberty and the rights of citizenship we are so proud of, gentlemen. So much for Gracchus' and Cato's laws. It makes a mockery of those long-lost tribunician powers which have just been restored to us this year. Yet this is the net result of all our struggles for reform: a Roman citizen, in a Roman province, in an allied city enjoying a special relationship with us, has been strung up and flogged by a man who holds his powers of death and punishment from this same Roman people here. I ask you, Verres, even if his frantic pleas and heart-rending cries could not move you while the fire, the red-hot metal plates, and all the other instruments of torture were being applied to him, could you not even be turned from your course by the tears and expressions of horror of all the Roman citizens who were there? How could you dare to crucify a man who claimed to be a Roman citizen? I did

not want to deal with this matter too emotionally in my first speech, gentlemen, because, as you saw, popular feeling against Verres was running high as distress, disgust, and fear for the safety of the state took control of people's passions. That was why I deliberately toned down my own language and the evidence of my witness, the knight Gaius Numitor, whom you all know so well. And I was delighted that Glabrio very wisely decided to adjourn the hearing while Numitor was actually giving evidence, for there was a real danger that the Roman people would take the law into their own hands and lynch Verres for fear that the law-courts and your verdict, gentlemen,

164 might not exact from him the penalty he deserved. But now that it is quite clear to everyone that you are doomed, Verres, I can safely tell

166 the whole story. . . . So you did not know who he was, Verres, but you thought he was a spy? Why? Of course; you've told us – because he said he was a Roman citizen. But if you were arrested in Persia, or even some outlandish place like India, and were being carried off for punishment, that is exactly what you would cry out too. And if the universally respected status of Roman citizen could save some anonymous creature like you in the heart of an unknown, barbarian country, was it not reasonable for Gavius, unknown as he was, to be given some remission, or at least a postponement of the death penalty by a Roman praetor when he claimed citizenship and appealed to a citizen's legal rights?

167   After all, poor and humble men traverse the seven seas to countries they have never seen before, where they are unknown and un-identifiable, relying only on their Roman citizenship to give them protection not only from our own magistrates, who are bound by law and public opinion, and from our own citizens, who share with them ties of language, law and social behaviour, but also from the inhabitants of any country they may care to visit. Remove this pro-

168 tection, gentlemen, destroy the power of the proud claim that 'I am a Roman citizen', and allow a praetor to inflict whatever penalty he likes on anyone claiming Roman citizenship, simply because he does not know who he is, and what is the result? In every province, every client kingdom, every independent allied state, indeed through-out the whole wide world to which our people now have access, you will be depriving Roman citizens of their right to protection. Was it, after all, so very difficult, Verres, to send a letter to Panhormus to check Gavius' story with Lucius Raecius, the Roman knight he had

named, who was then actually in Sicily? You could have kept the
man safely guarded by your Mamertine supporters, locked up in
chains, till Raecius arrived from Panhormus. If he recognized him,
you could have remitted part of the full sentence; if he didn't, you
could then – if you so wished – have established the principle that
anyone unknown to you who could not produce someone reliable
to vouch for him would be crucified even if he was a Roman
citizen.

169   But I have said enough about Gavius. The real issue is not so much
your cruel treatment of Gavius as the threat your action constitutes
to the name, status, and rights of Roman citizens generally. What
was the point of ordering the cross to be set up in the part of Messana
over-looking the straits when the inhabitants had already put it up
in their traditional spot behind the city on the Via Pompeia; and of
remarking, as you then did – and you cannot deny it, since everyone
heard you say it quite openly – that you had chosen the place
deliberately so that a man who claimed to be a Roman citizen could
see Italy from his cross and have a good view of his homeland? Yet
that is the only time in the whole history of Messana that a cross has
been erected there. He chose that view of Italy deliberately,
gentlemen, so that as he died in grief and agony Gavius should discover how narrow is the gap between slavery and freedom, and so
that the free land of Italy could see its own child nailed to a cross
170   suffering the harshest penalty even a slave can know. To bind a
Roman citizen is a disgrace, to scourge him a crime, but to kill him
is tantamount to murder. As for crucifixion – words fail me. And
even that was not enough. 'Let him look upon his fatherland', he
said, 'and die with law and liberty before his eyes.' But, Verres, it
was not just one ordinary individual called Gavius you tortured and
crucified to death, but the whole basis of a Roman's rights and
freedom.

One final point; one last monstrosity. You can only conclude from
all this, gentlemen, that it irked him not to be able to crucify a
citizen, and through him all citizens, here in Rome in this forum (the
centre of justice), in this *comitium* (where all citizens assemble), upon
this rostrum (the home of all free speech). So he chose the next best
thing: a city most like Rome for its crowds, and nearest to Italy in its
situation. For he wanted the monument to his abominable crime to
stand in full view of Italy and at the very gates of Sicily, where all

who come and go upon the sea could not but view the dreadful spectacle.

Verres was a particularly vicious governor; for Cicero's positive advice to his brother, his theoretical treatment of provincial government, and his own efforts in practice (in Cilicia, in 51–50), see Chapter VII below, (Sections 65–67).

12. CICERO AND THE NOBLES OF SULLA'S PARTY

Honesty in public life, and the claims of 'new men' form the remaining themes of this book. Cicero had spoken of his aspirations for his own aedileship (35–7), and in his peroration he makes an attack on the nobles of Sulla's *res publica*, with renewed threats that he will lead a crusade against judicial corruption.

Actio secunda in Verrem, v, 171–183:

Were I not speaking now, gentlemen, to citizens of Rome, to friends of our state, and men who know the great name of our city, if rather I was addressing brute beasts instead of human beings, or even, I dare say, pouring out my anger and distress to the rocks and crags of some deserted wilderness, nevertheless the whole dumb, inanimate creation would stand appalled at such a tale of dread monstrosities. But, as it is, I speak to the senators of Rome, men who are the very source and fountain-head of law and order and justice – and so I need not fear that they will fail in their verdict to adjudge that one Roman citizen is deserving of that cross and all

172 others totally undeserving. It was but a moment ago, gentlemen, that we could scarce restrain our tears at the shameful and tragic fate of the captains of the Sicilian fleet – and we were very right: for they were innocent men and our own allies. But how must we now react to the death of our own kinsfolk – for it is our duty to regard every Roman citizen as bound by ties of blood-relationship: that alone is the way of safety and of truth. Every Roman citizen here today, every Roman citizen wherever he may be, yearns for a savage sentence, prays for you to keep faith, demands that you defend his rights. For they all realize full well that on your verdict

hang their rights and privileges, the protection and the freedom of
173 the Roman world. What I could do I have done. But if I fail I shall
do more than they have asked of me. For if by some machination
he escapes the sternest censure of this jury – not that I fear it, gentlemen, for I cannot see how it can happen – but if, as I say, my
calculations are wrong, the Sicilians will rightly complain that their
case was betrayed and will be no less bitter than I. Nevertheless, as
aedile I have the powers to summon the assembly; and summon it
I shall. And before January is out, gentlemen, the Roman people
by their own votes will have recovered what is theirs by right. And
if you ask me how that will affect my ultimate chances of distinction,
gentlemen, I shall answer this: that it cannot prejudice my interests
that by a travesty of justice a man escapes the verdict of this court
and comes to judgement before the people. The case will have a
wide publicity and will gain me considerable credit and an easy
victory, and the people will be delighted. Perhaps I have given the
impression, quite unintentionally, of trying to win a quick reputation at Verres' expense; but let me assure you, gentlemen, that his
acquittal will implicate so many that, if he gets away, I shall have
plenty more to make my reputation from.

But for your own sakes, gentlemen, and for that of the *res publica*
I should hate so august a jury as yourselves to be found to have
committed such a crime, I should hate a jury whom I myself
accepted and approved to walk about this city not so much smeared
174 as blackened by the stain of his acquittal. And for this reason,
Hortensius – if the prosecutor may give a little advice to the defence – I beg you again and again to take care and examine the full
implications of your present course of action, as well as the character
of your client and the methods you are using to defend him. Far be
it from me to put any limitations on the ingenuity and eloquence
which you may choose to bring to bear on this case. But if you think
you can usurp the functions of this court by achieving your objectives by underhand activities elsewhere, if you are planning to
proceed by trickery, guile, power, influence or bribery, I most
earnestly advise you to stop it now; as for the devices Verres has
already used or begun to use, I know all about them and can only
suggest you abandon them forthwith and proceed with them no
further. You break the law in this trial at your own peril, and it is
175 a big risk, much bigger than you think. You may perhaps imagine

that as consul designate you have reached the highest office in the land and need fear no longer for your reputation; but believe you me, the honours and rewards of popular favour are as hard to keep as they are to earn. We have all endured as long as we could and as long as we had to the tyrannical monopoly of power of the nobles in the courts and the whole *res publica*; but the day that saw the tribunate restored to Rome marks the end for your class – if only you knew it – of all your domination. The eyes of the world are focussed on each one of us here today to judge our worth: my loyalty as prosecutor to my clients, your integrity, gentlemen, as judges,

176   your honesty, Hortensius, as defending counsel. If any one of us veers but slightly from the path of honour, we shall not face the unspoken protests of a public opinion which you nobles have so long despised, but a mighty and unfettered condemnation by the Roman people. My dear Hortensius, this man is neither relative nor friend of yours; you cannot here excuse an excess of zeal as you have on certain previous occasions by such appeals to sentiment. Indeed you must rather take great care not to give substance to Verres' own frequent claims in Sicily that whatever he did he could rely on you

177   to get him off. I am confident that I have discharged all my obligations even in the eyes of my bitterest opponents, since in the short space of the first part of this trial I proved him guilty to the satisfaction of every man alive. It is not, therefore, my integrity nor Verres' career which now remains on trial, for the one has been vindicated and the other condemned – but this jury and, to tell the truth, yourself, Hortensius; you are the one on trial now.

But one important question still remains: what will be the general climate of opinion if and when this next trial takes place? That is always an important consideration, and in the *res publica* it is vital to assess correctly these shifts of opinion. But in this case the answer is obvious: the trial will be held amid a general popular demand for another class of men, men of a different calibre altogether, to run the law courts here; indeed a bill has already been promulgated on this very subject, and the man responsible for its promulgation is not its official sponsor but Verres here, the defendant – he has caused this bill to be both drafted and published because of his confidence that you would acquit him and the low opinion of you

178   that implied. When this trial began the bill had not been heard of;

when Verres, alarmed by your stern demeanour, gave every appearance of refusing to face his trial, no-one mentioned such a bill; it was only when he had apparently regained his confidence and found new reason to hope for acquittal that it was at once made public. And though your conduct throughout this trial has been the best possible argument against the bill, gentlemen, it is the monstrous impertinence of his misplaced confidence in your decision that is playing into the hands of its advocates. And the result is that if any one of you in this case lays himself open to any blame at all, he will be put on trial either before the Roman people, who will be judging a man whose corruption they have already obviously assumed in transferring control of the courts, or else before new men, expressly appointed judges under the new law because of the scandalous conduct of the courts and their previous jurors, the

179   senators. As for myself, I need hardly say that I must press on with this case to the end; that much must be obvious to anyone. Can I be silent, Hortensius, can I pretend that all is well when I see the *res publica* so grievously wounded, our provinces fleeced, our allies harassed, our temples sacked, citizens crucified and murdered while the criminals go unpunished, and my prosecution fails? Could I now in mid-course just lay aside my heavy burden here in this court or simply put up with it and keep my mouth shut? No, gentlemen, when men have sunk so far in crime as to corrupt our juries, or the jurors themselves so far as to let themselves be corrupted, I must fight on, I must make the matter public, I must appeal to the honour of the Roman people, I must threaten these criminals with ruin or the rigour of the law.

180   It is, indeed, a massive task I am undertaking, as some of you may very well point out; it will probably win me widespread hatred in certain quarters. None of this gives me any pleasure I can assure you, gentlemen. But I am a newcomer in politics and can hardly expect to enjoy the privileges of the aristocracy who are given magistracies by the Roman people without their having to lift a finger to deserve it. I have to make my own way under very different conditions. In this connection I am reminded of the career of that wise champion of the Roman people, Marcus Cato. He realized that he was getting on in politics by his own merit and not by family influence. He was determined to achieve high rank himself and thus be the founder of a new noble family. So he was prepared to incur

the hostility of powerful men, and thanks to his untiring efforts he
181 did win great renown and lived to a ripe old age. Quintus Pompeius,
too, was a man of humble birth, and he too won the highest honours
in the state at the cost of much unpopularity, physical danger, and
prodigious effort. More recently we have seen Gaius Fimbria, C.
Marius and C. Caelius overcoming the bitterest opposition, and
by sheer hard work achieving the status which you, gentlemen, have
inherited despite a life of idleness and neglect of duty. Theirs is the
way we 'new men' must tread. And we are also very well aware that
the good qualities and unsparing efforts of 'new men' like us are
offensive to certain noble gentlemen; we know that if we relax for
a moment, they will ensnare us, if we give them half a chance to
smear our reputations, they will instantly ruin us. So we must be
182 for ever on our guard; we must labour night and day; we must face
the hostility and endure the hardships, knowing all too well that
those we really have to fear are the enemies who work in secret and
unseen rather than those who openly declare their opposition. For
to almost every member of the nobility we are anathema for the
very vigour we display, and no good service of ours can ever win us
their goodwill. Their whole outlook is as different as if they
were another breed of men. So really, gentlemen, one has little
more to fear from the hostility of men who have viewed us with
suspicion and dislike before we ever crossed swords with them
at all.
183   Nevertheless for all these reasons I should dearly like to end my
prosecution here, gentlemen, as soon as I have done my duty by the
Roman people and my friends from Sicily. But if I find my confidence in you misplaced, I am absolutely determined to bring to
trial not only those who will have been most closely implicated in
the corruption of this jury but anyone even faintly connected with
the affair. Let me therefore make a public declaration: let any man,
be he powerful, or foolhardy, or a man of guile, let any man, I say,
beware of seeking to pervert the course of justice in this trial – for I
shall be his enemy and the Roman people his judge. And if he has
found me eloquent, ruthless and determined in my prosecution of a
man the Sicilians made my enemy, let him realize that to any man
who becomes my enemy when I am champion of the Roman people
I shall be an opponent far more ruthless, far more determined, far
more deadly.

13. POLITICAL MANIPULATION

Abroad, Sulla's death had left the Senate with two principal problems; in Spain, Sertorius, a leader of Marius' party, had declared his independence; in Pontus, Mithridates utilized the breathing-space given him by Sulla to consolidate his position, and to harass the Romans by negotiating with Sertorius and encouraging piracy by sea and brigandage on land, especially in Macedonia. Sulla's party attempted no reconciliation with Sertorius, but sent Pompey to Spain in 77 to help Metellus Pius to crush the Spaniards, a mission successfully accomplished by 71. Mithridates himself kept the peace till 74, when the Bithynian king died, bequeathing his kingdom to the Senate and Roman people; Mithridates thereupon intervened, while in Rome intrigue began amongst rivals for the command of what appeared to be a promising field for plunder and wealth.

PLUTARCH, *Life of Lucullus*, V–VI (abridged):

When Lucullus obtained by lot the province of Cisalpine Gaul, he was extremely indignant, since it offered no expectations of military achievement . . . He was at loggerheads with one Cethegus. The latter enjoyed enormous influence: he courted popularity with everything he did and said. Lucullus however was always criticizing his morals and arrogant defiance of the laws . . . The death of Octavius, governor of Cilicia, was then announced. Many people aspired to the post, and made up to Cethegus as being most able to procure it for them. Lucullus did not care in the least about Cilicia itself, but thought that if he got that province, which was adjacent to Cappadocia, he was bound to be the only candidate for the war against Mithridates. So he strained every nerve to prevent its allocation to someone else . . . There was a woman called Praecia amongst those well known in the city for their attractiveness and promiscuity; what marked her out from ordinary loose women was the fact that she used her sleeping-partners to further her friends' political ambitions. She added to her other charms the ability to be a real partner to her lovers in the sense that she was able to get things done, and thus she became a powerful figure in politics. So when she attracted Cethegus at the height of his influence, and became his mistress, he brought the whole city with him, and all political power fell into her grasp; nothing now was done in politics if Cethegus did not support it, nor anything if Praecia did not put Cethegus up to it. Lucullus therefore sought her out; he gave her

gifts; he flattered her – and indeed it was a fine feather in her cap
for an arrogant bitch who liked to make a show to be seen sharing
the political aspirations of Lucullus – and this immediately brought
Cethegus over to singing his praises and canvassing for Cilicia to
be given him. But when once he got Cilicia, Lucullus no longer
needed the support of either Praecia or Cethegus – everyone was
equally anxious to put the Mithridatic War into his hands.

14. SPARTACUS: THE SLAVES REVOLT

While Lucullus campaigned in Asia Minor and Pompey campaigned in
Spain, the Italian countryside was ravaged for three years (73–71) by a
revolt led by Spartacus. He was a Thracian, one of a party of 74 gladiators
who escaped from their training school at Capua, occupied Mount Vesuvius,
and, having broken through the force besieging them, raised the slaves of
the South of Italy in arms. Eventually, Spartacus' own forces amounted to
perhaps 30,000, and those of an ally called Crixus to some 10,000. Both
consuls of 72, the proconsul of Cisalpine Gaul, and one praetor, Cn.
Manlius, were defeated by Spartacus; another praetor, Q. Arrius, defeated
and killed Crixus and was then defeated by Spartacus. The consuls were
then withdrawn from the war, which was entrusted to M. Licinius Crassus,
who had won a military reputation at the battle of the Colline Gate.

PLUTARCH, *Life of Crassus*, X–XI (abridged):

'Many of the leading citizens joined his forces because of their
friendship and their esteem for him . . .' and later, after his lieutenant
Mummius was defeated in central Italy, 'when Crassus re-armed
his troops, he demanded that they give him security for their arms
to ensure that they would not throw them away; moreover, he
decimated the 500 who had been the first to give way, and the most
cowardly, by dividing them into 50 squads of 10, and executing one
man per squad, whoever was drawn by lot. This was a reintroduction
of a traditional punishment long disused. It is carried out under the
eyes of many witnesses. Death in this fashion is in itself shameful,
and it is inflicted in a way which has many features calculated to
fill the onlookers with revulsion and dread'.

Dissension broke out in Spartacus' forces after Crassus had pursued him to southern Italy, and prevented him from crossing to
Sicily. The two parts of the slaves' forces were brought to battle

separately: 'Crassus decided to attack those who seceded from Spartacus first . . . and sent 6000 men to seize a piece of high ground without being detected. However, despite the fact that they had camouflaged their helmets, his men were sighted by two women who were making a sacrifice for the enemy forces. They would have been overwhelmed had not Crassus quickly appeared and joined in what was to be the bitterest battle of all. 12,300 of the enemy fell, all but two from blows on the front part of their body, sustained in hand to hand fighting with the legions'. Spartacus withdrew, and was eventually killed in another battle after inflicting a reverse on Crassus' quaestor. The remnants of his force were intercepted and killed by Pompey on his return from Spain, who 'wrote to the Senate that Crassus had beaten the runaway slaves in battle, hand to hand, but that he himself had ended the war, root and branch'.

15. PIRACY AND CONDITIONS IN ASIA

The problem of piracy, stimulated by Mithridates, but having as one of its more important causes the economic ruin of the Roman province of Asia caused by Sulla's exactions, also required attention; in 74, M. Antonius (father of Mark Antony), who was then praetor, was invested with proconsular *imperium* not restricted to any particular area and the task (*provincia*) of suppressing the pirates. He decided to attack Crete first, where he died after being heavily defeated; the campaign was then abandoned. The war against the cities of Crete was resumed in 68 under Q. Metellus, consul of 69, who was governor of Crete and Achaea (southern Greece), but the general problem of piracy was not solved until the lex Gabinia was passed in 67, under which Pompey was given a command similar to that of Antonius. A lightning campaign completed the task in 40 days; it was no doubt materially aided by a general policy of mercy to those who surrendered. Plutarch describes the conditions in Asia.

Life of Lucullus, XX (abridged):

Lucullus turned to the administration of justice . . . (sc. in Asia, while a mission was engaged in negotiations for the surrender of Mithridates). The province had long been without it, and had suffered unspeakable and unbelievable depredations; it was being devastated and enslaved by tax-contractors (*publicani*) and money lenders (*faeneratores*); individuals were being driven to sell the bodies of their handsome boys and virgin daughters; communities to sell their temple-treasures and works of art, and the statues of their gods; the end of it all for themselves was slavery when adjudged the property of their creditors, before which the tortures to which they were subjected . . . made their slavery seem like a blessed release . . . Lucullus, however, first fixed the maximum interest rate at 1 per cent per month (12 per cent per year); he then cut off all accumulations of interest above the original debt; third, and most important of all, he forbade a creditor to demand more than 25 per cent of a debtor's income; loss of his entire credit was decreed to be the punishment of a creditor who tried to add interest to principal. The result was that in less than four years all debts were paid off, and those who had pledged their (public) properties had redeemed them unencumbered. The origin of this public debt had been the 20,000 talents demanded by Sulla to punish Asia; the creditors had already received 40,000 talents, but by adding interest to principal the moneylenders had built up their credits to a total of 120,000 talents.

16. POMPEY AND MITHRIDATES

Successful though his policy was, Lucullus' campaign against Mithridates proved to be abortive. Negotiations with the Armenian king, Tigranes, were grossly mishandled by Lucullus' brother-in-law, Appius Claudius Pulcher; another brother-in-law, P. Claudius, (who favoured the 'plebeian' spelling of his name as Clodius, the name by which we usually know him) encouraged seditious elements in the army. How far this was influenced by the businessmen who had lost money by the settlement of Asia we do not know, though it is often alleged, and is not improbable. Lucullus was not able to bring either of the kings to a decisive battle, and, following the defeat of a lieutenant at Zela in 67, his soldiers mutinied, demanded their discharge, and threatened mass desertion if Lucullus attempted a new campaign (Plutarch, *Life of Lucullus*, XXI, XXXIV–V). Pompey was by now in the Black Sea area at the end of his campaign against the pirates; his troops were fresh, their morale was high; early in 66 a tribune, C. Manilius, proposed that the command against Mithridates should be transferred from Lucullus to Pompey. Cicero, encouraged by his electoral success in winning the praetorship, came forward to support the bill.

In *Pro lege Manilia*, after a few preliminary words for himself (1–3), Cicero passes first to the Romans' duty to aid their ally, king Ariobarzanes of Cappadocia, the province of Asia, and the substantial revenues to be derived from it, and the *publicani*, whose interests, he argues, cannot be divorced from those of the citizen-body as a whole.

Pro lege Manilia, 4–8, 11–19:

4   Let me start, then, at the beginning of the whole affair. War has been declared, a grievous war which threatens your revenues and your allies, by two most mighty kings, Mithridates (of Pontus) and Tigranes (of Armenia), the one encouraged by our negligence, the other provoked by our attentions, and both thinking they have a golden opportunity to seize the province of Asia. Every day I get letters from financial friends there, honourable men who have invested fortunes in collecting your revenues for you. Because of my close connections with their class it is to me they have sent these reports describing the menace to the *res publica* and the threat to

5   their own livelihood: Bithynia, now one of your own provinces, has had a number of villages burnt to the ground; Cappadocia, the

kingdom of Ariobarzanes which is next door to your tribute-paying allies, is totally in enemy hands; our general Lucius Lucullus, despite his great achievements, is giving up his command; his successor is too inexperienced to cope with such a war; there is only one man to take supreme command – everyone wants him, everyone longs for him, ally and Roman alike; this same man is feared by our enemies, and that cannot be said of anyone else. You see the situa-

6 tion. What are we to do? It is you, gentlemen, who must decide.

Now there are three aspects of the problem which I think I should discuss; the character of this war, its extent, and the choice of general – in that order. It is exactly the kind of war which should most inspire and inflame your hearts to see it through to the end. Rome's glorious achievements, the achievements of your forefathers which are your heritage, achievements remarkable certainly in every sphere but unsurpassed in the annals of war; the safety of your friends and allies for which your fathers fought many long and cruel campaigns; Rome's largest and most reliable source of revenue whose loss will cost you the adornments of peace and sinews of war; the property of many citizens for which both individual and national interest makes it your duty to show concern; all these are now at

7 stake. Furthermore, above all other nations you have yearned for glory and honour; yet there is a blot upon that honour, inflicted in the last war against Mithridates, which has stained too deep and marred too long the fair name of Rome. This you must eliminate. Remember that one man, by one despatch, at one nod of his head, procured the murder, the butchery of every Roman citizen through-out the innumerable city-states of the whole province of Asia. And that one man has so far suffered no punishment to match his crime; indeed he has remained king of his country for the last twenty-two years. And in ruling it he is not content merely to lurk concealed in his lairs in Pontus or Cappadocia, but wants to leave the kingdom which is his birthright and wreak havoc among your tribute-paying

8 states under the very noses of all Asia. For hitherto the battles which our generals have fought with Mithridates have yielded the rewards of victory without the substance. Lucius Sulla got a triumph; so did Lucius Murena; both for defeating Mithridates. They were both brave men and great generals. But though they got their triumphs and he was driven back, defeated, he is still there, and king. Nevertheless those generals deserve our praise for what they

did achieve and our pardon for what they left undone: it was political necessity that brought Sulla back to Italy, and Sulla that brought Murena. . . .

11   Our forefathers often went to war if the rights of merchants or ship-owners were infringed; what then ought you to do when thousands of Roman citizens have been butchered at one fell swoop? When our ambassadors were insulted, our forefathers wanted to blot out Corinth, the fairest city in all Greece; will you then leave unpunished a tyrant who loaded a senior ambassador of Rome with chains, flogged him, put him to every form of torture, and finally murdered him? Our forefathers would not tolerate the loss of one iota of the rights of Roman citizens; will you tolerate the loss of their lives? They punished a merely verbal infringement of diplomatic immunity; will you allow an ambassador to be cruelly

12 done to death? If so, let me warn you that, as it was their greatest glory to have bequeathed you this vast and noble empire, so it will be your ultimate disgrace to have failed to protect and guard your own inheritance.

Very well then. Since your allies are menaced as never before, how ought you to react? King Ariobarzanes, the friend and ally of the Roman people, has been expelled; instead, two tyrants, the implacable enemies of yourselves, your allies, and your friends threaten the whole of Asia. And now, because the menace is so vast, every state in Asia and Greece must look to you for help. They dare not ask you for one particular general (especially since you have already sent them someone else): in fact they think it would be

13 dangerous to do so. But they are very well aware, as you are too, that there is one man supremely well qualified to do this job, and since he is nearby they resent his absence all the more bitterly. Indeed, with his great reputation, the mere fact that he is there at all, albeit for a naval campaign, makes them feel that the enemy's attacks have been restricted and curtailed. They cannot ask aloud; but in the silence of their hearts they beg you to show that you value their safety as much as that of others by entrusting it to this great man. And there is, too, one special reason for this prayer: the governors we have sent out to other provinces have been so corrupt that their progress through the allied cities differs little from the assaults of the enemies from whom they may sometimes have protected them; but Pompey they know, first by reputation and now

by experience, is a man of such restraint, such mild temper, and such civilized demeanour, that men measure their blessings by the length of time he stays among them.

14 If, then, on behalf of their allies, without having suffered any loss themselves, our ancestors fought Antiochus, Philip, The Aetolian League, Carthage, is it not your duty to show far greater determination to defend your allies and your own self-respect as an imperial power, when you have already suffered personal loss, especially since you may also lose your largest source of revenue? For the revenue from the other provinces is such that it scarcely pays us to defend them; but Asia, gentlemen, Asia is so wealthy and so fertile that she easily excels all other countries in richness of soil, variety of produce, extent of grazing lands, and volume of exports. This province, in fact, finances our wars and makes our peace worthwhile; if you want to keep things that way, Men of Rome, you must protect it not just from danger but from the fear of danger.

15 For usually loss comes only in the wake of disaster; but when it is a matter of money, it is not disaster but loss of confidence that brings ruin in its wake. For when an enemy approaches, even if he does not actually invade a country, pastures are abandoned, fields deserted and merchants quit the seas. And so the taxes on imports and exports are lost, and so are the agricultural tithes and the poll-tax on beasts. And that is why, very often, one hint of danger, one

16 threat of war can often cost a country a whole year's revenue. And how do you think they feel about it, the tax-payers and the tax-contractors and collectors, with two kings, commanding vast forces, breathing down their necks? How do you think they feel when one cavalry raid can cost them a whole year's revenue; when they think the large staffs they have in the salt-works, on farms, in harbour offices and posts in the outback are in danger? Do you imagine you can continue to enjoy the fruits of Asia unless, as I have said, you protect the men who supply those fruits not merely from disaster but also from the fear of disaster?

17 There is another matter, too, which you must not neglect, though it is the last item in my discussion of the character of this war. It concerns the property of many Roman citizens, and if you have any sense, gentlemen, you will give it your most careful attention. First, then, the tax-contractors, who are a respected and distinguished body of men, have invested their money and resources in Asia, and

that in itself should make you feel concern for their welfare. For we
have always regarded our revenues as the sinews of the state, and so
we would certainly be right to call the class who collect those

18 revenues the backbone of our society. Secondly, there are working
in Asia at this time many representatives of all sections of society,
hard-working and devoted men, for whom it is your duty to take
thought in their absence. And there are others, too, who have
invested large sums of money in the province. It is only natural,
therefore, that you should strive to protect so many citizens from
disaster; it is only common sense to see that a disaster to so many
citizens must be a disaster for the whole *res publica*. There is, after all,
little point in trying to dun the tax-contractors for the missing
revenues when you have defeated the enemy. The disaster will have
made them too poor to pay up, and everyone else will be too
frightened to risk taking on the contract.

19   Mithridates it was, too, that taught us a lesson at the start of the
Asian war – it was a lesson so calamitous that we should never forget
it. At that time too, thousands lost large fortunes in Asia and we all
know how confidence was shattered by the postponement of debt
settlements. For one cannot have large numbers in a single state
losing every penny they possess without their dragging still more
down to ruin with them. Do not let it happen again. For believe
you me, (as you know, of course, very well yourselves) financial
confidence and the whole monetary system based on the forum here
at Rome is bound up with and depends upon those Asian investments. They cannot collapse without bringing this whole structure
crashing to the ground. Now can you hesitate, I ask you, gentlemen,
to devote your utmost endeavour to this war, in which you are
fighting for your honour, the safety of your allies, the bulk of your
revenues, and the fortunes of so many citizens at the same time as
you fight for the *res publica*?

17. POMPEY THE GENERAL

Cicero discusses the gravity of the war and concludes that it is 'large enough
to require our involvement but not so large that we need hestitate to enter
it'. He praises Lucullus for his achievements while making it clear that the
danger is now such as to require Pompey's presence; he then passes to a
laudation of Pompey, together with a brief résumé of his career up to that

moment. We note especially the inclusion among Pompey's virtues some qualities not usually associated with the Romans, approachability (*facilitas*) and warmth (*humanitas*), but these were qualities upon which Cicero himself laid considerable stress. More unusual to us appear the claims that Pompey enjoyed divine support (47–48), as Sulla had claimed to do, in proof of which he had taken the cognomen of Felix himself, and given the twin children born to Metella his wife the hitherto unknown *praenomina* of Faustus and Fausta.

Pro lege Manilia, 27–46, 49–50:

27   I think I have said enough to show you why its nature makes this war necessary and its size makes it dangerous. It only remains for me to speak, I think, about the choice of general to take command of the extensive operations involved. I only wish, gentlemen, that we had so many brave and incorruptible men available as to make it difficult to decide who is best qualified for such a responsible post. But now, at this moment, there is only one, Gnaeus Pompey, and he has won more glory than any known man, living or dead.

28   So why do you hesitate? It seems to me that a great general needs four qualities: experience, ability, leadership, and luck. No one has ever been, or could be, more experienced than Pompey. He left school and the classroom to become a soldier in his father's army in a major campaign against the fiercest foes; so at seventeen, as a common soldier, he served under a great general; in a year or two he was himself a general commanding a great army; Rome's enemies he has fought more often than anyone else has ever quarrelled with his own; he has fought more wars than anyone else has read about; held more posts than anyone else has ever dreamed of; and as a young man he learned the art of war at first hand from his own experience as a commander, without ever being defeated and winning a triumph for every campaign he undertook. In short, there can be no kind of war which he has not been through at his country's call: civil war, war in Africa, in Transalpine Gaul, in Spain against Romans and against warrior tribes, a slave war, a naval war, wars of every sort and every kind against a variety of enemies, all of them waged, and all of them won by this one man. All this proves, gentlemen, that there is nothing in soldiering outside the range of his experience.

29   As for Pompey's ability, words cannot do it justice. Nothing any-

one could say would be adequate, interesting or original. He has more than the popular conception of a general's abilities, though these he has in such full measure that no other general past or present seems to have had any at all: conscientiousness, courage,

30 vigour, speed, efficiency, imagination. If you want proof, look at Italy which Sulla, its conqueror, admitted was freed with Pompey's help and by Pompey's skill; look at Sicily, which is released from the many perils that beset it not by brute force but by quick thinking; look at Africa, which he soaked in the blood of the vast enemy forces which oppressed it; look at Gaul, through which, by the slaughter of the inhabitants, he opened the route to Spain for the legions of Rome; look at Spain, where so very often thousands of our enemies were overwhelmed and laid low by him; and again and again, look at Italy: when she was writhing under the pressure of that disgraceful slave war which threatened her very existence, she sought help from Pompey who was far away. Once he was expected, the danger seemed so much less; when he arrived, the war was dead

31 and buried in a moment. If you want proof, look at every clime and country, every nation and tribe, every sea and every gulf and harbour therein; all, all are proof indeed that what I say is true. For what place in recent years has been so well guarded as to be safe from the pirates, or so insignificant as to escape their attentions? Did anyone even set sail without risking death in the winter gales or slavery from the pirates who infested the seas in a sailing season? Did anyone ever seriously imagine that so vast a war, one so pernicious and long-standing, could ever be brought to an end in one year even by the united efforts of all our generals, or by one general in any number of years? In all this time no province has been free

32 from their ravages; no revenue safe. You could not defend your allies; your fleet was useless; God knows how many islands in your alliance were deserted, either abandoned in terror or captured by pirates.

But why tell of things so far away? In the good old days Rome used to fight at the far-flung bastions of her empire to defend her allies not herself. Why should I mention that over these last few years your allies could not cross the seas, when your own armies never dared leave the harbour of Brundisium except in the depths of winter? Why should I complain that foreign embassies were captured, when your own ambassadors had to be ransomed? Why

recall that the sea was unsafe for merchants, when twelve lictors, the
33 praetors' own bodyguard, fell into the clutches of the pirates? Am I
to remind you that those magnificent cities, Cnidos, Colophon, and
Samos were captured, as well as countless others, when you know
very well how your own harbours, and those from which you draw
your life-blood, were themselves in pirate hands? You all know the
story of how Caieta, a port world-famous and crowded with ship-
ping, was sacked before the very eyes of the praetor, and how the
children of the very man who had previously led the war against
the pirates were kidnapped by them at Misenum? We suffered a
defeat at Rome's own port, Ostia, which brought shame and disgrace to the *res publica*. But why complain of that when you yourselves almost literally saw a fleet commanded by a consul captured
and sunk by those same pirates? And yet, in the name of Heaven,
it passes belief that one man's amazing, god-given genius should so
quickly bring us to the light of day that, while a few weeks ago you
saw an enemy fleet knocking on the doors of Ostia, today it is
reported that there is no pirate this side of the Straits of Gibraltar.
34 And although you all know the speed at which this was done, I
cannot ignore it in this speech of mine.

Has anyone ever, even in the pursuit of business or profit, managed to visit so many places or make so many journeys in so short
a time as Pompey's military machine traversed the Mediterranean?
Before the sailing season had begun he visited Sicily, inspected
Africa, and sailed from there to Sardinia with his fleet, and thus
guaranteed the protection of Rome's three 'granaries' by land and
sea. Then he returned to Italy and organized strong garrisons of
men and ships for the two Spanish provinces and Transalpine Gaul;
he also sent ships to the coast of the Illyrian Sea, to Achaea, and
the whole of Greece, and in this way made the Adriatic and
Tyrrhenian Seas completely safe by protecting them with strong
garrisons and mighty fleets. Forty-nine days after leaving Brundisium he had added the whole of Cilicia to the Roman empire and
the pirates who had swarmed there everywhere were all either
captured and killed, or had surrendered to the power of Pompey
alone. When the Cretan pirates sent him an abject embassy all the
way to Pamphylia, he demanded hostages and kept their hopes in
surrender alive. And so, this vast and protracted war with its end-
less ramifications which had harassed all nations and all tribes was

dealt with by Gnaeus Pompey; he planned it at the end of winter, started it in early spring, and completed it by midsummer.

36　That is the kind of genius he is – inspired, incredible. But there is more. His other qualities which I began to elaborate a short while ago are numerous and remarkable. After all, a great general must be more than a superb war-leader; he needs many supporting talents. He must be, to a high degree, a man of honour and self-control, trustworthy, sociable, intelligent, generous. And has Pompey got these qualities? Yes, gentlemen, all of them, and in the highest degree. Indeed, in Pompey they so abound as to obscure their individual worth. Perhaps we can appreciate them best by a

37　comparison with those of other men. What, after all, are we to think of a certain other general in whose army promotion is for sale, and has been bought? He is an important and distinguished figure; but what are we to think of his loyalty to the *res publica* when he has drawn money for the war from the Treasury and then used it to bribe government officials in his greed to get a provincial governor's post, or else, out of sheer avarice, left it on deposit at Rome? I see from your reactions, gentlemen, that you know who I am talking about. But I am mentioning no names, so no-one can get angry with me without first giving himself away. As for the disasters such commanders bring upon our armies wherever they go, it is common

38　knowledge. Remember the way our generals went through Italy, and the devastation they caused in town and country to the property of Roman citizens; then you will find it easier to imagine what goes on among mere foreigners. Where do you think your soldiers have done more damage in recent years: to the cities of your enemies or the states of your allies when they were quartered there for the winter? No general can control an army if he cannot control himself; he cannot judge others by one standard and expect them to

39　judge him by another. In this context it seems remarkable that Pompey should be so pre-eminent: indeed we hear that when his vast army reached Asia, they left no trace of violence or indeed of their passage through the lands of those they had subdued. And now daily reports and letters reach us of the disciplined behaviour of these soldiers in their winter quarters. Not only is no one compelled to contribute to a soldier's expenses; he may not, even if he wants to. For our forefathers wanted the homes of our friends and allies to shield our soldiers from the winter not our avarice from the law.

40 Look, too, how restrained he is in all his other activities. How do you account for the incredible speed of his movements? He did not have specially mighty oarsmen, or some secret knack of navigation, or some new winds to carry him so fast to the far corners of the earth: but he was not held up by a general's usual 'distractions'. Avarice did not draw him from his planned route to plunder, lust did not lead him away to licentiousness, nor frivolousness lead him to some light pastime, fair cities to play the tourist, nor even hard work to seek for rest. Finally, the statues, the pictures, and the art treasures of Greece, which to others seem to be there for the taking,

41 he did not even think worth going to look at. And the result is that all the inhabitants of those parts look on Gnaeus Pompey not as the agent of Rome but as a god come down from heaven; now at last they are beginning to believe that Rome did once produce men of such legendary self-control, though foreigners used to think it the fabrication of a false tradition; now your empire begins to shed its lustre on those peoples; now they are realizing that their own ancestors were right when they preferred to surrender their sovereignty to the service of Rome rather than be the rulers, in the days when Rome's officials were men like that. For now indeed so easy of access is Pompey to individuals, so ready to listen to complaints about abuses that he, whose glory is greater than that of all the kings of the earth, seems as approachable as his meanest slave.

42 As for his statesmanship and his powerful eloquence backed by the weight of a general's prestige, you, gentlemen, have often encountered them in this very forum. Judge, if you can, how our allies trust him, when our enemies, one and all, of every nation, would never doubt his word. So generous is he, too, by nature that it is hard to say whether his enemies feared his courage more in battle than they loved his mercy in defeat. Does anyone doubt that this is the man to run this gruelling war? Indeed rather he seems to have come into the world by divine dispensation to put an end to every war we have ever known.

43 And furthermore, if you are going to run a war or lead an army, you must have prestige: and everyone knows that Pompey has more than anyone else. Any child could tell you that our generals' reputations with friend and foe are vital to their success, since we all know that on such occasions of crisis men are moved by their own prejudices and other people's opinions, as much as by any

rational process, to respect or despise, to hate or love a given commander. Well then, who in all the world has ever been better known
than Pompey? Whose achievements are a match for his? And the
greatest contribution to his prestige was made by yourselves when
you gave him more distinguished appointments than any other man.

44 Do you suppose that anywhere in the whole wide world is so desolate
that it has not heard the story of that great day when the whole
population of Rome packed the forum and every temple overlooking
it to demand as commander-in-chief for a war that threatened the
safety of the world one man, and one man only, Gnaeus Pompey?

I have said enough, and I do not need second-hand proofs of the
extent of Pompey's military reputation; but perhaps I might take
one example, which concerns him directly, as typical of his remarkable influence upon events. Immediately before his appointment,
the shortage of grain had been acute and the market price excessive.
Yet it is some indication of the measure of hope his name inspired
that on the day you appointed him commander-in-chief of the naval
operations against the pirates, the price dropped so sharply that it
fell to a level scarcely found after a bumper harvest in stable peacetime conditions.

45   And now you have suffered disaster in Pontus as a result of the
battle which, alas, I have had to discuss with you since your own
allies were panic-striken, your enemies' resources and confidence
increasing, and your province inadequately defended. You would
have lost Asia, too, gentlemen, had not Pompey by some miraculous
stroke of good fortune been in the crisis area at the vital moment.
His arrival halted a Mithridates elated by his unaccustomed success,
and forced Tigranes to hesitate at the moment when his huge forces
threatened Asia. Clearly the general whose mere prestige can do
that will do far more when his talent is actually put to the test; if
his reputation and the news of his arrival protected Asia, he will
certainly find it easy to save our allies and our revenues when he is

46 backed by his own army. And again, how Rome's enemies must
respect and fear him when, in such a short space of time, and from
places far afield and wide apart, they all sent their surrender to him
alone. For example, although we had a general and an army
actually in Crete itself, the Cretans as a body sent envoys almost to
the ends of the earth and offered Pompey the surrender of all their
states. Or again, did not this same Mithridates send his representative

all the way to Spain to see him? Some people were furious that he had been sent to Pompey specifically and chose to regard him as a spy, not an envoy. But not so Pompey.

So you can decide for yourselves, gentlemen of Rome, how enormously those foreign kings and foreign nations will be impressed by Pompey's prestige, enhanced as it is by his own great deeds and the vast honours you have heaped upon him . . .

49   To summarize then: you have here a war too vital to neglect and so large that it must be efficiently run; you have a man to put in charge of it of vast experience, enormous courage, incomparable prestige, and unprecedented good luck, a veritable gift from heaven for the defence and glorification of the *res publica* – you cannot
50   hesitate to give him the command. Had he been a private citizen at this time, you would still have had to go through all the elaborate procedures of appointing him and sending him out; but as it is, as well as all his other advantages, by a lucky coincidence he is already on the spot, with an army, ready to take over at once from those in charge – so what are you waiting for?

18. PRECEDENTS

The last portion of the speech consists of a skilful refutation of the objections to Manilius' proposal which had been advanced by Q. Catulus and Q. Hortensius, leading supporters of Sulla's settlement. Cicero's answer to the former – who had argued against setting precedents – is to quote examples from Pompey's earlier career and from elsewhere of precedents which had been vindicated by results.

Pro lege Manilia, 60–8:

60   Now you may argue that we should do nothing contrary to precedent and tradition in this matter. I need hardly remind you, gentlemen, at a time like this that our forefathers obeyed tradition in peacetime but followed expediency in war, and always adapted their policies to meet the requirements of each new situation. The Punic and Spanish wars were both brought to a successful conclusion by a single general; Carthage and Numantia, two of the most powerful cities ever to threaten our dominions, were both

destroyed by Scipio; more recently, as you know, you and your fathers decided that our empire's safety rested on C. Marius alone, and you gave that one man conduct of the wars against Jugurtha, the Cimbri, and the Teutones. As for the case of Pompey, Quintus Catulus has argued that we should not give him any unprecedented powers, but it is worth remembering how many he has already been given – with Catulus' full approval, gentlemen.

61   For example there can be nothing more unprecedented than a private citizen raising an army in a national crisis while he is barely out of his teens and then taking command of it. Pompey did both, and proved a successful leader. Or what about a man, far too young to be a senator, being given an army and a general's powers together with the provinces of Sicily and Africa and full control of the war out there? Yet as a governor he displayed an exemplary integrity, capability, and devotion to duty, finished off a major war in Africa, and brought his army home again victorious. Who ever heard of a mere knight celebrating a triumph? But all Rome saw it, and greeted

62 the spectacle with enthusiastic celebrations. Again, what could be more exceptional than a knight being sent out with consul's power to take control of an important and very dangerous war, when there were two very distinguished and courageous consuls available for the job? Yet that is what happened to Pompey, although some senators at the time deplored the fact that a private citizen was being given a consul's powers. However Lucius Philippus is reported to have said that he was voting for Pompey to get the powers of both consuls – and that is some indication of the hopes for success which the city placed in a single, remarkable young man. Nothing could be more unprecedented than the senatorial decree which released him from his constitutional obligations and allowed him to become consul before he was of a legal age to hold any magistracy whatever. Again, unbelievably, as a Roman knight he was granted a second triumph by senatorial decree. In short, the sum total of all the unprecedented decisions in our history would be less than those that

63 have been taken for Pompey alone. And all of them, many and remarkable though they are, have been taken on the authority of Quintus Catulus and his most distinguished senatorial colleagues in honour of that one man, Gnaeus Pompey.

In fact, gentlemen, if they are not careful, an unreasonable and quite intolerable situation will arise if you, the people of Rome, have always endorsed the Senate's authority in heaping honours on Pompey, yet they refuse to support your judgement of him now and so deny you your constitutional rights. Yet you, gentlemen, might very well defend your judgement of this man against all opposition, since it was you who selected him from all the candidates to run the

64 war against the pirates despite the senate's vociferous objections. If in so doing you displayed too little concern for the safety of the *res publica*, they are right to seek to force their advice upon you on this occasion. But if at that time you showed more wisdom and insight than they and, despite their opposition, brought distinction to our empire and safety to the whole world, then it is high time those princes of state confessed that they too, like everybody else, must bow to the authority of the assembled people of Rome. The war in Asia against Mithridates, gentlemen, requires not only the talents of a soldier, in which Pompey is pre-eminent, but many other qualities as well. It is not easy for a Roman general on operations in Asia, Cilicia, Syria and their hinterlands to think only of defeat for the enemy and glory for Rome. Whatever his qualities of moderation and self-control no other general will be believed to possess them because of the enormous temptations to which he will

65 be subject. It is a hard thing to say, gentlemen, but we are loathed abroad because of the damage our generals and officials have done by their licentiousness. No temple has been protected from them by its sanctity, no state by their oaths, no home by its locks and bars. In fact there is now a shortage of rich and prosperous cities for us to

66 declare war on so that we can loot them afterwards. And I am quite prepared to defend my statement in public debate with my honourable opponents Catulus and Hortensius, since they know the damage done to our allies, have seen the evidence, and heard the complaints. Do you think that when we send out an army against an enemy it is to protect our allies or rather to use the war as an excuse for plundering them? There is not a state in Asia which can satisfy the ostentatious arrogance of a single Roman military tribune let alone a general or his deputy. So it will not do, gentlemen, merely to produce a general who could probably defeat King Mithridates' forces in pitched battle; for unless he is also a man who can keep his hands, eyes, and mind off our allies' property, their wives and children, the treasures of their temples and cities, and from the gold and jewels of the king, he is not the man we can send out to fight

67 an Asian ruler. Think about it, gentlemen: do you know of a single state we have subdued that is yet rich, or a single rich state which our generals have yet subdued? The coastal dwellers asked for Pompey not merely for his military successes but also for his known restraint. They saw that year after year almost every praetor was making his fortune at the state's expense while our mighty fleets did nothing except ruin what little reputation they had left by suffering further defeats. Anyone who does not think that the whole command should be given to Pompey alone obviously has no idea of the avarice, the bribery, the secret agreements that are made before a governor sets out. Anyone would think that Pompey's greatness was merely a reflection of the shortcomings of others rather than his

68 own manifest good qualities. Do not hesitate, gentlemen, to entrust the whole conduct of the war to the only man for many years to be welcomed by our allies in their cities with his army.

But if you want me to produce men of prestige to give the weight of their authority to my arguments, let me introduce first one of our most experienced generals and wisest statesmen, Publius Servilius (Isauricus). His great deeds by land and sea make it obvious that no-one ought to have greater influence with you than he. Next, here is Gaius Curio – you have heaped honours on him for his great deeds; he is able, he is wise. Next, here is Gnaeus Lentulus – the great honours you have paid him testify to your appreciation of his worth. And then there is Gaius Cassius, a man of proven loyalty, honesty, and principle. The authority of men like these is surely adequate answer to the opponents of this measure.

The speech closed with a few claims for himself, and suggestions about his own motives, which we need not necessarily believe. The *lex Manilia* was passed, and Pompey remained away from Rome for nearly five years.

PARTIES AND PROGRAMMES AFTER 70

In Rome, the reforms of the year 70 broke up the new conventions for government established by Sulla. The passing of the *lex Gabinia* in 67, followed by the *lex Manilia* in 66, left politics in a state of flux. In military terms, contemporaries must have known that Pompey's power could not be opposed, if he were successful against Mithridates, and his earlier career must certainly have suggested that he would not hesitate to use it, if need be as unscrupulously as Sulla. In political terms, the breaking of the power of the nobles of Sulla's clique had left a vacuum which various groups tried to fill. A young aristocrat, C. Julius Caesar, who had been appointed to the post of *flamen Dialis* by the government of Cinna, and deprived of the post by Sulla, proclaimed in 65 the revival of the party of Marius; others, led by L. Sergius Catilina (Catiline), announced that they would tackle the problem of debt; a third, led by M. Crassus, tried to establish a new command which would create some military power other than that of Pompey in the Roman world; a fourth, amongst whom were most of Sulla's nobles, remained watchful and suspicious, largely withdrawn from politics, but eagerly looking for an opportunity to avenge the injuries, real or imaginary, they had suffered from Pompey; a fifth comprised Cicero and his friends, upholding the interests of the propertied classes, critical of Sulla's party, but maintaining that Sulla's settlement could not be overthrown without causing worse confusion and injustice, and maintaining that integrity in government and support for law and order were the prerequisites of stable government.

19. THE CIVIL LAW AND SOCIETY

In his indictment of Verres, and especially in his publication of the whole of the *Actio secunda*, Cicero had made the above point (Sec. 18, end); in 69, while speaking in defence of A. Caecina he again spoke of the fundamental importance of the law in society.

Pro Caecina, 65–75:

But the most remarkable thing about your whole defence, Piso, seems to be your assertion that we should not accept the opinion of experts in jurisprudence (*iuris consulti*) in interpreting the meaning of this law. Of course this is not the first time I have heard such a suggestion either from you or anybody else, but I am very surprised that you should make it here. Usually it is the tactic followed by men who believe they are defending a principle of equity, and if their opponents fight them on the strict letter of the law, they try to resist such unfair proceedings by appeals to fair play in the name of the dignity of the legal profession. They affect to despise such shilly-shallying, deriding their opponents for resorting to quibbles and legal peculiarities. That is the kind of occasion on which they appeal to equity and maintain that the matter should not be settled on the basis of some devious and complicated interpretation of a word or letter. It is, they insist, pure chicanery to stick to the letter of the law; good judges should uphold the intentions of those who framed it or

66 they will destroy the very foundations of all law. But in this case, Piso, it is you who are fighting by the letter, arguing that you could not have 'ejected' Caecina from a place where you stopped him even entering, and that he was merely 'refused entry' and not 'ejected'. But you have admitted collecting a body of men, arming them, and threatening to murder Caecina; you concede that you are bound by the intention and legality of the praetor's injunction to refrain from so doing, but claim to have found a loophole in the wording of the injunction, since you say you have not 'ejected' him from a place where you never allowed him to enter. And on that basis you presume to denounce the experts in jurisprudence who gave it as their

67 opinion that the principle not the letter of the law holds good. It is remarkable, too, that you cite the example of Scaevola who lost a case like this in the Court of the Hundred. On this occasion he was using your tactics, albeit with some justification, though you have none, but – as I have explained – he failed entirely to carry his point for the very reason that the letter of the law was not consistent with the principles of equity. I am, therefore, somewhat surprised to find you taking this line of defence when it is inappropriate and contrary to the interests of your client. But I do concede that in trials it is frequently asserted, even by able lawyers, that the experts' opinion should not be taken nor should civil law always prevail in

68 an actual lawsuit. But such an argument can only be defended from two angles: first, that the experts are wrong, in which case they are incompetent and not experts at all, and to reject their opinion is legitimate; secondly, that their opinion was right in principle but wrong for the particular case in question, in which case counsel are asking the experts to produce opinions based on bad law. For you cannot ask them to enunciate a legal principle and then make an exception nor can you regard any expert as worthy of the name who

69 propounds a principle which cannot be applied in practice. Of course there are cases where an expert's opinion is contradicted in court, and the question then arises whether the court was at fault or correct. If it was correct, then its judgement stands as good law; if it was at fault, then obviously you must blame the jury. But any particular judgement given in a court of law is no more a denial of the authority of an expert like, say, Scaevola if it contradicts him than it is an assertion of the infallibility of another expert like, perhaps, Manilius if it happens to agree with him. After all, when

the great Crassus argued a case before the Court of the Hundred,
he was not denying the authority of the experts so much as asserting
that on a particular point Scaevola was not making good law, and
to this end he himself adduced arguments and many learned
authorities, such as his father-in-law Quintus Mucius.

70   For the man who denies the validity of the civil law is not merely
destroying the whole basis of the administration of justice but also
overturning the very foundations of civilization. If he slanders an
individual lawyer and says he is incompetent, he is attacking a man,
not the civil law. But if he refuses to accept the judgement of an
expert, he is not just attacking a man but threatening the very
principle of legality. And you, gentlemen, are unlikely to forget just
how precious the civil law is, and how important it is that we fight
to defend it above all else. Remove the civil law and the individual
has no way of deciding what is his and what another's; there can be

71   no guarantee of a common standard of justice for all. And so, in
disputes or trials in a court of law questions may arise about whether
something did or did not happen, or whether a particular statement
is true or false; and indeed false witnesses are sometimes suborned
or false evidence produced resulting in an honest juror giving a
wrong verdict in all good faith or a dishonest juror getting a chance
to bring in a false verdict apparently in accordance with all the
evidence. But in a matter of law, gentlemen, there is nothing like
that – no false evidence, no dishonest witnesses, none of that undue
pressure which is brought to bear in a political case, since in this
kind of question alone there is no opportunity for such things, no
means of getting at a juror, no chance even to lift a finger to affect

72   the verdict. A man of influence rather than honour can always force
a jury to decide that this or that was or was not done, or to believe
this witness or that piece of evidence; but he cannot make them
decide that a man's will is not invalidated by the subsequent birth
of a son or that a woman's promise is binding without the guarantee
of her guardian, for that is a question of law. Neither power nor
influence can affect the verdict in such a question; and perhaps
more important, more vital to society, the juror cannot be bribed.

73   That witness of yours, Piso, who dared to say that he thought
my client was guilty when he could not even tell what you were
trying to prove he was guilty of, even he would never dare to
say that a woman's dowry is the property of her husband when

she has made it over to him without the authority of her guardian.

The civil law, then, gentlemen, is a precious thing, and it is your duty to preserve it. Consider its characteristics: it cannot be swayed by influence, destroyed by power, corrupted by money. If we allow it to be threatened, if we fail or are half-hearted in our efforts to defend it, no man will be able to be confident of his title to his property or his inheritance, or his childrens' right to what he leaves

74 them. For what is the use of having a house or estate, whether inherited or otherwise legally acquired, if you cannot be certain what is yours by right of contract and whether you are entitled to keep it, when the civil law has been so undermined that it can no longer guarantee your title to possession against an influential claimant? What use is it to own an estate, if the carefully-established legal boundaries of the property, its title deeds, the water rights and rights of access can be annulled or altered at random? Believe you me, gentlemen of the jury, the civil law and its regulations governing ownership have given to every single one of us a far, far more valuable inheritance than those who have left us their property. For I may acquire a property by someone's will, but I can only keep possession of it by means of the civil law. A man may inherit property from his father, but the right to take possession of it – that is, a confident and undisputed title to it – is not the legacy of his father but of the civil law. The right to draw water or to pipe it from well or stream, and rights of way for people or animals may be inherited by the act of a father, but legal entitlement to them is established from

75 the civil law. And so it is your duty to protect that civil law, which is your national inheritance, as diligently as you defend your own private property, not just because that property is protected by the civil law, but because, while the loss of an inheritance may be a misfortune for one man, the loss of the civil law must be a disaster for the state.

20. THE RANKS OF SOCIETY UNDER THE LAW

In 66, after *Pro lege Manilia*, Cicero defended a certain A. Cluentius. In the course of his speech he contrasts the career of Senator and *Eques* (knight); the former has the higher privileges, therefore must live under stricter laws. But the law itself is supreme, and both classes must defend it.

Pro Cluentio, 145–6, 150–9:

146   Attius complains that it is deplorable that a senator should be prosecuted for judicial murder while a knight is not. I am not really very impressed by that argument, gentlemen, and if for the moment I concede that it is regrettable – though I shall consider the question again shortly – he must concede to me that there is nothing more regrettable in a state living under the rule of the laws than to have them broken. For the laws are the chains which secure our position in the *res publica*; they are the foundation stone of liberty and the source of all equity. The laws are the mind and soul of the state, the basis of the wisdom and will of the community. In a body the nerves and sinews, the blood and the limbs cannot function without the brain; in a state none of its parts can function without the laws, whose servants are the magistrates, whose interpreters the courts, and whose bondage we all accept in order to find perfect freedom. . . .

150   You think, then, Attius, that it is unfair that every body is not bound by the same laws. I admit it is very unfair, but that means we need different laws, not that we can stop obeying the ones we have. And is it not also true that any senator is only too willing to accept stricter obligations under the laws in return for the higher position and status which the Roman people have conferred upon him? There are indeed great drawbacks to being a senator: it involves a lot of trouble and hard work; but we receive considerable privileges and honours in return for this. If you inflicted that sort of life on the equestrian or any other class, they would not put up with it, since they believe that men who could not reach or did not want the highest offices of state should not be so closely bound by all the ramifications and restrictions of the legal code.

151   But now I just want to look at one law which affects us senators and no-one else. It was brought in by Gaius Gracchus, and states that 'No man shall seek to compass the death of another by misuse of judicial proceedings.' Now the object of this was quite simply to protect the ordinary Roman, and in due course Lucius Sulla, who was as far removed from a popular leader as any man could be, set up the very court which you are administering today in order to try this offence under the Gracchan law. But even he did not dare to extend its jurisdiction to include the people of Rome who had hitherto been exempt. Yet if he had thought he could get away with

it, he so loathed the equestrian order that he would have been more than happy to include this court in the proscription which he conducted against the equestrian jurors of his own day.

152 So I must ask you, gentlemen, to handle this issue very carefully, for I can assure you it is merely the case of a few people trying to ensure that the knights are included in the provisions of the Gracchan law. It is not flattery, gentlemen, when I say that most senators – like yourselves – whose lives have not been corrupted by avarice, and who are amply protected by their transparent honesty and integrity, only want to see the knights as close to the Senate as possible in status and mutual respect. It is only the few who, in their search for a monopoly of power and reluctance to share it with any individual or class, reckon that they will have the knights under their thumbs if they can frighten them by getting it established that anyone who has served on a jury can be prosecuted under this law. For they see that the knights' prestige is growing, and that your strict administration of justice, gentlemen, is as popular in the state as it is irksome to themselves, and so they hope that these threats of pro-

153 secutions by reducing your zeal will diminish your severity. No man, after all, is going to pluck up the courage to return an honest verdict against a defendant even slightly richer than himself, if he knows he will then be prosecuted himself for conspiring to pervert the course of justice. Hitherto the order of knights has shown exemplary courage in resisting this, as for example when they fought the powerful nobleman Marcus Livius Drusus who, as tribune of the people, united the nobles of his day in a campaign to make all jurors liable to prosecution in courts like this. But Cluentius, my client, is of course afraid that if he refuses to face trial under this law he will appear to have something to conceal. Fortunately such scruples did not deter those popular champions of the past, men like Flavius Pusio, Titinius, Maecenas and others of that order. They fought the measure tooth and nail, refused to accept it, and made no bones about their motives, pointing out that if they had cared to make the effort to seek high office they too could have won the consulship from the Roman people. But without intending any disrespect to the distinction, honour, and value of a senator's position they were perfectly satisfied with their own status, as their fathers were before them, and preferred to live a life of peace and quiet away from the politi-

154 cal rat-race and its weapons of malicious prosecution. They argued

that the only fair thing to do under the circumstances was to give them back their youth and let them start again on the hunt for high office, or else, since that was impossible, to accept the *status quo*. It was manifestly unfair, they argued, that men who had sacrificed the prospect of high office and its privileges because of the many dangers involved should now still be deprived of such perquisites of popular esteem yet face the very dangers of prosecution which they had originally tried to avoid. Senators, however, had no such grounds for complaint since they knew the terms when they started on their political careers, and anyhow they had innumerable compensating advantages such as standing, prestige, social position, an international reputation and influence, the purple border on their togas, chairs of office, badges of rank, the lictors' rods, powers of life and death, armies to command, and provinces to control. And just as our fathers ordained splendid rewards for those senators who did well, so they intended that the penalties for malpractice should be specially severe. Pusio and his friends did not object to prosecutions under that law, the *lex Sempronia* – now the *lex Cornelia*, under which Cluentius is being tried – since they realized that it was not even applicable to knights anyhow; what they were fighting to prevent was the law being arbitrarily extended to include them,
155 thereby creating in effect a totally new law. Cluentius, however, has not refused to defend his career under this law even though it does not apply to his class. And if that is what you really want, gentlemen, we must all work together to get your jurisdiction extended to cover all the classes in the state.

But until such time as that is done, for God's sake let us stand foursquare upon the laws, since they are the source of all the privileges we now enjoy, our rights, our freedom, and our very lives. And let us at the same time be aware that, inequitable though it seems to be, the Roman people are not as yet aware of the problem, having left you, gentlemen, as guardians of the *res publica* and their destiny in the sure and easy confidence that a few jurors would never shackle them to a law they never sanctioned in a court they believed could never touch them.

156 Now Titus Attius, the prosecutor, is taking the line that every citizen is bound by every law. Well, he is rather young and very eloquent, gentlemen, though of course you are listening to him with all the silent attention which your position requires of you. But

Aulus Cluentius is a Roman knight, and is having to answer charges under a law which states quite specifically that only senators and magistrates are bound by it. And yet he will not let me make this law the bastion of my defence and refuse to answer the charge. If Cluentius wins, as we assume he will in view of your high sense of justice, everyone will conclude - and rightly – that he was acquitted because he was innocent, since that is the argument of the defence; but they will also assume that the law on whose protection he

157 refused to rely could afford him none. Now the particular point I want to make is one that I have often made before, but it is my duty to bring it to the attention of the Roman people, since my whole life is dedicated to defending with all the powers and ability I possess men who are threatened with the law. And it is quite clear to me that the attempt of the prosecution to extend to the whole body of the Roman people the provisions of a law which was drawn up to apply only to senators will turn this law court into a huge, dangerous and all embracing monster. Listen, gentlemen, to the actual wording of this law: 'Whosoever shall have combined . . .' that could mean anybody – 'or conspired . . .' – that is equally ambiguous and imprecise – 'or consented together . . .' – that is so vague as to be positively oracular – 'or borne false witness . . .' – is there any Roman who has ever appeared as a witness in court whom you cannot see as threatened by the menace of Attius' new proposal? I can guarantee that, if this law is made to apply to all the Roman people, no-one

158 will ever give evidence again. But I can also promise you this that, if anyone gets into trouble as a result of this law which does not apply to him, and asks me to defend him, I shall base my whole case on the question of legality and shall certainly have no trouble in winning it before this or any other similar jury by appealing to the very protection of the law which I am debarred from seeking by the wishes of my client, to whom I must defer. For I dare not, I must not doubt, gentlemen, that any man prosecuted before you under a law to which he is not liable – be he the vilest, most loathesome, and most hateful creature upon earth, whose acquittal you would unanimously deplore – such a man would be acquitted none the less, since you would put the high cause of justice before your own

159 personal prejudice. The true judge knows that his powers are limited precisely to what the Roman people have seen fit to entrust to him, and that the powers so vested in him are a high trust from that

people. He may acquit the man he hates; he may condemn the man he has no cause to hate – for he will pay no heed to his own feelings, but only to the dictates of his conscience and the law. It is his duty to know the act under which the accused is being tried, to examine his character, and note the evidence. And when all this is done and the moment comes to record his verdict, then, gentlemen, the best and wisest juror will not say to himself, 'I am alone; I can write what I like'; he will remember his duty to the law and the principles of justice, to his conscience and his juror's oath; he will outlaw from his heart all greed, malice, and unkind thoughts, all fears and all desires, and remember only that a clear conscience is the gift of heaven which none may take from him. For the serenity of a clear conscience, gentlemen, is a constant witness to honesty of thought and deed, and its gift is the gift of a life freed from fear to walk along honour's high road.

21. THE EMERGENCE OF CAESAR

Between his praetorship and the consular elections for 63, due to be held in 64, Cicero worked hard to promote his candidature. He defended Manilius, author of the *lex Manilia*, Cornelius, a reforming tribune of 67, and at least three other people. The political temperature rose, as is attested by the deprivation of the consuls first elected for 65, when they were condemned under a new bribery law; this was followed by the quarrels and resignation of the censors elected in 65, and Caesar's restoration of the trophies of Marius as aedile this year.

SUETONIUS, *Divus Julius* XI:

'Caesar tried to get Egypt assigned to him as a sphere of duty (*provincia*) through the tribunes' services . . . Caesar did not get the job because of the opposition of the party (*factio*) of the nobles. (Suetonius calls them *optimates*, but this is inaccurate, as are some of the other statements omitted in this passage). He therefore set about retaliating by undermining their prestige in every way he could. He restored the trophies which C. Marius set up for his triumphs over Jugurtha and the Germans (Cimbri and Teutones) which Sulla had previously demolished, and when he was president of the court to deal with murderers (*quaestio perpetua de sicariis*) he included amongst those culpable of murder the men who had been paid out of the Treasury for bringing in the heads of citizens who had been proscribed in the (Sulla's) proscriptions. This was despite the fact that they had been indemnified by Sulla's laws on this subject.'

III. Cicero's *Res Publica*

In 64, new censors failed even to revise the roll of the Senate, the first part of their task. The growth of coercion in politics is attested by the decrees of the Senate intended to curb the number of attendants permitted to candidates for office, and declaring illegal the *collegia* similar to those which Sulla had organized in order to bring pressure to bear on the assembly. It is evident that Cicero's rivals were using these pressure groups. Sallust (*Catiline*, 17) believed that the conspiracy of Catiline was formed in June, 64, and that it was the leakage of information about Catiline's plans which led to Cicero's election as consul (*Catiline* 23). It is more usually believed that the account of Asconius commenting on the now lost speech *In toga candida* is correct, and that it was this speech that swung the support of the leading families to Cicero's side, quite suddenly.

A political pamphlet purporting to have been written by Cicero's brother Quintus survives, the *Commentariolum petitionis*. Though usually thought to be spurious, it probably reveals something of the political situation of the day, and certainly shows how far politics were not a matter of programmes and policies, but of personally satisfying individual voters.

In the election, Cicero was elected, easily first, with C. Antonius. The disappointed Catiline, who had spent large sums of money on his election-campaign, was left with a further burden of debt.

22. *Consul Popularis* AND LAND REFORM

On January 1st, 63, when Cicero entered office, and presided over the Senate as the senior of the two consuls, the political atmosphere was excited and strained. A tribune, P. Servilius Rullus, who had been in office since 10th December, the customary date for tribunes to enter their office, had proposed a grandiose scheme for distributing lands to the poor. Features peculiar to this bill were: there was to be a commission of 10, who were to be charged with this task, and were to be given very wide powers; the conditions for membership appeared to have been drawn up with the specific object of ensuring that Pompey could not be elected to it, although his troops were among those who would soon be requiring lands, and most of the money for the scheme was to come from the proceeds of the Mithridatic War, now virtually finished.

To counter these plans, Cicero delivered his first two speeches as consul;

the bulk of the surviving parts is concerned with criticism of the details of
the schemes, but the surviving introduction and the perorations are concerned with the point of view that the new self-styled people's champions
(*populares*) are frauds, who are in fact working in the interests of sinister
figures in the background, whose aim is power. The first speech was in the
Senate, the second was a harangue to the people in the forum.

De lege agraria I, 22–7, II 1–16, 100–3:

(*a*)

I can assure you, honoured gentlemen of the Senate, that I shall
fight these proposals to the bitter end, and as long as I am consul I
shall allow no-one an opportunity to give effect to deep-laid plans
23 to overthrow the constitution. You are indeed making a big mistake,
Rullus, you and some of your colleagues, if you have hoped that your
activities, which strike at the very vitals of our state, will let you
wrest his leadership of the people from a consul who is genuinely a
people's man, not a sham. I denounce you and challenge you to
public debate and let the Roman people be our judge. For I
sincerely believe that of all the things that makes a leader popular,
there is nothing to match the gift of peace, harmony and quiet times.
But I have inherited from you a state seething with suspicion,
harassed by fears, and driven to distraction by all your legislation,
propaganda, and colonial enterprises. You have boosted the morale
of every crook in Rome and frightened the life out of every man of
standing; you have destroyed confidence among businessmen and
24 subverted the respect men feel for the *res publica*. The situation in
fact has been so chaotic, and men's expectations so confused, that to
the ordinary man in the street it came like a breath of fresh air
suddenly to hear the authoritative voice of a consul firmly in control
of things explaining that all was well, there was no need to panic, no
fear of gangs or private armies, no new colonies nor pawning of
revenues, no new powers vested in ten tyrannical commissioners, no
second Rome, no new capital of the empire, and that as long as he
was consul peace and good order would be his absolute priority.
Altogether, Rullus, even with your precious agrarian bill I do not
think there is much prospect of your producing a more popular
policy than that.
25　And then I shall uncover the whole ugly story of your illegal

activities, your fraudulent law, and the plots which the tribunes are laying against the very people they were elected to defend.

I suppose, Rullus, you think I dare not even face you in debate because of the threat of your veto, but you are entirely wrong, because it is my avowed and deliberate policy to conduct my consulship in the only possible way that is consistent with the dignity of the office and the free traditions of our society. I have decided that I shall accept none of the perquisites of that office, neither province, nor honours, nor trappings, nor profit, indeed 26 nothing which it is open to a tribune's veto to deny me. And since there are so many senators here to witness what I say, on this the first day of January and of my consulship, I hereby declare that, so long as there are no new developments or troubles bringing obligations which I cannot honourably avoid, I shall accept no province, gentlemen. For I intend that my consulship shall leave me free to restrict the activities of the tribunes when they lose patience with the constitution and to despise them when they lose patience with myself.

So therefore I beg you in the name of heaven, tribunes of the people, pluck up your courage, abandon your friends, who will very soon abandon you if you are not careful, and make common cause with me, and with the men of standing in Rome, and with one heart and mind let us all defend the *res publica* in which we all have a stake. Many are the secret wounds it has sustained, many the vicious plans of the criminal elements within. Here we have no danger from abroad; no king, no tribe, no nation threatens us; the evil lies within, a cancer gnawing at the body politic, and it is the duty of each and 27 every one of us, as far as in him lies, to seek and find the cure. And if you think that what I say is all very well in the Senate-house but hardly fit for popular consumption, you are very much mistaken. Every citizen who values his life will follow the consul's lead unselfishly and with conscience clear, facing danger with caution and discord with resolution. And if any of you thinks to further his career by fostering sedition, you can forget it, as long as I am consul. But if any of you really wants to know how to win honour and high position, let him follow my example, a mere knight by birth, risen to the rank of consul – that is the easiest way for any man of quality. And as for you, gentlemen of the Senate, if you will only give me your support in my efforts to preserve the respect we all feel for our society, I shall give you what the *res publica* needs above all else, the long-awaited restoration of the traditional authority and prestige of the senatorial order.

(b)

II, 1 There has been a long-standing tradition, men of Rome, that those on whom you have so kindly bestowed high office, and with it the right to bequeath their portraits to posterity, should make their first speech to you a combination of expressions of gratitude to yourselves and of adulation of their ancestors. But I am afraid that such speeches only occasionally suggest that the speaker shares the qualities of those distinguished ancestors, but more usually that his elevation is due rather to a sense of obligation to them on your part which can only be adequately expressed by doing honour to their descendants. But I have little to say about mine, gentlemen, not because they do not deserve full credit for the training and upbringing they gave me to make me what I am, but simply because they lived sequestered lives

2 far from the blaze of publicity or popular renown. And I am also afraid of seeming arrogant if I speak of myself too much, and ungrateful to you if I say nothing. It has been a long hard struggle to win this position and it would be a lengthy tale to tell, yet I can hardly say nothing of my gratitude to you for conferring it upon me. So in all that I say I shall try to show a decent reticence, recalling briefly the favours you have done me, and explaining my reasons for thinking I am not unworthy of them and the great compliment you have now paid me in electing me to the highest office in the state; and I shall do this as modestly as I can on the assumption that your view of me is unlikely to have changed since the time that you elected me.

3 I am, gentlemen, the first 'new man' you have elected consul for a long time, almost indeed within living memory. For the consulship has become a bastion of aristocratic privilege, jealously guarded by every means the nobles know; but you have torn down those barriers and shown through me that you want it to be an office open to merit for ever after. Nor is it just that you have made me consul, itself a signal honour I agree, but you have done so in a manner granted to few nobles and no 'new man' before me. For if you look back, gentlemen, I think you will find that all 'new men' elected at the

first attempt have managed it only by nursing their support for years and awaiting a favourable opportunity, long after they had been praetors and a good deal later than the age when the law made them eligible; no-one who was a candidate in the first year he was eligible got elected. I am literally the first 'new man' that any of us can remember to make the attempt in his first possible year and to be elected at his first attempt. As a result the position of honour you have granted me, which I sought as soon as I could, makes it clear that it was won by my own deserts, not as the by-product of a running-mate's popularity, nor the result of prolonged solicitation.

4 All these things that I have just described, gentlemen – the fact that I am the first 'new man' so honoured for so long, that it was at my first attempt in my first available year – all this, as I say, is a remarkable tribute; but it is as nothing compared with the quite extraordinary honour you did me when you showed your affection and support for me not by the silent testimony of the secret ballot but by the public acclamation that you gave me. It was no marginal victory depending on the last votes counted that made me consul, but a stampede rather of the earliest voters, not the voice of each century's

5 official teller but the unanimous shout of the whole Roman people. This distinguished, and quite unprecedented compliment, gentlemen, gives me remarkable pleasure but also an even greater cause for anxiety. For there occur to me many grave considerations which trouble me night and day – above all, how to defend my consulship: this is a hard task for anyone, but especially for myself, since I shall get little mercy if I fail, and little but grudging praise if I succeed. For when I am in doubt no nobleman will give me honest counsel,

6 nor reliable support if I am in trouble. But even though I met the dangers all alone, my friends, I could bear them with a calmer mind were it not that I see that there are certain men who will use the least mistake of mine, be it wilful or accidental, to castigate and denounce you all for choosing as consul an upstart like myself before a nobleman. But let me assure you, gentlemen, that I will do anything rather than allow my policies or actions as consul to reflect anything but credit on your policies and actions in appointing me. Then, too, I have made my whole task that much more difficult because I decided that my consulship should be radically different from my predecessors'. They never came near the assembly and avoided you like the plague, or certainly never sought your company

with any enthusiasm. But I shall say here, where it is easy, what I have already said in my opening speech on the 1st of January to the Senate, where there seems little welcome for such sentiments, that I intend to be a 'popular' (*popularis*) consul, (that is, a consul devoted

7 to the interests of the people). Of course I am bound to *seem* popular, both in office and out of it, since I know that I owe my election to the popular vote rather than the support and influence of a powerful minority. But you, in your wisdom, will have to help me make it clear exactly what it really means to be 'popular' in this sense. Considerable misunderstandings exist at present thanks to the dishonest claims of certain dangerous elements, whose whole policy is aimed against the welfare and indeed the safety of the people, but who think they can best achieve their ends by claiming to espouse

8 the popular cause. Yet I have only to look at the *res publica* on the 1st of January, gentlemen, when I entered office, to realize the damage they have done. Alarm and despondency were everywhere: good men feared the worst and bad men hoped for it. Rumour had it that there were conspiracies against the *res publica* and public order, some still being plotted and others hatched from the moment it was known that I was the next consul. Business confidence was shattered, not by any national disaster but because opinion was so sensitive, and it was thought that the law-courts would be in chaos and verdicts overruled, and that a new breed of rulers would arise and seize the powers

9 not of mere dictators but of kings. Once my suspicions were confirmed and I realized all this was going on – and there was little attempt at concealment, gentlemen, – I stated in the Senate that my policies as consul would be popular. But is there anything as 'popular' as peace? It does not just bring joy to men and animals but even seems to make our homes and countryside happy. Is there anything as 'popular' as freedom? You all know it is the greatest blessing man or animal can seek. Is there anything as 'popular' as a quiet ordered state? It is so precious that you, your fathers, and every hero of our land have felt that they must spare no effort to ensure that one day they might enjoy such good order in the state, especially when it brings them power and honour as well. And therefore we have every reason to bless our ancestors and honour them for the great boon of lasting peace which their efforts have afforded us. These are what the people want and when I see all these, their greatest blessings, entrusted to my honour and my care as consul – peace abroad,

freedom, the proudest right of every Roman, stability at home, and all else that is so precious and so dear to the hearts of every one of you – how can I wish to be anything but a 'popular' consul?

10   But there is nothing 'popular' or indeed attractive, as you ought to realize, about Rullus' proposals which are nothing more than large scale bribery, and, though they can be made to sound attractive enough in theory, can in fact only be implemented by national bankruptcy. There is nothing 'popular' either about chaos in the courts or judicial decisions over-ruled or restoration of the condemned, for these are all the last desperate resorts of ruined states which are tottering on the brink of disaster. Nor does anyone deserve the title 'popular' if he promises distributions of land to the Roman people but tricks out his proposals in gaudy and attractive terms for his own sinister and secret devices.

Now to tell the truth, gentlemen, I have nothing against agrarian legislation as such. Indeed I can think of two very able and distinguished patriots, true lovers of the Roman people, Tiberius and Gaius Gracchus, who distributed to the people public land which had hitherto been held as private property. I am certainly not, too, the kind of consul to follow public opinion slavishly and think it a crime to praise the Gracchi, whose wise and statesmanlike legisla-

11   tion gave to our state some much needed reforms. And so, when as consul-designate I first heard that the new tribunes of the people were drafting an agrarian bill, I wanted to know what they had in mind, because I felt that, since we were going to be magistrates together, we ought to have a common interest in making a success

12   of our jobs for the good of the *res publica*. I tried making friendly approaches to them but I found myself fended off and cold-shouldered, and when I offered my support and sponsorship for their measure if it seemed beneficial to the Roman people, I was snubbed for my pains and told that nothing would ever make me approve of any general distribution of wealth. So I offered no more help for fear that my efforts should seem subversive or impertinent. In the meantime they went on with their secret gatherings, calling in citizens with no official position, and having hole-in-corner meetings in out-of-the-way places at dead of night. You can easily imagine how alarmed I was when you remember your own anxiety at the time, gentlemen.

13   The tribunes of the people at last took office (on the 10th of

December) and everyone waited for a speech from Publius Rullus, who was primarily responsible for the bill and obviously more belligerent about it than the rest of them. From the moment he was elected he had been practising for the role, changing his appearance, speaking voice, and general demeanour, wearing worn out old clothes, neglecting to wash or shave, letting his hair and beard grow long, and cultivating the appearance and manner of a revolutionary tribune whose power was a threat to the whole *res publica*. I was waiting for him to make a speech to introduce the new bill. He made no formal proposal, however, to begin with, but summoned an assembly for the 12th of December. We met amid tremendous excitement. He made a speech, full of fine words and certainly very long. I had only one criticism, and that was that in the whole enormous crowd no-one could be found who had understood a word of it. Whether he did this deliberately to further his plan or because he enjoys that sort of oratory I do not know. But certainly his more perceptive listeners got the impression that he was trying to say something about an agrarian bill. However at some moment between my election and entering office at long last the terms of the bill were published. I got several clerks to record its provisions

14 simultaneously and they brought me the details. And I can promise you, gentlemen, that my whole attitude to the bill as I read and studied its proposals was that I should support and sponsor it if I felt that it would help or benefit you in any way at all. After all, there is no deepseated antagonism or dislike which makes a feud between consul and tribunate part of the law of nature, as it were, despite the fact that in the past courageous and patriotic consuls have obstructed the activities of seditious and malicious tribunes and, on occasion, the power of the tribunes has resisted the excesses of a bad consul. It is difference of outlook rather than any contradictions implied by the two offices whch has caused their opposition to each other.

15 And so, as I say, I began to study this bill hoping to find it conducive to your interests and so framed that a truly 'popular' consul could support it fully and with a clear conscience. But from beginning to end, gentlemen, I am afraid I found that its sole purpose, the whole object and intention of this bill, was that ten kings should be appointed to rule the treasury, the revenues, all the provinces, the whole *res publica*, the client-kingdoms, and the free peoples, in fact to lord it over the whole wide world -- and all this under the guise

and title of an agrarian bill. I swear, gentlemen, that this fine, 'popular' bill gives you nothing and ten specially selected men everything; it dangles the carrot of a little land before the people and deprives them of their liberty, it swells the bank-balances of a few individuals and empties the national treasury, and – worst of all – by the agency of a tribune of the people, whose office was devised by our ancestors to guard and protect our liberties, it seeks to establish 16 kings in our republic. And when I have tried to prove this to you, gentlemen, if you think I am wrong, I shall bow to your authority and change my mind; but if you now realize that this ostensible largesse is in fact a threat to your own freedom, I trust you will not hesitate to defend that freedom which you have never had to work for, but have inherited from the blood, sweat, and toil of your forefathers – and I will help you all I can. . . .

(c)

100 And that you, Rullus, should have made these your objectives seems to me entirely consistent with your stupidity and impudence, but that you should have hoped to achieve them while I was consul seems to me well nigh incredible. After all, it is every consul's duty to be tireless and meticulous in his defence of the *res publica*, particularly if he owes his election to his ability in public life, and was not destined from the cradle to succeed. I had no noble ancestors to commend me to the people; but you have trusted me, gentlemen, and now you have the right to demand repayment of my debt in my own name. As a candidate I could not appeal to a long line of ancestors to prove my worth; so, too, if I should fail in anything, I have no ancestors in whose name I can appeal to you for mercy. And so, men of Rome, if I survive – as I shall try to do despite the plots and threats of my opponents – I swear to you by all that I hold precious that you will find you have entrusted the *res publica* to a man of 101 vigilance, courage, perseverance, and devotion. I am not the consul to shun controversy in the assembly, to cower before a tribune of the people, to panic at the slightest provocation, or fear imprisonment at a tribune's command. You have given me weapons for the fight: a consul's power, prestige, and extensive prerogatives. I do not fear to come before you and with your support to fight the armies of unrighteousness; nor do I believe that this our *res publica*, armed and

guarded by defences such as these, shall ever be trampled by the ranks of villainy. Had I been apprehensive hitherto, this massed assembly of the people would by now have stiffened my sinews. Did ever man move a motion to support an agrarian bill amid half the cheers with which I have moved the motion for rejection – or rather

102 for its destruction and demolition? And by this I know, my friends, that there is nothing which I, your 'popular' consul, can bestow on you of half such popularity as peace, tranquillity, and public order. What you feared between my election and January 1st, this I have prevented by my skill, judgement, and foresight. You shall have the public order that was always your hearts' desire. And as for those to whom such peaceable public order is anathema, I shall see that they are the most peaceable and orderly of all. Their rank, power, and wealth depend on domestic fury and fierce civil strife; but as for you, gentlemen, your influence depends on your votes, your freedom on the law, your rights on the courts and the impartiality of the magistrates, your prosperity on peace – and so you have a vested interest in preserving public order. Men seek the quiet life sometimes out of sloth, and in their slothfulness derive great pleasure from that quiet. But you, gentlemen, who have not desired quiet through sloth, and have certainly won it by your own determination, how blessed will

103 you be if you can now embrace it and ever hold it fast. For myself, however, and my colleague, our unity is established; we are of one mind, despite the opposition of those who prophesied that we would be at loggerheads, and claim that we are. I have tried to plan for everything: I have organized the corn supply, restored business confidence, and warned the tribunes not to make trouble so long as I am consul. But the safest and surest guarantee of all our interests, gentlemen, will be if you will continue to support the *res publica* in the same kind of way as you have rallied so massively to my support today in this assembly when your own safety was at stake. And I give you now my most solemn word and promise that the very men who envied me my elevation will finally confess that in unanimously electing me your consul, you, gentlemen, have shown the greatest foresight of them all.

Cicero was successful, and Rullus' bill was defeated.

23. SENATUS CONSULTUM ULTIMUM

Caesar was a candidate for the praetorship this year (63), and also, when the *pontifex maximus* died, for his post; the revived 'Marian' party acted with vigour, led by T. Labienus, who was tribune this year, and was subsequently to become Caesar's chief liutenant in Gaul. The particular form their propaganda took was to prosecute for murder an elderly senator called Rabirius, on the grounds that he had struck the blow that killed Saturninus in 100. The trial, which was technically an appeal by Rabirius, took place in the *Campus Martius* before the *comitia centuriata*.

The fundamental issue raised, as Cicero saw it, and as perhaps the prosecution also intended, was the rights of the magistrates when the Senate declared a state of emergency by urging the consuls (or others) 'to see to it that the *res publica* come to no harm'.

(a)

In Sallust's opinion their rights were clear and extensive.

SALLUST, *Catiline*, 29, 3:

This declaration by the Senate traditionally gives a magistrate the widest possible powers; he can call up the army, wage war, and exercise compulsory powers over allies and citizens in a variety of ways; he has supreme military and civil authority, and the right of summary jurisdiction – though normally the consul can exercise none of these powers without a decree of the Roman people.

(b)

In 63, the issue was seen less clearly. Cicero undertook to defend Rabirius; part of his speech survives; clearly, some of the claims are rhetorical rather than realistic, but his concern to explode the claims of the 'popular front' by harping on the immunity of a Roman citizen was no doubt genuine.

Pro Rabirio, 1–20, 21–31 (abridged):

It is not my usual custom, gentlemen, to begin my speech with an explanation of why I am defending my client, since it seems to me a perfectly adequate justification that a Roman citizen is in trouble. However, on this occasion, when I find myself defending the life, reputation, and property of Gaius Rabirius, I feel some explanation is required for my action, because it must seem to you essential to

2 acquit him, as it is right and proper for me to defend him. Now our longstanding friendship, his high position, the claims of humanity, and my own unfailing practice as a lawyer of appearing always as defending counsel, all these required me to defend him; but that I should do so to the utmost limits of my capacity was required by considerations rather of the security of the *res publica*, and therefore by my own position as consul, since in making me consul, gentlemen, you made me also guardian of the safety of the *res publica*. For it is not a trivial offence, nor a general unpopularity, nor even some long-standing and well-founded feud that has brought Gaius Rabirius in peril of his life, gentlemen. No, the real purpose of this prosecution is to destroy one of the basic defences of our national security, one which we have inherited from our fathers; they seek to prevent an alliance of the Senate's influence, the consuls' powers, and the unanimity of all men of quality for the defence of the state and constitution when it is threatened with disaster or destruction; and the method used, gentlemen, is to attack a single, weak, lonely old

3 man. And so, if it is the duty of a good consul, who sees all the defences of the *res publica* being shaken and torn down, to bring succour to his country, to save the lives and fortunes of the community, to plead for the loyalty of the citizen body, and sacrifice his own safety to the common good, so it is the duty of all good men and true, such as you, gentlemen, have always proved yourselves to be in every crisis of our history, to close the gateways to conspiracy, to strengthen the defences of the *res publica*, to regard the powers of the consuls as supreme, and the Senate's decisions as authoritative, and to deem Rabirius, who did exactly that long ago, worthy of praise and honour rather than

4 condemnation and punishment. Thus, for the defence of Rabirius it is of course my duty to do the actual work, but it will also be for all of you alike to show a common determination to protect him.

For you must realize, men of Rome, that never in all our history has a greater, more dangerous, more perilous enterprise been devised by a tribune, thwarted by a consul, and handed over for decision to the people. The real issue, gentlemen, is whether there is in future to be any deliberative body in the *res publica*, any common action by men of good standing against the madness and audacity of scoundrels, any guarantee that our lives will be afforded

5 adequate protection in a grave crisis. We have, therefore, gentlemen, before us a vital case of life and death, a case which concerns the

lives, reputation, and property of every one of us; it is altogether fitting, therefore, that I should appeal first to Jupiter, the Lord of all Power and Goodness, and all the other immortal gods and goddesses by whose mercy and protection, far more than by the wisdom and counsels of mankind, our *res publica* is governed, that they give us peace and pardon, and grant that this very day may see the successful defence of Rabirius' life and a re-affirmation of the laws of our *res publica*. And then I beg and beseech each one of you, gentlemen, whose power is second only to the powers of heaven, that since upon your verdicts depend the life of Gaius Rabirius, poor innocent man that he is, and the safety of the *res publica*, you should show mercy to his misfortune and your usual wisdom in defending the safety of the *res publica*.

6   Now, I have done much work upon this case, gentlemen, but Titus Labienus, the counsel for the prosecution, has sabotaged my efforts by enforcing a time limit on my speech. So, instead of a carefully prepared address of normal length, I am limited to a mere half-hour, and I have no choice but to accept the prosecution's terms – which is manifestly unjust – and to allow myself to be blackmailed into agreement by a threat of veto – which is quite deplorable. In fact this time limit which he has forced upon me is adequate for the purposes of defence, but allows me no time to discuss, as a consul should, the further implications of the case; it gives me just about enough time to defend my client, but too little to protest at this prosecution.

7   Even so, he cannot, of course, expect me to have time to examine at length the subsidiary charges such as that of violating shrines and sacred graves, though the only evidence that can be produced for this is the fact that Gaius Macer once accused him of it. Indeed, I find it rather remarkable that the prosecution should remember Macer's accusation, which was motivated by personal spite, yet for-

8   get the verdict of the jury who were impartial and on oath. Perhaps the prosecution also want a long speech on the charges of embezzlement and destruction of public accounts? Well, Gaius Curtius, a relation of Rabirius', received an honourable and absolute discharge when accused of this, thanks to his known integrity and honour, but Rabirius has not only never been prosecuted for such a crime, but has never been even remotely suspected of it. Perhaps you want me to take seriously your charge of murdering his nephew in an effort to delay his brother-in-law's trial on the grounds that he

had a death in the family? It seems singularly unlikely that he
would have loved his brother-in-law so much more than his own
sister's son as to murder the one in order to get the other's trial
delayed for a mere two days longer. There are other petty charges too
about which I can find little more to say, for example that he broke
the *lex Fabia* by arresting another man's slaves, or the *lex Porcia* by
flogging Roman citizens, some even to death. The facts of the matter
are that Gaius Rabirius is popular and admired throughout all
Apulia and Campania (where he has estates), and, as you can see,
not only individuals but whole districts have rallied to his defence from
much too far afield to be the result of mere local and neighbourly
goodwill. As for the charge that he debauched himself and others,
it is hardly worth wasting my time on a matter which was adequately
dealt with when the attempt to have him fined for it failed – indeed,

9 I suspect that Labienus' reason for limiting me to half an hour was
to stop me discussing the charge of debauchery further. So you see,
gentlemen, that for the charges that need a barrister's skill the half
hour allowed me is more than adequate.

But it is in the other part of my speech – that which concerns the
death of Saturninus – that you have been trying to restrict me exces-
sively, Labienus. And here there is a crying need for the voice of
political authority, such as the consul's, rather than the skill of a

10 lawyer. You say that I have tried to abolish the crime of high treason; if so, that is a charge against myself and not my client, Labienus.
But in fact I only wish I could claim credit for being the first and
only man to do so. For, though Labienus says it is a crime, it would
be my chief claim and title to renown. Could I, or any man, hope to
do anything better in my consulship than eliminate execution of
citizens as a political weapon and their crucifixion as a national
institution? But credit for that must go, gentlemen, first to our
ancestors, who drove out the kings and then suffered no vestige of a
royal tyranny to remain among a free people; and then to the many
brave men who sought to fortify your freedom by moderate legal
penalties rather than savage punishments.

11 Which of us, therefore, Labienus, is showing greater concern for
the true interests of the people? You, who seek to bind and execute
a Roman citizen at a public meeting, you, who have ordered a cross
to be erected to crucify a Roman citizen in the *Campus Martius*, a
hallowed place of national assembly, or I myself, who refuse to

allow any meeting to be desecrated by a sacrilegious execution, and maintain rather that the forum of the Roman people should be purified and made clean of all traces of so dreadful a deed, and by my stout defence have sought to keep our places of assembly, the *Campus Martius*, and the whole body of the Roman people sacred, holy, and undefiled, and our rights of freedom undiminished and

12 inviolate? A fine 'popular' tribune of the people Labienus has proved to be, gentlemen, a true champion and defender of our right to freedom! The *lex Porcia* forbade any Roman citizen to be beaten with rods; so the ever-merciful Labienus has brought back the scourge. The *lex Porcia* denied the lictor access to a free citizen's person; so the 'popular' Labienus has allowed an executioner to do so instead. Gaius Gracchus passed a law that no-one could condemn a Roman citizen to death without your consent; so our hero Labienus has not merely handed a Roman citizen over to two commissioners to be tried without your consent, but to be sentenced to death with-

13 out a trial. It is hard to believe that he can speak to me of the *lex Porcia*, of Gaius Gracchus, of the freedom of our citizens and their champions, when he has sought to use unprecedented punishments and formulae of unheard-of cruelty to desecrate our freedom, to test the people's capacity for mercy, and to undermine their traditions. As for this so-called man of mercy, this champion of the people, one can imagine him gloating as he gives the traditional order, 'Lictor, arrest that men: fetter his arms'. Yet such words have nothing to do with liberty or mercy or even the acts of kings like Romulus and Numa Pompilius. Only the proudest and most cruel of the tyrants, Tarquinius Superbus himself, could have used with such lyrical delight as our merciful popular champion the classic formula of crucifixion, 'let his head be covered; let him be hung upon an accursed tree'. Such dark words, gentlemen, our *res publica* has not heard these many years, for they are veiled by the mists of antiquity and banished by the bright light of freedom.

14 But if, Labienus, your prosecution of Rabirius were truly in the popular interest, or indeed if it had anything reasonable or just about it at all, surely Gaius Gracchus would have used the same procedures to avenge his brother's death? You cannot seriously argue that you were more distressed by the death of an uncle, slain among the followers of Saturninus, than Gracchus was by that of his own brother; or that you feel more bitterly the loss of an uncle you

have never seen than Gracchus the loss of a brother to whom he was very close. You cannot argue that you are seeking to avenge your uncle's death on exactly the same principles as Gracchus would have avenged his brother's death had he wanted to resort to such methods; nor even that your uncle Labienus – whoever he was – was felt to be as great a loss to the Roman people as Tiberius Gracchus was. But perhaps you have a more highly developed sense of family feeling than Gaius, or greater determination, intelligence, wealth, prestige or eloquence? Alas, no. A tiny endowment of Gracchus' resources and abilities would seem riches indeed com-

15 compared with what you have. And since, in fact, he was pre-eminent in all these attributes, you cannot begin to estimate the gap between you. But Gracchus would have died a thousand times by the cruellest of deaths rather than bring an executioner into a meeting of his, a creature whom the censors by decree have forbidden to use the forum, the city, and the very sky we see and air we breathe. Labienus, gentlemen, dares to claim that he is acting in the popular interest and I against it, when he has searched not through our recent or nearly recent history, but through our barbaric past, and dug out all the most vicious forms of punishment and physical torture he could find from the public records and the archives of the kings, while I have fought and struggled to resist such savagery with all my resources of judgement, eloquence, and action. I don't suppose you want to see yourselves reduced to a state which even a slave would

16 only find tolerable if relieved by hope of ultimate freedom. To be found guilty in a court of law, to be fined or to have to go into exile, all these are miserable enough; but at least we see in them some remaining shreds of liberty. And if we must be condemned to death, let us at least die free men – let the Roman citizen be spared the executioner, the muffled head, the very mention of the cross; let them indeed be banished from his thoughts, his eyes and ears. To experience and suffer such things, indeed to live in a country where such things happen or are expected or even mentioned ill becomes a Roman and a free man. A kindly master can set free a slave from all fear of these dread punishments by one touch of the symbolic staff of manumission; will not then our achievements, our lives, and our honours received at your hands, gentlemen, suffice to set us free

17 from the lash, the hook, the terror of the cross? And so, Labienus, I am proud to confess that by my skill, courage, and authority I have

thwarted you in your cruel, barbaric prosecution, which would do more credit to a tyrant than a tribune. In it you have flouted tradition, the laws, senatorial authority, religious observance, and official regulations for the auspices – but of all this I shall say nothing in the short space at my disposal; I shall have plenty of time to do so on another occasion.

18 I shall now say a few word about the charges concerned with the Saturninus affair and the death of your illustrious uncle. You say, Labienus, that Saturninus was killed by Rabirius. This charge has already been shown to be untrue with the help of many witnesses and by a lengthy discussion of the matter by his defending counsel Quintus Hortensius. Now if this was a fresh charge, as yet unheard, my own line would be to welcome the accusation, acknowledge it, and confess to it. I only wish the case made it possible for me to proclaim that it was by the hand of Gaius Rabirius that Lucius Saturninus, enemy of the Roman people, met his death. (That uproar from the public gallery does not disturb me, gentlemen; in fact it is most encouraging: it suggests that there are still some citizens who are politically uneducated – but not many. As for the disturbance, the masses of the Roman people standing here so silent would never have made me consul had they thought I could be frightened by such shouts. Less noise? That's better, gentlemen. But why don't you shut up altogether? Your outcry only proves that

19 you have neither brains nor numbers on your side.) Let me repeat myself: if this was a fresh case, as yet unheard, I would confess, if I could, that Saturninus was slain by the hand of Rabirius, and in my opinion it was a boon to all mankind. But since I cannot do so, I shall confess instead to something which lessens the glory without weakening the accusation. I hereby confess that Gaius Rabirius took up arms with the intention of killing Saturninus. Well, Labienus, do you want a yet graver confession or a more serious charge against my client? You do not imagine there is any difference between murder and taking arms with intent to murder? If it was wrong that Saturninus was murdered, it must have been wrong to take up arms to murder him. If it was right to take up arms, you must admit it must have been right to murder him.

20 Now the facts, gentlemen, are these. The Senate passed a decree that Gaius Marius and Lucius Valerius, the consuls, should summon such tribunes and praetors as they thought fit and 'see to it that the

power and majesty of the Roman people take no harm'. So they summoned all the tribunes, except Saturninus, and all the praetors, except Glaucia, and ordered all who wished the *res publica* to be preserved to take up arms and follow them. Everyone obeyed. Weapons were drawn from the temple of Sancus and the public armouries, and distributed to the people under the personal super-vision of Marius, the consul. Now the one thing I really want to ask you, Labienus, is this: Saturninus had control of the Capitol under arms, supported by Glaucia, Saufeius and the notorius gaol-bird, Gracchus – and, of course, if you insist, your uncle Labienus was there too. But in the forum were the consuls, Marius and Flaccus, with the whole Senate in support – the Senate, be it noted, of which you, its critics, so often sing the praises so as to blacken the present one by comparison. The order of knights was there too, great men who in our fathers' time played a notable role in the affairs of state, and alone enjoyed the honour of jury-service. Every man of every order in the state who believed his safety rested on the preservation of the *res publica*, all took up arms in its defence. Now, Labienus, in such a situation what should Gaius Rabirius have done?

21   Answer me, Labienus, yourself, I ask you. When the consuls had acted on the Senate's decree and called the citizens to arms . . . what ought C. Rabirius to have done? Should he have shut himself up, or hidden in a funkhole, or saved his cowardly life by hiding in the darkest corners of his house? Or should he have gone to the Capitol and there joined your uncle and the others who had with-drawn there to die for their criminal careers? Or should he have joined with Marius and Scaurus, Catulus, Metellus and Scaevola, with every man of standing, in a gathering to seek safety through
22   facing dangers? And what would you do, Labienus, if you were
23   faced with such a crisis? . . . For my part, I would assert that nobody has ever yet admitted what you now tell us about your uncle; nobody has ever been found such an abandoned villain, so destitute of even the pretence of virtue, as to admit that he would have been on the Capitol with Saturninus. But your uncle was there. He may have been, yes, he may have, without coercion or compulsion from despair or bankruptcy; his friendship with Saturninus may have induced him to put personal relationships above patriotism; but why should this make Rabirius desert the *res publica*, or fail to take up his arms and join up in the ranks of the men of standing, and

31 obey the orders given by the consul? . . . I tell you that on that day
which is the subject of your prosecution there was not one man there
who was of age, and who did not take up arms and follow the
consul.

The trial reached no conclusion; almost certainly through collusion with
Labienus, the red flag on the Janiculum was lowered, and the assembly
broke up before the voting on the verdict took place.

24. CATILINE

Later in the year, the extent of the magistrates' powers became immediately
important; Catiline, unsuccessful again in his attempts to obtain the consulate, planned a *coup d'état*, the exact limits and objectives of which are
obscure to us, but they certainly included the assassination of Cicero and
other senators, and the raising of military forces by a confederate called
Manlius. The plot was betrayed to Cicero, who revealed it to the Senate;
a state of emergency was declared on either 21 or 22 October. Cicero brought
troops into the city, and sent officers to secure law and order in various parts
of Italy; the date planned for the *coup* passed off uneventfully. Catiline did
not give up, however; he attempted to procure the assassination of Cicero
early in November, but was again thwarted because of Cicero's informant
among the conspirators.

(a)

On the 8th November Cicero rose in the Senate and addressed Catiline,
reminding him and the rest of the audience of the background to the present crisis.

In Catilinam, I, 1–10:

In God's name, Catiline, for how much longer will you try the
limits of our patience? How long will your madman's schemes
frustrate our wishes? Are there no bounds to your unbridled insolence? Can nothing halt you in your mad career – neither the
night guards on the Palatine, nor the watches in the city, neither the
general terror, nor the united defiance of all men of standing, neither
the Senate's meeting in this fortress, nor the stern resolve you see on
every face? Do you not know that all your plans are revealed? Do
you not see your schemes cannot prevail, since these men know them

all? Your actions in the dark hours of the last night and the night before, where you were, whom you summoned, what you decided – which man here do you imagine does not know them all? Our age

2 has lost its bearings, gentlemen. Here we have a Senate which knows the truth, a consul who sees it all happening – and yet this villain remains alive. Yes, he even enters our Senate-House, sits in our council of state, and coolly marks each one of us for ultimate assassination. And yet we say we have bravely done our duty to the *res publica* if we can but escape this madman's weapons. O Catiline, you should long ago have died by order of the consul, and suffered a taste of that same medicine you have brewed so long for all of us!

3 The great Publius Scipio (Nasica), Rome's high priest, did not require an office of state to eliminate Tiberius Gracchus when he rather upset the stability of the *res publica*. Can we then, the consuls, endure to watch Catiline seek to devastate the whole wide world with fire and slaughter? Let me say naught of precedents too long ago, when Gaius Servilius Ahala with his own right hand slew the revolutionary Spurius Maelius. Gone are the days, alas, when courage ruled our land, and men of steel stood up to slay a traitor much more cruelly than even their bitterest foe. We have already a decree which the Senate has passed against you, Catiline – an outspoken decree; a mighty decree. So it is not the council of the *res publica* and the authority of this Senate that has failed. It is we – let me confess it openly – it is we ourselves, the consuls, who have failed.

4 Once upon a time the Senate passed a decree 'that Lucius Opimius, the consul, should see to it that the *res publica* take no harm'. And there and then, that very day, for a vague suspicion of conspiracy, despite the distinction of his lineage, Gaius Gracchus fell, and with him the ex-consul Marcus Fulvius and all his children. By a similar decree the consuls Gaius Marius and Lucius Valerius were given full charge of the *res publica*. Not for one single day did they delay to inflict the punishment of death decreed by the *res publica* on the tribune Saturninus and the praetor Glaucia. But we, for twenty days, have now watched the bright edge of their authority grow blunt. We have the same decree to back us – but it lies buried in our records as if justice had sheathed her sword. Yet, Catiline, by that very same decree you should have died at once. And yet you live; you live, I say, strengthened in unrepentant arrogance. No man likes to condemn himself, gentlemen, but I only wish that at this crisis of

the affairs of the *res publica* I could claim to have acted with due
energy; but I fear I must even now convict myself of sloth and
5 indolence. At this very moment there stands in Italy, at the gateway
to Etruria, a military base that threatens Rome; the enemy increases
every day; and the general who commands that base, the leader of
our enemies, is here before your eyes within our walls, within this
very Senate, a cancer in the body politic, daily seeking to compass
the doom of the *res publica*. If I now have you arrested and executed,
Catiline, I must expect all men of standing to blame me for my
delay rather than any man for my cruelty. There is, however, one
thing and one alone that makes me hesitate to do what I should long
since have done. Those who in the past executed our enemies did so
at a time when there was no man so villainous, so depraved, so like
yourself as to cry out that it was not rightly done. But now, so long
6 as one man remains who dares defend you, you shall live – but you
will live as now, surrounded and so fenced by my precautions that
you can make no move against the *res publica*. Many are the eyes and
ears that will guard against and watch your every move, though you
are unaware of it, as they have done up to now.

So what more can you hope for now Catiline, when neither the
darkness of the night can conceal your clandestine meetings, nor
your own house conceal within its walls the very whispers of conspiracy, when everything is seen, everything revealed. Reform yourself – I promise you, it is the only way; forget your plans for murder
and arson. You are hemmed in on every side; your plots are clearer
7 to me than the light of day. Let me remind you of them: do you
remember that on the 21st October I told the Senate that on a certain day, the 27th October to be exact, Gaius Manlius, your minion
and partner in crime, would take up arms? I was right, Catiline, in
my facts, wasn't I? – dark, terrible, and incredible facts though they
were; and, even more remarkable, I was right about the date. I also
told the Senate you had transferred the murder of our leading
citizens to the 28th October, – this was at a time when many of them
had escaped from Rome to thwart your plans, rather than to save
their skins, of course. Can you deny that on that day you were so
hedged in by my careful preparations for defence that you could not
lift a finger against the *res publica* and had to say you were content
8 to slay those of us who remained and had not fled? Though you
thought, did you not, that on the 1st November you could seize

Praeneste by a night attack – but then you found that the colony was
defended on my orders by guards and armed men on the watch. I
know what you do, Catiline, I know what you plan, I know what
you think – I see it, I hear it, I feel it in my bones. And now let me
remind you of the events of the other night; as you shall see, I am
much more alert to save the *res publica* than you to destroy it: late
the evening before you came to the shoemakers' street – well, let us
not mince matters – to Marcus Laeca's house, where a number of
your supporters, as mad and criminal as yourself, had foregathered.
Dare you deny it? Why won't you answer, Catiline? I can prove it
anyhow, since I see some of those men here today in the Senate-
9 House. In the name of heaven, are we barbarians? What sort of *res
publica* do we live in? What sort of city is this? Here, gentlemen,
among our own number, in this, the most sacred and august council-
chamber in the world, are men who are plotting our deaths, and the
destruction of Rome, and indeed the ruin of the civilized world.
And here am I, the consul, confronting them, asking them their
opinions on the *res publica,* and refraining even from attacking them
verbally though they should long since have been put to death by
the sword. So, you were at Laeca's house that night, Catiline, and
there you drew up areas of command in Italy, decided where each
conspirator should go, chose the men to stay in Rome and the ones
to go with you, selected which parts of the city would be burnt by
which fire, and confirmed that you yourself were leaving very soon,
but that there would be a short delay since I was still alive. Two
knights volunteered to relieve you of that problem and promised to
kill me in my bed that very night just before dawn. Almost before
10 the meeting broke up I knew these facts. I put a still larger guard
upon my house to make it secure, I refused to see the men you sent to
greet me that morning, as I had told a number of eminent witnesses
exactly who would come to see me and at what hour – and sure
enough they came.

(b)

Cicero then points to the actions of the senators in the House, which
proved Catiline's lack of support among them, and to the garrisons of
equites and others with which Cicero had guarded the city. He urges
Catiline again and again to leave the city.

In Catilinam, I, 10, 13–21:

So, Catiline, wherever you were going, go! Leave this city now; it is high time; the gates are open; get out! Manlius and his henchmen in that camp of yours have done without their commander far too long. And take your whole gang with you – or, at least, as many as you can – and rid the city of these vermin. I will not relax until I have a city wall between us two. There is no room for you now within

13 this city – I refuse to put up with you a moment longer. . . . Come now, Catiline, why do you hesitate to do what you intended to do before I encouraged you? It is the consul who is ordering you, a public enemy, to leave the city. 'Does that mean exile?', you want to know. Well, since you ask me, preferably yes, though I do not insist. Just get out. There is surely nothing to attract you here now? Every decent, lawabiding citizen fears and hates you. You are blackened by every kind of family scandal; your personal reputation is in shreds. Your eyes are glutted with lust, your hands are stained with blood, your body is corrupted by debauchery. Every youngster whom you have ensnared with the delights of your own low life you have equipped with weapons for murder and shown the way to seduction.

14 You killed your own first wife to make room in your home for another, and then heaped another crime upon this dreadful one. All this I willingly will say no more of; I am happy that men should not imagine such crimes could ever have existed here, or been unpunished. I say no more either of your ruined finances, which you will discover all too fully at the next settlement of accounts on the Ides. Rather than plumb the depths of your own disgusting private vices and the tangled crimes of your family life, let me turn now to matters of vital concern to the *res publica* as a whole and our own

15 lives and safety. How, Catiline, can you bear to see the light of day or breathe the air of heaven when you must realize that every man alive knows that on the 31st December, in the consulship of Lepidus and Tullus (66), you stood, sword in hand, in the assembly-place of Rome, having organized a gang to kill the consuls and the leading citizens, and that your mad crime was only prevented by the kindly deity of fortune rather than any scruples or fears of yours? But say no more of that – there have been many notorious crimes since then, such as your frequent attempts on my life as consul-designate and as consul. Indeed, many of your seemingly deadly attacks I have

avoided by some subtle swerve or side-step, as they say. You get nowhere; you achieve nothing; but you never stop trying and hoping.

16 I cannot imagine how many times that dagger of yours has been struck from your grasp or slipped from your fingers by mistake. Heaven knows what blessings or magic incantations you poured over it to make it stick in the consul's body.

What kind of life are you leading now? I shall try to speak of it in such a way that men may see that I am moved by pity – though you deserve none – rather than by the hatred it is natural I should feel. You entered the Senate just now. It was crowded, but not a friend or relative greeted you. Why wait for insults when this unprecedented and unheard-of silence condemns you far more eloquently than words? When you came, all the seats round you emptied, since all the ex-consuls you had so often marked for murder left the benches near you bare and unoccupied as soon as you sat down. How should

17 you feel about that? If my slaves felt the same kind of fear for me as all your fellow-citizens for you, I should feel obliged to leave my home at once; should you not leave the city then? If I found that I was an object of such even undeserved suspicion and dislike to all my fellow-citizens, I should prefer to shun their sight rather than meet their hostile gaze. But you know what crimes you have committed, and how long overdue and well deserved such loathing is – so how can you hesitate a moment to remove yourself from the sight of those to whom you are an offence to mind and eye? If your parents feared and hated you, and you could find no way to win them over, I think you would betake yourself somewhere out of their sight. But now it is your country, the common parent of us all, that declares its hate and fear of you, and has long since believed only that you plan its destruction; can you then not respect its authority, bow to

18 its judgement, or even fear its power? Imagine, now, your country comes before you and makes, as it were, this silent appeal to you. 'For many years, Catiline, you have been responsible for all vice and crime; the deaths of many citizens can be laid at your door; your plunder and ruin of our allies went free and all unpunished; you were strong enough to ignore and overturn and nullify the laws and the courts of justice. Intolerable though such crimes were, I tolerated them as best I could. But now the fact is that I, your country, live in utter terror of one man, and that is you; that at any hint of trouble Catiline is feared; that every conspiracy against me stems

from you – all this I can no longer tolerate. Therefore get out, and
rid me of my terror, so that, if the terror prove well-founded, I may
not be destroyed, and if unfounded, I may at least cease to be afraid
19 at last'. Now surely, Catiline, if such is the plea of your own native
country, she should be allowed to have her way, even if she cannot
get it by force? Did you not, after all, agree to go into custody before
your trial, and suggested the house of Manius Lepidus so as to place
yourself above suspicion? But he would not have you; so you had the
nerve to come to me and ask me to take charge of you. I too refused;
I told you that, since I was in danger while you were inside the city,
I could hardly be safe with you under my own roof. So you then
tried the praetor Quintus Metellus. Rejected there, you turned to an
old bosom-companion, Marcus Metellus, a worthy citizen, who I
suppose you thought would be careful to guard you well, would
trust no-one, and be resolute in your defence. But surely a man who
thinks he needs to be in custody should really already be locked up
in prison? Why, therefore, Catiline, do you delay? If you cannot die
with a clear conscience, at least go off abroad and devote the life
which you have snatched from the rich punishments you deserved
to the loneliness of exile.

20   You suggest I should refer the matter to the Senate, and if they
decide on exile for you, you assure me that you will obey. I will not
do so; it is unconstitutional and against my principles. But I shall
make it clear to you what they do think of you: Catiline! Get out of
this city; free the *res publica* from fear! Into exile – if that is what you
expect me to say – depart! What's the matter? Why are you waiting,
Catiline? Do you not see these silent rows? Silence means assent,
Catiline. You need not wait for senior senators to speak – their
21 silence makes their wishes clear. Had I said this to young Publius
Sestius here, or the heroic Marcus Marcellus, the Senate would
have assaulted me here in this temple, consul though I am – and
quite right too. But in your case, Catiline, their quiet signifies assent,
their assent is tantamount to a vote in favour, their silence is a
veritable shout of agreement. And it is not the senators only that
agree, the senators whose authority is apparently as dear to you as
their lives are cheap, but also the Roman knights, a most excellent
and loyal body of men, and all the other brave citizens who are
massed about the Senate here; you have seen the crowds, you have
realized their wishes, you have heard their murmurs of assent just

now to what I said. Indeed, I can scarcely keep them from tearing you to pieces any longer, Catiline. But I can easily persuade them to escort you to the gates, if you will leave the city you have so long sought to destroy.

25. CATILINE'S DEFENCE

Catiline was demoralized by Cicero's speech, (Section 24 above), though he attempted to reply, and was shouted down; he left the city. As he left, he wrote letters in defence of his conduct to certain men of influence. If they are correctly reported by Sallust, they shed a great deal of light on the attitude of the Roman nobles to the *res publica*.

SALLUST, *Catiline*, 34–35:

'On his journey Catiline wrote to a number of people, especially to the leading nobles; he had been trapped, he said, by false accusations; since he was unable to stand up to the party intrigues of his enemies he was going to submit to his fate; he was going into exile at Marseilles, not because he had a guilty conscience about the alleged atrocities, but that the *res publica* might be free from civil discord, and that there should not be a crisis arising from his opposition. Q. Catulus however read a letter out in the Senate which he said he had been sent in the name of Catiline. The following is a copy: "L. Catilina greets Q. Catulus. Your complete loyalty in the case you pleaded for me, and which I was particularly happy to have because of the predicament I have been in, gives me confidence to speak for myself. I have decided not to prepare a defence of my unusual behaviour; I have decided to lay before you an explanation. This is not because I have a guilty conscience, but I have every confidence that you will acknowledge that it is true. I have been driven by injuries and insults; since I have been robbed of the fruit of my conscientious labour, and do not occupy the place of honour that is my due, I have taken up in public life the cause of those in want, as I have always done; my motive is not that I cannot pay my own debts from my own property – and besides the generosity of Orestilla with her own and her daughter's fortunes would suffice for the sums for which I am surety–; no, it is because I see worthless men honoured with office, and myself driven into the wilderness by falsely-based suspicions. It is for this reason that I have pursued the hope of preserving what remains of my reputation in a manner honourable enough for one in my position. Though I wish to write more, I am told that force is being organized against me. Now I commend Orestilla to you, and entrust her to your loyalty. I beg you in the name of your children to defend her from any injury".'

26. CATILINE'S SUPPORTERS

Cicero meanwhile addressed the people; he had said that he would be a *popularis* consul who would appear in the forum; he was as good as his word. He describes Catiline's supporters, eloquently, if not very precisely.

In Catilinam, II, 17–23:

But I should not have talked so long about a single, self-confessed enemy of the state, whom I have no longer any reason to fear since we are now separated by the walls of Rome – as I have always wanted. But I must say something about the rest, the secret men who are still in our midst in Rome. Now these, if it is possible, I have no desire to punish, only to cure, to reconcile them to the *res publica* – it should be perfectly possible, if only they will listen to my advice. Let me first explain to you, gentlemen of Rome, from what type of men these forces of revolution are recruited. And then I shall suggest for each in turn the best cure my counsels can supply.

18   The first type are men who, though heavily in debt, have more than enough property to meet it, if they could only bear to part with their possessions. They make a great parade of honesty – for they are very rich – but they are utterly unscrupulous. My advice to them is that, richly endowed as they are in land, houses, silver, slaves, and property of all kinds, they should not hesitate to sell some of it to increase their credit. It is folly for them to wait for war or cancellation of debts. There will be nothing sacrosanct about their property in the general devastation of war, and anyone who thinks that Catiline will cancel debts is mad. I am the only person around here likely to cancel them, and I shall do so by compulsory auction of all debtors' property. What I advise is the only hope for men who still have capital; if only they had done it sooner, instead of sense-

lessly running up huge loans whose interest they can hardly settle out of income, they would all be the richer and better citizens for it. But this category should give us no real cause for alarm; they can be persuaded to change their minds, and, if not, I think they will assail the *res publica* with prayers for mercy rather than weapons of destruction.

19 The second type are those who are also heavily in debt, but are hoping for a tyranny and general revolution, and to get control of the state and the high offices which they cannot expect to win while the country is at peace. My best advice to them, and indeed to all the rest, is this: they should give up hope of getting what they want, first because I am for ever on the watch, I am everywhere seeing to the defence of the *res publica*, and secondly because of the stout resolve of all men of standing, the unanimity of all the orders of the state, the vast numbers who support us, and the large army under our control, and thirdly because the immortal gods themselves will stand beside us and bring aid to our unconquered nation, our glorious empire, and our lovely city against a crime as monstrous as revolt. And if by some remote contingency they should attain their mad desires, do they really imagine they can ever be consuls, dictators, or even kings in a city they have reduced to ashes, amid citizens whose blood they have spilt, to gratify their lunatic and criminal ambitions. Can they not see that, even if they achieve their ends, some exiled renegade or professional thug will come out on top and seize the power?

20 The third type are the army veterans – they are old now but still as hard as nails, thanks to their military training; that scoundrel Manlius, whom Catiline has gone to join, is one of them. These are men from the colonies which Sulla founded. Now I know that on the whole these colonies are made up of worthy and courageous citizens. But some of their members got rather above themselves and lived beyond their means, encouraged by their sudden and unexpected acquisition of wealth – and these are the ones I am talking about. They have built themselves houses fit for millionaires, wallowed in their rich estates, large establishments of slaves, and extravagant banquets, and have fallen so heavily into debt that they would need to resurrect Sulla himself from the dead to get them out of trouble. They have also managed to persuade some of the poorer, small-time peasant farmers to share their hopes of another bout of robbery such

as made their fortunes in the proscriptions long ago. Men of both these types are nothing more than brigands and robbers as far as I am concerned, and my only advice to them is to abandon this madness and cease to hope for proscriptions or dictatorships. Our memories are for ever so seared with the horrors of those times that neither we nor even the brute beasts themselves will ever tolerate its like again.

21   The fourth type is certainly a hotch-potch collection of unruly elements, men who have been in difficulties for years and never made the grade, men who through idleness, incompetence, or extravagance are staggering under a load of long-term debt, many of them ruined by forfeit of bail, loss of law-suits, and confiscations of their property. They are now all said to be flocking to Catiline's camp from the city and the countryside, apparently more eager to fight than pay their creditors. Well, if they cannot stand by their obligations, let them fall, and as soon as possible – as long as their ruin does not affect their country or their neighbours. But I cannot understand why men who cannot live honourably should choose to die dishonourably, or why they imagine it will hurt them less to die in company than alone.

22   The fifth type are the murderers, assassins, and criminals of all sorts. And as far as I am concerned Catiline is welcome to the lot. They will stick to him like leeches; and I hope it kills them, since certainly our prisons have not room to hold them all.

    Finally there are the lowest of the low, Catiline's Own Battalion, his special recruits, his bosom-companions. They are a familiar sight to you, gentlemen, with their long styled hair, their sleek looks, some effeminate and beardless, others as shaggy as satyrs, dressed like women in ankle-length, full-sleeved tunics and veils instead of togas. They burn up their energy and the midnight-oil in all-night feasts.

23 Amongst this pack you will find the gamblers, adulterers, and professional debauchees. They are mere boys, sweet and delicate, trained to give and receive love's sweet caresses, skilled dancers and singers, but experts too with the dagger and the poisoned phial. If these vermin are left in our city and not destroyed, I can assure you, gentlemen, that even Catiline's death will leave us in our state this breeding-ground of future Catilines. And what do these wretches want anyhow? They surely can take their women to camp with them. But how will they do without them, especially at night? How will they stand the frosts and snows of the Apennines? But perhaps

they think those naked dances at their banquets will have toughened them to endure the cold of winter. All in all, this will clearly be a fearful war, when Catiline's bodyguard is this battalion of harlots.

27. THE CONSPIRATORS BETRAYED

The conspiracy did not break up however; an embassy of Allobroges, Gauls, who had come to seek redress for grievances, was solicited for military aid, and agreed to carry letters to their fellow-countrymen. They betrayed the conspirators, handing over the letters; the conspirators were unmasked and denounced in the Senate. On the 3rd December, Cicero narrated the course of events to the people.

In Catilinam, iii, 3–15:

A few days ago, Gentlemen, Catiline broke out of the city. But he left behind in Rome all his partners in crime, who are the real hard core of this conspiracy and the brains behind the military organization. I have, therefore, been for ever on the watch since then trying to ensure our safety against these dark and terrible plots. At the time when I threw Catiline out of Rome – yes, threw him out, gentlemen: I use the word confidently, since the only odium I am likely to incur will be because I threw him out alive instead of dead – my only objective was to get him out of the city, since I thought that the rest of the conspirators would either go with him or be utterly helpless

4 without him. But then I found that all the most violent and criminal of his followers had stayed behind among us here, and so I made it my business night and day to smell out and discover exactly what they were doing and plotting. I knew that if I tried to tell you all the facts behind this vast and well-nigh incredible conspiracy you would refuse to believe your own ears; so my aim has been to catch them red-handed in the hope that you might then start to take the problem of your own safety seriously, once you had before your eyes and ears the evidence of their nefarious activities. I managed to discover that Publius Lentulus had approached a deputation of the Allobroges, who were in Rome for negotiations, in an effort to persuade them to stir up war and revolution among the tribes of Transalpine Gaul. He sent them back to their own people there, and gave them letters and orders to deliver to Catiline *en route*. Titus

Volturcius went with them, and he too had letters for Catiline. This seemed to me the very chance I had been hoping and praying for, the rare opportunity of uncovering the whole plot and making a clear case to you, gentlemen, and to the Senate.

5   So yesterday I summoned the praetors, Lucius Flaccus and Gaius Pomptinus, who are both brave men and true patriots, told them the whole story, and explained what I wanted done. Their whole attitude was absolutely splendid, and without hesitation or delay they got on with the job, and as night was falling made their way secretly to the Mulvian Bridge and stationed themselves in the nearby houses in two detachments separated by the bridge and the river. With them they had a large number of stout-hearted citizens, and I had armed and sent to join them a hand-picked group of young men from the Reate district, who have been of regular assistance to me in policing the city. All these they managed to get into position with-
6   out arousing any suspicions. It was between two and three o'clock in the morning when the embassy of the Allobroges, together with Volturcius and a large escort, began to cross the bridge. When the party were actually in transit, we closed in on them; both sides drew their swords, since only the praetors knew what was going on and the rest had no idea at all. Then Pomptinus and Flaccus arrived and everything calmed down; all the letters the party were carrying were handed over to the praetors with their seals unbroken, and as dawn was breaking the men were brought to me under arrest. I then immediately summoned Cimber Gabinius, the real villain of the piece, before he had any reason to become suspicious. Then I sent for Lucius Statilius and Cethegus. Lentulus was rather slow to arrive, presumably because his correspondence had kept him up rather later than usual that night! Meanwhile the news had got
7   around, and my house was beseiged that morning by a host of lead-ing and distinguished citizens. They all advised me to open the letters before presenting them to the Senate, in case we found no incriminating evidence and it would look as though I was making an enormous fuss about nothing. But I refused and said that this was a national emergency and it was my duty to give an unvarnished report to the council of the nation. It did not seem to me, gentlemen, that excess of zeal was anything to be ashamed of in a crisis of the *res publica*, even if I failed to find the evidence I had been led to expect. As you know, I quickly convened a full meeting of the Senate.

8 Meanwhile the Allobroges suggested I should send the praetor Gaius Sulpicius, who has a cool nerve in a crisis, to see if he could find any weapons in Cethegus' house – and he did, gentlemen; a huge number of swords and daggers. I brought Volturcius into the meeting, without the Gauls, to give evidence, and on the Senate's authority I gave him a solemn guarantee of indemnity, urging him not to be frightened to reveal everything he knew. He was still obviously under considerable stress, but he managed to tell us that he was carrying a letter from Publius Lentulus addressed to Catiline, and suggesting that he should take a bodyguard of slaves and come to Rome with his army as soon as possible. The plan, you see, gentlemen, was that, once the incendiaries had set the city on fire by areas as detailed in the master-plan and the general massacre of citizens had begun, Catiline should be in the immediate vicinity to mop up the fugitives and link up with these subordinate commanders in the city.

9 Then the Gauls were brought in, and they described how Lentulus, Cethegus, and Statilius had solemnly promised them support and then given them letters for their tribe, and, together with Lucius Cassius, told them to send cavalry to Italy as soon as possible, since, as far as infantry was concerned, they would have enough for their requirements. Lentulus had then explained to them that the Sibylline books and the predictions of the *haruspices* (interpreters of omens) all showed that he was the 'third Cornelius', who was destined to rule the city and the empire, his predecessors of that name having been Cornelius Cinna and Cornelius Sulla. The same prophecies had stated, he said, that this was indeed the year of destiny, which would see the end of Rome and her empire, since it was the tenth year after the acquittal of the Vestal Virgins and the

10 twentieth after the great fire on the Capitol. The Gauls also said that there had been a split between the conspirators, Lentulus and the rest wanting to start the massacre and arson at the Saturnalia (19th December), and Cethegus arguing that this was too long to wait.

Well, gentlemen, to cut a long story short, I ordered the letter that each man was supposed to have written to be produced. I showed Cethegus his letter first, and he acknowledged the seal. I cut the string; I read the letter. It was written in his own hand to the Senate and people of the Allobroges, assuring them that he would carry out the promises he had made to their representatives, and begging them in their turn to put into effect the undertakings made to himself by them. To account for the swords and daggers found in his house, Cethegus had already just produced the remarkable excuse that he had always been a connoisseur of good metal-work. But when his letter was read out, he lost his self-assurance and, as the full realization of his predicament began to dawn on him, he suddenly had a good deal less to say for himself. Next came Statilius, who likewise acknowledged his seal and hand-writing. His letter said very much the same thing and he confessed his guilt. I then showed Lentulus his letter, and asked him if he would acknowledge the seal. He did so; but, of course, as I pointed out to him, it was so well known that he could hardly do anything else. It was the portrait of a famous ancestor of his, who loved his country and his fellow-men as few have ever done; the mere sight of it should have been enough to stop him committing such a dreadful crime. His letter to

11 the Senate and people of the Allobroges was then read out in the same way, and I gave him a chance to defend himself. At first he refused, but when all the evidence had been revealed, he got up and asked the Gauls, and likewise Volturcius, what business had brought them to his house. Their answer was short but unequivocal. They explained who had made the contacts, how often they had come, and challenged him to deny his remarks about the Sibylline oracles. At this point we saw clearly the power of a guilty conscience: he lost his head and, instead of denying the charge, he suddenly and most unexpectedly, confessed. In fact, so utterly damning was the evidence of his guilt that not only did his very considerable eloquence desert him, but also that over-weening self-assurance which is the envy of his fellow criminals.

12 But then Volturcius suddenly asked for the letter to Catiline which he had been given by Lentulus to be produced and opened. At this Lentulus was really shaken, but he had to acknowledge that the seal and the writing were his. It was unsigned, but went as follows: 'Who I am you will be told by the bearer of this letter. Be resolute and remember you are playing for high stakes. Take all the necessary precautions and see that you get all the help you can from every source, even the lowest of the low.' After that we brought in Gabinius, but after trying to bluff his way out, he was finally unable to deny any of the Gauls' allegations. And as far as I was concerned,

13 gentlemen, although the letters, the seals, the handwriting, and the

individual confessions were cast-iron proof of guilt, I found even more convincing the ashen faces, the way they looked, their terrified expressions, and their silence. The way they looked so overwhelmed and gazed at the ground, occasionally exchanging furtive glances with each other, was far more damning than any amount of outside evidence.

Once this evidence had been revealed in detail, men of Rome, I asked the Senate what action they thought was needed for the defence of the *res publica*. The forthright, and indeed violent, opinions of the leading senators who spoke first found unanimous accord among their fellow-members. And since their decree has not yet been published, let me quote it to you, gentlemen, from memory.

14 First, a vote of thanks was passed to me, couched in the most fulsome terms, for the courage, skill, and foresight with which I had saved the *res publica* from the most terrible dangers. Then, as was only right and proper, the praetors Flaccus and Pomptinus were praised for the courage and loyalty which they had put at my disposal. Credit was also given to my brave colleague, Gaius Antonius Hybrida, who had refused to allow any of the conspirators to have access to his discussions on matters of national interest. The degree then ordained that Publius Lentulus should be arrested as soon as he resigned the praetorship, and that Cethegus, Statilius, and Gabinius, who were all in the Senate at the moment, should be taken into custody forthwith. The same provisions were passed with regard to Lucius Cassius, who had volunteered to organize the incendiaries in the city, Marcus Ceparius, who, it emerged, had been given the job of inciting the shepherds of Apulia to revolt, Publius Furius, one of the colonists whom Sulla had put into Faesulae, Quintus Annius Chilo, who had always been involved with Furius in the attempts to seduce the loyalty of the Allobroges, and Publius Umbrenus, a freed slave who was agreed to have made the first contacts between the Gauls and Gabinius. Note, gentlemen, the extraordinary moderation and leniency of the Senate: this was a vast conspiracy involving an enormous number of treacherous elements within our state – and yet they thought they could save the *res publica* and bring the rest of the conspirators to their senses by making an example of only the nine most utterly corrupt and depraved criminals involved. In addition to all this, a Public

15 Thanksgiving to the immortal gods was decreed for the great

benefits we had received at their hands; it was decreed in my honour, and the reason for this distinction, never before in all our history accorded to a civilian, was, as the resolution put it, 'because I had saved the city from fire, the citizens from slaughter, and Italy from civil war.' And the thing that makes this thanksgiving different from all other such occasions is that the others have celebrated the glorious achievements of our city, but this one the preservation of the *res publica*.

28. THE PUNISHMENT OF THE CONSPIRATORS

On 4th December, Cicero consulted the Senate about what he should do with the imprisoned conspirators. No conclusion was reached, but the proposal that they be put to death was almost certainly made, since we are told that it was proposed by D. Junius Silanus, the consul-designate, who spoke first. During the following night, an attempt to free them by force was made; it failed. On 5th December (the Nones) the debate was resumed. Cicero, spoke; he was the centre of attention; threats had been levelled against him, perhaps in the course of the debate. The two proposals under discussion were that of Silanus, that they be put to death, and of Caesar, praetor-elect, that they be imprisoned under stringent conditions.

In Catilinam, IV, 1–7:

Gentlemen of the Senate, I am very well aware that I am the focus of all your attention, and I can see that your relief to find the threat to yourselves and to the *res publica* now passed is tempered by your deep concern for my own continued danger. That you should be so concerned is indeed no small comfort to me in my anxieties and an encouragement to me in my misfortunes, but I must urge you once again by all I hold most sacred to forget my danger and give your undivided attention to your own and that of your children. I can easily endure, if needs must, the bitterness, the miseries, the hardships of a consul's lot; I can endure it undeterred and indeed with joy, given only that by my labours and exertions I can restore to you and to the Roman people that honour and security which once was

2 yours. After all, gentlemen, as consul I have had no respite from insidious plots against my life, neither in the forum, which is the source and fountain-head of justice, nor in the *Campus Martius*, a place hallowed by the auspices so often there consulted by consuls,

nor in the Senate, which is the guardian of all men's rights, nor in my home, which is to every man his castle and defence, nor in the very bed, which is my resting-place, nor even in this the consul's honoured throne – nowhere gentlemen, have I found safety. And yet I have not complained; indeed I have shut my eyes to much that I should not; I have relieved your fears often at no small cost to myself. And if it is the will of heaven that the outcome of my consulship should be that you and all the Roman people should be saved from bloody assassination, that your wives, your children, and the Vestal Virgins should stay unmolested, that our temples, shrines, and this fair country should be spared the horrors of arson and Italy the devastation of war, then let me face whatever destiny may bring my own poor self with a high heart, for it is a small price to pay. If Publius Lentulus was so intoxicated by his prophets that he believed himself the man of destiny, ordained for the destruction of the *res publica*, why should not I myself rejoice to find my consulship the instrument of providence, ordained for its salvation?

3   And therefore, gentlemen of the Senate, take heed unto yourselves, take counsel for your country; protect your own lives and those of your wives and children; preserve your property; defend the Roman people and their glorious name. Spare not a thought for me or for my safety, first because I have every right to hope that all the gods who watch over this our city will reward me according to my deserts; and secondly because, if anything should happen to me, I am not afraid to die. Death can not disgrace a brave man, nor overtake a man of consular rank before his time, nor bring distress to a philosopher. Yet I confess I am not so iron-hearted that I am unmoved by the tears of my own dear brother here beside me, nor the grief of all my colleagues that you see about me. I do not find it easy to prevent my thoughts from turning homeward when I see my wife, my daughter, and my darling little son all out of their minds with fear – although the *res publica* herself seems to me to protect him, since he guarantees that I shall do my duty as consul. And over there, among the audience, I see my son-in-law, standing and waiting anxiously to see the end of this day's events. All this, gentlemen, moves me deeply, as I say, but only to a stern resolve that they and you should all be saved together, though it cost me my life, rather than allow them and all of us to perish together among the ruins of

4 the *res publica*. Therefore, gentlemen of the Senate, bend to your

task; save the *res publica*; make all provision to face the storms that may otherwise come upon you unawares. For here we bring to judgement, to face the strictness of your justice, not a Tiberius Gracchus, accused of seeking a second tribunate, nor a Gaius Gracchus, accused of stirring up sedition over land-reform, nor yet a Lucius Saturninus, accused of murdering a Gaius Memmius – no, gentlemen, here we hold in custody men who stayed in Rome to fire the city, to butcher you all, to welcome Catiline; we have their letters, signed and sealed; we have each man's confession. They are inciting the Allobroges, stirring up the slaves, calling for Catiline. The conspiracy has begun; and its ultimate objective is that when we are all dead, there will be no-one left to sing a requiem for the passing of the Roman people's name, or to lament the doom of a great empire.

5 All this, gentlemen, you have heard from my witnesses; the accused have confessed to it; and you have already declared your verdict in many different ways: first, you passed a vote of thanks to me in terms of unprecedented generosity, and declared that thanks to my courage and devotion to duty a criminal conspiracy had been unearthed. Then, you forced Publius Lentulus to resign his praetorship, and voted that he and the others whom you found guilty should be taken into custody. Then, most remarkable of all, you decreed a public thanksgiving in my name, an honour never before accorded to a civilian. Finally, yesterday you bestowed most generous rewards on the legates of the Allobroges and on Titus Volturcius. All these actions amount to a public and unqualified verdict of guilty passed on those whom you have specifically named and put under arrest.

6 Nevertheless, gentlemen of the Senate, it has been my intention to treat the whole question as still an open one, and to ask you to reach a decision both about the actual offence and about the penalty we should impose. Let me merely give you my views in my capacity as consul. I had long been aware that a mighty demon of unrest was at work in the *res publica* and that fresh calamities were brewing, but I never dreamt that so monstrous and disastrous a conspiracy could be the work of citizens. But as a result, this is now the moment for decision, and whatever that decision may be, however you may incline to vote, that decision must be reached by nightfall. You are aware of the enormity of the crime; and if you think that only a few are party to it, gentlemen, you are making a big mistake. It is a

poison that has spread far more widely than you think; it has permeated Italy and even crossed the Alps, and already in its unseen and tortuous course it has corrupted many of the provinces. It is quite impossible to stop it now by delay and procrastination; you must exact punishment at once in whatever way you choose.

7 Now on this point I am very well aware that opinion is still divided. Decimus Silanus represents one view, which is that men who sought to destroy the state should be punished by death, while Gaius Caesar rejects the penalty of death but would welcome the severest of any other kind. They are men of high standing and this is a grave crime – that the penalties should be severe is common ground between them. Silanus maintains that men who have sought to deprive us all, to deprive the Roman people, of the right to live, who have sought to overthrow the nation and blot out the name of Rome, should not be allowed to enjoy this life nor to draw breath among us a moment longer. He reminds us that there are ample precedents in the *res publica* for the use of such a penalty against traitors. Caesar, however, holds the view that death was established by the immortal gods, not as a punishment but rather as part of the processes of nature, to be a quiet end to all our labours and our miseries, and that this is why philosophers have faced it willingly and heroes often even joyfully. But imprisonment, he says, even imprisonment for life, if necessary, is certainly an appropriate and dire penalty for a dreadful crime. So he recommends that the guilty men be imprisoned in various provincial towns. But this seems a very unfair imposition if you make it an order, and unlikely to succeed if you make it a request. However, if that is what you want, gentlemen, that is what you must decree.

29. CONCORDIA ORDINUM

After brief counter-arguments against Caesar, Cicero passes to the main theme of the speech, the *concordia ordinum*, a uniting of men of all ranks and classes in the interest of preserving order and the rights of property, and peace. In doing so, however, he makes it very clear that he himself was incurring unpopularity on this account, and that there were some who would seek to victimize him if he carried out the sentence proposed by Silanus.

In Catilinam, IV, 14–24:

But I would be less than frank, gentlemen, if I failed to report what I hear. And it has come to my ears that some men are afraid that I shall not have adequate protection to give effect to what you have decreed today. But have no fear; I have foreseen everything, prepared everything, arranged everything with all the care and thoroughness at my command, backed as I am by the yet more resolute determination of the Roman people to retain their sovereignty and protect their common interests. My support is to be found in men of every rank, every class, and every age; they have packed the forum, the temples round about it, all the approaches to this, the Temple of Concord, and to the Capitol. At last, for the first time in the history of this city, we have found a cause which has united the whole nation, except those men who, knowing they must die, have chosen to drag that nation wholesale down to death beside
15 them, rather than die alone. But such men I except and willingly discount; for I do not regard them as unruly citizens so much as the most vicious of public enemies. But for the rest – words fail me, gentlemen. Their crowds, their enthusiasm, their courage, all testify to their united concern for the common safety and the grandeur that is Rome. Here we have the knights, in rank and influence yielding pride of place to you, gentlemen of the Senate, but challenging you to match their patriotism. After the long years of struggle, the crisis of today has brought them back to harmony and concord with your order. And if this harmony, which my consulship has established, can but survive for ever in the *res publica*, I promise you that never again hereafter shall we see in any part of the *res publica* the horrors of civil and domestic strife. With no less zeal for its defence I see the Treasury officials have assembled here today; the civil servants have also come here to a man – chance brought them to this spot today to draw lots for the allocation of their duties, but I see that their thoughts have turned from the excitement of the
16 draw to higher things, the safety of the state. Here in their thousands, too, are all the freeborn citizens of Rome, however poor. And is there one among them, gentlemen, to whom this temple, this fair city, his own freedom, the very light of day, this soil which is a Roman's fatherland, is not a precious, sweet, and lovely thing? You might note, too, the loyalty of our freedmen, gentlemen, who by their own

efforts have made a place for themselves in this city and rightly now regard it as their country, while others – born on this soil and into high estate – have chosen rather to regard it as the city of their enemies.

But I need say no more about these orders and these men, who have leapt to the defence of their country to protect their own possessions and their common share of the *res publica*, and, above all, the freedom that is their greatest treasure. After all, there is no slave, unless his lot is quite intolerable, who would not shudder to see citizens commit such dire crimes, who would not wish to see our heritage preserved, who would not offer to the common cause all

17 the support his courage and his powers can allow. You may have heard – some of you – gentlemen, with some alarm that one of Lentulus' pimps has been canvassing round the markets to try and bribe the poor and ignorant into violent action. Well, he certainly tried; but he could find no-one so wretched or depraved that he did not wish to preserve the place where he worked and earned his daily bread, where he relaxed and slept, and lived the even tenor of his way. The vast majority of those who work in shops and businesses – indeed I should say rather that whole working class – are passionately devoted to the cause of civil peace. All their equipment, their work and livelihood depend on having plenty of customers; in fact it is by civil peace they live. They lose money when they shut up shop, so what would have happened to them if their shops had been burned down?

18 So then therefore, gentlemen of the Senate, the Roman people will not let you down; but it is also your duty not to let them down. You have a consul who has been preserved from innumerable dangers, ambushes, and death's very clutches to fight, not for his own life, but for your survival. Every order in the state has united with heart and mind and voice for the protection of the *res publica*. Menaced by fire and the weapons of an ungodly conspiracy, your own dear motherland stretches out suppliant hands towards you and entrusts herself to your safe-keeping along with the lives of all her citizens, the citadel, the Capitol, the altars of her domestic gods, the eternal flame of Vesta, goddess of hearth and home, the shrines and temples of all its gods, the walls and houses of the city. On your decision hang today, gentlemen, your own lives, the lives of your wives and children, the fortunes, homes and hearths of every citizen

19 of Rome. But you have a captain for the fight whose thoughts are centred on your safety and never on his own, and this is rare indeed. And furthermore, every citizen of every rank, indeed the whole populace of Rome, is united and at one in a manner never known before in any time of civil strife. Remember the price this people paid to establish this nation, remember the courage it needed to ensure our freedom, the blessings of heaven by which our prosperity has increased; yet one night has nearly led to the destruction of it all. It is, therefore, your duty to take such measures today as will ensure that never shall it be possible for any citizen to do or even contemplate such things again. And I have said all this not to arouse your zeal, which has been so often well nigh greater than my own, but because as consul it is my duty to the *res publica* to give the lead, and my concern to be seen to have done so unequivocally.

20 But before I return the debate to the House, I shall deal briefly with my own position. The number of the conspirators is, as you know, gentlemen, considerable; and I am very well aware that every single one of them is now my enemy. But that does not concern me. I regard them as depraved, debilitated, and demoralized. But if there ever comes a time when that same gang of villains, encouraged by the criminal madness of some politician, should prove too powerful for you or the *res publica* to restrain, for all the weight of your combined prestige, never for a moment shall I feel the least regret for the deeds that I have done and the counsel I have given. They may threaten me with death perhaps; but that is a fate in store for all men. And in my life the honour which your decrees have heaped upon me is such that no man ever won before. To others you voted public thanks that they had done the state good service; to me and to nobody else that I had proved the salvation of the *res publica* . . .

23 And therefore, gentlemen, I have sacrificed a high command, a province, a triumph and such other signal marks of honour as I might have won, in order to ensure the safety of our city and yourselves; I have foregone the privilege of winning clients and friends in the provinces, though I have tried as best I could from Rome to win such friendships as much as to keep them. And for all these sacrifices, and no less for my devotion to your cause and my conspicuous determination to preserve the *res publica*, I ask but one thing in return: that you remember this time and the whole

achievement of my consulship. For as long as that memory remains fixed in your hearts, I shall think myself protected by the mightiest of defences. But once the powers of evil men suffice to cheat or vanquish the hopes I place in you, then I commend to your safe keeping my tiny son. And you will have given him adequate protection for himself and his career if you but remember that he is the son of the man who all alone risked his life to preserve your heritage.

24   Therefore, gentlemen, for the ultimate safety of yourselves and the people of Rome, for your wives and children, your hearths and altars, the shrines and temples of your gods, your homes and houses throughout this city, for your government and freedom, the safety of Italy, and the whole fabric of this *res publica*, with all the care you have shown hitherto, be bold, be resolute – and vote. Your consul does not fear to carry out your orders; and while he yet lives, whatever you decide, he has the power to defend and guarantee it.

Cicero's speech was followed – probably after an interval occupied mainly by speakers supporting Caesar – by that of M. Porcius Cato, whose speech on this occasion turned the tide of opinion back in favour of the death-penalty. It was in one sense his political *début*, a speech which at one blow established him as a leader of a substantial group of nobles and those who supported them. After Cato spoke, Cicero put the motion in the terms proposed by Cato; it was passed, and Cicero personally supervised the execution of the prisoners. Catiline himself was subsequently brought to battle, nominally by Antonius, Cicero's colleague, and died fighting bravely.

30. THE END OF CATILINE'S REVOLT, AND THE AFTERMATH

(a) The Military Victory

SALLUST, *Catiline*, 61:

'When the battle was over, you could not fail to appreciate the desperate courage which had inspired Catiline's army. Almost every man's body was found on the same spot where he had taken up his post. In the centre, where the praetorian cohort had broken into the line, a very few were slightly scattered, but every single man had fallen with his wounds on the front of his body, facing the enemy.

Catiline was found far in advance of his own men, among the
corpses of the enemy, still breathing slightly, and showing on his
face that spirit of dauntless valour that had been characteristic of
him in his lifetime. In short, there was not one single freeborn
citizen captured out of the whole army, either on the battlefield or
in the pursuit; they had all been as unsparing of their own lives as
of their opponents'.'

(b) Clashes with the Nobles

Cicero's actions were not universally approved, even in 63. Catiline and
Lentulus were patricians, and many nobles resented Cicero's attitude to
themselves and the claims of their class. Metellus Nepos, for example, who
became tribune on 10 December, 63, attacked Cicero, and prevented him
from addressing the people on 31st December. Cicero defended himself early
in 62, and Metellus' brother, Metellus Celer, wrote an abusive letter to
Cicero about his conduct. This letter survives, as does Cicero's reply (*Ad
fam.* V, 1 & 2). Other nobles evidently sympathized with Metellus, and in
consequence Cicero felt isolated, and sought political allies in various places.
Pompey was on his way home, his task completed; Crassus, no friend of
Cicero's, despite his aid in the Catilinarian conspiracy, went to Asia to meet
Pompey, though whether this was from fear, as is alleged by the ancient
sources, or in pursuit of political support or business opportunities, we do
not know. Cicero wrote to Pompey to canvass his support, and was rebuffed,
as is plain from the surviving part of the correspondence (*Ad fam.* V, 7).

(c) Defence Counsel Defends Himself

In Rome, Cicero sought to obtain allies by resuming his legal practice.
P. Sulla, a nephew of the dictator, had been elected consul in 65, but
had never taken office because he had been condemned for bribery along
with his colleague Autronius. He was now accused of having taken part in
the conspiracy of Catiline. For Cicero, to defend him was a means of drawing closer to Sulla s and his family's many influential friends. A young
patrician, L. Manlius Torquatus, was the prosecutor. He had attacked
Cicero for having established a cruel '*regnum*' and for being a 'foreigner'.
Cicero's reply is based on the arguments that most people approved of his
actions, and that not everyone can be a patrician. The participation in
trials by the spectators is well illustrated.

Pro Sulla, 1–2, 21–35:

How I wish, gentlemen of the jury, in the first place that Publius
Sulla could earlier have held on to the high position which his

election to the consulship had conferred upon him, and afterwards, when disaster struck him down, could at least have had something to show for the restraint and moderation which he has since displayed. But alas, this was not to be; Fate was against him, and he was toppled from the highest office in the land by the general envy which is the lot of all successful politicians and the unprecedented hatred felt for his fellow-consul, Publius Autronius. And even amid the misery and degradation of what little he could salvage from his previous success, he still found enemies whose malice could not be appeased even by the dire penalty which he had paid. However, despite the deep distress which this man's misfortunes have caused me, I have derived some small grain of comfort for myself in the midst of my own misfortunes, in that I have been given the opportunity of reminding all men of standing of the moderation and generosity of judgement for which I was once renowned but have had to suppress of late, and of forcing all criminals and traitors, who have recently been tamed and brought to heel, to acknowledge that in the days when the *res publica* was falling I was implacable and courageous, but once it was preserved I was willing to be merciful

2　and to pardon . . . . For my opponent, Lucius Torquatus has clearly perceived that anything he can do to reduce my standing with you, gentlemen, will reduce proportionately the effectiveness of my defence of Publius Sulla. But I believe that if I can successfully vindicate my own actions, and convince you that I am consistent in allowing my friendship for my client to persuade me to undertake his defence, then I shall in fact vindicate Publius Sulla too . . .

21　　Now Torquatus says, gentlemen, that he cannot bear my 'tyranny', but it is rather hard to see what he is referring to. I can only assume he means my consulship, in which, so far from giving orders like a tyrant, I actually took my orders from the Senate and the men of standing in our state – proof, surely, that my tenure of office was devoted to the suppression of tyranny and not its imposition. But perhaps he calls me 'tyrant', not referring so much to the time when I held the high office and extensive powers of consul, but rather to the present time when I am a private citizen, on the ridiculous grounds that all those I gave evidence against have been convicted while my client is hoping to be acquitted. Of my evidence, gentlemen, I can only say in reply that if it was false, then so was Torquatus' evidence against the self-same men; and if true, it is hardly characteristic of a tyrant to vindicate the truth of his evidence given

22 under oath. As for Sulla's hopes of acquittal, let me just say this: Sulla expects nothing from me in the way of money, influence or anything else – only the loyalty one is entitled to expect from one's own lawyer. Torquatus also argued that Sulla would never have defended his case but would have allowed it to go by default and himself gone into exile had I not taken it up. The logical conclusion of that argument must be that a man as distinguished as Quintus Hortensius here, and men as eminent as this jury, have no minds of their own but rely on my judgement. Furthermore, if his incredible allegations are true and this jury would really not have stood by Publius Sulla had I not done so too, then who, I should like to know, is the real tyrant in the case – Torquatus, the irresistible, the scourge of the innocent, or Cicero, the champion of the underdog? As for his unnecessary and flippant remarks about my being the third foreign tyrant that Rome has had (Tarquin and Numa being the first two), ignoring for the moment the slur of 'tyrant', what does he mean by 'foreign'? After all, if he is right, the remarkable thing is not that I was a foreign tyrant – since, as he says, Rome has had two of them before – but a foreign consul. What he means, of course, is

23 that I come from a provincial borough. Yes; and I am proud of it, since it is the same borough that has now saved Rome for the second time. But tell me, Torquatus, what makes you think that a man from a borough is a foreigner? That is an insult which no-one ever threw at that grand old man of Rome, Marcus Cato, although he had innumerable enemies, or at Tiberius Coruncanius, or Manius Curius, or even at my own fellow-townsman, Gaius Marius, though he too was the object of much envy. I must confess, it gives me great pleasure that the only insult you can find to hurl at me, for all your efforts, is an insult to most of the citizens of Rome.

Now you are an old friend of mine, Torquatus, and so I have excellent reason to repeat again and again the advice I have given you before. Men cannot all be patricians – indeed, if you really want to know, many of them do not even want to be – nor do your own contemporaries regard themselves as your inferiors just because

24 they are not patricians. So if you think that men like myself are foreigners when our fame and reputation have been established for

years in this city and been a talking point for all its citizens, then you are bound to regard your rivals for the quaestorship as foreigners too, since they are the pick of all Italy and are competing with you for office and every position it leads to. But I would not use the word too readily, if I were you; you may be swamped by all those 'foreign' votes. If they bring their energy and determination to bear in the forthcoming election campaign, believe you me, they may yet turn the tables on you and make you eat your arrogant words, and cost you a few sleepless nights into the bargain. Anyhow, they are prepared to lose to you on merit but nothing else.

25 And even if you and I, gentlemen, were rightly regarded as foreigners by all other true-blue Romans, I would not have expected our deficiencies to be pointed out by Torquatus of all people. After all, he is a provincial himself on his mother's side; for very distinguished, very honourable though his mother's family is, nevertheless they are from Asculum. So he either has to prove that people from the district of Picenum, such as the men of Asculum, are the only non-foreigners in the provinces, or else heave a sigh of relief that I am not claiming that my family are more upper-class than his. So do not call me a foreigner again, Torquatus, or I will refute you with a few less pleasant home truths; and do not call me a tyrant or I will make a complete fool of you. But perhaps by tyrant you mean a man who lives in such a way that he is a slave neither to any man nor to his own passions, but has conquered desire and lacks neither gold, nor silver, nor any other material possessions; a man who speaks his mind freely in the Senate, caring more for the welfare of the people than for their whims, refusing to be browbeaten, and standing rock-like for his principles. If you think that that is being tyrannical, then a tyrant I am, I confess: but if any power I enjoy, any superior position, or indeed any haughty or arrogant remarks I may have made infuriate you, why not cast those in my teeth instead of descending to cheap abuse and malicious insults.

20 I have done the *res publica* some service in my time, gentlemen, and if the only reward I sought from the Senate and people of Rome was to be left alone in a position of honour, no-one would refuse me. Other men could then have the high offices, the power, the provinces, the triumphs, and the other trappings of distinction; I would be left to contemplate with quiet satisfaction the city which I had

saved. But what if I do not ask such things? What if I choose to put at the service of my friends and make available to all the citizens of Rome those same qualities of unremitting industry as of old, the painstaking effort, the high sense of duty, the grinding toil, and the sleepless nights? Suppose my loyalty is still at the service of my friends in the law-courts and of the *res publica* in the Senate; suppose I claim neither the rest from labours nor the release from toil my age and high achievements might expect; suppose my goodwill, my industry, my home, my faculties, and my attention are open to the service of all, and I cannot even find a moment to record and examine all that I have done for the common safety of the state; must I nevertheless still endure the slur of 'tyrant' when no man else
27 can be found willing to take my place? In fact, Torquatus, to be a tyrant is alien to my character. If you want to know who really were the men who sought to seize despotic power in Rome, you need turn back the pages of history no further than your own family tree. For myself, I have won more than enough glory from my achievements already, and they may perhaps have led me to an excessive opinion of myself. But famous, unforgettable though they are, I think I may say of them that for me it will be sufficient reward for snatching our city and all its citizens from the very jaws of destruction if such great benefits to every man alive shall bring no consequent disaster to
28 myself. You see, gentlemen, I know my Rome; I understand the nature of the city which is the scene of my past triumphs and present policies. The forum here is packed with those whose yoke of tyranny I lifted from your shoulders but cannot shake from off my own. For of course you do not imagine, I assume, that it was a mere handful of men who pitched their hopes and ambitions so high as the destruction of a mighty empire like our own. I was able to tear the firebrands from their hands and wrest the swords from their grasp – as indeed I did – but I was not able to cure or take away the vile and criminal desires that drove them on. As a result, I am deeply conscious of the danger in which I live, surrounded as I am by so great a multitude of criminals, since I realise that single-handed I am
29 engaged in war to the death with all the hosts of evil. So if perhaps, Torquatus, you begrudge me my bodyguard here, or if it seems to you to smack of tyranny that every decent citizen of every class and kind has identified his safety with my own, at least take comfort from the fact that I alone am the object of all the hatred and hostility of

all the ciminal classes, not just because I thwarted their unholy enterprise and mad conspiracy, but far more because they believe that while I am alive they can make no similar attempt again.

30 And yet why should I be surprised at the vilification I endure from criminals, when Torquatus himself from time to time indulges in unrestrained abuse? After all, unlike them, he himself has laid the foundations of a public career with his eyes set on the one great goal, the one high hope of winning the consulship. Moreover he is the son of Lucius Torquatus, an excellent consul, a resolute senator, and always a most patriotic citizen. And yet he did not raise his voice when he spoke in condemnation of the treachery of Publius Lentulus, and the brazen audacity of all his fellow-criminals; he merely whispered his account barely loud enough for you to hear who agree with what he said. But when he came to speak of their punishment – the execution and imprisonment of those same traitors – he issued his complaints at the top of his voice. It was a ludicrous proceeding,

31 gentlemen. You see, he wanted your approval for his whispered condemnation, which he did not want the bystanders to hear at all; but when it came to his public pronouncements he failed to realize that he could not stop you hearing other sentiments, which were designed to commend him to those whose goodwill he was soliciting, but of which you most certainly disapproved. Furthermore, Torquatus, you broke another of an orator's cardinal rules by failing to realize what is appropriate to each case. It is singularly bad tactics for a speaker who accuses one man of conspiracy to be seen to be distressed at the punishment and death of other conspirators. It is not surprising to find a tribune like Bestia distressed, since he seems to be the only survivor left to mourn them; and, since his grief is genuine, it is presumably hard to conceal. But I find it very remarkable that a young man like you should feel grief in the very case in

32 which he seeks to bring conspirators to justice. But the most deplorable aspect of the whole affair is that with your endowments of ability and common sense you should not espouse the cause of the *res publica*, but imagine that the common people of Rome do not approve of the actions taken in my consulship by all the men of standing in the interests of our common safety.

Here you are, Torquatus, trying to win the goodwill of men reluctant to bestow it on you – but do you seriously imagine any single one of them was so depraved as to have wanted our country to

perish, so wretched as to have willed his own destruction or the loss of all he wished to keep? Does anyone at all condemn your namesake and ancestor, Titus Manlius Torquatus, because he executed his own son to prevent the subversion of the discipline of his army? How then can you condemn the *res publica* for executing the traitors who
33 threatened her survival? So listen, Torquatus, while I reiterate the principles on which I exercised my consulship – for in this I am a model of consistency. At the top of my voice, publicly, and for all to hear, I make this declaration which I shall continue to make until my dying day. Come and hear it anyone who is listening; the more the merrier! Get your brains to work and listen while I tell you what I think about the actions which Torquatus professes to believe so unpopular. I was consul at a time when an army of depraved and vicious citizens, hell-bent upon their secret treasons, had devised the cruellest and most lamentable end that ever came upon a mother-country; I was consul at a time when both Catiline with his army and Lentulus here in this city, among our temples and under our very roofs, were the appointed leaders for the destruction and ruination of the *res publica*. By my own devices and my own labours, at the risk of my own life, without panic or fuss, without calling up reserves, without weapons and without an army, by arresting five men and extracting their confessions, I saved the city from conflagration, the citizens from death, Italy from devastation, and the *res publica* from ultimate destruction. By punishing five lunatic criminals I saved the lives of all our citizens and the peace of the world; above all, I saved this city, which is to all of us our home, and to foreign kings and nations a bastion of defence, a shining example, and the heart
34 of the empire. Did you believe, Torquatus, that I would not say here in court, where I am not under oath, what I have already said under oath before a vast assembly of the people? One futher point, in case some irresponsible person should leap to your side, Torquatus, and count on you for help later on; and let me shout it at the top of my voice so that everyone can hear this too: everything I did or tried to do for the salvation of the *res publica*, I did with the backing, help, and support of Lucius Torquatus – that man there, gentlemen. He was my personal assistant in my consulship and in my praetorship, and alike in thought and action the leader, director, and guide to all the young men of Rome. As for his father, that great patriot, that man of courage, wisdom, and steadfastness, despite his illness he

took a personal share in everything we did; he never left my side; he helped me to the limit of his powers with encouragement, advice, and personal influence, overcoming his infirmity of body by sheer

35 force of will. You see, Torquatus? I am trying to rescue you from your new found favour with the irresponsible elements of our society and to restore you to the good graces of all men of standing. Among them there is an enormous fund of goodwill and affection for you, which will not be easily dissipated. So even if you are temporarily at odds with me, they will not let you make that an excuse for taking sides against the *res publica* to the detriment of your own character and political standing.

However I must return to the case in hand, gentlemen, and I must ask you to bear witness for me that Torquatus left me no option but to speak at length about my own record. Had he confined his accusations to Publius Sulla, I too would have confined my present speech to a defence of the accused. But since Torquatus' speech is from beginning to end an attack on me, and, as I have already said, an attempt to weaken my defence by destroying my authority, my client's interests would have made me speak as I have done, even had my own indignation not required me to do so.

31. POLITICAL RELATIONSHIPS IN ROME

(*a*) *Amicitia* and *Inimicitia* in the courts; opposition does not mean personal enmity.

Pro Sulla, 48–50:

I really cannot see why you should be annoyed with me, Torquatus. Certainly, if it is because I am defending the man whom you are prosecuting, I should have thought I had at least as much reason to be angry with you for prosecuting the man I am defending. I can match your claim to be prosecuting a personal enemy by pointing out that I am defending a personal friend. Nor is the claim valid that I have no right to defend any man accused of conspiracy; in fact, no one has a better right than I to defend a man against whom there was no breath of suspicion, when I collected a mass of evidence against others who were implicated. Why, then, you may ask, did I give evidence against all the other conspirators? Quite simply, because I had to. And why were they convicted? Because the jury believed my evidence. And it is no use argiung that it is character-istic of a despot to pick and choose whom one will defend or prosecute, because it is most certainly equally the mark of a slave's con-dition not to do so. And if you ask yourself whether you or I was under a greater obligation, you will have to admit that it is much more honourable for you to abandon your personal vendetta than

49 for me to ignore the obligations of friendship. During your father's struggle to obtain the office of consul, the question at issue was the attainment of the highest honours in the state by your family. But your father, who is a man of admirable good sense, certainly did not hold it against some of his closest friends when they defended Publius Sulla and testified to his high character. He fully under-stood that it is a long-standing tradition of ours that ties of friendship should not hinder us from helping a defendant in his hour of need. What a difference between that case and this! On that occasion your family stood to win the consulship – and indeed did so – once Sulla was convicted. You were fighting for high political honours and made no secret of your claim to be seeking in the courts restitution of an office of which you were robbed in the elections. And yet some of your closest family friends fought for Sulla's acquittal on that occasion, and you did not resent it; yet they were seeking to deprive you of the consulship and to obstruct your path to high office, with-out damaging in any way their relationship with you or seeming to fail in their obligations as friends. And the reason was simply the excellent precedent afforded by the long traditions of men of stand-

50 ing in this city. Yet in this case today I am not depriving you of any distinction or blocking your path to high office by opposing you. In fact I am at a loss to discover your motives for this prosecution at all. Your father got his consulship and you the distinctions consequent upon it. In fact, laden as you are with the spoils of that victory, you have taken his life, as it were, and now seem to be wanting to hack the corpse. And all I am doing is to try and defend the poor naked corpse as it lies there, while you abuse and rage at me for doing so. Nevertheless I am not going to be angry with you nor even criticize you for that, since I assume that this course of action is a deliberate choice and that you are perfectly capable of deciding where you think obligations lie.

(*b*) The Influence of a *Patronus* in the affairs of
an Italian *Municipium*.

Pro Sulla, 60–2:

Now Torquatus has also alleged that the citizens of Pompeii were induced by Sulla to join the conspiracy of Catiline and support his criminal plot; but this accusation absolutely defeats me, gentlemen. Do you mean, Torquatus, that they actually conspired? That is a completely new idea, and there is not a shred of evidence to support it. Torquatus' actual words were that 'he poisoned relations between the natives of Pompeii and the retired soldiers in the colony there, so that in this antagonism the general dissension between the two communities would enable him to get control of the town with the help of the natives'.

Well, to begin with, the dispute between the colonists and the natives of Pompeii was a long-standing grievance, which had been causing trouble for years. It was then referred to the city's patrons for arbitration, and when they had eventually investigated the matter Sulla found himself in agreement with their conclusions on every point. Finally, the colonists themselves certainly reckoned that Sulla

61 had protected their interests no less than those of the natives. And you have only to look, gentlemen, at the crowds of colonists here today, excellent men all of them, and all of them anxious about the fate of Publius Sulla here, their patron, their protector, the champion of their colony. Even though they were not able to ensure his safety and success on every occasion or in every struggle for office, they are most anxious for you to help and protect him with your assistance, gentlemen, in this particular misfortune which has afflicted him. Also here to day, and matching the enthusiasm of the colonists for his cause are the men of Pompeii whom the prosecution have denounced as well by implication. These men may have had their disagreements with the colonists over public promenades and voting rights, but they obviously agree with them when it comes to the

62 question of where their common safety lies. And I certainly must not ignore Sulla's own personal qualities. He was responsible for launching this colony originally, and though the requirements of the *res publica* were clearly incompatible with the interests of the natives of Pompeii, he so managed to endear himself to both sides that they

felt he had not deprived one party of their property so much as guaranteed security of tenure to both.

(c) Convictions and Sentences

Legislation – even in a relative's interest – must distinguish between convictions and sentences; the former must never be tampered with, but the latter may be for reconsideration.

Pro Sulla, 62–5:

Let us now examine your next complaint, Torquatus. You say that strong-arm tactics were organized to force through Caecilius' proposed bill: gladiators, thugs, and all other such weapons of brute force; and you have made this an excuse for a virulent attack on Lucius Caecilius, a most respectable and highly distinguished citizen. I need not dwell upon his admirable qualities and high principles: suffice to say that, when he brought in his proposed decree, he aimed only to alleviate, not to remove, the penalties inflicted on his brother, and he refused to allow his concern for his brother's welfare to over-ride his obligations of loyalty to the *res publica*. As a result, although brotherly affection was responsible for his proposals, he also 63 abandoned them in deference to his brother's wishes. Now these attacks on Caecilius are also a means of attacking Sulla. Yet the behaviour of both of them in this affair has been exemplary. Caecilius may have proposed the restoration of Sulla, and in that he apparently proposed to rescind a decision of the courts there is legitimate ground for complaint. After all, the concept of legality is one of the fundamental sources of stability in the *res publica*, and is based on the inviolability of judicial decisions. We cannot afford to make concessions to brotherly affection to the extent of allowing the welfare of our relatives to blind us to our obligations to the common safety. But Caecilius' proposals did not raise the question of the verdict at all; they only concerned the statutory penalties for bribery, which were a comparatively recent innovation; in other words, the bill aimed to correct a defect in the law, not to overthrow a verdict. To criticize a sentence is to find fault with the law, not the verdict. A verdict is for a jury, and the verdict stood. But a statutory penalty is a part of a law; it was this that Caecilius sought to reduce. 64 Do not, therefore, Torquatus, I beg of you, alienate the sympathies of the various orders who are responsible for our courts, and who act so impressively and with such distinction in them. No-one has tried to reverse their decision; that is not what Caecilius' proposals were about. Even though it was his brother that was suffering, he always believed that the authority of the juries must be upheld, and so he merely sought to mitigate the extreme severity of the law.

I hope I have made my point. I could and would willingly say much more, if loyalty and affection for his brother had driven Lucius Caecilius to abnormal or unreasonable lengths; I would then appeal to your emotions, gentlemen, begging each one of you to remember your own affection for your friends, to look into the secret places of your hearts, and out of common feelings of humanity

65 to forgive Caecilius for his mistake. But though his bill was published, it never reached the stage of formal proposal, and after a few days it was decently interred. The actual day was the 1st January, and I had called a meeting of the Senate. It was the first piece of business that came up and Quintus Metellus, the praetor, announced that he had Sulla's full authority to say that Sulla himself did not want the proposal about himself to be brought forward. And ever since then Caecilius himself has been heavily involved in public affairs – he promised to veto the agrarian bill, which I myself had vigorously denounced wholesale and utterly rejected; he opposed the irresponsible demands for large-scale distributions in cash or kind; he co-operated with the Senate in every way. In short, throughout his tribunate, once he threw off the burden of what he owed his family, he thought only of the welfare of the *res publica*.

IV. The *Res Publica* of the Noble *Populares*

32. A TRIAL FOR SACRILEGE,
AND POMPEY'S RETURN

Late in 62, Pompey returned, and to the astonishment of all disbanded his army at Brundisium on landing; from there he returned on foot to Rome as a private citizen. When he arrived, early in 61, the city was in a ferment.

(*a*) The Scandal Breaks

Ad Att. 1, 13, 3:

On 25th January, Cicero wrote to Atticus:

'I suppose that you've heard that when public religious rites (those of the Bona Dea, the Kindly Goddess) were being conducted at Caesar's house, a man was present, wearing women's clothes. . . . The question was raised in the Senate by Q. Cornificius – it was he who took the initiative, just in case you think it was one of my friends. The Senate decreed that it be referred back to the Vestal Virgins, and to the *pontifices*; they pronounced that sacrilege had been committed. Then, as voted by the Senate, the consuls put forward a bill (sc. to deal with the matter, because there was no court available to deal with cases of sacrilege). Caesar has sent his wife a letter divorcing her. In this business, (Pupius) Piso, the consul, has been led by his friendship for P. Clodius to secure that the bill which he himself is proposing, and moreover is proposing on the strength of a Senate's decree, and is concerned with the state's religion, is defeated. So far, Messalla (the other consul) is acting vigorously and uncompromisingly. Men of standing (*boni*) are being won away from the business by the pleas of Clodius, gangs of thugs are being collected. I myself, though I was a veritable Lycurgus at first, am cooling off every day. Cato presses on, and rallies others. Why make a long story of it? I much fear that this affair may be the source of great mischief for the *res publica*, owing to its abandonment by the men of standing, and its support by the rascals.'

(*b*) Pompey's First Impact

Ad Att. 1, 14, 1–4:

Cicero's account of Pompey's return to the city is lost, but a letter of 13th February reveals the poor impression he made, and the atmosphere of the Senate in 61:

'I've already told you what Pompey's first address to the common people was like; the poor didn't like it, the rascals could see nothing in it; the rich were not pleased with it, to men of standing it hadn't the (expected) dignity; so it left everyone cold. Then Fufius, a most irresponsible tribune, introduced Pompey to one of his meetings – he was put up to it by the consul Piso. The meeting was in the Circus of Flaminius; it was on a market day, and there was a great holiday crowd there. Fufius asked him if he thought it right that the praetor who was going to preside at a hearing should himself empanel the jury – that was what the Senate had decided should be the procedure in the case of Clodius' trial for sacrilege. (2) Pompey then replied like a real aristocrat, and said that the Senate's judgement always seemed to him of prime value in everything, and that that had always been the case; at great length too.

Afterwards the other consul Messalla asked Pompey in the Senate what he thought about the sacrilege case, and the bill that had been drafted. The drift of his speech was that he commended all the decrees of that body on principle, and, as he sat down, he remarked to me that he hoped that he had now given enough replies on his own views on these questions. (3) When Crassus saw that Pompey had been applauded because people understood that he was expressing approval of my consulship, he got up and made a most complimentary speech about it. He said that the fact that he was a senator, a citizen, a free man, alive, he regarded as a gift from me; every time he saw his wife, his house, his native land, he thought that he looked upon my bounty. In short, he embroidered very impressively that whole scene which I am in the habit of sketching in various colours in my speeches, all about fire and sword – you are my critic, you know my genuine productions. I was sitting next to Pompey, I could see he was put out. I didn't know if it was because Crassus was stealing a chance for popularity which he had missed, or because my achievements were signficant enough for the Senate to be happy to

hear them praised so much, especially when the praise came from a
man who didn't owe me much praise; after all, in all my writings
what is due to Crassus has always lain in the shadow of my praises of
Pompey.   (4) Today has really aligned me with Crassus, and yet I
was glad to receive all the oblique tributes that Pompey offered. As for
me, ye gods, what a display I made in front of my new audience . . .
the periods . . . the figures of speech . . . if they ever came to my aid,
they did that day. In short, shouts of applause. My theme was the
dignity of the Senate, the sympathy being shown by the *equites*, the
support of the Italian towns, the dying embers of the Catilinarian
conspiracy, the cheapness of the food-supply, the lack of civil disturbances. You know already how I can thunder on these themes.
The noise was so loud that I can summarise now because I suppose
you must have heard it all the way to Greece.'

(c) A Rigged Vote

Ad Att. I, 14, 5:

'This is how things are in Rome: the Senate is a High Court,
determined, strict, resolute – nothing could be more so. You see,
when the day came for the vote on the bill drafted in accordance with
the Senate's decree, all those fashionable little beards flocked together, that whole gang of Catiline's, little fancy-boy Curio at their
head, and they began to beg the people to reject it. Piso the consul
too, the bill's proposer, spoke against it. Clodius' gangs had taken
possession of the gangways for the voters to pass through; the tokens
for voting were being given out without the 'aye' tokens being
available. Hereupon Cato flies up, I tell you – lays into Piso quite
astonishingly – if you can call it 'laying into a man' when a speech
is so impressive, so powerful, such a public service you might say.
Hortensius our friend rallied round too, and many men of standing;
but Favonius' effort was especially remarkable. At this show of
upper-class solidarity the voting assembly was dissolved, and the
Senate was summonded to meet. A full meeting was in the process
of deciding that the consuls should urge the people to approve
the Senate's decree; this despite the opposition of Piso the consul,
and the grovelling pleas of Clodius to individuals. When Curio
proposed that the decree of the Senate be void he got only about

15 votes against 400 on the other side; so the question was settled. Fufius the tribune vetoed the decree. Clodius launched into a wretched stream of harangues, in which he hurled abuse at Lucullus, Hortensius, C. Piso, Messalla the consul; the only charge he levelled at me was the gibe that I sniffed everything out. The Senate resolved not to deal with the provinces for the praetors, nor with the embassies (from allies and foreign peoples), nor with anything else until the bill had been voted on in the assembly.'

(d) A Rigged Trial

Ad Att. 1, 16, 2–6:

Eventually the trial was held in April. In July, Cicero replied to a letter from Atticus enquiring how it had happened:

'If you want to know the cause of the acquittal, . . . it was the empty pockets and disreputable quality of the jury; and that it happened at all was due to the plan of Hortensius. He was afraid that Fufius would veto the bill that was proposed in accordance with the Senate's decree; he did not see that it was better for Clodius to be left in disgrace, and eating humble pie, than for the trial to be held before an unreliable jury; but he was led by his hatred to bring the case to trial quickly, since he said that Clodius' throat could be cut even by a sword made of lead.   (3) As to the trial itself, if you want to know, it was quite incredible how it went. . . . You've never seen a bigger bunch of crooks seated in a gaming-club: tarnished senators, threadbare *equites*, and tribunes, not moneyers so much as money-makers; yet there were a few men of quality whom Clodius could not put to flight at the scrunity of jurors. . . .   (4) In the court, as each question was referred to the court during the preliminaries, their opinions were unanimous, and as strict as could be. The accused was granted nothing, the prosecutor was given more than he asked for. Well, Hortensius began to gloat about his foresight; there wasn't a soul who thought Clodius still on trial and not condemned 1,000 times already. When I was called as a witness I think you must have heard the story – the supporters of Clodius shouted, the jury rose and stood around me, baring their throats, and indicating to Clodius that they would die for me. . . .   (5) And so, when I was thus being defended by the jury as if I were the saviour of my country, the defendant was shattered by their voices, and all his counsel collapsed. Moreover, the next day, a crowd gathered at my house every bit as large as the one which escorted me home at the end of my consulship. Our splendid High Court clamoured that they would not come unless the court was guarded. The question was referred to the court; there was only one vote against a guard. The question was raised in the Senate. A decree was made, very impressive, very complimentary; the jury was praised, the magistrates were told to act. Nobody thought that Clodius would offer any defence.

"But tell me now, Muses, (as Homer says) how first the fire was lit" . . . You know that Calvus, one of the young sparks, the singer of my praises (reading "*Calvum ex νεανίαις illum*", with T. P. Wiseman in C.R. (n.s.) xviii, 299) . . . Inside two days, using one slave, and he a one-time gladiator, he fixed the whole thing. He got people to come and see him, he made promises, he stood as surety, he made gifts. On top of all that – ye gods, it's scandalous – some of the jury even got – as the final titbit of their reward – nights with certain women, and introductions to some of the young nobles. So, there was a complete flight of the men of standing; the forum was full of slaves and yet 25 of the jury were still brave enough to prefer even to risk their lives in the face of instant danger than to bring the whole state to ruin. There were 31 more anxious to be paid than to have a worthwhile reputation. Catulus saw one of them: "What did you want to ask us for a guard to protect you for?" he said, "Were you frightened that your profits would be snatched?" (6) There you are, as briefly as I can, what the trial was like, and why Clodius got off.'

33. POMPEY IN POLITICS

(a) Pompey, the Popular Hero

The aftermath of Clodius' trial was that Cicero took the lead in attacking the perpetrators of the scandal, and Clodius in person; this further alienated him from the young nobles. He drew closer to Pompey, however, and this in turn brought him popularity with the city populace, at least temporarily.

Ad Att. i, 16, 11:

'This is how I stand personally; among men of standing I'm as I was when you left; among the dregs of the city and the riff-raff much better than when you left. It's no discredit to me that my evidence was seen not to be decisive; my unpopularity has had a painless reduction in blood-pressure, and this is all the more true because all those who approve of this scandalous affair admit that a cut and dried case was bought off from the jury. There's also the point that that agitating bloodsucker on the treasury, the wretched, hungry rabble, thinks that I am the Great Pompey's number one favourite – and I tell you that there's many a pleasant personal contact which links us; it goes so far that our young drinking-conspirators, with their fashionable little beards, call him their slang "Gnaeus Cicero". And so at the games and the gladiators I get wonderful ovations and never a whistle to be heard.'

(b) Afranius Elected Consul

Pompey's leadership was not universally acceptable, however; it was only by overt bribery that he succeeded in obtaining the election of L. Afranius to the consulate of 60. It was probably his hope that Afranius would secure for him the ratification of his settlement of the East, and allocations of land for his veteran troops.

Ad Att. 1, 16, 12:

'Now we are awaiting the elections. Our Great Pompey is pushing Afranius (Cicero actually calls him, for a reason we cannot certainly fathom, "Aulus' son"), everyone is against it; in his campaign he is not using either his prestige or his popularity, but the weapons with which Philip of Macedon used to say that any castle could be stormed, if only an ass laden with gold could be got up to it. That supporting actor of a consul is said to have taken on the organization of it, and to have the bribery-agents in his house. This I do not believe, but two pretty distasteful decrees of the Senate have already been passed, which are thought to be directed at him; Cato and Domitius were the instigators. One is that magistrates' houses should be liable to search, the other that anyone who gives houseroom to bribery-agents is acting against the *res publica*.'

[The word for bribery-agent is *divisor*; the fact that the Romans in this period had a name for this occupation shows how rampant was the practice of bribery.]

Afranius was elected, despite Cicero's view (*Ad Att.* I, 16, 13) that his election would reduce the consulate from being almost equivalent to an apotheosis to a low farce – 'a rat's tail', as Shackleton Bailey translates it.

34. THE END OF *Concordia Ordinum*

(*a*) Quarrels between Senate and *Equites*

Early in December, 61, it became clear that Cicero's alliance between Senate and *equites* could no longer be held together; Cicero tried vainly to stem the tide.

Ad Att. I, 17, 8–9:

'Here the *res publica* is tottering, wretchedly weak, and fickle; I suppose that you have heard that my supporters the *equites* have virtually broken with the Senate. They were first offended because it was proposed, in accordance with a senatorial decree, that anyone who had received money on jury-service should be liable to prosecution. As it happened that I was not in the House on the occasion that the motion was passed, and as I saw that the *equites* were deeply offended, though they had not said anything in public, I told the Senate off; I used all my influence, I thought, and though the cause was rather disreputable, I was impressive and fluent. Then there comes along another treat for the *equites* – quite intolerable too – but I not only served it up, I garnished it too. The tax-collecting syndicate who had bought from the censors the right to collect in Asia complained in the Senate that they had slipped up in their anxiety, and had bid far too much; they asked that their contract be annulled. I was the first to take up their case, and thus became the second to do so, – Crassus, you see, it was who put them up to making this bold demand. The thing stank; the demand was a disgrace, an admission of their recklessness. There was the gravest danger that if they achieved nothing they would be absolutely alienated from the Senate. We came to the rescue here too, myself especially, and got them to meet a full Senate, and a very friendly one too, and I made a long speech about the standing of the two orders, and about their harmony; I spoke on the first of December, and on the next day too. So far the question is not settled, but we have tested the reactions of the Senate. The only unfriendly speech was that of Metellus (Celer), the consul-designate; Cato was going to oppose too, heroic champion that he is, but we did not get to him because the days are short now.'

(b) Cicero's Isolation, and Failure

In January of 60, however, Cicero knew he was losing. Ostensibly successful, he yet lacked friends with whom to discuss public affairs.

Ad Att. 1, 18, 1–3:

'I am so deserted by everyone that the only time I can relax is the time I spend with my wife and daughter, and my darling Cicero. (His son Marcus; we should note that it is the *cognomen* and not the *praenomen* that Cicero uses in this affectionate reference). For these specious, careerist friendships of ours shine brightly enough in public, but they bring no return in social terms. And so, though my house is nicely crowded with morning callers, and when I go to the forum I am escorted by swarms of friends, I can't find in all that great throng any one with whom I can exchange a jest freely, or anyone to join me in regretting what's going on. So I'm waiting for you, longing for you, begging you even to come. There are many things to worry and vex me, which I believe that I can get out of my system if I can have your ears, and have one good walk and talk. . . .

(2) In the *res publica* however, though the spirit is there, again and again the very course of treatment injures it afresh. To give a brief résumé of what has occurred since you left; you will cry out that it is impossible for the Roman state to remain on its feet any longer. Well, after you left, there was the first production of that tragedy of Clodius' (Section 32 above); in this, I thought to myself, I had a part to play in pruning back licentiousness and getting control of the young. I blew hot and strong, I poured out all the resources of my mind and my strength, not that I was motivated by any enmity, but in the hope of healing the state's injuries rather than reforming it.

(3) Then the *res publica* was hit by that bought and corrupted jury-court. Have a look at the consequences: we have got a consul wished on us whom nobody could look at without a sigh of regret, except philosophers like you and me – what a savage blow that was! There

was a senatorial decree about bribery, and one about the courts; no law was passed, though. The Senate was criticized, the *equites* antagonized because the decree said "anyone who takes bribes in court". So this fine year has destroyed the two supporting pillars I put under the *res publica*, since it has destroyed the Senate's good name, and shattered the harmony between the orders.'

35. DEADLOCK IN THE SENATE

(*a*) A Senate Without a Policy

The future looked dark too; the campaign to enable the patrician Clodius to become a plebeian in order to hold the tribunate had begun, and an agrarian measure was mooted by Flavius, one of the tribunes of 60. Those to whom Cicero looked for leadership remained silent, or cultivated their fishponds, except for Cato, whose sole desire seemed to be to frustrate the *equites* over their contract.

Ad Att. 1, 18, 6–7:

'But here in the meanwhile there's not the ghost of a sign of a real statesman to be seen. The one who could do it, my close friend – for he is that, I'd have you know – Pompey, holds his tongue as he keeps that lovely little triumphal robe of his out of trouble. Crassus won't say one word that might cost him any popularity. The rest of them – you know them already; they are so stupid that they seem to hope that even if the *res publica* collapses they'll still have their fishponds. The one man who cares is Cato, but it is determination and integrity, in my opinion, rather than judgement and intelligence, that is his suit; he has been harrassing the wretched tax-contractors for over two months now, though he was very much in their good books, and will not let the Senate give them an answer. The result is that we are not allowed to pass decrees on any of the rest of the business until the tax-contractors have their answer.'

(*b*) The Agrarian Law of Flavius (60)

When the law of Flavius came up, Cicero criticized it in detail rather than in principle; others were more extreme. Pompey backed Flavius. On March 15th, Cicero wrote again.

Ad Att. I, 19, 4:

'The Senate is opposing this whole agrarian business; it suspects that some new commission for Pompey is in mind; Pompey certainly has set his heart on the law getting through. For my part, I am seeking to confirm the validity of the tenure of all private individuals, and am very popular amongst the tenants of the public domains; that is my army of supporters, as you know, the well-to-do. However, I am satisfying Pompey and the people – I want to please them too – by arguing for the purchase (sc. of lands); if this is set in train energetically, I think that this cess-pool that is the city can be drained and the uninhabited parts of Italy settled. But the whole thing has gone cold because of the intervention of the war (in Gaul, the first stirrings of the population-movement which Caesar was to deal with in his Gallic Wars). Metellus (Celer) is a really good consul, and very friendly to me; that other fellow (Afranius) is such a nobody that he does not know what it (i.e. the consulship) is that he has bought.'

36. NEW POLITICAL ALLIANCES

(*a*) Cicero's Alliance with Pompey in 60

Flavius' bill later in the year met with implacable opposition from Metellus the consul, and Flavius went so far as to imprison him; riots ensued. Cicero and Pompey drew closer together, and Cicero decided to try to win Caesar over to his own political standpoint. On Cato's instigation, the *equites'* two requests were thrown out. In about June of 60, Cicero again assessed the situation. It is clear that Atticus had written to Cicero reproving him for his association with Pompey, and questioning his decision to try to make an alliance with Caesar who must have been newly returned from his province in Spain. There, as Suetonius tells us (*Divus Julius*, 18), 'he pacified the province, and, with a speed that matched his speed in setting out for it, set off for Rome with a view to securing both a triumph and the consulate, and without waiting for his successor to come.'

Ad Att. II, 1, 6–7:

'You write about the agrarian law; it seems to have gone quite cold now. As for the dig in the ribs you give me for my friendship with Pompey, I would not have you think that my joining up with him has anything to do with my need for a protector. But the situation was that if we crossed swords at all there was bound to be a major political battle in the *res publica*. So I have taken measures to forestall this. It doesn't involve my abandoning my own firm stand for the constitution, but it is to make Pompey more one of our party, and less inclined to court popularity. I would have you know that, though many people had prompted him to attack my achievements, he is more complimentary about them than he is about his own. He himself has served the *res publica* well, he claims, but I have preserved it. I do not know how much good this does me, but it certainly is good for the *res publica*. And what of it, if I try to make Caesar more one of our party? He's certainly got the wind in his sails at the moment. Is this to damage the *res publica* so much?   (7) Why, if I had no envious critics, if everyone supported me, as they ought to do, even then a dose of medicine that healed the affected parts of the *res publica* would have more to be said for it than a treatment that involved amputation. But as things are, since that order of *equites*, which I once stationed on the Capitoline Hill with you as my standard-bearer and lieutenant, has deserted the Senate, and since those senatorial leaders of ours think that they have reached the seventh heaven if they have bearded mullets in their fishponds which will eat from their hand, and don't give a rap for anything else, surely I'm doing well enough in your eyes, am I not, if I keep those who could damage the state from doing so?'

(b) Cato's Intransigence

Ad Att. II, 1, 8:

'As for Cato, I'm as fond of him as you are; he means well, his principles are impeccable, but sometimes the damage he does is appalling; you see, he speaks as if he was in Plato's Republic, not in Rome's cesspool. "Jurors who take bribes should be liable to prosecution" – what could be fairer than that? This was Cato's view; the Senate supported him; the result? – war with the *equites* – not with me, for I was against it. The tax-contractors repudiated their contract – what could be more impudent? Yet we ought to have put up with the loss in order to keep their support, but Cato opposed it, and won the day. So now we have had the consul shut up in gaol, riot after riot, and not a whisper from any of those who used to rally round for the defence of the *res publica* in the year when I was consul, and under my successors. "What then", you will say, "shall we pay these *equites* for their support?" What else shall we do if that's the only way to get it? Or should we prefer to take our orders from the slaves, and the freed slaves?' (that is, from the poorest in the city-populace who formed the gangs known as *operae* and *collegia*).

(c) The Scene is Set for 59

The consular elections were held, Caesar waiving his claim to a triumph when it was blocked by a filibuster in the Senate by Cato. The leading supporters of Cato and the other implacable opponents of Caesar joined together to subscribe to a huge fund for the purpose of securing the election of Bibulus as Caesar's colleague. He was a rigid and incorrigible opponent, one it would be impossible for Caesar to do a deal with. Caesar and Bibulus were elected. Caesar announced that he would propose an agrarian law, assured Cicero that he would act upon his advice and that of Pompey, and sought to win over a large body of opinion in the Senate by gaining the support of Crassus. So the coalition usually – and quite anachronistically – called the 'first triumvirate' appeared to Cicero towards the end of December, 60.

Ad Att. II, 3, 3–4:

'I come now to the month of January, and to the foundations of my political position; I shall be a Socrates and cross-question each of them (sc. the consuls), but in the end, like his followers, I shall declare my choice. Certainly the issue needs careful thought. I must either put up a stout resistance to the agrarian law, in which case there will be a battle but plenty of credit to be gained, or I must hold my peace, which is equivalent to going off to Solonium or Antium, or I can even give it a hand, which they tell me Caesar is confident that I shall do. Cornelius – Balbus, that is, Caesar's confidant – called on me. He swore that Caesar will rely entirely on my advice and on Pompey's, and will set to work to bring Pompey and Crassus together. Here you are then, the closest association with Pompey, with Caesar too if I want, reconciliation with my enemies, good terms with the common people, peace and quiet for my old age. But that finale that I wrote in the third book (sc. of the poem *On His Consulate*) influences me: "Meanwhile that course, which from the

earliest paths of youth, And which as consul too thou didst pursue
with spirit bold, Uphold it, and make swell thy fame and choruses
of good men's praise." . . . So I don't think that I can hesitate to
follow Homer when he says: "one sign is always best – to fight for
your native land".'

37. THE YEAR 59

(*a*) Caesar and Bibulus

The year 59 began. After a moderate start, as soon as it became evident
that Bibulus, with the backing of Cato and their friends, would make no
concessions, Caesar revealed that he would not be thwarted in his plans.
Lands were found in Italy for Pompey's troops, and for any of the poor of
the city who had three or more children, Pompey's Eastern settlement was
at last ratified, the tax-collecting syndicate in Asia received their revised
contract, Ptolemy Auletes was recognized as the rightful king of Egypt, the
laws about provincial government were revised and made more stringent,
the Senate's proceedings were made public (which could have made for a
more informed public opinion, as well as preventing cliques of nobles from
securing the passage of self-interested measures), and the origninal distribution of provinces for the consuls of 59 was upset by the lex Vatinia, which
granted Cisalpine Gaul and Illyricum to Caesar for 5 years instead of the
internal security of Italy (reported in our ancient sources as *silvae callesque*,
the woods and paths). This last grant was subsequently augmented by the
addition of Transalpine Gaul by vote of the Senate, perhaps when Metellus
Celer died during the course of the year.

Criticism of Caesar's proceedings began early in the year; Pompey tried
to equivocate; whether to Cicero in private conversation or in the Senate
he had said that he approved of Caesar's proposals, but that Caesar's
methods of implementing them were Caesar's concern, not his. Cicero was
hopelessly compromised; he was known to be close to Pompey, he had
solicited Caesar's support in 60, he was known to have wanted to make
concessions to the *equites*. Caesar tried to involve him more deeply in the
fortunes of the coalition; commissions and embassies were offered to him.
Although these tempted him, he refused them all, and in March he came
out in open criticism of their actions while defending (unsuccessfully) C.
Antonius, his colleague of 63. The coalition reacted sharply. P. Clodius, who
had been trying for two years to become a plebeian in order to be tribune,
was now enabled to do so; Pompey and Caesar officiated at the ceremony.
The conviction of Antonius was claimed as the first step in the avenging of
Catiline and his supporters; his grave was decked with flowers, a banquet
was held to celebrate the success (*Pro Flacco*, 95). Once he was a plebeian
Clodius proclaimed his intention as tribune to square the account with
Cicero.

Cicero felt himself quite alone again; his old enemies remained unrelenting, and gained new strength; those he thought his new allies demanded support, whatever they did, or silence. In early April, he left Rome in disgust, and stayed away till June. When he returned, he found only young Curio still in public opposition to the coalition, and high in popular favour. Ad. Att. II, 18, 1: 'We're held down on all sides; now we no longer refuse an abject obedience, we're frightened of death or expulsion from the state, as if these were greater evils, though in fact they're far less . . . . One person alone makes speeches and openly opposes them – young Curio – ; he gets rounds of applause, a most flattering welcome in the forum, innumerable indications of approval from men of standing. Fufius (sc. Calenus, praetor this year) is pursued by shouts and abuse and hisses. This sort of thing provokes no hopes, only fury, when you see that public opinion is free, but the spirit to act in chains.'

The rest of the opposition had, as Cicero said, been silenced. Bibulus had been assaulted in the forum, and had had his fasces smashed; tribunes and others who tried to block bills had been assaulted and nearly killed. In April, Bibulus decided that the only powers of obstruction left to him were to use his right as consul to watch for omens, and thus to render any legislation passed invalid, and liable to challenge on religious grounds. This policy had the support of Cato and the other nobles who were irreconcilable to Caesar's programme. If they could make the whole programme technically invalid, they could afford to bide their time.

(*b*) Cicero, Pompey and Caesar

On his return to Rome, Cicero was met at first with renewed offers of jobs to win his support; the threats of Clodius tempted him to accept, but he was reassured by repeated assurances of support from Pompey.

Ad Att, 11, 20, 2:

'For my part, I don't battle against that programme because of my friendship for Pompey, but I don't support it either, to avoid condemning my past successes'.

Rome, however, was full of criticism. There were demonstrations in the theatre; Gabinius (probably) was hissed at his own show, Caesar was received in silence; the *equites* and people gave young Curio a tumultuous welcome (*Ad Att.* II, 19, 3); Bibulus' edicts against his colleague were copied down and read, and so were the addresses he issued to the people: 'Nothing', says Cicero 'is so popular as hatred of the popular party' (*Ad Att.* II, 20, 4). Of this party Pompey seemed to be the leader; certainly the storm of unpopularity, in Cicero's view, affected him more seriously than it did Caesar. Those who had supported the coalition's measures began to desert (*Ad Att.* II, 23, 2), and an attempt to discredit their principal opponents by alleging that they had plotted to assassinate Pompey was a flop. Cicero appealed to

Atticus to return to Rome and help him: 'I think that if Crassus presses him Pompey may waver, but if you (Atticus) are in Rome, since you can discover via Lady Ox-eyes (Clodia) from Publius (Clodius) himself how far they are to be trusted – *Ad Att*. II, 22, 5, Shackleton Bailey's proposed text and supplement – , I shall either be untroubled, or left under no illusions.'

Caesar's offers to Cicero had evidently been withdrawn by about mid-July; negotiations with Clodius were then 'in hand' (*Ad Att*. II, 20, 2), but there is no further mention of them, and Cicero decided to defend himself: 'I hope I shall have the backing of men of all ranks', he wrote in late July, (*Ad Att*. II, 21. 6). 'I have nothing to do with the *res publica*', he wrote a little later (*Ad. Att*. II, 22, 3), 'I'm totally engrossed in legal work, and in that practice of mine at the bar, which I notice wins friends remarkably well, not only among those who use my services, but also among the common people. My house is full of people, I am accosted in the street, people speak of how they remember my consulate, and tell me that they support me.'

38. CATILINE'S FRIENDS SEEK REVENGE

Among the cases which Cicero took up was the defence of L. Valerius Flaccus. He had been accused of misgovernment in Asia; the prosecutor was D. Laelius. As praetor, Flaccus had commanded the force which arrested the Allobroges at the Mulvian Bridge in 63, and had brought the documents to Cicero which had incriminated the principal conspirators (Section 27 above). In his defence of Flaccus, Cicero plunges straight into the theme that this prosecution was an attack on Cicero's consulate by the surviving sympathizers of Catiline's party.

Pro Flacco, 1–5:

At a time of dire peril for our city and empire, when the *res publica* was facing the most serious and dreadful crisis of its history, I, gentlemen, preserved from massacre yourselves, your wives, your children, and I saved your temples and shrines, your city and all Italy from devastation. And my right-hand man amid all the anxieties and perils of that time was the defendant here, Lucius Flaccus. At that time, gentlemen, I had hopes that I would help him later to high office in our city; little did I think that he would be in danger and that I should have to plead for mercy on his behalf. For surely, I thought, there could not be any honour which the Roman people would deny him. They have always awarded them to his ancestors, and here, on what was almost the quincentenary year of the *res publica*, was Lucius Flaccus, who, like his ancestor Valerius,

was restoring the freedom of his country and reviving thereby the
2 ancient glories of his ancestry. It did seem possible, of course, that
enemies might arise from time to time to denigrate his achievements,
denounce his courage, or begrudge him the honour he had won; but
I always assumed that Flaccus would come to trial, if come he must,
before the people, who could hardly appreciate the value of his
efforts (though even they would not condemn him, I believed), not
before some of the choicest and wisest spirits of our age. For these
were the men who had been the very centre of resistance in those
troubled times – they had defended and preserved the safety of
citizen and foreigner alike the whole world over. I never dreamt
that one of them would be a source of danger and conspiracy against
the fortunes of Lucius Flaccus. And yet, if it were going to happen
that some one of them would plot disaster for him, never for one
moment did I think, gentlemen, that Decimus Laelius, whose father
is a man of such standing in our city, who himself has such high
hopes of winning the consulship one day, would ever undertake a
prosecution more suited to the crazed malice of a criminal than to
the integrity and honourable upbringing of a young man like him.
I have often seen our noblest men abandon feuds with other worthy
citizens, fully justified though those feuds were; but I never thought
that any man who loved the *res publica*, who had seen Flaccus'
patriotism so well proven by events, would ever pick a quarrel with
3 him which had no justification whatsoever. Alas, gentlemen, so
many of my hopes both for myself and for the *res publica* have gone
awry, and we bear our destiny as best we may. One thing alone I
beg: that you realize the true issues at stake today – the whole
framework of the *res publica*, the very foundations of our state, all
our traditions, our present safety and our future hopes, all these
rest in your power, depend on your decision, and hang utterly upon
the outcome of this one trial. If ever the *res publica* cried out for
wisdom, responsibility, skill, and vision in her judges, this, this is
the moment, gentlemen. The case you are called upon to try does
not concern states out on the outposts of your empire, whose members have been badgered and bribed to attend this trial, but rather
your own *res publica*, the foundation of your state, national security,
and the hopes of all men of standing, if hope indeed can still exist
today to give strength to the hearts and minds of all brave citizens.
For all those other principles on which men of standing depend, the

protection of the innocent, the institutions, the deliberative cham-
bers, the means of redress, and the courts of justice of the *res publica*,
4 all these have collapsed and fallen to the ground. To whom then
can I turn, whom call upon, from whom can I beg for aid? Certainly
not the Senate, which itself begs for your help and knows all too
well that you are vested with the power to shore up its crumbling
authority. The knights? Well, we shall have to see the views of the
fifty leading members of their order when they declare their verdicts
with their fellow-jurors. The people of Rome? Certainly not, since
they have delegated to you, gentlemen of the jury, all their powers
over us. And so, unless in this court, before you, gentlemen, and by
your agency we can restore not our long-lost prestige but rather the
national safety, which hangs on such a slender thread of hope, we
shall have no resource left; we are doomed, gentlemen, unless you
realize the true motive for this trial, the real issues, and the ultimate
5 target of the men who have initiated this prosecution. The man
who slew Catiline as he marched against his country has already
been condemned; good reason this for the man who expelled him
from the city to feel afraid. The man who got the evidence of their
plans for the general massacre is being haled away to punishment;
why should the man who had the evidence brought to light and
published feel anything but the gravest apprehension?

39. GREEK COMMUNITIES' DECREES

Cicero complains that Pompey's name had been used to gain support by
his opponents, contrasts Greek and Roman political methods, and casts
aspersions on his opponents' methods of obtaining evidence. The theme of
Roman unpopularity again recurs. Compare Section 18 above.

Pro Flacco, 14–19:

I do not want to say anything about the violent methods employed by the commission which went to Asia to gather evidence
against Flaccus. But they resorted to many other tactics too, not
actually illegal since they are part and parcel of the normal practice
of a prosecutor, but certainly objectionable none the less – and for
the following reasons: first because the news was spread about the
whole of Asia that Gnaeus Pompey had persuaded Laelius, an old

friend and close associate of his father's, to prosecute Flaccus, of whom he was a bitter opponent, and had thrown the whole weight of his authority, influence, wealth, and support into the scales against him in the hope of securing his condemnation. The story gained more credence among the Greeks because they had seen the close connexion of these two men in that province quite recently. And Pompey's influence which, as you might expect, is everywhere considerable, is particularly powerful in the very province which he has recently freed from a war with the pirates and the two kings, Tigranes and Mithridates. Secondly, Laelius actually terrorized those who were unwilling to leave home to give evidence at Rome by threatening to subpoena them, and gave to those who had good reason to leave home the added incentive of an extremely generous

15 expense account. In fact, with considerable ingenuity this young man has put pressure on the rich by fear, the poor by cash incentives, and the foolish by deceit. And that is the way those splendid resolutions from the various Asian communities which we heard read out in court were extracted; they were not passed by any process of proposal and debate, nor was their accuracy ensured by oath; they were merely extracted by a show of hands amid the disorderly clamour of an excited mob.

In fact, gentlemen, although in Rome we have an admirable tradition and a long record of orderly behaviour, we may be unable to preserve it much longer; it seems somehow to be slipping from our grasp. For in their wisdom and respect for order our ancestors were unwilling for a public meeting to have any power to act. The will of the people – whether for or against a proposal, and whether expressed in resolution or decree – they wanted to be ascertained only when an orator's audience had been dispersed, and the partisans split up and reorganized by tribes or centuries according to rank, class, and age, when the proposers and supporters of a measure had been given a formal hearing, and the contents had been published and scrutinized for a considerable period of time.

16 Greek states, however, are governed entirely by the whims of a mass assembly which even sits to do business. I need not therefore remind you of how the Greece of today has long been plagued and afflicted by assemblies such as these. But even the Greece of old, which once enjoyed such vast wealth, power, and renown, was destroyed by this same single constitutional flaw, the absence of any

control or limit to the powers of its mass assemblies. When all those
ignorant citizens, men with neither experience nor knowledge of
affairs, took their seats in a theatre they entered upon useless wars,
put revolutionaries into office, and expelled all the best elements
17 from the city. And if that sort of thing went on in Athens, which at
that time was probably the most civilized city in the whole world,
let alone Greece itself, what sort of restraint do you think was to be
found in the mass assemblies of Phrygia or Mysia? Our own public
meetings here often degenerate into riots thanks to the activities of
members of those states; what on earth do you think goes on out
there when they are on their own? There was that fellow Athenagoras of Cyme, who was flogged for daring to export grain during
a famine. When Laelius held an assembly to hear about it, in the
usual Greek fashion Athenagoras came forward and protested about
his own punishment – not a word about whether he was guilty or
not. So they took a show of hands and – abracadabra – there's your
decree! Instant evidence, gentlemen! Or another example: the
people of Pergamum were first softened up with bribes and then
entertained to a huge feast, and immediately after it these small-
time tradesmen, cobblers, beltmakers, and the like, voted for
Mithridates' proposals with acclamation; in fact he controlled the
whole lot of them not through his own authority but through their
bellies. You could hardly describe that as the collective opinion of a
nation. I myself have of course brought witnesses at public expense
also – from Sicily. But their evidence was that of a Senate under
18 oath, not a disorderly rabble in an assembly. So it is not that I am
objecting to any particular evidence, gentlemen, so much as asking
you to decide whether you can in fact call it evidence at all.

And this is how it was collected: a nice young man, with an
admirable pedigree and an accomplished speaker, enters a Greek
city with a vast and elaborate retinue. He demands a public meeting
and deters all the rich and respectable citizens from giving any
evidence he does not want by threatening to subpoena them all.
Then he goes to work on the local paupers and men of straw, offers
them bribes, a free trip to Rome, all expenses paid by the state, and
a bit extra on the side from private sources. It is an attractive offer
and so it is no trouble at all to work up the feelings of the artisans,
tradesmen, and the scum of the city against their late governor, a
man whose high office was hardly calculated to inspire deep feelings

19 of affection among them. Nevertheless, I do find it remarkable how quick those people are to take any chance they are offered of paying us back for all those features of our rule they so dislike – those insignia of officialdom which they loathe the sight of, the very name of Rome which is anathema, and all those taxes, the pasture taxes, the land taxes, the harbour taxes, which they regard as worse than death itself.

So remember, gentlemen, when you hear those resolutions, that it is not evidence you are listening to but a rabble running riot, the cries of every penniless spendthrift, the howls of the ignorant, and an unruly assembly of the most irresponsible nation in the world.

40. RACIAL PREJUDICES

Roman prejudices against other peoples are skilfully exploited; note the anti-Jewish feeling in Rome even in this day.

Pro Flacco, 64–8:

Yet anyone who has ever taken the slightest trouble to study the subject knows that there are really three kinds of Greek: Athenians who are said to be of Ionian stock, Aeolians, and Dorians. Yet this whole country which we call Greece, whose reputation and renown, whose scientific and cultural achievement, whose military and imperial success has been so vast, occupies – as it always has done – only a tiny corner of Europe, together with the coastal fringe of Asia Minor, which it conquered and girded with city-colonies whose aim was to guarantee possession rather than be the bastions of

65 imperialism. Yet it is not with the Greeks but with the men of Asia, gentlemen, that we are mainly dealing here. And I should like to suggest to any Asian witnesses who want to know how much their evidence is really worth in this court that they should take a hard look at the kind of image Asians present of their own nation – not what foreigners say about them, but what they say about themselves. Now I think that for you Asians your country consists of Phrygia, Mysia, Caria, and Lydia. And isn't there a proverb which says that 'a good flogging makes a Phrygian better' – is it one of

your proverbs or one of ours, I'd like to know? Then, haven't you
got a well-known saying in your country which applies to Carians
in general that 'if you are trying something dangerous, use a Carian
for preference'? And again, it is a hackneyed cliché in Greek to say
of someone you really despise that he is the 'lowest of the Mysians'.
As for Lydia, well, in every comedy that has ever been written by a
Greek the leading slave is always a Lydian. So you can hardly
66 blame us when we take you at your own valuation. However, I
think that is more than enough about Asian witnesses. I leave it to
you, gentlemen, to use your own imaginations to make up for the
deficiencies in my account of their totally frivolous, unreliable, and
grasping character.

Now let us take a look at the Jews and their mania for gold.
They are, presumably, the reason why this trial is taking place near
the steps of Aurelius. You chose this site, Laelius, and the crowd
which frequents it, with an eye to this particular accusation,
knowing very well that Jews with their large numbers and tendency
to act as a clique are valuable supporters to have at any kind of
public meeting. So I shall keep my voice down so that only the jury
can hear; I would not put it past some people to incite those Jews
against me and against all the men of standing here, and I do not
67 want to make it any easier for them to do so. Every year the Jews
used to export gold to Jerusalem from Italy, and indeed from all our
provinces. So Flaccus decreed that in Asia it must stop, and very
rightly, gentlemen, as I think you would all agree; and besides, the
Senate has roundly condemned the practice during my consulship
and also on many previous occasions. It is, indeed, a mark of high
moral principle that Flaccus sought to take a stand against such a
barbarous and superstitious religion, and an act of commendable
courage to have refused to be deterred from acting in the best
interests of the *res publica* by the frequently furious demeanour of the
crowds of Jews in our public meetings. And it is quite irrelevant to
argue that Pompey never laid hands on anything in the Temple in
68 Jerusalem even as victor after he had captured the city. It was, like
much else that Pompey did, extremely prudent of him not to leave
himself open to any kind of criticism in a state so prone to slander
and suspicion. Pompey is our greatest general, and I do not believe
that he was put off by any religious scruples of his enemies, the
Jews, but by his own, because he is a considerate person.

41. THE POLITICAL CHARACTER OF TRIALS

Men on trial are always judged by the whole of their public careers; their whole political standpoint is considered. A vote against Flaccus is a vote for Catiline.

Pro Flacco, 94–102:

94 But I am wrong, gentlemen, to spend so much time discussing the letters of Falcidius, the Andro Sextilius affair, and the census returns of Decianus, and not to say anything about the safety of every one of us, the welfare of our country, and the vital interests of the *res publica*. For these are the things which are at stake in this trial, and the whole burden rests on your shoulders, gentlemen, and yours alone. I need not remind you that we live in tumultuous times, and that confusion and chaos threaten the world we know. There are amongst us certain persons who are laying many plots against us, whose aim is above all to ensure that your attitudes, gentlemen, your judgement, and your verdicts should prove to be utterly opposed and implacably hostile to all the best elements in our society. The numerous stern censures you have already passed on the crimes of the conspirators accord well with the honour of the *res publica*; but these schemers will not rest content in their efforts to undermine the *res publica* till they have forced our worthiest citizens

95 to share the punishment of those criminals. Gaius Antonius has fallen. Be it so; he had achieved a certain notoriety. Yet I think I can confidently say that he would not have been found guilty had you been the jury, gentlemen; for when he was condemned, Catiline's tomb was decked with flowers, and criminals and traitors met to celebrate. But now that Catiline's 'funeral' is over, they are trying to get you to punish Flaccus in revenge for Publius Lentulus' punishment. But Lentulus was the man who sought to butcher every one of you, gentlemen, with your wives and children in your arms, and to burn you to ashes in the flames of your own fatherland; could you then offer his ghost a more welcome sacrifice than to let him gorge his perverted hatred of you all on the blood of Lucius

96 Flaccus? But if you do so, then let us offer prayers to Lentulus, oblation and satisfaction to Cethegus, recall to the men we have exiled; and if you so wish, I too must pay the penalty for my ex-

cessive loyalty and extreme devotion to my country. Already the
informers are denouncing me; charges are being laid against me;
dangers threaten my life. And if the instruments chosen were other
citizens, or even if in the name of the Roman people my enemies
had roused the masses in their ignorance against me, I could bear
it all with greater equanimity; but what is unendurable is that my
enemies think that they can use the very knights and senators of
Rome, whose unity, singleness of purpose, and courage in the cause
of our common safety guided their every action, to hound from the
state and plunder the possessions of the self-same men who were the
foremost leaders and directors of the operations against the conspirators. For you see, they realize that the hearts and minds of the
common people of Rome remain unchanged; in every possible way
they make their feelings clear; they are unanimous in their thoughts,
97 their feelings, and their words. And so, if anyone summons me to
trial before the people, I accept; far from refusing to be judged by
them, indeed, I demand it. Only let there be no violence; lay aside
your words and stones; let the strong-arm men depart and the
slaves be silent; for there is no man so unjust – so long as he is a
free man and a citizen – but when he hears me he will believe it is
his duty to discuss the question of rewards not punishment for my
service to the state. Things have come to a pretty pass, my friends,
when I, who wrenched the sword and firebrands from the hands of
Publius Lentulus, can trust the judgement of the ignorant masses
98 but fear the verdict of the best and noblest of our citizens. In the
good old days Manius Aquilius was charged and proved guilty of
many acts of extortion, but then acquitted by the court because he
had fought so bravely in the slave war. A short time ago as consul
I defended Gaius Piso, and he survived unharmed to serve the *res
publica* again because he had been a brave and resolute consul. As
consul I also defended Lucius Murena, my successor-to-be. None of
the jury then imagined that they should listen for one moment to
the charges of bribery and corruption, despite the great distinction
of the prosecution witnesses, because they realized the truth of my
contention that with Catiline still at war it was essential to have
both consuls entering office on the 1st January. An innocent, upright, and most distinguished citizen, Aulus Thermus, has been
twice defended by me this year and twice acquitted to the general
delight and pleasure of the Roman people, who saw it as a blow

struck for the *res publica*. It has always been the practice for our grave and learned judges to consider the best interests of our community, the national security, and the immediate needs of the *res publica* when they make their judgements.

99   So when that voting tablet is handed to each one of you, gentlemen, the verdict you will be required to reach will be a verdict not just for Lucius Flaccus here, but also for all those who led the defence of the state, for all the men of standing in society, for your own selves, your children, your lives, your country, and the national security. You are not here discussing the interests of foreign nations

100   or your allies, but those of yourselves and your own *res publica*. But if you feel a greater concern for the interests of your provinces than of yourselves, so far from refusing to agree with you, I must insist that you allow yourselves to be influenced by what your provinces have to say. There is, I admit, evidence from Asia against Flaccus – but I can set against that the evidence from a large part of that same province too, whose members have sent delegations to sing his praises in his hour of danger; and I can add the evidence of the provinces of Gaul, Cilicia, Spain, and Crete. Against the prosecution's Greeks from Lydia, Phrygia, and Mysia I have the men of Marseilles, Rhodes, Sparta, Athens, all Achaea, Thessaly, and Boeotia. Against the evidence of Septimius and Caelius I shall produce that of Publius Servilius and Quintus Metellus to testify to the honesty and integrity of my client. In fact our law-courts will teach those Asians what justice really means; the prosecution's charges refer only to one brief year; but Flaccus' defence will be his

101   whole life and career. For it must stand to Flaccus' credit, gentlemen, that in all his duties, whether as military tribune, quaestor, or lieutenant of distinguished generals, amid mighty armies, and in provinces so vital to our interests, he proved himself a worthy scion of his ancestors. But how much more should it weigh with you that, in the midst of the dangers which we all endured, with your own eyes you saw how he linked his fortunes to mine, how he was given formal testimonials by all the most respected colonies and allied townships of Italy, and that he was accorded a similar testimonial

102   as remarkable as it was sincere by the Senate and people of Rome. I remember too well that grim night which nearly plunged our city forever into darkness. The Gauls were being called to war, Catiline to march on Rome, and the conspirators to fire and sword. Then it

was, Lucius Flaccus, that I invoked the darkened heavens to be
my witnesses, and with tears that matched your own I sought your
aid and entrusted to you, the most tried and loyal Roman of them all,
the safety of the city and her people. And it was you, Flaccus, as
praetor, who arrested the messengers of our general destruction,
you who confiscated the letters which held their scheme of ruin for
the *res publica*, you who brought to me and to the Senate both the
evidence of danger and the means to overcome it. How well I
remember those votes of thanks to you which were proposed by
myself and passed by the Senate, and by all the men of standing in
the state. Who could have imagined at that time that any man of
standing would ever again refuse to you, or the heroic Gaius
Pomptinus, whatever honour you demanded, let alone the bare
right to be a citizen? Alas for that fatal 5th December in my
consulship – a day which I could well call the birthday of the state –
103 or at least its independence day. For it may well prove, I fear, that
the night which preceded it ensured the city's safety but my own
destruction. Yet I salute your heroism, Lucius Flaccus, – to say
nothing of my own – I salute your patriotism, your courage, and
your stern resolve. But such salutes are worthless. For when those
deeds were done, Rome and the whole world joined heart and
voice to do them honour; but now I fear that those same deeds may
prove no glory but the cause of our undoing. For I realize now
that the memories of our enemies are sometimes longer than the
memories of our friends.

Flaccus was acquitted. From what we hear of other trials also, we must
conclude that the political message which Cicero delivered did not fall on
deaf ears.

42. CLODIUS, CICERO'S EXILE AND RETURN

In 58, Gabinius, a 'new man', whose political sympathies lay with Pompey,
his old commander, and L. Calpurnius Piso, Caesar's father-in-law, were
the consuls. Among the tribunes was P. Clodius, who lost no time in
launching a legislative campaign directed in part against abuses, such as
the religious obstruction practised by Bibulus in 59, and perhaps the cen-
sorial quarrels which had prevented any census being completed in 65 or
64; in part it was to gain popularity with the urban poor, by abolishing the
small payment demanded for the grain distributed by the state. Whether

he foresaw, or could or should have foreseen, the resulting problem we do not know; men purchased slaves in order to liberate them, perhaps for money, and thus obtained large numbers of freedmen supporters, fed free by the state, who had no interest in the Roman state or loyalty to it, but were bound by their obligations of *obsequium* and *officium* to do what their ex-master wanted; in addition, any free man who had no work, or no wish to earn his living, was enabled to come to Rome and be fed by the state. The immense size of the Roman mob, and its political exploitation, was immeasurably increased, if not actually founded, on this piece of legislation.

But most seriously for Cicero, Clodius undid the measure of 64 which had tried to curb the amount of violence employed in politics; he re-established the *collegia* or clubs, which were ostensibly workers' associations of various sorts, but were in fact also used as cells of activists available for political intimidation. He then secured the support, or at least the acquiescence, of the consuls by promising them the provinces they coveted, Syria and Macedonia, provided that they let his next measure pass; this was the re-enactment of the ancient *lex Valeria de provocatione*, which prohibited the execution of Roman citizens without trial and appeal before the people. Cicero knew that it was directed at him, as the executioner of Catiline's imprisoned supporters in 63. He tried to rally support; there were demonstrations by senators and *equites*, and it was rumoured that the towns of Italy were willing to rise in arms; to resist would have meant to stir up an armed conflict in Italy, and Cicero was not willing to start a civil war. 'Peace', he had always said, and was to say again, 'peace with honour is the best political condition for a state', but the peace of the state held a higher place than the honour of any one man – even when Cicero was the man. Pompey's support collapsed; had he wanted, his name could have raised a military force quite large enough to crush Clodius, but he preferred to abandon Cicero as he had abandoned Carbo in 84 and Lepidus in 78, and was to abandon Caesar in 50. The other military force available was Caesar's, preparing to go to Gaul. Caesar had decided that, since Cicero had refused all offers, he was too powerful an opponent to leave behind unscathed; Caesar therefore himself remained in the neighbourhood of the city with his praetorian cavalry until the bill was passed – no doubt to see that there was no use of force by the other side.

The day after Cicero left Rome, Clodius carried his bill, and simultaneously published another, formally accusing Cicero under the terms of the new bill, and declaring him an outlaw – 'forbidden fire and water' in the Roman phrase – and confiscating his property. The sentence was subsequently modified to allow him to live within the Roman world, so long as it was 500 miles from Italy. That same day too the consuls were granted their provinces, and Caesar left for Gaul; the former was a clear indication that their support had been obtained in part by blackmail, in part by their ambitions. Cicero bitterly resented their failure to support him, and especially the failure of Piso, who was a relative by marriage, since Cicero's son-in-law was a Piso; Piso's support also indicated that Caesar was personally involved, though Dio Cassius, an historian not normally favourable to Caesar, declares that though Caesar believed the Catilinarian conspirators to have been wrongly put to death in 63, nevertheless he thought that it would have been better to let byegones be byegones. (Dio LXXXVIII, 17, 2).

Cato in Cyprus

At the same time Cato was sent away from Rome. The pretext was that he should see to the annexation of Cyprus, though Cicero alleges that the real motive was to prevent him from attacking such special commissions (*De domo sua*, 22). Moreover, whether Clodius intended it or not, it did make Cato resent wholesale attacks on the tribunate of Clodius, and on his right to have been a tribune at all, since such attacks contained the implication that Cato had been acting illegally. Cato was also perhaps aware of the possibility that the commission might be used to furnish grounds for prosecution if he were not careful. He guarded against this by having two copies of his accounts made, but he was unlucky: one copy, which he sent separately, was lost at sea, the copy which he brought back with him perished in his tent on the way home. It may have been this which made him proceed carefully when he first arrived home. He was not impeached, however, and the laudatory tradition of the ancient sources claims that his settlement was impeccable. It is an unpleasant fact, however, that when Cicero governed Cyprus, in 51–50, the principal usurer in the island, demanding interest at 48%, was none other than Cato's kinsman, Brutus.

Cicero's Return

Cicero remained in exile in various parts of Greece until August, 57, when his recall was at last secured by the joint efforts of Pompey, P. Lentulus Spinther, one of the consuls, and 8 of the tribunes of 57, led by Q. Fabricius, P. Sestius, T. Annius Milo, and T. Fadius. The agitation had begun as early as June, 58, and had been renewed by the tribunes of 57 as soon as they came into office (on 10 December, 58), but it had been frustrated by some timely bribery (according to Cicero), and subsequently by the open use of force by Clodius and his henchmen. By August, 57, however, the opposing tribunes and Metellus Nepos, the other consul, had withdrawn their opposition, and the gangs of Clodius had been overborne, but by no means crushed, by the rival gangs organized by Milo. These had secured from attack the meeting of the assembly which voted Cicero's recall – how far they had intimidated the opposition we do not know – and they also secured a hearing for Cicero himself when he arrived, and when he thanked the Senate on 5th September, and the people two days later, for his recall, in the two speeches *Post reditum*.

43. ROME IN CICERO'S ABSENCE

(a) Riots and Disorders

In the senatorial speech *Post reditum*, Cicero pictured vividly the chaotic
state of the city, a state which continued until Clodius left during 57.

Post reditum in senatu, 3–7:

And so, gentlemen of the Senate, I feel that I have received at
your hands such a gift as no man can have reason to expect – the
gift of a kind of immortality. For time shall never take the record of
your kindness to me from the lips and memories of men. In those
days, when violence, assassination, terror and threats of every kind
surrounded you, with one voice you called me back to you again
one brief year after my departure into exile. Lucius Ninnius
proposed the motion, and I applaud him for his courage and his
sense of honour. For through the grim year of my exile he was the
most loyal of friends, and would have proved the staunchest of my
champions had there been a general recourse to arms. As for yourselves, gentlemen, you were denied the right to vote for my recall
by that villainous tribune Publius Clodius, who skulked behind the
crimes of another once his own attempt to lacerate the *res publica*
was frustrated. But never for a moment were your protests stilled;
never did you cease to badger with demands for my safety the very
4 consuls who had traded it away. And so by your diligence and
prestige you have ensured that, for the very year which I had resolved should rather prove fatal to myself than to my country,
eight tribunes of the people were elected of sufficient courage to
move a motion for my recall and to bring it before you repeatedly
for action, gentlemen. For the consuls themselves had such a strict
regard for constitutional propriety that they felt themselves obliged
to observe the law which my enemy, Clodius, had passed – in terms
which threatened them rather than myself – to the effect that I
should not return until such time as those conspirators who nearly
wrecked the state should have returned to life and Rome again.
Yet these terms constituted in fact a twofold indictment of himself
by Clodius, since they were in effect a confession first that he wished
that they were still alive, and second that, if those murderers and
traitors should return, then the *res publica* would indeed find itself

in desperate danger were I not recalled. And yet, gentlemen, throughout that year when I was far away, when Pompey, our leading citizen, relied for his safety on the stout walls of his house and not on the bulwark of the law, when the *res publica* had no consuls and had been bereft of its permanent guardian, the Senate, and of the magistrates, its annual champions, when you were denied the right to vote and the terms of my exile were proclaimed about the streets, never for one moment did you cease to believe
5 that my safety and the safety of the state were one. Then, gentlemen, thanks to the supreme courage of the consul, Publius Lentulus, on the first of January, after the gloom and darkness of the previous year, you glimpsed the first faint streaks of the new dawn of the *res publica*. For Quintus Metellus, a man whose lofty character so well accords with his high position, put his unrivalled influence at the service of the *res publica*, while the praetors and almost every tribune of the people threw their loyalty and courage behind him; at last Gnaeus Pompey, whose heroism, greatness, and achievements are the glory of the world, the centuries, and all recorded history, felt himself safe to enter the senate-house once more; and your desire for my return was so unanimous that already in spirit, if not in body,
6 my honour had come home once more. That same January brought home at last to you the real difference between myself and my enemies. For I had cast my safety to the winds lest the *res publica* be stained with one drop of the blood of citizens. But they thought to hinder my return, not with the votes of those same citizens but with rivers of their blood. And for that reason public business had to cease: you refused to answer deputations from citizens, allies, or client kings; the law-courts closed; the popular assembly did not meet to vote nor the Senate to pass its weighty resolutions; you all became aware that silence had settled on the forum, the senate-house had been struck dumb, the state was cowed and dared not
7 raise its voice. And in these days, gentlemen, when I, who with the backing of your authority had stood firm against assassins and incendiaries, was far away, throughout the city you saw dim figures flitting through the streets with fire and sword, the houses of the magistrates attacked, the temples of your gods set alight, your noble and most honoured consul's rods of office broken, and the inviolable person of your splendid and heroic tribune not merely desecrated by the touch of men's hands, but wounded, mortally wounded, by

their swords. Such butchery dimmed somewhat the enthusiasm of
certain magistrates for my cause, either through fear of death or
despair of saving the *res publica*; but the rest were men whom neither
the terror of violence nor the horror of lost hopes, neither bribes
nor menaces, fire nor sword could turn from their loyalty to your
high office, gentlemen, to the honoured name of the Roman people,
and the cause of my salvation.

(*b*) Cicero's Recall

After insults to his opponents, and thanks to his supporters, he refers to the
measures the Senate took for his recall.

Post reditum in senatu, 24–8:

For what could be more glorious, what could redound more to my
credit than the resolution proposed by Lentulus, the consul, and
carried, gentlemen, by you, that men from all over Italy who
cherished the safety of the *res publica* should gather together to
ensure my safety and my restoration? Yet I was but an individual
citizen, gentlemen, my career broken and virtually shattered; only
three times before in all our history had the terms of that resolution
been employed by a consul – and always as a general summons, to
those who were there to hear it, to rally to the defence of the *res
publica* as a whole. Yet in my case the Senate used it to summon the
citizens from every territory and township in all Italy to the defence
of a single individual.

25   I could bequeath to my posterity no prouder boast than that the
Senate had declared that any citizen who did not leap to my defence
was a traitor to the *res publica*. And, of course, your prestige was so
tremendous, gentlemen, and the general respect for the consul,
Lentulus, so high that any man who did not answer that call felt
himself guilty of a dreadful crime. The response, in fact, was
unbelievable; people flocked to Rome in their thousands till all
Italy was there; and then our great consul once again took action;
he summoned a full meeting of the Senate on the Capitol, and
thereby allowed you all to see clearly how powerful a force for good
are the inherent virtues of a true nobleman. For Quintus Metellus,
who with his brother-in-law has long been an opponent of mine,

recognized the general feeling of that meeting and abandoned his hostility to me. He was powerfully influenced by Pubius Servilius – a dear friend of mine, and a citizen of the highest reputation and standing – who persuaded him in a speech of positively Olympian authority to remember the honours and achievements of his family and the ancestors they both revered. Indeed, there rose to counsel him, it almost seemed, the ghosts of his buried kinsfolk – his brother, once a staunch supporter of mine, and all those glorious members of the Metellus family, roused from their slumbers under Acheron, and even the great Numidicus himself, whose own departure from his native country was viewed by all his fellow-citizens with ad-

26 miration mingled with dismay. Thus a near miracle occurred, and he who had been my enemy till this great act of generosity emerged as champion of my safety and defender of the honour of my name. On that day, gentlemen, four hundred and seventeen of you were present at the meeting, including every magistrate; and the only voice that broke the harmony was that of the man who by his measure clearly sought to raise the conspirators from the dead. On that day, too, when you had passed a long and most impressive resolution to the effect that my counsels had saved the *res publica*, that same consul, Lentulus, undertook to see that a similar resolution should be read next day to a mass meeting of the people by the leading figures in the state; then he himself, in person, pleaded my cause with all the eloquence at his command – and with all Italy standing there to hear. As a result, no-one heard that day the voice of any corrupt or vicious person uttering their bitter denunciations of the men of standing in our city.

27   Such sentiments and resolutions helped to bring about my recall from exile, and added in no small measure to my personal prestige. But you were still not satisfied, gentlemen, and passed a further resolution that no man should seek in any way to thwart your wishes; that any who did so would be visited by your gravest displeasure; and that, since he would be acting contrary to the welfare of the *res publica*, the safety of all men of standing, and the unity of the citizen body, you would immediately censure him in the Senate. Meanwhile you ordered me to return forthwith, even if such slanders continued unabated. Need I remind you of the votes of thanks you passed to the members of the Italian boroughs who had flocked to Rome; of your request to them that on the day when business

returned to normal they should make an equal effort to be present once again? Then, above all, there was that great day, which Publius Lentulus has made a second birthday for me, for my brother, and for our children not only during our lives but as long as men remember the events of our time. For it was in the assembly of the centuries, which our ancestors always wished to be regarded as our premier assembly, that he moved my recall to my native land, ensuring that the assembly which once gave me the consulship

28 should also signify its approbation of my conduct of that office. And on that day every citizen felt bound by his conscience to cast his vote for my safety, whatever his age, whatever his state of health. Did you ever see, gentlemen, a crowd to match it in the *Campus Martius*; did you ever see so glorious a gathering of every rank from every part of Italy; did you ever see the officials – the polling-clerks, the counters, the supervisors – perform their duties so impressively? And so, by the supreme and superhuman gift of Publius Lentulus, I returned to my native land, not simply recalled, as has happened to a number of most distinguished citizens, but borne back in triumph in a golden chariot behind bedizened stallions.

But Cicero claims he would not use force; he declares: 'When I was consul, I defended the lives of us all without drawing the sword. Therefore I did not want to draw it for my own life. I thought that if I alone was put to death, so much the worse for me, but if many others fell with me, it would sound the death-knell of the *res publica*' (ibid., 34). Concluding the speech, he declares that the circumstances attending his exile and return were such that he would not be humiliated by his exile: 'Since my restoration was also the restoration of the *res publica*, I shall not in any way surrender my freedom of action in its defence; I shall regard it as all the greater' (ibid., 36).

44. THE PLEASURES OF A RETURNED EXILE

In the popular speech, though Cicero lays much stress on public life, and public position, his family circumstances are strongly emphasized, and his claim that he will not be humiliated is repeated (19).

Post reditum ad Quirites, 2–5:

My friends, one of the greatest blessings life has to give to the human race is the gift of children. And I, because I am naturally

soft-hearted and they are highly talented, love my children more
dearly than my life itself. And yet, when first I took them in my
arms, the joy I felt then did not compare with what I now feel to
3 have them back again. My brother, too, is dearer to me than the
dearest treasure any man possesses; and yet, when blessed with his
company, I did not feel this half so much as when we were divided,
and when later each was re-united with the other by your generosity.
Each man, indeed, loves his own possessions; yet the poor relics of
my fortunes now restored to me give me far more delight than the
secure possession of my former property. Friends and companions,
neighbours and clients, secular and religious holidays – all bring me
now a pleasure heightened by their temporary loss. High office,
4 prestige, position, rank, and those distinctions which you heaped
upon me, have always seemed to me most glorious; but now they
seem far more so for having been lost to me a while. And then there
is my own dear country. By heaven, words cannot express the joy
and adoration which I feel for it – the lovely land of Italy, its busy
cities and fair countryside, its fields, its crops, its beauteous capital,
its warm-hearted citizens, their proud *res publica,* and the majesty of
your assembly, gentlemen. My pleasure in these things has always
been as great as any man's; but just as health is always more
precious to the man who has survived a grievous illness than to the
man who has never been ill, so all these delights are much the
richer for their temporary loss than if my enjoyment of them had
been uninterrupted.
5   What, then, is the point I wish to make, men of Rome? It is simply
this: I want you to understand that there has never been a man
blessed with such a gift of eloquence, or endowed with such inspired
or fabulous a gift of speech, that he could even satisfactorily enumerate and list the many and mighty acts of kindness you have done
myself, my brother, and my children, let alone adorn them with the
arts of elevated oratory. For, though I owe my birth, of course, to
my parents, it is to you, men of Rome, I owe my life in consular
rank. My parents gave me a brother; but they could not tell his
future worth. But you have given me that brother back again – and
now his worth is tested, his loyalty proved. Through my parents I
was heir to a *res publica* on the brink of destruction. But now that
same *res publica* – once saved, as all agreed, by one man's efforts – I
have regained through you. The eternal gods gave me my children;

but you restored them to me. Many, too, are the gifts that heaven has given me in answer to my prayers; but without your goodwill I would have lost all those same gifts from heaven. And finally, the various offices, which one by one I earned from you as I made my way, are now all mine again together thanks to you. In short, gentlemen, all that I owe to my parents, to the eternal gods, and to yourselves, all these now at this time I also owe no less to the Roman people as a whole.

Cicero's claims in these two speeches must not be taken too literally, but they were made at the time, when events were still fresh in men's minds, and the bare facts correspond to what he said to Atticus in a letter the day he returned (*Ad Att.* IV, 1); there was no point in trying to deceive Atticus. Moreover the style of these speeches has often been criticized as being unlike Cicero (sc. at his best), and this suggests that they were probably not touched up much before going into circulation, and that there was not much delay before this took place. It seems, therefore, impossible not to believe that Cicero's recall had very wide support, both in Rome and in Italy.

V. Religion, Law, and Violence in the *Res Publica*

45. THE ROMAN STATE RELIGION I. THE *Pontifices*

In politics, Cicero at first felt obliged to tread warily in order to obtain from the Senate the restoration of his property, and compensation for its destruction. The Senate referred the question to the *pontifices*, because Clodius had dedicated the site of Cicero's house on the Palatine Hill to '*Libertas*' – Freedom. Cicero appeared before the *pontifices* on 29 September, and delivered the speech about his house (*De domo sua*).

(a) Their Social Standing

The speech begins with an account of why the Roman priesthoods were held by the leading political figures of the day, and not by a separate caste, as in Christian societies.

De domo, 1–2:

Many indeed are the institutions, lords of the priesthood, which our ancestors devised and established through the inspiration of our gods. But perhaps the greatest of all their decisions was that the same men should control both the religious observances and the most vital affairs of the *res publica*. For by this means they ensured that all our most distinguished and respected citizens should by the wise conduct of the *res publica* guard and preserve its religion, and by their wise understanding of that religion guard and preserve the *res publica*. In times past, I do not doubt, important questions have been referred to the priests of the Roman people for judgement and decision; but here now before you, my lords, is a case of such profound significance that one might reasonably say that to your wisdom, honour, and p⸝wer are committed and entrusted this day all that glorifies the name of the *res publica*, the safety of all its citizens, their lives and liberty, their altars, hearths, and household

2 gods, their possessions, their property, and their homes. It is for you
to decide this day whether in time to come, when crazed villains win
the offices of state, you wish them to be denied the support of other
unprincipled and criminal-minded citizens, or rather to be actually
protected by the dread powers of heaven. For if it should turn out
that Clodius, the bane and scourge of the *res publica*, has successfully
used the powers of our sacred religion to defend his pestilential and
disastrous tribuneship – though it was, in all conscience, indefensible
by human standards – then our religion is indeed ripe for reforma-
tion, we need new priests to serve our immortal gods, and new
interpreters to declare to us the way of truth. For these madmen
have done terrible things to the *res publica*; some have oppressed it,
others abandoned, and some actually betrayed it. But if you, my
lords, by the authority and wisdom that is yours are now prepared
to obliterate what they have done, then, indeed, we shall have true
and excellent cause to praise our ancestors for appointing our
noblest citizens to the offices of the priesthood.

(*b*) Intimidation

Turning to the political violence of the day, Cicero hotly denies Clodius'
allegations about intimidation.

De domo, 8:

In the first place I maintain that it is a good senator's duty always
to attend the Senate; I do not agree with those who think they ought
to stay away when things are not going too well. Such men fail to
realize that by their excessive adherence to principle they only
delight those they intended to insult. You say, Clodius, that certain
members stayed away because they thought they were not safe in
the Senate. I do not blame them, nor do I question the sincerity of
their apprehensions, since I believe that every man must calculate
the risks for himself. And if you want to know why I felt safe, it was
simply because, as everybody knew, you were not amongst those
present. If you want to ask why certain men of standing did not feel
safe in the Senate when I did – the reason is the same as why earlier
they stayed in Rome when I did not believe myself to be safe anywhere in the whole country. If other men, quite rightly, do not feel

themselves endangered by threats to me, must I alone feel threatened by dangers to them as well as to myself?

(c) Adoptions

It was the duty of the *pontifices* to supervise adoptions, because of the religious implications for the family cults; Clodius' adoption had been a complete fraud, however, defeating all the objects of a real adoption, and damaging the state's religious life.

De domo, 34–7:

Let us examine, my lords, the law of adoption. It states, does it not, that a man may adopt a child provided that he is no longer able to beget one, and made the attempt when he was so able. And it is normally the function of the college of *pontifices* to investigate the reasons for each particular adoption and how it will affect the situation of the families and their standing and religious cults. But in this case, when we have a man of twenty or less adopting a senator, which of these questions was investigated? If he wants children, he can beget them; he has a wife and will doubtless in future produce children from her. So here, in effect, we have a father proposing to 35 disinherit his own son. And, on the other side, why should you, Clodius, be allowed (so far as it lay in your hands) to destroy the religious integrity of the Clodian clan? This was the kind of question which should have been the primary concern of the *pontifices* when they were looking into the question of your prospective adoption. The only possible justification for their failure to do so would have been that they were investigating your real motives for seeking adoption, ensuring perhaps that it was not your purpose to stir up havoc and sedition in the *res publica*, and that you did not aim to become that man's son only so as to be eligible for the tribunate – and thereby enabled to disrupt the state utterly. No doubt you told them that this was so, and, doubtless, it seemed to the *pontifices* a legitimate reason for your adoption – and so they gave it their blessing. As a result they never asked about the age of the adoptive parent, as they had done in the cases of Gnaeus Aufidius and Marcus Pupius, who we remember as very old men adopted Orestes and Piso respectively. But, as happened on a large number of other occasions, these adopted sons also inherited their new father's names, wealth, and religious affiliations. But you, Clodius, are not now a Fonteius, as you should be; you are not your new father's heir; you have not abandoned your own family's religious ties to assume his. In fact you have thrown the rites into confusion by confounding both the families, the one you have abandoned and the one you have infected with your presence; you have contravened the age-old Roman law of tutelage and inheritance; you have become the son of a man whose father you are old enough to be; you have become an offence to heaven.

36   And so, at the risk of teaching the *pontifices* their business, I assert that your adoption was contrary to the principles laid down by the college of *pontifices*; first because your respective ages are such that your 'father' could have been your son, or even . . . well, I prefer not to dwell upon his real relationship with you. Secondly, it is normal for an investigation to be made into the reasons for any adoption, so as to ensure that the adopter is trying to get, in a manner consistent with the laws of god and man, the children which he can no longer produce by natural means. And on these occasions careful precautions are taken to ensure that the adoptive child is a credit to both families and does not bring discredit on the religious rites of either. But above all these precautions aim to eliminate any scandal, trickery, or guile, and to ensure that adoption procedures, artificial though they are, should be seen to reproduce as closely as possible

37   the realities of parenthood and all its implications. Can you imagine, then, a more flagrant scandal than for a beardless youth, married and in excellent health, to come before them claiming that he wished to adopt a senator of Rome, when everyone knew perfectly well that the only reason for the adoption was to let Clodius abandon his patrician status and become eligible for the tribunate – and not because Fonteius wanted a son? And they made no bones about it either; for the moment Clodius was adopted, his new 'father' released him from his legal control, so that in the eyes of the law he was no longer a son of his adoptive father. It makes the whole adoption procedure pointless. And if you once allow that sort of adoption, my lords, it will be an end to everyone's family religion, which it is your duty to protect, and we will soon have no patricians left. For why should any man be willing to remain ineligible for the tribunate, restricted in his opportunities for the consulship, or barred from the priesthood because of the limitations of his patrician

status, when he has such a simple remedy? As soon as a man finds it more convenient to be a plebeian, he will get himself adopted in just the same way.

(d) Laws concerning Individuals

The law which deprived Cicero of his citizenship and confiscated his goods was equivalent to a proscription; this was a very dangerous precedent. Rome's laws existed to prevent measures against individuals being proposed and passed.

De domo, 44–7:

Is it, therefore, your intention, gentlemen of the pontifical college, to allow a tribune of the people to proscribe any citizen he may choose, protected by your verdict and defended by your authority? For the terms of Clodius' bill certainly amounted to proscription, since the intention, if not the letter, of his resolution asked you to 'will and command that Marcus Tullius Cicero be no more a citizen, and that his property be forfeit to myself'. You certainly could not describe that as a legal resolution of either the people, the state, or an individual. It must be intolerable, gentlemen, both to yourselves and to the nation at large, that any individual should be so casually disfranchised. For myself, of course, I fear neither violence nor assault; I have been through the mill already. Detractors have done their worst to me, criminals have gorged their hatred of me, traitors have exercised their treachery and crimes upon me to the full. But my record, gentlemen, which may have seemed to leave me an easy victim to every traitor in the land, has been vindicated by the judgement of every city, every class, and all
45 the hosts of heaven and earth alike. And so your high position and your reputation for statesmanship demand that in reaching your verdict you consider the interests of yourselves, your children, and your fellow-citizens. Remember the safeguards which our ancestors established for the control of the popular courts: first, that no charge involving loss of personal rights should ever be associated with a charge involving financial penalties; second, that no man should be prosecuted without due notice; that a magistrate should state the accusation three times on alternate days before inflicting a fine or reaching a verdict; that the accusation should be stated for the

fourth time a full fortnight before the trials. Besides, defendants are given every opportunity to win favour and ask for mercy; the people are easy to appease; it is easy to gain access to them to solicit votes for acquittal; finally, if the day of trial is rendered unacceptable for religious or any other reasons whatsoever, the whole proceedings and the trial itself are cancelled. And if this is what happens in a properly conducted case where there is a charge, a prosecutor, and witnesses, what could be more disgraceful than that gangs of assassins, beggars, and criminals should vote in a trial involving the rights, the children, and the entire property of a man like myself, who received neither summons, nor indictment, nor accusation – and

46 that their vote should be thought to be a law? Now I, gentlemen, was protected by my high position and reputation, the justice of my case, and the interests of the *res publica*; also by the fact that Clodius was not after my money, and that the only thing to tip the scales against me was a national crisis and the general decadence of our age. Yet, if Clodius could go as far as he did with me, what hope is there going to be for men who have led sequestered lives far from the honour and glory of a high political career, especially if their wealth is such as to arouse the envy of our rabble army of nobles with their empty pockets and extravagant tastes? If you once give the tribunes

47 their head in this way, then look out for the future, and especially for all the youngsters who seem even now to pose a threat to us as they fix their greedy eyes upon the tribunate; as sure as I am alive, if you establish this principle, you will soon find united groups of tribunes working in syndicates to get the property of all our richest citizens, which will have become fair game for the mob with everybody hoping for his share.

(e) A Family's Gods

Cicero then speaks of his family gods and shrines, contrasting them with Clodius' 'Goddess of Liberty', a statue which Cicero alleges was a funeral memorial to a courtesan of Tanagra in Boeotia.

De domo, 108 – 112:

No man laid a hand on any of my property without being condemned forthwith by one and all as a prince of criminals. Can we

therefore believe that the immortal gods coveted my home? Or that Clodius' lovely goddess, Liberty, expelled the gods of my home and the holy spirits of my family in order to instal herself like a queen in
109 a captured palace? Never, my friends! For the most sacred, the most hallowed place on earth is the home of each and every citizen. There are his sacred hearth and his household gods, there the very centre of his worship, religion, and domestic ritual. Indeed, it is a sanctuary so universally held sacred that for any man to be dragged from it is a breach of the ordinances of heaven. All the more reason for you, therefore, gentlemen, to refuse to listen to this man's sacrilege, seeing that he has not merely undermined the very places which our ancestors most earnestly wished to protect and guarantee for us by religious sanctions, but has actually destroyed them in the name of the religion he affects to defend.

110 Now, Clodius, let us examine this goddess of yours. Who is she? She must be kindly, of course, since you were the one who made the dedication (Section 32(a) above). You say her name is Liberty? It seems remarkable that you have established in my house a statue of the goddess whom you have driven out of all the rest of Rome. Look at your record, after all: you treated your own colleagues like slaves, although they were vested with supreme power by the state; you denied anyone access to the temple of Castor; with all the Roman people there to hear you, you ordered your minions to do physical violence to this most distinguished nobleman here beside me, a man who has enjoyed high honour from the people, was a *pontifex*, an ex-consul, and renowned for his gentleness and moderate opinions – indeed, I am amazed that you have the nerve to look him in the face; you claimed the prerogatives of a tyrant and drove me into exile without a trial; you kept the foremost citizen of all the world locked up and confined within his home; you ruled the forum with the dregs of the populace. And yet you actually sought to instal a statue of the goddess Liberty in my house, a house whose very existence was a living proof of your tyranny and the wretched slavery which you had inflicted on the Roman people. Could the goddess Liberty ever expel from his house the one man above all whose career prevented the whole state from surrendering its liberty to slaves?

111 Surely not? And so, for that reason, I have conducted a careful enquiry to establish where you discovered this goddess Liberty. The account I have, gentlemen, is that she was a harlot of Tanagra,

whose marble statue stood on a tomb not far from that city. A certain nobleman, related to our pious priest of Liberty here, appropriated it to adorn his aedile's show, which he had intended to celebrate with unprecedented magnificence. And so with heroic disregard for his own enrichment and simply for the greater glory of the Roman people, of course, he carried off to his home all the statues, paintings, and adornments that remained in the shrines and public places throughout Greece and all the islands of the Aegean. Then 112 he realized that the consul, Lucius Piso, might return him as praetor if he renounced the aedileship and could only find a competitor with an initial letter the same as his own (so that the voting tablets could be easily altered). So he laid up the reserves he had gathered for his aedileship partly in his own bank account and partly in his pleasure gardens. As for the statue of the harlot he had taken off its tomb, he gave it to this fellow to be the patroness of these libertines rather than a statue to the liberty of the *res publica.* For surely no-one would dare to violate this goddess, one made in the likeness of a harlot, derived from a tomb, stolen by a thief, and set up by a sacrilegious criminal! Is this the goddess you will allow to drive me from my home, gentlemen? Will she be allowed to celebrate her victory over Rome, adorned as she is with the spoils of the *res publica*? Will she be allowed to stand on a monument dedicated to commemorate the ineradicable disgrace of that day when the Senate was defeated?

(*f*) Experience in Religious Matters

In dealing with religious questions, nothing is as important as experience.

De domo, 117-118:

He tells us, gentlemen, that a member of the pontifical college attended the consecration ceremonies. You should be ashamed, Clodius, to assert in a trial before the pontiffs that one member attended and not their whole college, especially since as tribune of the people you were entitled to request or even require their collective presence. However, be that as it may; since you did not summon the whole college, which one of its members turned up? Certainly the occasion required a man of authority, which, of course, all pontiffs possess. But seniority and high office certainly enhance a pontiff's personal prestige. The occasion also required a certain religious expertise which, though all pontiffs possess it in some degree, 118 clearly increases with age and experience. So who turned up, do you think, gentlemen? He has told us the answer – his wife's brother! So if we look for authority, his brother-in-law, Lucius Pinarius Natta is hardly old enough to have any, and such little standing as a junior pontiff does possess must clearly be discounted on this occasion by the close marriage-ties he has with Clodius. As for expertise – you could hardly get less than that of a man who had then only been a member of the college for a few days, and anyway must have felt himself more obliged to you than most, Clodius, for the high compliment you paid him in inviting him to the ceremonies, and preferring to have the presence of a brother by marriage than a brother by blood. But I suppose you have taken good care to see to it that your brother cannot lay any accusations against you for malpractice.

So much, then, for your so-called dedication ceremony, Clodius. You could not invite the pontiffs as a college; you could not invite a member who was distinguished by his public offices; you could not even ask one of its other younger members, though your relationship with some of them was as close as it could be. In fact, the man who came – if indeed he really did come – was forced to do so by pressure from you, his sister's entreaties, and his mother's orders.

The *pontifices* decided in Cicero's favour, though somewhat ambiguously: 'If the person who claims that he dedicated the site had not been commissioned by name for that purpose either by command of the people, or by vote of the plebs, nor ordered by such command or vote to do so, it is their opinion that that part of the site could be restored to me without any bar on the grounds of a religious objection'. Clodius claimed that the *pontifices* had decided against Cicero; the Senate was summoned on 1st October to decide the question; the *pontifices* who were senators were asked to speak. M. Lucullus said that as *pontifices* they had decided the religious question, it was now up to them as senators to decide the legal question as to whether Clodius had been commissioned to act as he did. Clodius tried to filibuster; he spoke for three hours until he was shouted down; the Senate's decree was vetoed, but the following day the vetoing tribune withdrew, and the Senate decided in Cicero's favour, and appointed the consuls as assessors to judge the question of the compensation due. Needless to say, Cicero thought the sums assessed very inadequate.

46. THE ROMAN STATE RELIGION
2. THE SIBYLLINE BOOKS

On January 1, 56, new consuls entered office; Lentulus Spinther went to Cilicia; a relative by adoption, Lentulus Marcellinus, became consul. The question before the Senate was whether Ptolemy Auletes, King of Egypt, should be restored to the throne from which his subjects had expelled him, no doubt when he sought to repay his Roman sponsors for their support in getting him accepted by Rome as the rightful king, which in fact he was not. The bribe, according to Suetonius (*Divus Julius*, 54), had been 6,000 talents. Cicero's letters to Lentulus show the Senate in session, and reveal how little that body could achieve when opinions were sharply divided (*Ad fam.* I, 1–6).

One theme in these letters is the 'religious question'; an account of what happened is given by Dio Cassius (**XXXIX**, 15, 1–3): 'The very first thing that happened at the start of the year (56) was that a thunderbolt from heaven struck the statue of Jupiter on the Alban Mount . . . When they consulted the Sibylline Books, they found in them the following 'If the King of Egypt comes asking for help, do not renounce your friendship for him, but do not support him with any large body of men (literally, with a crowd); if you don't obey, you will have severe troubles and dangers'. Men were astonished at the coincidence between the verses and the current situation; they annulled all their decrees about the king in response to the promptings of Gaius Cato, a tribune. These were the words of the oracle, and they were published by C. Cato, though in fact it was forbidden for any of the Sibylline verses to be made public unless the Senate voted that they should be.'

Regardless of this irregularity, popular feeling was aroused, and the Senate felt that they had to take note of the Sibylline Books, and voted, as Cicero told Quintus, (*Ad Q.f.* II, 2, 3) 'that it would be a danger to the state if Ptolemy were restored by a large body of men', which was said to mean an army. A great variety of proposals was made: Cicero lists at least 5 in a letter to Lentulus, and the Senate became deadlocked in procedural quarrels, some of which were deliberately allowed to waste the time of the House, as Cicero said (*Ad fam.* I, 1, 3, *ib.* 2, 1–3). In the second half of January, Cicero wrote (*Ad fam.* I, 4, 2): 'The view of the Roman people is that the sham religious excuse for not acting has been introduced by those critics of yours who envy you, not so much to tie your hands as to prevent anyone wanting to go to Alexandria because he wants to have an army at his back'. The Senate in fact never did solve this problem; Gabinius, while governor of Syria, solved it by force some two years later.

47. THE ROMAN STATE RELIGION
3. THE *Haruspices*

The state's religion was brought into politics again by Clodius when a strange noise was reported from the countryside near Rome. It is always indicative of a crisis in Rome that unnatural phenomena were readily reported, and as readily believed. The portent now said to have been heard was publicized by Clodius, and was referred to the *haruspices*, a college of non-senatorial priests. Their reply was, characteristically, ambiguous. Clodius seized upon a reference to 'the use for non-religious purposes of places that were sacred to the gods, and had been consecrated' to make an attack on the restoration of the site of Cicero's house. This was at a public meeting; Cicero replied in the Senate, in the speech *De haruspicum responso*. Cicero argues that it was not his house that was the subject of the response; he then sketches the different departments of the Roman state religion, and makes the claim (evidently widely held) that the Romans were the most religious people of their age.

De haruspicum responso, 18–19:

But now, gentlemen of the Senate, that I have disposed of my own affairs, let us turn our attention to what the *haruspices* say. For I confess that I have been deeply disturbed by the extent of this prodigy, by the serious tone of the reply of the *haruspices*, and by the unswerving unanimity with which they have made their pronouncements. For though it may seem to some that my devotion to letters is extreme compared with others whose commitments are as heavy as my own, I must insist that I have no affection for, nor any interest whatsoever, in the literature of atheism or dissent. In religion I am a traditionalist, regarding our ancestors as my prime authorities and guides to my religious practices. Indeed, so preeminent do I think them in such matters that if any man today can show some understanding of the measure of their achievements, let alone measure up to the standard they have set, I regard him as more than adequately advanced in his religious development. Now they believed that the *pontifices* were responsible for all the prescribed high ceremonial in the religious calendar; that it was for the augurs to pronounce their support for the success of future policies; that the holy books of the soothsayers contained Apollo's age-old predictions of the fates, the manuals of the Etruscans the ritual purifications necessary after portents. And indeed these same manuals have given remarkable proof of their efficacy in recent years: shortly before each event they foretold in unambiguous terms the start of that disastrous Social War (91–87 B.C.), then those catastrophic emergencies under Sulla and Cinna, and finally the recent 19 plot to burn down our city and destroy the empire. Furthermore, gentlemen, such leisure time as I have had has enabled me to become familiar with much of the teaching of the scholars and philosophers of old, which have come down to us in their theological writings. Certainly these works bear the marks of divine inspiration, and yet my own feeling is that they had nothing to teach our ancestors and plenty to learn from them. Only a simpleton could scan the heavens and not believe in the gods; only a simpleton could seriously ascribe to chance a universe constructed by such a wondrous intelligence that the highest flights of human art can scarce describe the order and the laws that govern it; only a simpleton could perceive that there are gods, but fail to realize that it is to them this vast empire of ours owes its birth, its growth, and its stability. Prone though we are, gentlemen of the Senate, to blowing our own trumpet, we cannot honestly claim to have surpassed the Spanish in the size of our population, the Gauls in physical strength, the Carthaginians in low cunning, the Greeks in creative talent, nor indeed our own neighbours the Italians and Latins in our common native wit and characteristic common-sense; but in our deep devotion to religion, and our unique perception that the world is guided and governed by the providence of heaven, we have conquered the world.

Cicero was successful in his plea, and Clodius again frustrated.

48. RIOTS

Clodius did not take his defeats lying down. On 3 November, 57, Cicero's building-site was attacked, and Q. Cicero's house was set on fire; Cicero went about with an escort. *Ad Att.* IV, 3, 2; 'On 11 November, as I was going down the Sacred Way (*Via Sacra*), Clodius came after me with his men. Shouts, stones, clubs, swords – all in a flash. I beat it into the forecourt of Tettius Damio; my escort easily prevented the hooligans from getting in. Clodius himself might have been killed, but I'm beginning to look for a physician's regime for the state, not a surgeon's; I'm fed up with surgery'. That is, Cicero was beginning to feel that a working formula to enable men to co-exist in the state must be found, and that getting rid of men like Clodius would not cure the state's troubles. Riots, however, went on; Milo's house was attacked the next day in broad daylight, though he was still tribune, by a gang in full armour – 'with swords and shields' as Cicero describes it. 'Clodius', he says, 'had taken the house of P. Sulla as his base for the assault' (*castris*, the military word, is used). Yet family loyalty prevailed; when the Senate debated these occurrences on the 13th, 'Clodius was at home; Marcellinus, the consul-designate, was splendid, everyone was in full cry. However, Metellus (Nepos) the consul took up the time with a filibuster, Appius (Claudius, Clodius' brother) supported him, and that good friend of yours about whose self-consistency you write most truly'.

Later in 57, public opinion turned against Milo, as his counter-attack on Clodius involved constant postponement of the elections in order that he might bring Clodius to trial for violence (*de vi*), and prevent his election as aedile. We hear of the sort of religious obstruction which Bibulus had used in 59, and of Milo's open declaration that he would kill Clodius if he caught him. *Ad Att*, IV, 5, 3: 'I don't think there'll be any elections; I think Publius (Clodius) will be put on trial by Milo, unless he is killed first. If he gets in Milo's way in a scrimmage now, I can see him being killed by Milo with his bare hands. He has no hesitation about it; he advertises the fact. He's not worried about getting my medicine; he's never going to take the advice of a jealous and treacherous you-know-who, nor rely on a spiritless noble class' (Shackleton Bailey's text).

Cicero was wrong. Clodius was elected aedile, and when Milo's tribunate ended, Clodius prosecuted him for violence (*de vi*). The case came up on 6 February, 56. The hearing ended in a riot, as Cicero described it to his brother Quintus, who was then in Sardinia as one of Pompey's lieutenants for the corn-commission.

Ad Quintum fratrem, II, 3, 2:

'Milo appeared in court on February 6th. Pompey made a speech– at least he tried to. When he got up, you see, Clodius' gangs began to shout; they kept it up all through his speech – not just shouting, but curses and swearing too. Pompey refused to be stopped, he's got courage. He said all that he had to say, sometimes even getting a bit of silence.... Anyway, as he finished, Clodius got up. He was greeted with such a roar from our chaps (for we'd decided to return the compliment) that he completely lost control of himself and couldn't speak. Pompey's speech ended about an hour after noon; the din went on for two hours, swearing and the filthiest ditties about Clodius and his sister being bandied about. Pale with fury, he began to shout to his supporters, "Who's starving the people to death?" "Pompey", the gangs replied. "Who wants to go to Alexandria?" he asked; "Pompey", they replied. "Whom do you want to go?" "Crassus" came the answer – he was there too, not wishing Milo any good either. About an hour later, it seemed as if someone had given Clodius' men an order to start spitting at us. Our men's tempers rose; they began to jostle us to make us give ground. Our men charged, the gangs took to their heels, Clodius was thrown off the speaker's platform. I took to my heels too, in case anything happened in the crowd. Pompey went home. I didn't go to the Senate either, to avoid having to hold my tongue on such an important question, or to tread on the toes of the men of standing in a defence of Pompey. Bibulus, Curio, Favonius, young Servilius were all criticizing him.' "

49. OLD *Populares* AND NEW

In *De haruspicum responso*, Cicero first began to urge his contemporaries to mitigate the violence of their political rivalries, and abandon the use of force in politics. In this interest, one of his lines of attack was to question the genuineness of the support enjoyed by the *populares* of his day, and to argue that they did not represent the real aspirations of the common people of Rome in the way that the *populares* of earlier generations had done.

De haruspicum responso, 40–6 (abridged), 60–end:

But I have said enough about what the *haruspices* claim has been done wrong by mortal men; so let us now consider what those same *haruspices* maintain that the gods have declared by this portent. I quote: 'Let not the discord and dissensions of the *Optimates* bring death and danger upon the senators and leaders of our state; let them rely upon the help of heaven to prevent a return to tyranny, with the defeat of Rome's armies, and a diminution of her power'. (Reading: 'ne ad unius imperium res redeat, exercitusque pulsus deminutioque pecuniae accedat'.) Those are the exact words of the *haruspices*, gentlemen; I have added nothing. So the first question we must ask ourselves is who is stirring up discord among the *Optimates*? And the answer is – as usual – Clodius; thanks not to any skill or cunning of his own, but to the suicidal folly of our own order, a folly so transparent that he could not fail to see it. And what makes the damage done to the *res publica* more degrading still is that it is not even done by an honourable adversary; if it were, the *res publica* could be seen to meet its end like a brave warrior perishing from
41 honourable wounds in facing the foe in the heat of action. Tiberius Gracchus destroyed the stability of our state: but he was a man of

high principle, exalted eloquence, and great prestige; only in his desertion of the Senate did he deviate in any way from the exemplary standards of his father and his grandfather, Africanus. Gaius Gracchus after him had such abilities, such gifts of oratory, such a forceful and impressive style of speech, that good men could only lament that he did not find a better aim and object for such splendid talents. Even Saturninus' unbridled and almost lunatic rhetoric made him a force to be reckoned with, for he had amazing power to excite and inflame the minds of the ignorant. As for Sulpicius, I need hardly say that a few words from him were enough to impress and charm quite sensible men to acts of folly and patriots to toy with treason. Now I would be the last to deny that the rulers of the day found it an enormous burden to struggle daily with such men for the safety of the state – but at least it was a burden they could honourably shoulder....

43   But contrast the behaviour of such *populares* with that of Clodius. When he was quaestor to the consul, Gaius Mancinus, Tiberius Gracchus had a hand in signing a treaty with Numantia. The unpopularity this brought him together with the stern refusal of the Senate to ratify the treaty caused him such resentment and alarm that this courageous and distinguished citizen felt obliged to sever his connection with them. Gaius Gracchus' case was a little different. He was a man of passionate nature, and devoted to his brother; as a result, his resentment at his brother's assassination drove him to avenge his blood. Saturninus turned *popularis* out of pique, as we know, when the Senate sacked him from his job as quaestor in charge of procuring corn because the price had risen, and gave it to Marcus Scaurus instead. Sulpicius started well by resisting Gaius Julius' illegal candidature for the consulship. But the popularity he

44   earned made him go rather further than he intended. Now we cannot pretend that these men had right on their side – nothing that does damage to the *res publica* can ever be right. But at least they were all men of strong character, and they each had a grievance which lent some weight to their cause. But when Publius Clodius became a *popularis*, he certainly suffered a sea-change out of something rich and strange: for he laid aside his saffron-yellow robe and the ribbon in his hair, his woman's slippers and purple stockings, his girdle and his lute, his lust and his lechery, and in an instant was a *popularis*. If only it had not been our womenfolk who caught him

dressed up like that, and if only their servant girls had not so kindly allowed him to escape from a place where it was sacrilege for him to go, the Roman people would have no *popularis* leader now, and the *res publica* no citizen like that. But thanks to our lunatic quarrels, about which these prodigies are heaven's own warning to us, one man who had no right whatsoever to be a tribune of the people was

45 dragged out of the patrician order to take that office. A year before, Clodius' cousin, Metellus, prevented the same thing happening with the help of a still unanimous Senate and the full support of its leader, Pompey, thanks to the very unanimity of their vigorous resistance. But then the present divisions among the *Optimates*, about which we received such warnings, have made it possible, thanks to the confusion and turmoil they brought about. The very thing which Clodius' cousin, the consul, prevented, the very thing which his far-famed kinsman and companion, Pompey, thwarted, (though he did speak against putting him on trial), was brought about by the quarrels of our leading men and by the hand of Caesar, as consul, the very man who ought to have been Clodius' bitterest enemy, but claimed that his actions were prompted by an authority which none could question. The result is, gentlemen, that a firebrand bearing shame and dismay was thrust into the *res publica*; it threatened to devour your authority, the influence of the highest orders of our state, the unity of all men of standing, and the whole order of our society. Those I assure you were its targets. But I detected them all, and, as a result, the flames they lit were turned against me. I bore the brunt, and all alone I endured the flames of martyrdom for my country's cause. But you too were surrounded by that same blaze, gentlemen, and I was but the first you saw stricken and consumed for your sake. The quarrels did not die down; indeed no; instead a

46 wave of hatred began to swell against those persons thought to be my champions. But look, gentlemen, I am home again, thanks to the very men behind Clodius, and thanks to Pompey above all who, at a time when Italy yearned for my recall, when you were demanding it, and Rome desired it, roused you all to fight for my safety not only by his prestige but also by his prayers to you all.

At long, long last let there be an end to our strife; let us rest from our everlasting quarrels. Clodius, of course, the usual menace, will seek to prevent it; he goes on holding those meetings, stirring up trouble and dissension, selling himself to one group of supporters after another, but no-one thinks himself one whit the better for his praise; it is merely that they delight to hear his abuse poured out upon those they disapprove of. . . .

60   So I adjure you, gentlemen, to heed the final admonition in the *haruspices'* reply and see to it 'that the order of the *res publica* be not disrupted'. For as it is, even if on every side we all put our backs into it to shore up the crumbling fabric of the *res publica,* our united strength will scarce suffice to keep its edifice intact. There was a time long ago when this state of ours was so strong and so secure that neither senatorial incompetence nor the wicked actions of individuals could disturb it. But that is no longer so. The treasury is empty, the tax-collectors going bankrupt; respect for authority is non-existent; national unity is dissolved, the law-courts have gone to ruin, the right to vote is the close preserve of a chosen few. We senators will soon no longer be able to count on the men of standing in this city to be for ever at our beck and call ready to rally to our support, and you will look in vain for any citizen prepared to court unpopularity in his country's cause; he will soon be a thing of the past. For all

61 these reasons we will only be able to preserve our present standing – for what it is worth – if we all unite; and we certainly cannot even hope for any improvement until Clodius has been brought to book. Only death or slavery can make our condition any worse than it is now, and since human counsels failed us long ago, the very gods are warning us not to let ourselves be forced into such a condition.

What I have had to say, gentlemen, is grim and depressing, and I have been extremely reluctant to say it. For, though it would have been hardly consistent with the role and character which I have long felt it my duty to sustain in return for the high office given me by the Roman people and the honours heaped upon me by your-selves, it would have been easier by far to keep as silent as the rest of you. It is not my concern for my own position but our country's religion that has made me speak. Perhaps I have overstated my case; but all the views I have expressed merely echo those of the *haruspices* – and we should either be influenced by their pronouncements or

62 else stop referring our prodigies to them for interpretation. But if we have been troubled in our hearts before by other prodigies, more publicized perhaps though less impressive than these, then surely the very voice of heaven is bound to move us one and all. Do not credit the old wives' tales you see on stage, nor believe that some god

actually comes down from heaven to associate with men, to spend
a while on earth, and walk and talk with them. Consider the very
nature of the noise which our country folk have reported; bear in
mind, too, the report, which has not yet been referred to the *haru-*
spices, of the horrible earthquake which shook Potentia in the district
of Picenum at about the same time; remember all the many other
terrifying portents that accompanied it. Then surely you will
tremble to think of the danger which we can see looming over us.

63 For we must surely believe it is the voice of heaven, speaking to us
almost as clearly as I to you, when the whole world, the sea and land
alike, quake with an unprecedented shock, and presage the future
with a sound both strange and unbelievable. Let us then make due
expiation and intercession as we are commanded. But it is no hard
thing to pray to a kindly heaven which has deigned to show us the
·way of salvation; we must play our part too, and bring to an end
our feuds and bitter dissensions.

50. SESTIUS

(*a*) Sestius as a family man

Cicero's call to mitigate the violence of political enmities is repeated in the
great speech *Pro Sestio*, delivered on 11th March, 56. Sestius, who had
vigorously supported Cicero's recall, was indicted for violence (*de vi*);
Clodius and his party were the real prosecutors, while the leading speakers
of the prosecution were mere men of straw, and are never mentioned by
name in Cicero's speech. Cicero, who was the last speaker on his side,
begins by giving reasons why he should defend Sestius; he represents him
as a family man.

Pro Sestio, 1–7:

It may hitherto have been a source of some surprise, gentlemen
of the jury, that, despite the vast resources of the *res publica* and the
great glory of its empire, it has proved quite impossible to find enough
men of sufficient courage or resolution ready to risk themselves and
their lives to preserve the constitution and the general liberty. But
from this day onwards it will be more of a surprise to see even one
single citizen of such honesty and courage, and none at all to see any
number of them trembling with fear and thinking only of themselves

instead of the *res publica*. Yet it is not necessary for you at this juncture
to focus your attention on the misfortunes of each and every individual; for, at a single glance, you can see what has been the fate
of those who joined with the Senate and all citizens of standing in
seeking to resurrect the fortunes of the *res publica* in its affliction, and
to free it from the depredation of domestic brigands: they are all
victims of prosecution, a wretched band, reduced to rags and tatters
as they fight for their lives, their reputations, their rights, their
property, and their children. But the men who have defiled, broken,
destroyed, and overturned every ordinance of god and man are still
as free as the birds and on top of the world, confidently plotting the
2 ruin of all the best and bravest in our land. Now there is much in all
this that is indeed deplorable – but there is nothing more utterly
intolerable than that these same brigands are no longer seeking to
destroy us with the help of their own gangsters, beggars, and criminals
but have turned to you, gentlemen of the jury. They are trying to
use patriots to destroy patriots, and whoever they have failed to
eliminate by riot, assassination, arson, violence, brute force and
gangsterism they expect to be able to remove by the authority and
sanctity which attaches to your verdicts. I fondly thought on my
return that I should have to use such small talent for oratory as I
possess in offering my thanks to those who have deserved so well of
me and in putting their generosity on record. But now, since duty
compels me to use it rather to repel the dangers that encompass
them, it is my earnest prayer that this same talent may serve
particularly to help those whose efforts have given that talent back
to me, to you, and to Rome.
3   Now I know that my most distinguished and persuasive colleague,
Quintus Hortensius, has said all there is to say about the case of
Publius Sestius, omitting neither justifiable protests at the state of
the *res publica* nor reasoned arguments on behalf of the defendant.
Nevertheless I have ventured to address you, gentlemen, so that I
might clearly be seen to champion the one man who, more than
any other, has made it possible for me to champion every other
Roman citizen. And, as the last speaker in a case as serious as this, I
have decided to speak rather as befits a loyal son of Rome than an
advocate, and to give full rein rather to the depths of my distress and
resentment than to my eloquence and powers of speech. And so, if
4 perhaps I speak more bitterly or more bluntly than my predecessors,

I must ask you to make every allowance possible for an indignation born of patriotism, and a fury founded on the justice of my cause. For no man's resentment can be more of a duty forced upon him than mine is on me, inspired as it is by the perils of one of my noblest benefactors; nor does any man's fury merit your applause more than mine since its flames are fed upon the crimes of those who have
5   chosen to make war upon every champion of my safety. My colleagues have dealt adequately with the detailed charges against Publius Sestius, so I shall deal with the wider issues of his case, examining his position, way of life, character and behaviour, the unbelievable depth of his concern for men of standing, and his deep desire to protect the nation's safety and the civil peace. And I shall try, as best I can in a case as complex and of such general significance as this, to leave out nothing which could possibly be relevant to your investigations, my client's interests, or the safety of the *res publica.* And since by Fortune's blessing Publius Sestius was tribune at a time of national crisis in the days when the *res publica* was beset by enemies and falling in ruins about our ears, I shall leave till last his deeds at that time, for they are his greatest and most important achievements, and tell you briefly first about those early beginnings which laid the foundations of his later and most glorious reputation.
6   His father, gentlemen, as many of you will remember, was a wise man, a good man, a man of principle. He was first choice for tribune of the people in a most distinguished list of candidates during some of the happiest days our state has known. After that he showed himself more interested in deserving other offices of state than winning them. Encouraged by this father, Sestius married the daughter of Gaius Albinus, a most respected citizen of the highest standards of honour and integrity, and she bore him the son you see before you here in court, and a daughter, now married. These two grand old gentlemen, his father and Albinus, full of years and high distinction though they were, came first to respect and then to love him dearly and to delight in his company. When his daughter died, Albinus lost the status of a father-in-law, but the close ties of kinship and affection between the two men were never broken; indeed this love has persisted to this day, as you can see from Albinus' regular attendance here in court, and from the concern and anxiety he
7   displays. While his father was still alive, Sestius married again, this time the daughter of Lucius Scipio, a patriot but a most unlucky

one. Sestius' exemplary sense of family loyalty was universally admired and was evidenced by his immediate decision to set sail for Marseilles to visit and comfort his new father-in-law, who had fallen a victim to the wild storms of civil strife in the *res publica* and was languishing in exile abroad when he should have been here at home following in the footsteps of his ancestors. He brought Scipio's daughter with him too in the hopes that the unexpected joy of that meeting and reunion would alleviate, though not of course remove, his misery. Such acts of supererogation in the fulfilment of his obligations as a friend and relative did much to lighten the old man's burden of grief while he was alive and to solace his daughter in her enforced separation from him.

I could tell you much more, gentlemen, about his generosity and loyalty, about his achievements as a military tribune and the integrity he displayed in his service in his province. But ever before my eyes I see the honour of the *res publica*, which recalls me to speak of it and compels me to abandon matters of such minor import.

(*b*) Sestius' Political Career, and the Year 58

After recalling Sestius' services at the time of the conspiracy of Catiline, (8–12), and his public career up to and including his tribunate in 57, when he opposed Clodius (13ff), Cicero turns upon Piso who, as consul of 58, had connived at, if not encouraged, the activities of Clodius. Yet Piso, he argues, as a noble, had had the electoral support of the men of standing (*boni*): 'All men of standing', Cicero declares, 'always support the nobles in elections. We think it useful for the *res publica* if men who are nobles are as good as their forefathers. We are also influenced by the memory of distinguished men now dead who served the *res publica* well in their day' (21) Piso's politics were thus disloyal to his own supporters. Recalling the events of 58 (36–52), Cicero explains why he himself fled; Clodius had the overt or tacit support of those who had armies, or could raise them, and Caesar in turn was driven to rely on Clodius because of the nobles' attacks on his actions in 59. For Cicero to have fought would have meant civil war; on the other hand, suicide by Cicero would not have shown – as was needed – that the right would in the end prevail.

Turning to Sestius' mission, when he went to Gaul to see Caesar there late in 58, Cicero speaks of the policy of *concordia* and the need for civil peace (*otium*): 'Sestius undertook the first journey,' he says (71), 'for the sake of the *res publica*. He thought that to establish harmony in the state (*concordia*), and to carry out the purpose he had in mind, it was important not to have Caesar in opposition to my cause.'

51. VIOLENCE AS THE ANTITHESIS OF CIVILIZATION

Cicero recounts the riots of early 57, to show that Sestius was almost murdered, though a tribune, and that he did no more than Milo, whom the opposition had praised, in protecting himself with a bodyguard. Cicero asks (77), 'What are the causes of a riot?', as he contrasts the assaults of Clodius' gangs with the spontaneous outbursts of fighting that had occurred previously: 'A civil disturbance arises from time to time through the obstinacy or determination of a tribune, when, thanks to the deplorable irresponsibility of the proposer, some concession or largesse is offered to the politically uneducated; it arises when there is rivalry between the magistrates; its course is slow; it starts with some shouting; then a public meeting seems to separate into different sides; it is only late in the day, and on rare occasions, that men actually come to blows. But who has ever heard of a riot breaking out even before dawn, without any public meeting having been called, or the reading out of any proposal?' This, says Cicero, is not rioting, but organized hooliganism.

Civilization, however, is based fundamentally on the replacement of violence (*vis*), which is the law of the jungle, by the law (*lex*).

Pro Sestio, 91–92:

We would all of us agree, I think, gentlemen, that there was a period of evolution, before the concepts of civil or natural law had been defined, when man led a solitary and nomadic existence, and his possessions were what he could grab for himself by brute force, murder, and violence, and keep if he was able. It was due entirely to those first men of genius and sagacity, who realized the extent of man's innate capacity to learn, that these scattered elements of humanity were persuaded to congregate and were thereby brought from a state of primitive barbarity to the rule of law and the influence of civilization. Such societies soon acquired property for the general use – what we now call public property. Next they began to form associations of their members, which later came to be called states, and then to build closely grouped dwellings which we now call cities – and once the principles of religious and human law were established these various elements were embraced within a single 92 defensive city wall. Now the chief distinguishing feature between that early crude existence and this later civilized life which I have described lies in the difference between the rule of law and that of force. If you won't have the one, you must have the other. If you want to eliminate violence, you must accept the rule of law – and that means the law courts, which are the repositories of the law. If you will not bow to the courts, or if you ride rough-shod over them, then violence must of necessity prevail. Anyone can see that; certainly Milo did, and took action to eliminate the rule of violence, and put the rule of law to the test. He wanted to use the law so that right could prevail over might; he was compelled to use violence for fear that it was might that would otherwise prevail. Sestius had recourse to the same logic, though without the use of prosecution – for there was need for everyone to take the same course of action. But, compelled to fight for his own survival, like Milo he organized a bodyguard to resist the violent attacks of his enemies.

52. POLITICAL MORALITY; WHO WERE THE *Optimates*?

Political morality has been violated, Cicero argues, in a situation such as the present one; scoundrels like Gabinius and Piso were governors of great and rich provinces; Clodius, now an aedile, was stirring up agitation and prosecuting men of quality such as Sestius and Milo, who had themselves been prevented from prosecuting him by the delays of the Senate. This state of affairs was the direct antithesis of the rule of 'the breed of men of quality' (*natio optimatium*), a phrase of Cicero's which even then required explanation.

It is evident from this speech that the phrase was a new one, and that Cicero had used it, and been taken up by Vatinius who had asked what on earth he was talking about. This in turn suggests that the notion that there was always an 'optimate' party in Rome, calling itself '*optimates*' cannot be true. Note also that Cicero claims that this exposition is a lesson for the young.

Pro Sestio, 96–102:

In the course of your speech for the prosecution you made a special point of challenging me to explain who I meant by my phrase 'the breed of men of quality' – that was your exact phrase. That is a good question; it is vital for our younger generation to learn the answer, and I feel myself well qualified to give it. And so, gentlemen of the jury, if you will bear with me I shall discuss it briefly, since it will be a useful lesson for all to learn, and far from irrelevant to the case you have to try, and in the best interests of my client, Publius Sestius.

Politicians in Rome who are eager to get to the top have always fallen into two broadly defined categories, the *populares* and the *optimates*, the men of the people and the men of quality, and their choice of nomenclature is a good guide to their policies. Those who wish to commend themselves to the masses both in word and deed are described as *populares*, those who seek to commend their policies

97 to all the best elements in our society as *optimates*. What then do I mean by these 'best elements'? Their numbers, if you want to know, are very large indeed; if they were not, we *optimates* could not survive as a political force. They include not only the leaders of opinion in the Senate, but also those who follow their lead; they are not only the members of the highest orders who are eligible for the Senate, but also the Roman citizens living in the boroughs and the country districts of Italy; businessmen, too, and even freedmen – all these belong to the 'best elements' in our society. As I have said, their numbers are large, their backgrounds widely varied; but the whole class can be briefly and accurately described and defined as follows: all men are *optimates* who have neither criminal records nor criminal characters, who are not extremists, and whose private life is above criticism. Your so-called 'breed' of *optimates*, therefore, must include all men of uncorrupt life, right mind, and well ordered personal affairs. The men who seek to govern the *res publica* in accordance with the wishes, interests, and opinions of this class are called their champions and are generally regarded as the most influential of the best elements, the most eminent of our citizens, and

98 the leading figures in the state. What then are the ideals and objectives towards which these men ought to steer the *res publica*? They are the finest, the noblest aims of all men of wisdom, integrity, and substance – civil peace for Rome and honour for those who deserve it. Those who desire this are the *optimates*; those who bring it about are considered the best of men and the bulwarks of our country. For it is as wrong for a man to be so captivated by his desire for the honour of high office that for it he sacrifices the nation's peace as it is for a man to welcome any sort of peace that compromises the honour of public men. Moreover our rulers must guard and protect, at the cost of their lives if need be, those fundamental and essential elements upon which the objectives of civil peace and honour for public men depend. Let me enumerate them: religious observances and the auspices; the power of the executive

influenced by the Senate; laws and traditions; the verdicts of civil and criminal courts; loyalty towards our provinces and allies; the good name of the government, with its twin supports, the army and
99 the treasury. These elements are considerable both in number and extent; to defend and protect them calls for high courage, great ability, and unflinching resolution. For our citizen population is vast, and in it there are many whose awareness of their own misdeeds and fear of the punishment they are likely to incur leads them to desire chaos and revolution in the *res publica*; there are many others whose inborn anarchistic tendencies thrive on civil disorder and sedition; others again who, with their tottering finances would rather see the nation's fortunes than their own go up in flames. Once men like these get hold of advisers and leaders to suit their own depraved objectives, then the storm waves start to mount against the *res publica*, and this calls for the utmost vigilance on the part of those who have presumed to claim the right to rule their country, together with the utmost exertion and all the skill and diligence at their command, so as to ensure first that those essential elements which I have just described are defended, and then that the ship of state can hold its course and come safe home to that haven of civil peace and personal honour which is its ultimate
100 objective. It is a hard road, gentlemen, a steep road, full of dangers, full of the snares of the enemy; if I were to deny it, I should be a liar – especially since I speak from bitter personal experience.

But those who are against the *res publica* have a heavier armament than those that are for it, because the forces of evil and depravity are driven to act upon the instant, and to make their assaults upon the *res publica* spontaneously, without provocation. But good men somehow tend to act more slowly; they fail to nip trouble in the bud, and are eventually roused to action only by dire necessity. As a result, thanks to their lethargy and prevarication, sometimes even when they are prepared to sacrifice their honour to keep the civil
101 peace, they have managed to lose both. Aspiring champions of the *res publica* usually desert their posts if they are men of straw, and never even volunteer for service if they are cowards. A few alone remain, and for her sake they bear the whole burden; they are the men like your own father, Marcus Scaurus, who resisted every revolutionary in Rome from Gaius Gracchus (123) right down to Quintus Varius (91), and was deterred from the line of duty neither

by violence, nor threats, nor unpopularity; or like your great-uncle, Quintus Metellus, who as censor blackballed Lucius Saturninus, one of the leading *populares* of the day, and also disfranchised Lucius Equitius, the spurious son of Tiberius Gracchus, despite the threats of a frenzied mob of supporters; and then alone he refused to take the oath of allegiance to Saturninus' agrarian bill, because it had been illegally proposed, preferring to be forced to quit his country rather than desert his principles. There are innumerable other examples I could cite from past history, men whose number matches the glory of our empire, but I prefer to pass over them in silence. And since I do not wish to mention any living person either, let me name only one other, the late Quintus Catulus, a man who could never be forced to change his course either through fear when danger's storm-clouds lowered over him, nor through hope when the fair breezes of success were blowing.

102   Let these men be your inspiration, by the gods above, all you who seek high honour, glory, and distinction. Their example is noble, their deeds immortal, their glory grows not old; their names live ever on the lips of men; history is their sepulchre, posterity their memorial. That your task is mighty, I confess; that the perils are dire I do not deny. For, as the poet rightly says,

> 'Danger aye dogs the paths of righteousness',

but, as he also observes,

> 'What many grudge, the prize that many claim,
> 'Tis ignorance to seek, and earnest toil disdain'.

I wish I did not have to admit that this same poet, who has left all these other excellent precepts to guide our young, also coined a phrase for the traitors in our midst to take to heart,

> 'Hate me they may, if they but fear me too'.

53. REAL, AND FALSE POPULAR SENTIMENTS

(a) The Support Enjoyed by Real and False *Populares*

'Optimate' leaders of past ages were opposed by people who had a genuine sympathy for the common people, and a real political following; Clodius and his friends had no genuine support at all, as was shown at public meetings, assemblies of the voters, and the shows and games.

Pro Sestio, 103–127:

In the old days, however, those politicians who followed the policy and principles I have just described (see 52 above) had good ground for apprehension, since in many issues the basic interests of the *res publica* had little in common with the wishes or interests of the common people. For example, Lucius Cassius wanted to introduce a new law for secret ballot, which the people regarded as an essential guarantee of their liberties, while the leading figures in the state opposed it, since they feared that such relaxation of controls on voting was a threat to 'optimate' supremacy and an invitation to popular irresponsibility. Tiberius Gracchus sought to introduce an agrarian bill. It was popular with the masses since it seemed to hold out hope of profit for the poorer classes. But the *optimates* fought it tooth and nail, since they thought it likely to disrupt the harmony of the nation and deprive the *res publica* of its stoutest champions by removing the rich from property which they had long enjoyed by right of tenure. Gaius Gracchus sought to introduce a corn law: the people were delighted, since it seemed likely to provide a generous supply of free food. The men of standing were against it, since they regarded it as an open invitation to sloth instead of effort for the masses, and saw it was a drain upon the treasury.

104   I can myself remember many issues, which I deliberately refrain from resurrecting, which were sources of contention between what the masses sought and what was the considered opinion of the ruling classes. But at this moment now there is nothing to divide the people from their chosen leaders. They have no demands to make, no desire for revolution; they revel in the peace that they enjoy from civil strife, in the honoured position held by our men of standing, and the glory that thereby accrues to the whole *res publica*. And as a result, revolutionary and seditious elements are finding that nowadays no amount of extravagant promises can rouse the temper of the Roman people, because ordinary folk are sick to death of violent quarrels and civil strife, and are thoroughly enjoying their new found civil peace. So what do they do? They rent a crowd, and hold a public meeting, not with the intention of saying or

proposing anything that the meeting may wish to hear, but to ensure that, whatever they themselves may say, their hired crowd will pretend to want to hear it – at a price of course, and a large one at

105   that. I am sure, gentlemen, you cannot imagine the Gracchi or Saturninus or any of those who used to be called *populares* ever had a single hired supporter at any of their meetings. Of course not – for their proposals were generous enough, and held out enough prospect of improvement, to arouse the masses without any recourse to bribery. So in those days the *populares* may indeed have given offence to all the more responsible and worthy elements in the state, but at least they enjoyed regular demonstrations of popular support. They were cheered in the theatre; they got what they wanted by the votes of their supporters; they were household names; they attracted huge audiences; men loved to see them and watch them pass. But their opponents were also respected as men of weight and consequence, though it was in the Senate, and most particularly among the men of standing, that their views carried weight, since they were unpopular with the masses, who often thwarted their wishes by their votes; and indeed if one of them ever got a cheer his first reaction was to wonder what he had done wrong. And yet, in any issue of really major importance, they were the very men the people chiefly listened to.

106   But now, unless I am much mistaken, the situation is very different, and, if one could ignore these hired claques, in all that concerns the best interests of the *res publica* all men's views would be identical. For there are three places where the Roman people can most obviously express their views on current issues – public meetings, official assemblies of voters, and the mass gatherings for plays and gladiatorial contests. Has there been a public meeting in recent years, (a genuine one, that is, where the audience was not hired beforehand), at which the unanimity of the Roman people was not perfectly obvious? I admit that there were many meetings called by that arch-criminal and dagger-man, Publius Clodius, to discuss my fate – but they were never attended by any honest or upright citizen. For no-one of any standing was capable of even looking at his loathesome face or listening to that fiendish voice of his. With a bunch of crooks like that around, his meetings were

107   bound to be disorderly. But Clodius was not the only one to hold a public meeting to debate my case. Publius Lentulus, the consul, did

so too, and all Rome flocked to attend; every class, indeed all Italy
made up that meeting. And Lentulus urged his case with such
supreme dignity and eloquence, to a crowd whose silence amply
signified their unanimous approval, that you would have thought
it was the best proposal that a *popularis*, not a consul, ever let fall
upon the ears of the people of Rome. Then he handed over to
Gnaeus Pompey, who introduced himself not just as the champion
of my cause but also as a suppliant to the Roman people for my
safety. Pompey's speech was, as always, heard with respect and
welcomed with delight by the assembled crowd; but believe me, he
never spoke in a cause where his opinion carried such great weight
108 or his eloquence gave such delight. All Rome's leading figures were
listened to by a hushed and silent crowd as they spoke on my behalf.
But I will not name the speakers now, for it would be invidious for
me to give more weight to one man's contribution than another's,
and, if I did justice to them all, my speech would seem interminable.
Consider instead the speech which my arch-enemy Clodius made
about me on that same occasion in the *Campus Martius* before the
'real' people of Rome. So far from anyone approving of it, was there
anyone who did not think it was a most monstrous crime that he
should even be allowed to live, let alone make a speech? His very
voice was felt by one and all to be a slur upon the good name of the
res publica, and listening to him like an act of complicity in his
crimes.

109   Then there are the official assemblies of voters, whether you
want to consider those for electing magistrates or those for passing
laws. Laws indeed we see passed in plenty. But here I am not
referring to the ones that are passed when less than half a dozen
men, and those from the wrong tribe, are unearthed and brought
along to vote. Clodius, that scourge of the *res publica*, claims to have
passed a law about me, describing me as a tyrant and the ruination
of men's civil liberty. Yet I challenge him to find a single man who
would admit that he voted when that motion was being carried.
But when the Senate's resolution about me was being put to the
vote in the assembly, I challenge him to find a single citizen who
would admit he was not there, voting to save me. Which of the two
sides then should be regarded as genuinely popular? The one on
which every decent Roman citizen, old, young, high, or low united
to vote, or the one for which a bunch of fiends hastened to flock like

110 vultures round the carcass of the dead *res publica*? Or if a man like
Lucius Gellius Poplicola is there, does that make it a popular
demonstration? After all, he is a disgrace both to his brother, an
ex-consul and a man of great distinction and high standing, and
also to the *Equites*, to whose order he still claims that he belongs,
although he has long-since pawned the insignia. I suppose it could
be said that he is a dedicated servant of the Roman people – yes,
indeed, none more so. After all, in his youth he could have shared
the limelight with his step-father, Lucius Philippus, a man of the
highest rank who had won great political distinction; but no, he
preferred to squander on himself every penny he possessed, and only
on himself – so far was he from being a true *popularis*. Then, after a
lecherous and lascivious youth, having so frittered away his inheritance that it ceased to be the fortune of a vulgar millionaire and
resembled rather the threadbare poverty of a philosopher, affecting
the style of a foreign intellectual and man of leisure, he suddenly
turned 'litterateur'. He brought in Greeks to read for him, but got
no pleasure from them; he regularly had to pawn his books to raise
the cash for drink; his gluttony remained insatiable – till supplies
ran out. As a result, he dreamed endlessly of revolution – but as long
as the *res publica* stayed calm and peaceful his powers atrophied.

He was responsible for every conspiracy, the friend of every conspirator, the man behind every riot in our assemblies. He never had
a good word for any man of standing – indeed he subjected every
loyal citizen who had the courage to stand up to him to the most
villainous abuse. He even married a freedwoman not, I suspect, to
satisfy his lust, but quite simply to make it seem as if his taste in

111 women was as plebeian as his surname and his politics. He took part
in the vote that sent me into exile; he was present and feasting at
the celebration banquets of the traitors who expelled me. Yet he
avenged my exile for me on the same occasion, when with those
loathsome lips he kissed my enemies. He has not a penny to his
name – and he became my enemy for this, as though it was I who
made him bankrupt. But was it I, Gellius, who filched your inheritance – or was it you who frittered it away? You monument of
gluttony, you bottomless pit that swallowed all your estate, while
you were guzzling, I risked my life as consul to defend the *res publica*
against you and your boon-companions. And did I do it just to have
you try to drive me out of Rome? Your own relations hate the sight

of you; all Rome avoids you like the plague; they run when they
see you coming – anything to avoid meeting you or talking to you.
Your own nephew, Postumius, an admirable youth with an old
head on those young shoulders, showed what he thought of you
when he failed to make you one of the large number of guardians
he appointed for his children. Gentlemen, forgive me – I have
allowed my own personal feelings and the loathing I feel for him on
behalf of the *res publica* (and I do not know which of us he hates the
more) to distract me into saying more than I should against one who
112 is the most feckless and penniless of debauchees. Let me return to the
point: when our city lay a victim in the grip of felons and the bill
was brought forward against me, it was Gellius, Firmidius, Titius,
all men of a type, all demons of vengeance, who acted as the leaders
and instigators of those mercenary gangs, while Clodius himself
proposer of the bill, was a match for any of them in villainy, audacity, and all that is despicable. But when it was proposed to restore
me to my former high estate, no-one felt that ill-health or old age
was any adequate excuse for being absent from that meeting. All
believed that in recalling me they were simultaneously recalling the
res publica to its rightful home.

113   And now we come to the Assemblies for the elections of magistrates. Recently one of the bodies of tribunes was thought to contain
two *populares* and three members violently opposed to them. These
three so-called *anti-populares*, Gnaeus Domitius, Quintus Ancharius,
and Gaius Fannius, were quite unable to achieve anything positive
in the sort of rigged political meetings which I have been describing
Nevertheless, I see that two of them have now been elected praetors
by the Roman people. And as far as I can gather from general talk
and the way the voting went, the Roman people made no secret of
their belief that, though neither had achieved anything in his
tribunate, Domitius had shown high courage and consistent principle, and Ancharius a sense of honour and great resolution; as a
result, the people regarded this as sufficient proof of goodwill to
merit the gratitude. Certainly their high esteem for Gaius Fannius
is clear enough now: and no-one need have any doubt what the
verdict of the Roman people will be when he is a candidate for high
114 office. Compare this with the record of the two so-called *populares*,
Gaius Alfius Flavus and Publius Vatinius. Flavus was a man of
moderation; he proposed no bill; he was a good man, politically

naive, but always respected by the men of standing; his views on the *res publica* were just rather different from what people had expected. But alas, as tribune he was quite unaware of what the real people of Rome wanted, because he assumed that those who turned up at assemblies were the real Roman people. As a result he failed to get elected to the high office he would easily have attained had he not tried to be a *popularis*. As for Vatinius – the man who made so much of his 'popular' ideals that he rode roughshod over the auspices, the regulations for assemblies in the *Lex Aelia*, the Senate's authority, and the wishes of the consul, of his colleagues, and of all men of standing – he stood for the aedileship against men who had high standing and high reputations all right, but certainly lacked any great amount of money. And what was the result? He did not even win the vote of his own trive, not that of the Palatina tribe, which used to be allegedly the main source of support for all those scoundrels who so harassed the *res publica*; nor, unfortunately, apart from his rejection at the polls, did he get what all men of standing thought he richly deserved. But it all goes to prove, gentlemen, if I may say so, that the Roman people is itself no longer *popularis* in its politics, since it always rejects with indignity the very men supposed to be its leaders, and judges the men who fought against such scoundrels to be worthy of the highest offices.

115   Now let us turn to the games: and the concentrated attention which you are clearly giving me, gentlemen, makes me feel that I can speak rather more informally. The displays of popular favour which we see at elections and public assemblies are sometimes genuine, but sometimes spurious and rehearsed; but it is generally agreed that among the spectators at the theatre and at gladiatorial shows a thin and scanty applause can easily be raised by bribing a few unprincipled villains. However, on these occasions it is easy enough to see just where and from whom the applause is coming, and to assess the reaction of the main bulk of honest citizens. And there is no need for me to try to tell you, gentlemen, what sort of men or citizens it is that usually gets most applause. Every one of you knows the answer very well. Now you might argue that all this is of trivial significance; but you would be wrong, since we are dealing with an honour accorded to the men of highest standing. Indeed only a sterling character would find it trivial – while for

men who are on tenterhooks to catch the slightest shift in popular
opinion, who are, as they admit themselves, beguiled and led by
every murmur and every tiny shift in the people's feelings, of
necessity such applause must feel like immortality, and a hiss like
116 the knell of death. Now then, Scaurus, you organized the most
lavish and splendid games recently, so you are just the man to tell
us whether any of the *populares* I have just described turned up to
watch, or dared be seen in the theatre by the Roman people.
During his fire-and-brimstone tribunate even Publius Clodius, our
leading man of the theatre who happily takes the part of spectator,
actor, or clown, knows all his sister's best strip-shows, and plays the
flute-girl at women's gatherings, even he did not pay a visit either
to your games or to anyone else's, except the one from which he barely
escaped with his life. As I say, once and only once did this so-called
popularis show himself at the games, and that was an occasion when
virtue had met with its deserts, in the temple of Virtue. This temple,
built by Marius, the saviour of his country, had just been the scene
of the recall to safety of one who, like Marius himself, was a citizen
of Arpinum and the saviour of his country.

117   The Roman people made their views on the matter abundantly
clear at the time by two demonstrations of their feelings: first of all,
when the news of the Senate's resolution got around, they greeted
its actual provisions and the Senate itself with general acclamation,
before the members had even appeared out of the senate-house.
Secondly, as they left the Senate on their way to the games, individual members were cheered and applauded. And when the consul
himself who was giving the games took his seat, they gave him a
standing ovation, thanking him with outstretched arms and tears of
joy in their eyes, and showing all too clearly what they felt and how
they sympathized with me. But when Clodius stormed in with his
crazy mind whipped up to a frenzy of madness, the Roman people
could scarcely control themselves or keep their raging hands off his
vile and abominable person; they howled their abuse, shook their
118 fists, and called down imprecations on his head. At that time, after
years of slavery, they were catching a glimpse of freedom at long
last, and I need not dwell upon their mood of confidence and daring.
At the time Clodius was standing for aedile, but when he visited the
theatre, even the actors attacked him to his face. One of those
Italian comedies was on at the time – 'The Hypocrite', I think, –

and the whole cast leaned over in front of him and full in his loathesome face declaimed these words at the top of their voices:

> 'In villainy your life began and ended;
> This, Titus, this is now your just reward.'

He sat there flabbergasted; the man whose hired actors had made
his own meetings ring with their abuse was booed out of the theatre
by real live actors. And since we are talking about the theatre, I
must not fail to point out either that amongst the innumerable
comments which the poet made there was not a single point that
seemed to have any bearing on contemporary events to which the
whole people failed to react, or which was not given suitable em-
119 phasis by the individual actor. And I hope, gentlemen, that you will
not think me flippant or inappropriate for discussing poets, actors,
and plays during a trial. For of course I am not such an inexperienced
advocate and orator as to pounce on titbits of every kind for my
speech, or to flit here and there plucking and sipping butterfly-like
from other men's flowers. You take your duties seriously; so do my
colleagues for the defence; I am very well aware of my obligations
to this whole assembly, no less than to the reputation of Publius
Sestius, and his threatened position, to my own seniority and high
standing. Nevertheless, I have set out to explain to the younger
generation, as best I could, who the *optimates* were, and in so doing
it is essential for me to demonstrate that not all so-called *populares*
are anything of the sort. And the easiest way to do that is to describe
what is the true and unadulterated opinion of them held by the
people as a whole, and exactly what the people's innermost thoughts
on the matter really are.

120   So just listen to this: when the news came red-hot to the performance at the theatre about the decree of the Senate which was
passed in the temple of Virtue, Claudius Aesopus was playing before
a huge audience. He is indeed a supreme artist, an *optimate*, as it
were, no less in politics than on the stage. Yet he burst into tears
both with delight at the news and with sorrow and longing for my
presence. Then he turned to the Roman people and pleaded my
cause better than I could have done myself by the weight and point
he gave to his lines. His consummate skill, allied to the deep emotion
of the moment, enabled him to give full expression to the genius of
our noble poet, Lucius Accius. How forcefully he spoke of one who

'With dauntless spirit helped the state,
Gave it new life, and to his pledge stood true.'

And although the lines refer to one who fought loyally with the Achaeans of old, he contrived to suggest that it was I who had been true to my pledge to you, men of Rome, by pointing to your ranks. The whole audience roared for an *encore* when he said

'And when our fortunes stood at lowest ebb,
Without demur he risked his life, his head,
And all he had and was.'

121 Shouts of applause greeted these lines. Acting went by the board – what people were cheering were the poet's words, the profound sincerity of the actor, and the thought that I would soon be home again,

'Rome's greatest friend in this her greatest war,
A man with greatest genius endowed.'

This last line, which was added by the actor himself as an expression of his affection for me, was greeted with approval by the audience, perhaps because they too missed me just a little. A little later in the same play he also began the line

'O my father . . .',

only to be greeted with enormous groans from the people. For they thought that it was I, Cicero, whom Quintus Catulus and many others in the Senate had so often called the Father of his Country, who should be being mourned like a long-lost father. With tears in his eyes Aesopus lamented the flames that had ruined all I had, as he played the part of one who sorrowed for his exiled father, his stricken country, and his burnt and ruined home; finally, having spoken of his former blessings, he turned to the audience and cried

'All this I saw, burning before my eyes'

with such power that even my enemies and opponents burst into tears. By heaven, it was magnificent! How he spoke his lines! The language, the delivery, were so superb you would have thought it was Quintus Catulus himself, returned to life, declaiming them. For Catulus had no inhibitions about reprimanding and denouncing on occasion either the excesses of the masses or the errors of the Senate:

> 'You thankless Argives, stony-hearted Greeks,
> Strangers alike to thanks and gratitude.'

Yet that is not strictly accurate. The Greeks were not so much thankless as unfortunate, since they were vouchsafed no means of repaying a man who had won them their freedom; but certainly no single one of them was ever more grateful to anyone than the whole Roman people were to me. But the fact remains that the words which I am about to quote from our profoundest poet might have been written of me, just as they were most certainly made to refer to me by the best and bravest of our actors, when he pointed an accusing finger at all the ranks of our society, the Senate, the *Equites*, the whole Roman people, and proclaimed,

> 'You suffer him to be an exile still;
> And yet you raise no finger to remit
> The banishment you were the authors of.'

The whole audience erupted; the whole people of Rome declared with one voice their affection for a man who was supposedly not a '*popularis*'. But I am, after all, only reporting what I heard at second hand; those who were present at the time can evaluate this demonstration more accurately than I.

123   I have now gone so far that I must finish the story. Aesopus lamented my misfortunes so often and pleaded my cause with such powerful emotion that his lovely voice was choked with tears. The poets whom I have always loved came to my aid now, and the groans and applause which greeted their words testified to the approval of the Roman people. Yet if Rome had been free, would not her leading citizens have been the more appropriate choice rather than Aesopus and Accius to utter these words from the *Brutus*, which actually made mention of my name,

> 'Tullius, who made Rome's liberty secure'?

For this line Aesopus was encored a thousand times over. And does this not seem adequate proof of the Roman people's belief that I and the Senate had restored the very thing that those criminals had accused us of destroying?

124   But the clearest demonstration of the collective judgement of the
Roman people was made at the gladiatorial games given by Scipio
in honour of his adoptive father, Quintus Metellus Pius, and in a
manner that did credit to them both. It was one of those shows
which particularly appeal to the masses and attract a huge audience
of every class and kind. Publius Sestius, tribune of the people, who
had spent all his energies in my cause during his term of office,
entered this assemblage and made himself conspicuous, not in order
to court a reception for himself but to invite my enemies to see for
themselves a demonstration of mass goodwill for me. He proceeded
from Maenius' column, as you know, and there was such a tremendous roar of applause from all the spectators as far back as the
Capitol, and all along the railings in the Forum, that it was generally
acknowledged there had never been a more massive or unequivocal
demonstration of the wishes of the whole Roman people in any
125   man's favour at any time. Where were the bosses of the assemblies
then, I would like to know, the men who frame laws to suit their
whims, the men who hound citizens into exile? Perhaps they have
a different Roman people, one of their own, reserved for criminals,
to whom I am as hateful and offensive as they claim.

Yet for my part I cannot think of any time when there was a more
massive gathering of the people than at those same gladiatorial
games, whether for a public meeting or even for elections. This vast
uncountable multitude, this unprecedented and unanimous demonstration of popular feeling at a time when they believed my fate was
about to be debated, signified one thing, and one thing only: that
the safety and honour of citizens of the highest standing was a
matter of deep concern to the Roman people as a whole. But as for
126   that villainous praetor, Clodius' brother Appius Claudius, whose
habit it was, when putting motions about me to the vote, to ignore
the traditions followed by his father, his grandfather, his great-
grandfather, and indeed all his ancestors, and to ask instead in the
manner of mere Greeks, 'Do you want him back?', and then to
return a verdict of 'No' when a few half-baked mercenaries answered
him, he came to the games regularly – but he took good care to keep
out of sight. He crept in underground and popped out suddenly from
under the stage like a ghost in an old time melodrama crying
'Mother, mother, I want you . . .'. Anyhow, as a result, the underground route by which he used to come to see the games was duly

nicknamed the 'Appian Way', and every time he did appear he was frightened out of his wits by the sudden burst of hissing that erupted from the gladiators and even from their horses.

127   So I hope, gentlemen, you can now see the difference between the Roman people and a miscellaneous gathering. The political bosses who control these meetings receive every mark of popular disfavour; while those who are not allowed to appear in these gatherings, among the crowds of their paid hacks, are honoured by the general acclamation of the Roman people.

(b) The Popular View of Cicero's Return from Exile

A reply is then given to the charge that Cicero had sought to return to Rome by enlisting armed bands of slaves and freedmen; he recites the decrees and resolutions of the Senate and people by which he was recalled, and reminds the jury of the welcome he had had. All these people were, he claims, truly *optimates*.

Pro Sestio, 131–2:

Of course my homecoming has now assumed almost legendary proportions. The whole world knows how at my approach the men of Brundisium extended to me the right hand of friendship on behalf of all Italy and my own mother country. What a memorable day that was, that famous fifth of August. It was the day of my arrival there, and, as it were, the birthday of my restoration; it was the birthday, too, of my beloved daughter, Tullia, whom I saw then for the first time after all the pain and grief of separation; it was the birthday, too, of the colony of Brundisium, and of the Temple of Salvation. And on that day the household of Marcus Laenius Flaccus, his father and his brother – each of them a scholar, each a man of the highest standing – welcomed me with open arms, though the previous year they had greeted me in sorrow and given me protection at grave risk to themselves. Every city in Italy along my route seemed to have declared a public holiday to welcome my arrival; the roads were packed with hosts of delegations sent from all over the country to bid me welcome; the approaches to Rome were gay with vast holiday crowds to cheer me as I came; and such was my reception all the way from the Capena gate, up to the Capitol, and then along to my home that I wanted to weep in the midst of my joy as I thought that a state I loved so much had been the wretched victim of such tyranny.

132   That is my answer to you when you ask me who the '*optimates*' are. 'A breed' you called them – but you are wrong. They are a whole people. But 'breed' is a term I recognize: it was coined by Publius Sestius' arch-enemy, Vatinius, the very man who wanted this 'breed' destroyed, exterminated; the man who has often slandered Gaius Caesar, although he is a considerate man with a hatred of bloodshed, alleging that he would never be safe as long as this 'breed' survived.

54. PRINCIPLES OF POLITICAL LIFE

Pro Sestio, 136–9:

Gentlemen, I must finish my speech before your patience and attention are exhausted. I shall say no more about the *optimates*, their leaders, and the champions of the *res publica*, but simply issue a challenge to the younger generation: I shall urge every nobleman in my audience to live up to the traditions of his ancestors, and every man who has it in him to embrace those principles of political life by which so many 'new men' have won through to high position and
137   renown. There is only one way, I do assure you, to acquire honour, glory, and high office – first win the esteem and affection of such men of standing as are wise and naturally upright, and then seek to gain a full understanding of the principles on which our ancestors so wisely established our constitution. For when they found the rule of kings intolerable, they created a system of annual magistrates and a permanent council, the Senate, to control the *res publica*; but the Senate's members were to be chosen by universal suffrage, and the opportunity for election to this, the highest order in the state, was open to any man with the will to work and the ability to get there. So they made the Senate guardian of the *res publica*, its guarantor, and its champion; and they wanted the magistrates to act on its authority, and be the virtual agents of this venerable council; and they ordained that the Senate should guarantee the privileges of those orders immediately subordinate to it, and ensure that the freedom of the common people should be protected and their benefits extended.

138   It is the men who do their best to defend this constitution who are
our *optimates*, whatever rank they belong to, while the men who take
it upon themselves to bear upon their shoulders the principal
burdens of the *res publica* are always held to be their leaders, and
responsible as such for directing and protecting the state. I must
confess, as I have often done before, that such men have many
opponents, many enemies, many detractors; they face many dangers
and suffer many injuries; they must submit to undergoing herculean
labours. But my whole discourse is directed towards men of vigour
and energy, not men of sloth, men of high reputation, not volup-
tuaries, men who believe that they are born to serve their country and
their fellows, to seek honour and high reputation, not to spend
their days in sleep, feasting, and self-indulgence. But let men
who have given themselves over to vice and to the blandishments
of unhealthy desires, let them, I say, renounce high office and
avoid any place in the *res publica* and be content to enjoy the
civil peace and personal leisure which brave men's efforts have
afforded them.

139   Those, then, who seek to win the praise of men of standing, which
alone deserves the name of honour, must ever strive to win for others
the peace and pleasures which they must deny themselves. They
must toil and sweat for the common good; they must face hostility
and often endure danger for the sake of the *res publica*; they must
wrestle with many unscrupulous rascals and scoundrels; and sometimes they must even challenge the men of power. Such was the
policy, such the achievement of our most distinguished statesmen;
it is a tale made familiar to all of us by legend, tradition, and history.
And, I ask you, do we ever find held up as paragons for emulation
men who have at any time incited the people to revolution, or
clouded their innocent judgement by wholesale distributions of
largesse, or heaped calumny on any man of courage or distinction
who served the *res publica* well? The general verdict of our citizens
has always been that such men were irresponsible, reckless, criminal,
subversive, while those who thwarted their attacks and assults,
those whose authority, integrity, determination, and high resolve
stood firm against the counsels of Rome's enemies, those are the men
whom they have always called our men of principle, our most
influential members, our leaders, and the sources of our great
imperial achievement.

Cicero concluded his speech with appeals for pity for Sestius, and for Cicero's other supporters, then the victims of prosecution. He was triumphant; Sestius was acquitted by the unanimous verdict of the jury (*Ad Q. f.* II, 4, 1).

It is in the *Pro Sestio* that Cicero's political thought shows an important development. In his consulate he had spoken for *otium* (civil peace), and for harmony between the different classes in the state (*concordia ordinum*); he had also, on a number of occasions, spoken of the respect men ought to feel for the institutions of the state (*dignitas reipublicae*). Cicero now combined the ideas of *otium* and *dignitas* into the phrase *cum dignitate otium* (peace with honour), but with special reference to the idea of respecting the honour of individuals. This idea was certainly fostered by his own personal experiences and by the other events of the tribunate of Clodius, who had shown the chaos that the life of the *res publica* could be reduced to by politicians who did not acknowledge the need for mutual respect. That year had also shown the imperative need for a strong body of men who would actually stand up for law and order, and the jury who in 56 unanimously acquitted Sestius showed they accepted Cicero's point of view on this.

In *Pro Sestio* Cicero had claimed to be speaking to the young (see 52 above, ch. 96); he had supporters among the young men, and these included some, like P. Crassus, whose fathers were among Cicero's opponents, and others who were young men about town, like M. Caelius Rufus, who moved in the circle of Clodius and his sisters, and whom Cicero successfully defended (see 57–61 below). Caelius later wrote to Cicero the entertaining series of letters known as *Ad fam.*, Book VIII.

55. REALIGNMENTS, RAVENNA AND LUCA

Cicero's call to close the ranks and to renounce extreme enmities was badly needed. The situation early in 56 was that a bitter feud festered between Pompey and the leading nobles, perhaps even a majority of the Senate. Cicero told Quintus his brother in March, 56, that the acquittal of Sex. Cloelius, soon after that of Sestius, was caused by Pompey's unpopularity. *Ad Q.f.* II, 4, 6: 'The senators' voting urn was for acquittal by a large majority, that of the *equites* evenly divided, the *tribuni aerarii* condemned him'. Moreover, in 56, the return of Cato from Cyprus threatened to revive the bitter feud between him and Caesar, who was in Gaul winning victories, and in whose honour a thanksgiving of unprecedented length was voted late in 57. Domitius Ahenobarbus, a consular candidate for 55 and a member of Cato's circle, openly declared that he would do as consul what he had failed to do as praetor (in 58) – have Caesar recalled from Gaul. There can have been little doubt that this meant a recall to prosecution and not to a triumph, and Cato had also sworn to prosecute Caesar on his return. Even Clodius, whom Cicero said had been made tribune to frustrate Caesar's enemies, had challenged the validity of Caesar's acts in

59; Cicero declares that this was during his tribunate, and it was certainly before the end of 57 (*De domo sua*, 40).

In December, 57, Caesar's annexations of lands in Campania had also been discussed in the Senate, but Marcellinus, consul-designate for 56, had opposed discussion of the subject in the absence of Pompey (*Ad Q.f.* II, 1, 1). They were discussed again on April 5th, 56, in the context of the problem of a shortage of money, and the expense of providing grain (*sc.* for the free distribution). *Ad Q.f.* II, 5,1 ; 'There was a vigorous debate, the noise in the senate-house was almost like that in a meeting of the popular assembly'. It was on this occasion that Cicero subsequently asserted that the ambiguous phrase 'there was a vigorous debate' meant that he himself gave notice that he would propose a review of Caesar's law about Campania on 15th May (*Ad fam.* I, 9, 8). At the time, he wrote (*Ad Q.f.* II, 5, 3): 'After dinner (that day), I went round to Pompey's house. I was not able to see him before dinner because he was out. I wanted to see him because he was leaving Rome the next day, and going to Sardinia. I met him, and asked him to send you (Quintus) back to me as soon as possible. "At once", he said, "I'm going on April 11th, and sailing from either Leghorn or Pisa". So, my dear brother, as soon as he comes, do not fail to be on the first boat – so long as the weather is reasonable'.

Crassus, however, by that time must have been on the way to Ravenna to meet Caesar. What he said we do not know; Cicero told Lentulus in 54 only that 'he inflamed Caesar's feelings against me' (*Ad fam.* I, 9, 9). From Ravenna, Caesar crossed the Apeninnes to meet Pompey at Luca which, was on his way to Pisa. To Luca had been summoned (according to Plutarch's *Life of Caesar*, XXI) Appius Claudius from Sardinia, Metellus Nepos from Spain, several of the praetors and other provincial governors not named by Plutarch, in all about 200 senators; some came to seek support, some in gratitude for the support that Caesar had given them. Such a conference cannot have been the result of a sudden whim, or of one speech by Cicero a bare week or so earlier; it must have been carefully prepared, and since those attending included Appius, the eldest brother of Clodius, and Metellus Nepos, his cousin and sister's brother-in-law, who had defended him in 57, it included those capable of controlling him, if anyone could. In return, Pompey was to be asked to control Cicero.

From Luca, Pompey went on to Sardinia, as he had planned, and there met Q. Cicero. "Ha, it's you", he said, according to M. Cicero (*Ad.fam.* I, 9, 9–10), "yes it's you I want to see, just the man I wanted. If you do not get busy and take a strong line with your brother Marcus, you're going to have to pay up what you promised me when you went bail for him". Not to make a long story of it, he complained bitterly; he went over all the good turns he had done me; he reminded Quintus of all the agreements he had made with him about Caesar's legislation, and of all the promises Quintus had made him about me; he swore to Quintus that the steps he had taken for my recall had had the full agreement of Caesar. He commended the defence of Caesar's honour to me, asking, if I could not join in upholding it, that at least I should refrain from attacking it. When my brother handed on this message to me, and when Pompey had also sent Vibullius to me with the demand that I should refrain from raising the question of the lands in Campania before his own return to Rome, I pulled myself together . . .' Consequently, on May 15th, Cicero did not raise the question (*Ad Q.f.* II, 6, 2): 'The subject of the lands in Campania, about which notice of debate and a motion had been given for the Ides (the 15th) of May and the 16th, was not raised; on this subject my right to speak has been cut off'. In return for his promises Cicero must have been promised some sort of security from Clodius, since there is no further mention of attacks on him by Clodius.

At the conference it was also decided that Domitius must be taught a lesson; he would not be allowed to be consul in the most honourable year, the first year in which he was eligible; Pompey and Crassus would be consuls for 55, whatever Marcellinus, consul for 56, tried to do. They would then be granted armies and commands, Crassus in Syria, where he would take over from Gabinius, and Pompey in Spain, at least nominally; it is not impossible that it was always envisaged that he, as the senior partner, would take over the supervision of Rome and Italy, and that he would use troops to deal with any situation such as that of 58, should it occur.

It was also agreed that Caesar should remain in command in Gaul. As consuls Pompey and Crassus would get a law through to prolong his command, and in the meanwhile the Senate must be persuaded not to choose Gaul (or any of the provinces of Caesar) as a province to be allotted to one of the consuls for 55; this allocation, under the terms of the law of C. Gracchus (*lex Sempronia*), would take place before the election. Cicero was asked to speak against the choice of Gaul; the fact that he spoke for the choice of Macedonia and not Spain with Syria suggests that he was not fully aware of what had been planned, but it is possible that he merely took his chance to attack the two consuls, Gabinius and Piso, who had not prevented his exile. This speech is *De provinciis consularibus*, Section 56 below.

56. *Inimicitia* AND THE STATE'S INTERESTS

(*i*)

In his opening, Cicero argues that the interests of the *res publica*, which are paramount, coincide with Cicero's personal wishes in determining which provinces shall be allocated to the consuls of 55.

De provinciis consularibus, 1–2:

Gentlemen of the Senate, if any of you wants to know what provinces I shall propose be assigned to the consuls of next year, he has only to ask himself which governors it is most desirable for us to withdraw from their commands. And I think it will be clear to you all that my inclinations and my obligations must coincide in this matter. If I were being asked to speak first and then spoke as I propose to do, you would doubtless greet me with applause; if I were the only one to hold these views, I do not doubt you would forgive me; and even if you thought my views unhelpful, you would still make some allowances for my own personal feelings of resentment. So now, gentlemen, it gives me great pleasure to hear it proposed that Syria and Macedonia be the provinces assigned, both because it is in the best interests of the *res publica* and so my own feelings in no way conflict with the public interest, and also because I find myself seconding the proposal already made by my most distinguished colleague, Publius Servilius, whose loyalty and support has been as unsparing in the campaign for my recall as it has been unstinting in the service

2 of the whole *res publica*. Not only on this occasion, but whenever he has found the place and opportunity, Servilius has maintained that Gabinius and Piso should be censured. In language whose extreme severity accorded with his views, he claimed that these creatures of ill-omen had well-nigh ruined the *res publica* by their various crimes, and in particular by the primitive cruelty of that criminal vendetta which they waged against me. And if those were Servilius' views, gentlemen, how do you think I must feel when it was my career those villains were prepared to pawn to satisfy their own cupidity? But in my discussion of this matter I shall not be swayed by my own feelings nor ruled by my own personal resentment. My attitude to those men will be exactly what the attitude of every one of you should be. And as for the less restrained, more personal sense of grievance, which I know you have always felt represented your feelings no less than mine, that I shall suppress during this debate, keeping it in store until the moment for recompense has arrived.

(ii)

There follows some unedifying abuse of Gabinius and Piso. Turning then to Caesar, Cicero argues that, despite his personal views, the interests of the *res publica* will best be served by letting Caesar complete his work of pacification in Gaul. Note that Cicero was interrupted in his speech, paras. 18 and 29; cf. 40.

De provinciis consularibus, 18–20, 23–31:

But even if Gabinius and Piso were men of outstanding quality, I should still think it inappropriate as yet to relieve Gaius Caesar of his command. On this subject, gentlemen, I shall say exactly what I think and refuse to be put off by the remarks of my very good friend, the present consul, Lucius Marcius Philippus, who has just interrupted me to say that my hostility to Gaius Caesar should really be no less than to Gabinius, since Caesar was the one who both initiated and assisted in that storm of trouble to which I finally succumbed. My reply to him would be first that my concern is with the national interest, not with a private grudge, and I should hope to be able to justify my answer by appeal to precedents established by our most courageous and distinguished citizens. Did not Tiberius Gracchus senior – and I only wish his son had not fallen so far short of his father's standard of responsible behaviour – did he not win enormous credit for the fact that, as tribune of the people, he was the only member of his college to defend Lucius Scipio, although he was most bitterly opposed both to him and his brother Africanus? But Gracchus swore that the two of them had not made up their quarrel, but that it seemed to him wholly incompatible with the respect due to Rome as an imperial city that Scipio, who had once celebrated a triumph over Rome's enemies, should be hauled off to the self-same prison to which he had once in triumph conducted those enemies'
19 leaders. Did anyone ever make more personal enemies than Gaius Marius? He was opposed by Lucius Crassus and Marcus Scaurus, and hated by the whole family of the Metelli. Yet this personal opposition did not lead these men to propose the recall of their enemy from Gaul; rather, because that campaign called for special qualities, they voted it to him as an exceptional command in the province concerned. Now on the present occasion a great war has been going on in Gaul; great tribes have been subdued by Caesar, but not yet brought finally under the control of law; justice and a sufficiently abiding peace are not as yet established. As we can see, the war is well in hand; indeed, to tell the truth, it is well nigh over, but the situation is that the task will soon be done provided that the same man who initiated it puts the finishing touches to the job. But there is also the risk that, if someone else takes over, we shall find the dying embers of this vast war re-kindled and renewed. In my

capacity as a senator, therefore, for all that I may be a personal enemy of Caesar's, it is my duty to be the friend, as I have always
20 been, of the *res publica*. And if, for the sake of the *res publica*, I lay aside my personal ill-will, has any man the right to blame me for it, not least because I have always thought it my duty to model all my policies and my actions upon the actions of the leading lights of the *res publica*? For example, Marcus Lepidus was twice consul, and also *Pontifex Maximus* – and he has won high praise both in our folk-lore and in the history books as well as in the writings of our greatest poet because he at once made up his quarrel with his bitterest enemy, Marcus Fulvius, on the very day and in the very place in which Fulvius was elected as his colleague in the censorship, so that with hearts and minds united they might both defend the censor's noble
23 office. . . . Believe me, gentlemen; my love for Rome, as you well know, is a brightly blazing fire, like yours. And this same fire of love has in the past compelled me to come to her aid at the risk of my own life, when dire perils threatened her; and again, when I saw my own country menaced on all sides by the weapons of revolution, my love compelled me to submit to making myself their only target for the sake of all my fellow-citizens. Such is the quality of my love for the *res publica*; such it has always been, and always will be; and this is what has brought me back to Gaius Caesar; this has reconciled us and made us friends once more.
24   And so, whatever men may care to think, I cannot be the enemy of any man who is serving the *res publica* well. After all, I did not put myself merely on terms of enmity with those who sought to destroy the state with fire and sword; I declared war upon them, even though some were my associates and some my clients whose acquittal from capital charges I had managed to secure. If then the *res publica* could fire my fury against my personal friends, why should it not be able to reconcile me with my personal enemies? After all, my only reason for hating Publius Clodius was that I thought him likely to be the bane of my country, since his vile lechery had led him to violate in a single crime two of our most hallowed institutions, the rites of religion and the chastity of our womenfolk. Can anybody seriously doubt after what he did then – and still does today and every day – that in opposing him I was showing more concern for the security of *res publica* than for my own, or that those persons who sought to defend him have shown more concern for their own security than

25 for that of the community? I must confess, gentlemen, that in politics my views have coincided with yours rather than with those of Gaius Caesar – and no less so now than hitherto. For you are the men who greeted Gabinius' despatches with such a devastating and unprecedented mark of censure and disgrace by denying him a public thanksgiving, you are the men who decreed in unprecedented terms a longer public thanksgiving in honour of Gaius Caesar than has ever before been given in honour of one individual in any one war. Why then should I wait for someone to reconcile us? The highest order in the land has already done so, the very order which has been the supreme authority and guide in informing public policy as well as my own. It is your lead I follow, reverend fathers of the Senate, it is to your wishes I defer, with your counsels that I agree; as long as you did not wholly approve of Caesar's policies in the *res publica*, you witnessed how far apart he and I remained; but now that you have changed your attitude because of his achievements, you see that I not merely share your views but actually applaud them.

26   Further, gentlemen, I cannot really see why men should be especially surprised and criticize my actions now, when on so many previous occasions I have moved decrees which had more to do with Caesar's honour than the exigencies of the *res publica*. I was one of those who spoke in favour of Caesar's fifteen-day thanksgiving. The five days accorded to Gaius Marius were enough for the *res publica*; likewise the immortal gods would surely have regarded as sufficient the five-day period traditional after major wars; the additional ten days must therefore be regarded as a tribute of respect

27 to the individual concerned. Besides, in my consulship I personally proposed for the first time ever a ten-day thanksgiving for Gnaeus Pompey when he slew Mithridates and ended the Mithridatic war. It was on my proposal that the standard thanksgiving for a consul's achievements was thus doubled – and you all agreed to that proposal; I read out Pompey's despatches, which reported that all wars by land and sea were at an end, and you decreed that ten-day thanksgiving. And I cannot but admire Pompey's high-principled generosity since, despite the fact that the distinctions heaped upon himself were unparalleled, he was still prepared to allow another to receive yet greater honours than himself. It was the same in the case of the thanksgiving for Caesar which I seconded; by the proposal itself we

honoured our obligations to the immortal gods, tradition, and the
needs of the *res publica*; but the honorific terms and the unprecedented length of fifteen days was a tribute to Caesar's high achievement and his glory.

28   We have also recently had before us the question of pay for
Caesar's troops: not only did I give the motion my full support, but
I also did my best to persuade you all to pass it. I answered many
objections, and personally helped to draft the motion. In this too,
perhaps, I was more concerned with a great man than with some
pressing issue. For I reckoned that, even though he was perfectly
capable of keeping his troops together and finishing the war without
this particular sum, by using the booty he had won, it would never-
the less be undesirable to reduce the distinction or quality of his
triumph because we were in any way niggardly or mean. Then there
was the debate on the ten legates for Caesar's staff. Some people
wanted to refuse point-blank; others tried to explore the precedents;
others wanted to play for time; others again were willing to consent,
but in very grudging terms. Here too my own speech made it clear
to all that my actions were dictated by my view of the interests of the
res publica, but that my wish to be generous was stirred by my high
regard for Caesar.

29   On all those previous occasions I was listened to in silence. Now
however, when we are discussing which provinces to assign, I find
my speech being interrupted. Yet previously my proposals were
intended to enhance the marks of our esteem for Caesar; now my
only motive is the military requirement, and therefore the highest
interests of the *res publica*. After all, Caesar himself has no reason for
wanting to stay in Gaul except to finish the job he started, and then
to hand it over fully completed to the *res publica*. It might be
suggested, I suppose, that he finds the countryside attractive, the
cities beautiful, the native tribes paragons of civilization and charm,
victory desirable, and the chance to widen Rome's dominions keeping him irresistibly. In fact, of course, it is the most savage country
on earth, its towns the most primitive, its inhabitants the most
bestial; his victories are already impossible to match; Rome's
dominions can hardly spread beyond the Atlantic Ocean. Another
argument suggests that his return will be unpopular. With whom?
The people who sent him out to Gaul? Or the Senate which loaded
him with honours? People forget; absence never really makes the

heart grow fonder; the victory laurels for which he risked so much will quickly wither as the months slip by. And so, if Caesar has enemies, the last thing they should want is to recall him; for this means a return to glory, a triumph, and congratulations, the highest praise the Senate can bestow, the thanks of the *Equites*, and the
30 affections of the Roman people. And if Caesar does not hurry home to enjoy such signal marks of favour, and prefers to serve the *res publica* by finishing the job, what should I recommend, as a senator whose duty it is to consider what is best for the *res publica* even if it conflicts with his personal feelings?

In fact, gentlemen, to me the issue is quite clear. In assigning provinces at this moment it is our duty to pay regard to the need for world peace. For it must be perfectly clear to all that throughout our
31 other dominions there is neither threat nor likelihood of war. For some time now we have found the mighty Mediterranean, whose fury threatens cities and communications as well as those who occupy their business on its waters, almost a private harbour for the Roman people, safe and secure from the Atlantic to the Black Sea's furthest shores, thanks to the valour of Gnaeus Pompey. Thanks to Pompey too, the nations whose innumerable hordes could so easily overflow into the provinces of our empire have been either cut down to size or totally suppressed. And Asia, which was once the limit of our dominions, is now itself bounded by three new provinces. And what I say is true of every nation, every corner of the world: there is no people which has not been either virtually eliminated or else so crushed as not to stir, or made so docile that it actually enjoys the fruits of our conquest and dominion.

(*iii*)

The Senate should not wantonly insult leading citizens.

De provinciis consularibus, 38–40:

Now, gentlemen, I am very well aware that you have conferred signal and well-nigh unprecedented honours upon Gaius Caesar. If he deserved them, you displayed an appropriate sense of gratitude; but if your purpose was in fact to draw him into as close a connection with your order as possible, then indeed you revealed a supernatural perspicacity. For you have never, as a Senate, heaped honours and privileges on any man who did not think all other distinctions of far less worth than those which he obtained from you. No-one who has ever had the chance of becoming a leader of the Senate has preferred to be a *popularis*. But there are men whose shortcomings have made them lose confidence in their own ability; and others whose rejection by other senators has driven them to sever their connection with your order. It is only men like these who have abandoned, as it were, the safety of the harbour and have risked themselves perforce upon the storm waves of revolution. And if such men are tempted, after a tossing on the waves of a popular career, to turn their gaze back to this House and, having done the state some service, wish to win the goodwill of this venerable body once again, so far from spurning their advances, we should go out of our way to

39 win them back. We have just been warned by one of the best and bravest consuls in our history to ensure that we are not defied and, if we allocate Nearer Gaul to next year's consuls, to see to it that there is not a popular vote to re-allot the province to someone else. For the result of that will be that it will ever after be controlled by the demagogic and violent methods of the enemies of our order. That would indeed be a blow, gentlemen, and far be it from me to take it lightly, particularly when the warning comes from so great a statesman as the consul who has been one of the foremost champions of our nation's peace and order. Nevertheless I am far more afraid of seeming in any way to diminish the respect we pay our most distinguished and most powerful citizens, or to reject whatever overtures of goodwill such citizens may make towards our order. And after all the remarkable and unprecedented honours you have paid him, I cannot imagine that Gaius Julius Caesar will pass this province on to the men you would least like to see there, nor that he will deny free choice to the very order which gave him his highest honours. In conclusion, gentlemen, let me say this: I do not know how each of you intends to vote; but I do know what I hope. It is my duty as a senator, so far as in me lies, to see to it that no man of power or distinction can have any just cause for resentment against this order. And were I Caesar's bitterest enemy, I would still maintain this view for the sake of the *res publica.*

(*iv*)

Caesar's *inimici* have no right to seek Cicero's support against Caesar, when they had supported Cicero's *inimicus* against him. Cicero says that he himself will not pursue *inimicitiae*.

De provinciis consularibus, 44–7 (om. 46):

Now perhaps some people will not allow me to claim that I have sacrificed my own resentment and personal animosity to the good of the *res publica*, since such a claim is appropriate to a man of stature and sagacity. But a more modest claim I shall make; it may not perhaps bring me any great credit, but should serve at least to counter criticism; it is this, that I know how to be grateful not only for major acts of generosity but also for mens' smaller deeds of kindness. So let me make this demand of all those brave men to whom I am so deeply indebted: I did not in the past demand that you should share my labours or my sufferings; so do not ask me now to be a party to your personal enmities, especially since the resolution which you yourselves passed in the Senate has made it reasonable for me to defend the very acts of Caesar on which I have hitherto made no
45 public pronouncement whatsoever. And my reason has been that certain leading personalities, whose advice once helped me save the *res publica* and whose influence persuaded me to shun any political alliance with Caesar, have maintained that the Julian Laws and the other measures of his consulate were passed illegally, whereas the measure by which I was proscribed was legal because, although it constituted a threat to the *res publica*, it was none the less proposed without any breach of religious observances. In fact the matter was aptly summed up by one of our most distinguished and eloquent colleagues when he declared in all seriousness that my exile marked the death of the *res publica*, but that the *res publica* had at least been given a ceremonious funeral. It is, of course, gentlemen, the highest compliment I could be paid to have my own exile described as the death of the *res publica*; and rather than criticize the rest of what he said let me adapt it to defend my own viewpoint. My opponents have claimed that, because no-one had declared that he was watching the sky for omens at the time, the bill condemning me to exile was legally passed even though it was sanctioned by neither law nor precedent. But they appear to have conveniently forgotten that

Clodius, the man who brought it in, was made a plebeian by formal adoption while Bibulus, the consul, was officially observing omens. So he was not remotely entitled to be a plebeian. It follows, therefore, that he was certainly not entitled to be tribune of the people. So if Clodius' tribunate is legally valid, it is quite impossible to argue that any of Caesar's acts are invalid, and furthermore not only was Clodius' tribunate legal, but all his most vicious measures were equally so because, when they were passed, religious requirements were satisfied. . . .

47   In conclusion, gentlemen, let me say that if I had any personal hostility towards Gaius Caesar, I should feel it my duty to save it for some future occasion, but at this moment in time to think only of the interests of the *res publica*. I could even follow the example of some of our most distinguished citizens and, for the sake of the *res publica*, lay them aside for good. But since there has never been any personal hostility, his enormous kindness to myself makes it easy to forget whatever injury I might have imagined he had done me. And therefore, gentlemen of the Senate, I support the following: if Caesar's honour is the question, I shall vote to honour Caesar as a man; if it is his position, I shall vote for any measure which will promote harmony among the senators; if it is our concern to preserve respect for the decrees of the Senate, I shall support consistency by conferring further honours upon Caesar; if our concern is the war in Gaul, I shall vote for the best interests of the *res publica*; if my personal obligations are the issue, I shall be showing due gratitude for past favours. I should very much like to persuade every one of you to support me, gentlemen, but I shall not be unduly concerned if I fail to influence either those who gave their protection, against your wishes, gentlemen, to Clodius, my personal enemy, or those who have so venomously attacked my reconciliation with their own personal enemy, though these people in their turn did not hesitate to become reconciled with one who is no less their enemy than my own.

(v)

Men should restrict their pursuit of *inimicitia* to their own personal *inimici*, and not stretch their feuds to cover their supporters. In this case Cicero means that Caesar's *inimici* should not try to persecute Balbus. Balbus was a native of Gades (Cadiz, in Spain), who was given the Roman citizenship for military distinction, and was, at this period, serving Caesar as his chief agent in Rome, with the rank of Officer Commanding Rear Headquarters (*praefectus castrorum*). Cicero's speech shows that some of Caesar's opponents were determined to remain unrelenting.

Pro Balbo, 57–62:

Cornelius Balbus' personal detractors do not present us with a very formidable problem. The manifestations of their animosity are fairly typical – snubs at dinner parties or pulling him to pieces at social functions; and all this is actuated by malice rather than
58 enmity. But the detractors and enemies of his friends are a much more formidable proposition altogether. Balbus never had an enemy – nor gave anyone reason to become one. He was assiduous in his attentions to men of standing, paying due respect on all occasions to their rank and position. He was the intimate friend of one of our most powerful citizens, and during the recent crisis here when passions ran high, neither by action, word, or even demeanour did he ever give offence to anyone whose politics or policies were different from his own. It was my destiny, or that of the *res publica*, that I alone had to bear the brunt of a crisis which threatened us all. But so far from rejoicing at my downfall and your degradation, gentlemen, Cornelius did everything in his power, everything that tears, effort, and sympathy could do, to support and encourage my family
59 while I was far away. And it is they, my family, who are his witnesses for this; it is they who have begged me to help. It is indeed a service he has well deserved, and, as I said at the beginning of my speech, I am now repaying the debt of my deepest gratitude. I hope, therefore, gentlemen of the jury, that just as you have honoured and held dear the men who led the battle for my recall and restoration to a place of honour, so too you will demonstrate your approval and delight at what Cornelius has done – for it was all that any man could do in his position.

He is not, therefore, being attacked by his own enemies – for he has none – but by the many high-ranking enemies of his friends. And only yesterday Gnaeus Pompey, in the course of a long and powerful speech, challenged such enemies to do battle with himself, if they liked, but to abandon their unjust attacks on Balbus, who was no match for them. Certainly it would be a reasonable principle,
60 gentlemen, and one of advantage to ourselves and those whose

friendship binds their fortunes to our own, that we should confine hostilities to our own personal enemies, and not extend them to the friends of those same enemies. And if I had enough influence with Cornelius' opponents, especially since it must be obvious to them that I have learnt more than most from my own misfortunes and personal experience, I would try to persuade them to abandon their more immediate enmities as well. For I have always believed that it is the duty of all men of character and high position to fight for the *res publica*, for in so doing one is defending that which is our prize possession. Certainly I have never shirked this task, which is indeed a labour of love for me. Political struggles are only sensible as long as they benefit or at least do no damage to the nation's interest. I have had a policy for which I have fought and struggled, but without success. It brought indignation to others, but abiding grief to me. Yet is it right to destroy rather than endure what one cannot change? The Senate chose to honour Gaius Caesar with a national thanksgiving, unprecedented in extravagance and extent. Despite the empy coffers in the treasury, it also chose to pay his victorious army, and voted its general ten legates intead of six, and decided not to relieve him of his command under the provisions of Sempronius' law. I was primarily responsible for these decisions, thinking it my duty to bury the hatchet of my previous hostility and work for harmony during the present crisis of the *res publica*. But others, alas, did not agree: and perhaps they are more consistent in their policy. I am blaming no-one; but neither can I agree with everyone; and I do not think I am guilty of any inconsistency because, like any good helmsman, I have modified my course and direction in the face of the storms in the *res publica*. But if we are going to have men, as indeed I see we have a certain number, whose capacity for hate is so unlimited that once a feud is taken up they cannot lay it down, they should fight their principal opponents but not the opponents' friends and supporters too. To fight the principals will be called doggedness by some, or even high-mindedness by others, but to fight their supporters too will be regarded by one and all as a combination of injustice and cruelty.

VI. Social Aspects of the *Res Publica*

57. THE INTEMPERANCE OF YOUTH

Youth also found a defender in Cicero this year (56). Before the conference at Luca, perhaps about 3rd or 4th April, M. Caelius Rufus, who had been associated with Cicero when he first came to Rome, was prosecuted on a variety of charges. Those, however, which concern this speech were that he borrowed money from Clodia, sister of Clodius, and that he subsequently tried to murder her. The prosecutor was L. Herennius Balbus. Whether this was another attack on Cicero's friends we do not know, but it is at least possible, and Cicero's reply is unsparing of the whole of Clodius' family. Young men may be led astray, Cicero argues, but a wild youth may be followed by a sober and useful manhood. Generalizations about youth are not proofs.

Pro Caelio, 18, 25, 28–30:

The prosecution has sought to make capital out of the fact that Caelius no longer lives with his father. But at his age one cannot reasonably object to that. After all he is old enough to have scored a considerable political triumph, which was as honourable to himself as it was irksome to me, by successfully prosecuting Gaius Antonius. Futhermore, he is old enough to be eligible for public office, and the decision to live on his own was the result of his father's active encouragement, not just his consent. The facts are that Caelius' family lived a long way from the forum, and he wanted to be able to visit me more easily, and himself to be more accessible to his own friends. So, very reasonably, he rented a house on the Palatine quite cheaply, and lived there.

My honourable friend, Marcus Crassus, when denouncing the visit of King Ptolemy to Rome, recently quoted a line of Ennius of which I might remind you:

> 'If only in the woods of Pelion
> The good ship Argo never had been built.'

Perhaps I might also remind you of the later lines which claimed that 'then a wayward mistress never would' have caused us this trouble; the reference was, of course, to

> 'Medea sick-hearted,
> Wounded by the savage pangs of love.'

I hope to show you in due course, gentlemen, and to prove to your satisfaction that there was, here on the Palatine, a second Medea, and that the unfortunate young Caelius' move to her vicinity caused him all his 'trouble', or, to be more precise, made him the victim of much malicious gossip. . . .

25 But let us turn our minds to the main essentials of the case. I noticed, gentlemen, what a close and attentive hearing you gave my friend Lucius Herennius. His speech was a stylish and virtuoso performance and of course you were captivated by it. But I feared on occasion that this speech, which had been so subtly slanted to suggest my client's guilt, was imperceptibly distilling its sweet poison into your minds. He dilated at length about men's extravagance and lust, on the vicious habits of the youth of today, and the general decline in moral standards. And though in his everyday life Herennius is a broadminded gentleman, and perhaps the supreme exemplar of that particular form of easy-going charm in which almost all of us take such delight, yet here in court he has been as sour as a spinster, a puritan, or an old-fashioned schoolmaster. He tore Marcus Caelius to pieces more savagely than any father would his son, dwelling at length upon his wildness and lack of self-control. Needless to say, gentlemen, I can hardly blame you for having listened with such close attention. It made even my hair stand on

28 end to hear that searing, damning denunciation. . . . Yet from my own experience I can say that in this state I have seen and heard of large numbers who have not merely taken a preliminary sip of this kind of life, or, to coin a phrase, supped there with a long spoon, but have rather totally abandoned their youth to a life of dissipation; yet they have emerged later and brought forth the proverbial hundredfold of fruit, becoming responsible and distinguished citizens. By common consent, young men of this age are allowed to sow their wild oats, since adolescent desires are naturally intense. And as long as their manifestations do no damage to life or property,

29 they are generally tolerated and regarded with indulgence. But the

prosecution's tactics, gentlemen, seemed to me to consist of wanting to smear Caelius with the prejudice that attaches to all the vices of youth. And so the close attention which was accorded to the prosecution's speech was due to the fact that, though there was only one defendant, the vices described were the vices of many. Anyone can make general accusations of dissipation. I could myself, and it would take me all day to exhaust that particular topic. The same goes for seduction, adultery, lechery, and extravagance. As long as you pillory the vices and not the vicious, you have ample material for a prolonged and formidable denunciation. But you, gentlemen, are much too intelligent to be diverted from the facts of this particular case. If the prosecution delivers a general attack on vice, immorality, and the decadence of the present generation, you must not allow your high regard for principle to arouse your wrath against an individual defendant, when he is unjustly denounced not

30 for his own crimes but for the failings of a whole generation. For this reason I dare not answer the prosecution's censures as I ought by pleading for the generosity and indulgence which is usually shown to youth. As I say, I dare not. So I enter no plea of youthful folly, no claims for the indulgence to which all young men are entitled. All I ask is this: there may be at this time a general prejudice against the debts, the wildness, the licentiousness of youth, – as indeed there is, a strong one – nevertheless, you must not, I beg of you, allow the misdemeanours of others or the general depravity of youth and present society to bias you against Marcus Caelius. But in making that demand I also make you a promise in my turn, that I shall willingly refute in detail whatever specific charges are laid against him.

58. ADVICE TO A NOBLE WOMAN

(a) An Ancestor Speaks

Cicero argues that the two accusations against Caelius reveal a love-hate relationship. After a brilliant and scathing apology for attacking a woman, Cicero addresses Clodia in the guise of her ancestor, Appius Claudius the Censor, who was blind.

Pro Caelio, 30–4:

Now there are only two serious charges – fraud and poisoning; both involve one and the same person. It is alleged that Caelius obtained money from Clodia and procured poison to use on her. All the rest of the charges are mere abuse, the vulgarities of street-corner oratory not the formal indictments of a law-court. 'Adulterer, fornicator, bribery-agent': these are insults, gentlemen, not accusations. They lack substance and foundation. They are provocative and unfounded abuse hurled out by a prosecutor who has lost his temper.

31 But the two serious charges are a different matter; they spring from somewhere; they have a source – and I know who it is. I know the name; I know the person. Caelius allegedly needed money. He got it from Clodia, without witnesses, and kept it as long as he wanted. All this points to a really remarkable intimacy between them. He also wanted to kill her – allegedly. So he got hold of poison, suborned what slaves he could, prepared the fatal dose, fixed a rendezvous, and brought the poison to the spot in secret. Obviously here we find evidence of a really remarkable dislike, doubtless the result of a spectacular rift in their relationship. So the whole issue centres round the person of Clodia, a lady whose rank is as formidable as her reputation is notorious. I shall. therefore, say no more than is

32 necessary to refute the charges. Being a wise and understanding president of this court, you will of course be well aware, Gnaeus Domitius, that it is only with Clodia that we have to deal. If she denies having fixed up Caelius with cash, if she does not claim that he had prepared to poison her, then we are guilty of most ungentle-manly conduct in dragging the good name of a respectable married woman through the court and failing to treat her with the respect due to our wives and mothers. But in fact we have only to eliminate this woman from the case and the prosecution are left with neither charge nor ammunition against Marcus Caelius. Hence the only thing left for the defence to do is to refute her evidence, since she is the real source of the charges against Caelius. And I would have far more energy for this were it not for my feud with her husband – I mean her brother; I am always making that mistake, gentlemen. So I shall treat her lightly and go no further than my obligations to my client and the truth compel me. But I must confess that I never thought that I should have to deal with a woman's feuds, least of all a woman who is said to be no man's enemy but to love them all.

33 Of course I do not really know if she would like me to deal with her in the old-fashioned style, with an uncompromising severity

rather than with an indulgent and civilized leniency. So let us try
the old-fashioned style. I had better therefore resurrect one of those
hoary old ancestors, one with a great shaggy beard like those we see
in old statues and paintings, not one of those trim little modern ones
that Clodia likes so much. Let him scold her on my behalf so that
she will not have a chance to get angry with me personally. And
therefore let us resurrect one of her own family – and best of all
Appius Claudius, the blind censor. For since he cannot see her he
will find her much less offensive than anyone else. If he was resur-
rected, this is the kind of speech he would make: 'What business have
you, woman, with Caelius, a young, vigorous fellow from another
family? Why was your relationship so close that you lent him money,
why so distant that you feared his poison? Did you not know that
your father, your uncle, your grandfather, your great-grandfather,
and his father and grandfather before him were all consuls? Are you
not aware that you are the wife of Quintus Metellus, one of Rome's
most distinguished and heroic patriots, who, from the day he entered
public life, surpassed almost all his fellow-citizens in achievement,
honour, and high position? You are yourself a member of one of our
highest families and married into another of comparable distinction
– why then this close connection with Caelius? Was he a relative, an
in-law, or one of your husband's friends? Certainly not. So it must
have been a reckless infatuation. And even if the men of your family
failed to influence you, surely my own grand-daughter, Quinta
Claudia, of blessed memory, should have inspired you to strive to
match the honours which our womenfolk have brought to our house,
women like Claudia, the Vestal virgin, who when her father celebrated his triumph over the Salassi, clung to him and would not let
a hostile tribune drag him from his chariot? Why do you emulate
your brother's vices rather than the traditional virtues of your father
your grandfather, and your family – virtues which from my own day
have never failed to find expression in both the men and women of
our line? Did I once prevent Rome making overtures to Pyrrhus
merely so that in later years you would be safe to swear your daily
allegiance to your vile paramours? Did I build Rome's first aque-
duct merely for your post-incestual ablutions? Did I build Rome's
great highway just to let you romp along it in the company of other
women's husbands?'

34

(*b*) A Modern Philosophy for Girls

Cicero now speaks in the mouth of her brother Clodius.

Pro Caelio, 36:

But perhaps you would prefer the more modern type of suave criticism. So away with Appius Claudius, that uncompromising, almost uncouth veteran of the past; and from among your contemporaries, Clodia, my first choice will be your youngest brother, that arch-exponent of elegant criticism. He loves you very dearly. When he was a small boy, being of a nervous disposition, I suppose, and absurdly frightened of the dark, he always used to creep into his sister's bed – for comfort. The conversation might perhaps go like this: 'What's the fuss about, my sister? Are you crazy? Why all this clamour and making mountains out of molehills? It was only that next-door neighbour of ours you saw. Of course he is fair, tall, good-looking, and has beautiful eyes – in fact, he quite bowled you over. You wanted to see him again and again; you contrive sometimes to meet him in the park. Fancy an aristocrat like you wanting to waste your money on keeping the affections of a boy whose father is so mean, so parsimonious. You can't do it; he walks all over you, treats you like dirt, refuses to have anything to do with you, and doesn't think much of your presents. Try someone else. You've got your gardens along the Tiber; they are strategically placed where all the young men go to bathe. You can take your pick there any day you like. Why go on importuning a youngster who won't even look at you?'

59. AN OLD-FASHIONED EDUCATION AND A MODERN ONE

Rome is a place of malicious gossip – who can escape it? (38) The ancient education is out of fashion; a modern one which still upholds the important principles is better. An eloquent speaker cannot have wasted his education.

Pro Caelio, 39–47 (abridged):

My arguments may very well provoke inquiries about the sort of education my pupils get. How would I bring up a young man nowadays? Did Caelius' father entrust him to my care so that he should spend his youth amidst amours and dissipations, and I should defend them? Believe me, gentlemen, if I thought that any man possessed such natural strength of character or such powers of self-control that he could resist all pleasures and devote the whole of his life to physical exercise and intellectual effort, taking no delight in rest, relaxation, his friends' activities, parties, or affairs of the heart, seeking nothing out of life save that which brought him honour and high position, I would indeed be convinced that such a man had been trained and endowed with superhuman qualities. There were men like that, I suppose, once upon a time, men like Camillus, Fabricius, and Curius, men whose achievements raised

40 Rome from her lowly origins to her present greatness. Yet you will find little evidence of such qualities in contemporary society or even literature; and there is no demand nowadays for the books which honour such unyielding adherence to principle. In Rome, where we have for so long practised as well as preached the virtues of such a way of life, new philosophies have now emerged. Even the Greeks, for all their education, have changed with the times, and failed in their actions to live up to the noble and honourable ideals which

41 they taught and wrote about. As a result, different schools of thought have now developed: one claiming that for a wise man pleasure is the sole criterion by which action should be judged – and many highly educated men find this degrading doctrine most attractive; another maintains that such pursuit of pleasure must be moderated by concern for one's own self-respect – as though two such incompatibles could be reconciled by so facile an approach as that. Meanwhile the men who taught us that the one true road to honour was the road of unremitting effort are now lone voices crying in their

42 academic wilderness . . . So let us abandon their route to honour; let us leave it deserted, untrodden, blocked by bushes and undergrowth. Let us allow youth to have its fling; down with regimentation; let us have some pleasure in our lives; the old way may be the true way, the right way – but you can have too much of a good thing. We must allow pleasure and enjoyment to get the better of ideals some of the time, provided that on these occasions young men observe the following golden rules of moderation: do nothing to corrupt your own morals or anyone else's; do not squander the family fortunes; do not get hopelessly into debt; do not attack

another man's house or family; do not pollute the pure nor start another on the downward path; do not tarnish an untarnished reputation; avoid violence and intimidation, conspiracy and crime; and once you have had your fling and allowed your youth time to enjoy its sport and frivolous self-indulgence, then remember your obligations to your family, your career, your *res publica*, that men may see that what your education could not forestall, satiety and the disenchantment of experience has encouraged you to despise and cast away . . .

44   But, of course, Marcus Caelius is quite different, gentlemen; and because I can rely on your understanding sympathy, I am able to tell you the whole story of his youthful and entirely honourable activities with far more confidence than I might have done. In him you will find no love of luxury, no hint of high extravagance, no debts, no lust for wild parties or general debauchery. And, as you know, a love of eating and drinking normally increases with age. But as for what are popularly described as affairs of the heart, well, they do not trouble men of character for very long; their attractions quickly fade and certainly Caelius has never succumbed to them;

45   they never interrupted his career. You have all heard for yourselves evidence of his power of oratory on two separate occasions, when he spoke in his own defence, and before that when he prosecuted Antonius – and this, I may say, gentlemen, is relevant to the defence and no mere eulogy of my client. Being educated men you will have noted, of course, the quality of his speech, the fluency, the richness of his phraseology and vocabulary. There, gentlemen, you heard clear proof not just of his ability, though I concede that ability can triumph even without the help of honest effort, but also, unless my affections have made me blind, a style which could only have been the product of an excellent education, long hours of labour, and late nights of toil. And you must be aware, gentlemen, that the vices of which Caelius is accused and the sort of education I am describing are unlikely to be found in one and the same man. It is quite impossible for a mind obsessed with lechery and love-affairs both old and new, handicapped by swinging between extremes of opulence and penury, to endure the sheer effort, whether physical or intellectual, that we orators endure, whatever style of speaking we adopt.

46   When further you think of the enormous rewards which a skilled speaker can command, the pleasure he derives from his oratory, the

honour, influence, and high position he achieves, can you think of any reason other than the sheer effort involved why so few men, past or present, have faced up to it? The would-be orator must forgo all pleasures, sacrifice all hobbies, relaxations, fun, social life, and even almost all association with his friends. That is why the effort involved is unacceptable to men and deters them from oratory's pursuit; it is not just that they lack either ability or the
47 elementary education. If then Caelius had lived the typical life of debauchery I have described, do you think that as a youngster he could have prosecuted an ex-consul? If he was frightened of hard work, up to his neck in the idle pleasures of the moment, would he be here doing battle daily in the law-courts, hungry for challenges, prosecuting at the risk of his career, fighting under the eyes of the Roman people month after month for his own position and the honour he might gain?

Nevertheless, I do admit that there is something fishy on the Palatine; there is some truth in the general gossip; Baiae has a few secrets to reveal, I am sure. And what does Baiae tell us? Tell us, gentlemen? No, it shouts aloud that there is one woman whose depravity has sunk so low that she no longer seeks to cloak her immorality in the secrecy of darkness, but delights rather to parade her grossest vices before a vast audience in the brightest glare of publicity.

60. AN IMMODEST WOMAN'S ENTOURAGE

(a) A Woman More Sinning than Sinned Against

Pro Caelio, 48–50:

Of course there may be some who think that young men should not be allowed to associate even with prostitutes. Such, I admit, are men of strictest principle; but they are rather out of touch with the more permissive views of modern society and indeed even with the measure of broad-mindedness habitual in our ancestors. Was there ever a time when whoring was not common practice, when it was denounced, forbidden, or any less permissible than now? I am not mentioning any names, merely describing a particular phenomenon;
49 I shall leave it to you to assess its significance. Suppose, now, a

woman without a husband throws open her house to every lecher in town, and blatantly lives like a prostitute, giving dinner parties for perfect strangers, and so on; suppose she does it in Rome, in her own country house, or in Baiae at the height of the holiday season, parading herself in provocative dresses, keeping loose company, making eyes at or flirting with one and all, and (worse still) kissing, embracing, importuning them at picnics, punting parties, dinners, till everyone would rate her not as a mere prostitute but as the most brazen, the most abandoned harlot in town. Then suppose a young man happened to associate with a woman like that, Herennius, would you regard this adulterer, this lover, as storming the breaches of a chaste woman's virtue, or rather as merely wanting to satisfy a perfectly natural desire?

50   You have done me terrible injuries, Clodia, and caused me bitter resentment; yet I have forgotten it and erased it from my memory. When I was in exile far away, you cruelly wronged my family; but I make no mention of that. You may take it that what I have said bears no reference to you at all, you may be sure. But since the prosecution claim that you are the source, and you personally are the witness in support of what they say, just answer me this: suppose there was a woman like the one I have described, so utterly unlike yourself, a woman who lived and acted like a whore; if a young man had a certain amount of business with her, would you regard it as so utterly deplorable or vile? And if you are not the woman in question – as of course I much prefer to think – what can the prosecution have against Caelius? But if you are, as they appear to insist, why should my client be afraid of being accused of vices which you regard as trifling? So please explain the line our defence should take: if you insist that you are chaste, then you must acquit Caelius of any improper behaviour; if you do not, then you will give Caelius and the rest an excellent platform from which to conduct a defence.

(*b*) Like Mistress, Like Slaves

In turning to the accusation of poisoning, it was alleged that Caelius had tried to administer the poison through Clodia's own slaves; the slaves of an immodest woman, however, are quite unreliable.

Pro Caelio, 57–58:

Finally then, who was in the plot with Caelius, who helped him, who was his assistant and accomplice, whom could he trust with the secret of his crime, and therefore with his own life and security? You at least gave Caelius credit for having a few brains, Herennius, whatever other qualities you may have denied him in that offensive prosecution speech of yours. Yet you suggest that he was so utterly lunatic as to entrust all his fortunes to a gang of slaves belonging to someone else. And look at the kind of slaves they were, too – for this is relevant. They did not live like ordinary slaves, as Caelius was very well aware, but enjoyed quite exceptionally lax discipline, freedom and familiarity with their mistress. It must be perfectly obvious to anyone of even minimal intelligence that in a household where the mistress lives like a prostitute, where all activities should be a dark secret, where you find experiments in lust and debauchery, and in fact all kinds of unheard of vice and depravity, there the slaves are slaves no more, since they minister to, conduct, and indulge in all the self-same vices I have just described, are entrusted with those same dark secrets, and make no small profit for them-
58 selves from her daily extravagance and debauchery. And yet you ask us to believe that Caelius was not aware of this, Herennius? If he was as intimate with Clodia as you would have us believe, he must have known that her slaves were very close to her. And if he was not as intimate as you maintain, then how could he have been close enough to suborn her slaves?

61. A PLOT AT THE BATHS

The tale of how the plot to poison Clodia was detected is utterly incredible.

Pro Caelio, 61–65:

The prosecution have failed to tell us where the poison came from or how it was prepared. They claim that it was given to Publius Licinius, a thoroughly respectable young man and a close friend of Caelius. Then, allegedly, an arrangement was made with Clodia's slaves to come to the Senian Baths, and there Licinius would meet them and hand over the poison phial. Now the first question that occurs to me is, what on earth was the point of arranging to take the poison to the baths? Why did the slaves not go to Caelius' house? If Caelius still had such close and intimate relations with Clodia, there would be nothing suspicious in one of her slaves being seen at his residence. But if the couple were now at loggerheads, and having broken it up were at each other's throats, then of course, 'Hell hath no fury . . .', as they say, and there we have the real motive for all

62 these accusations of attempted murder. But let us go on with the prosecution's story: apparently the slaves told the whole tale of Caelius' villainy to their mistress and she cunningly told them to co-operate with all Caelius' proposals. She also wanted Licinius caught red-handed actually handing over the poison. So she told them to fix up the Senian baths as a rendezvous, so that she could send some of her friends there to hide and then suddenly jump out and arrest Licinius when he arrived and was handing over the poison.

A child, gentlemen, could refute a story like that. Why choose the public baths, of all places? There is nowhere for a fully dressed man to hide. If they were on the entrance porch, they could not conceal themselves; and if they wanted to hide inside, they certainly could not do it conveniently in walking-shoes and fully dressed. They probably could not have got in at all indeed, unless perhaps their influential mistress had got onto friendly terms with the attendant

63 there – doubtless at her usual farthing price. However, I am simply dying to be told who these noble witnesses are who caught Licinius *in flagrante delicto*, actually handing over the poison. For we have not yet been vouchsafed any names. But I have no doubt they will prove to be highly respectable gentlemen – after all, they are friends of a great lady and took upon themselves the arduous public duty of being crammed into the baths like sardines – something which no lady, however influential, could have persuaded any but the most honourable and distinguished of gentlemen to do. But there is no need for me to extol the honour of her witnesses. Listen to the tale of their conscientious devotion to duty. 'They hid in the baths.' What brilliant sleuthing! 'They leapt out just too early.' What self-discipline! The story goes on like this: 'Licinius arrived with the phial in his hand, was holding it out, but had not actually quite handed it over, when these anonymous heroes leapt out at him. Licinius had his hand out in the very act of handing over the goods,

but he snatched it back when they suddenly rushed him, and fled hot-foot.'

Fortunately, gentlemen, truth is a mighty power. Despite the ingenuity, the cunning, the deviousness of the plots that are framed for its destruction, easily and all unaided it always prevails. The 64 author of this flimsy little tale is a lady of wide and long-standing literary experience, yet somehow it is devoid of plot or denouement. It seems strange that all those witnesses – for of course it needed large numbers to ensure an easy arrest and greater credibility for their evidence – should allow Licinius to escape from their clutches. Why was it any harder to catch him once he had snatched the phial back without handing it over than if he had actually done so? The whole purpose of the ambush was to catch him in the act, and to arrest him in possession of the poison or immediately after handing it over. That was the whole point of the woman's plan, the whole object of the exercise. I cannot see why, therefore, you claim that they were so careless as to jump out too early. They were asked to do one job, they were positioned to do one job, and that was to catch Licinius in the act and prove publicly the existence of poison, 65 plot, and crime. Could they in fact have rushed out at a more opportune moment than they did, when Licinius had arrived, with the poison in his hands? If the woman's associates had waited till he had already handed it to the slaves, and had then dashed out of the baths and arrested him, Licinius would have sworn to high heaven that it was not he who had given the slaves the poison. And those witnesses could never have proved otherwise, nor could they claim to have seen him do it, since it would have laid them open to exactly the same accusation themselves, not least because they would have been claiming to have seen something they could not possibly have seen from their hiding place. So in fact they showed themselves at exactly the right moment, when Licinius had just arrived, had got out the phial, and was reaching forward to hand over the poison.

The denouement is splendid farce, perhaps, but a rotten story. They could not find a satisfactory ending for the plot, so they let the villain get away, rang the cue-bell, and hauled up the curtain.

This Clodia was also the 'Lesbia' of the poet Catullus, and it has been suggested that it was Caelius who supplanted Catullus as her favourite lover. Her stormy love-affair with Catullus also ended in bitterness and vile abuse, as his poems to her show. Cicero's devastating attack in this defence of Caelius seems to have put an end to her salon.

62. POLITICS AFTER THE CONFERENCE AT LUCA

For a time after 56, Cicero's arguments for concord fell on deaf ears; though Clodius was reconciled to Pompey, according to Dio (XXXIX, 29, 1), Pompey and Crassus were resisted to the last ditch in their bid for the consulships of 55, and they succeeded in the end only by the overt use of force; bribery and force also secured the exclusion of Cato from the praetorship (Plutarch, *Life of Cato*, XLII). The consuls got the measures agreed at Luca passed, and they also put through various ineffective measures against the political clubs and judicial corruption. But they were very unpopular; even the magnificent games which Pompey gave at the opening of his theatre and the dedication of the temple of Venus Victrix turned out not to bring the expected popularity, as the common people sympathized with the hunted elephants in the arena (Pliny, *Natural History*, VIII, 21):

'Pompey's elephants, when they abandoned hope of escape, tried to gain the sympathy of the watching mob by entreating them with gestures impossible to describe, and bewailing their fate with a sort of moaning. They roused such sympathy among the people that they forgot the general and the splendid show he had taken much pains to devise in their honour. They burst into tears and rose as one man shouting curses and imprecations at Pompey, which were all too soon fulfilled.'

Crassus, moreover, when he left for Syria in November 55, left to the curses of the tribune Ateius Capito (Cicero, *de divinatione*, I, 30). Cicero himself was formally reconciled to Crassus, entertained him to dinner the night before he left, and spoke on his behalf in the Senate early in 54. He published this speech, though it is lost, and this shows that he wanted it to be on record. He also wrote to him (*Ad fam.* V, 8) a letter professing friendship and a willingness to serve him, though in his heart he knew, as he wrote to Atticus, that he was a rascal – '*O hominem nequam*' – (*Ad Att.* IV, 13, 2). His reconciliation did not extend to Piso, however, when he returned from Macedonia in 54. They were no longer related by marriage, since Tullia's husband was dead; Piso attacked Cicero in the Senate; he was met with a verbal onslaught, subsequently written up into the violent and undignified *In Pisonem*. Another pamphlet issued this year, 54, was the 'letter' *Ad fam.* I, 9, in which Cicero defended himself, ostensibly to Lentulus Spinther, for his support of Pompey, Caesar, and Crassus.

The same defence, in a rather shorter form, appears in a passage of the *Pro Plancio*, which was also delivered in 54.

Pro Plancio, 93–94:

I do not want, on this occasion, gentlemen, to refer to Pompey as the champion who organized and inspired my recall from exile –

that would be to confuse the permanent debt of gratitude I owe him for a personal favour with the question of the safety of the *res publica*, which is my present concern. But surely he does deserve my sincere respect for the fact that he is universally regarded as the leading citizen of the *res publica*? So too with Caesar – should I begrudge him my admiration, when I know very well that first the Roman people, and now the Senate too, whose authority I always regard as paramount, have honoured him with frequent and generous votes of confidence and gratitude? That surely would be tantamount to a confession that I regarded the interests of the *res publica* as subordinate to personalities when it came to deciding who were to be my

94 friends and enemies? If I were to find my ship running before the wind and heading for a harbour different from, but no less safe and sheltered than, the one which may originally have been my destination, I would be mad to insist on beating against the gale to my original destination at the risk of my life rather than to modify my course and bow to necessity, especially when it was likely to ensure my safety. The lessons of history, of my own experience and reading, the records and writings of the wisest and most distinguished statesmen of this *res publica* and elsewhere, all point the same lesson to us, that no-one's political views remain immutable but are always adapted according to the political situation, the mood of the times, and the cause of harmony within the state. And that, Laterensis, is my policy too, and always will be. You taunt me with not being a free agent – but you are wrong. I am a free agent, always have been, and ever shall be, but I believe freedom lies not in being obstinate but in being willing to accept compromise where compromise is necessary.

63. ROMAN ELECTIONS

Cn. Plancius had been quaestor in Macedonia in 58/7, stationed at Thessalonica. There he had helped Cicero in his exile by sheltering him from his enemies who were living in exile in Greece. In this his services were so conspicuous that he had been formally thanked by the Senate in 57 (*Pro Plancio*, 78), and again by Cicero in his senatorial speech after his return (*Post reditum in senatu*, 35, *Pro Plancio*, 74). In 54 he was prosecuted for electoral irregularities by a defeated rival for the aedileship, M. Juventius Laterensis.

(*a*) The Roman People's Right to Choose

After a preface in which Cicero explains that Plancius has friends and
enemies because of his services to him, he passes to the difficulty of speaking
against an opponent whom he respects, and to the reasons which motivate
men in making an electoral choice. He then asserts the people's right to
choose, and to have their votes solicited.

Pro Plancio, 5–13:

The issues in this case, gentlemen, are simple and straightforward;
but to defend my client is a complex and delicate task. Even if it
was only a matter of contradicting Laterensis, that would be unpleasant enough, since we are close friends and associates, and it is
an old-established principle of true friendship, such as we have long
enjoyed, that friends' wishes should always coincide. For friendship
knows no stronger bond than the sharing of one another's thoughts,
ideas, and aspirations. Even so, having to contradict my friend is the
least of my causes for regret on this occasion. Far more distressing
is the fact that in this case it is essential for me to make invidious
6 comparisons between the two parties. Laterensis himself raised the
matter and pressed it with considerable vigour by claiming to be
Plancius' superior in calibre, success, and status. What can I do? If
I concede the primacy to Laterensis – for indeed his distinctions are
considerable in quantity and quality – I am bound, by implication,
both to deny my own client's merits and to accept the suspicion that
he used bribes. If, however, I claim the palm for Plancius, I must
insult my opponent by accepting his challenge and asserting that in
merit he is Plancius' inferior. So either I must emphasize the shortcomings of a very close friend, if I fight the case on ground of his
choosing, or else I must sacrifice my own client, to whom I owe far
more than I can say.

Fortunately, Laterensis, it would be an admission of blindness and
immaturity of judgement if I claimed that either Plancius or anyone
else had greater merits than yourself. So I can ignore the battle of
personalities to which you challenge me and press on to the real
7 issues of the case. Do you seriously imagine that the people are
passing judgement on a man's merits when they choose their
magistrates? Occasionally they may be, and I only wish they always
were. In fact, however, it seldom happens, except on those occasions

when they appoint magistrates in times of apparent national emergency. At the lower levels office is won by a combination of hard work and popularity, not by the merits which you so manifestly possess. As for the people, it is always a poor judge – well, a judge influenced by prejudice for or against a given candidate. Nevertheless, I must insist that you, Laterensis, can claim no monopoly of merit; your virtues are shared in each particular by Plancius.

8 But enough of that – I will discuss the matter fully elsewhere. For the moment my concern is with the rights of the people, which, in its selection of magistrates, can, and often does, pass over men of impeccable quality. But the fact that the people has wrongly passed someone over is no reason for the law-courts to condemn a man they have selected. Indeed, if it were, the law-courts would be possessed of that very power of passing judgement on the elections which the patricians used to have in olden times but could not keep. That would be even more intolerable – for in the old days a man who had secured office did not hold it unless the patricians confirmed it; but what are you being asked to do today, gentlemen, is to censure the people's judgement by actually condemning the man of their choice.

So it looks as though I have approached the case from the very angle I had intended to avoid. Nevertheless, it is reasonable to hope, Laterensis, that my speech will give you no reason to suspect the slightest degree of personal abuse. I am indeed highly critical of the way you risk your reputation in so regrettable a fashion; but I am not seeking to blacken that reputation in any way whatsoever.

9 Because you were not elected aedile, do you really think that the Roman people have made light of or denied your qualities of self-control, industry, and loyalty to the *res publica*, of high principle, honour, integrity, and unremitting effort? If so, I disagree with you profoundly. I can assure you in all sincerity that if there were in Rome only ten men, and they were all men of honour, wisdom, integrity and merit, and if they had pronounced you unworthy of the aedileship, I would regard it as being a far greater reflection on your honour than you seem to think the people's verdict is. For in the elections the people do not judge; they are influenced. And they are influenced mainly by prestige, to some extent by entreaty; they elect the most assiduous canvasser. Indeed, inasmuch as they are led to form any sort of judgement at all, they do so not as a result

of rational choice or balanced assessment but usually on impulse and a wave of emotion. It is because the people are impervious to qualities of intelligence, consistency, sound judgement, and hard work that wise men have always declared that what the people decree must always be endured but not always respected. So when you complain that you ought to have been elected aedile, you are

10 in fact finding fault not with your rival but with the people. Let us suppose that you were a more deserving candidate than Plancius – and I intend to settle this issue a little later, but without decrying your merits – let us suppose, anyhow, that you were; it is not your opponent who is at fault for defeating you, but the Roman people for passing you over. And of course in any election, but especially in elections for the aedileship, what you have to capture are the people's hearts and not their heads. Votes are won by velvet gloves not iron fists. Voters tend to be swayed by a sense of personal obligation to a candidate rather than by their collective responsibilities as members of the *res publica*. And even if you insist on regarding their votes as expressions of a rational judgement, you are duty bound to accept that judgement; you are not entitled to

11 reverse it. It may have been a rotten judgement; but it was their judgement. It should not have been, perhaps; but that was for the people to decide. It may seem unacceptable, but many of Rome's greatest statesmen have managed to accept it. It is one of the fundamental rights of a free people, not least a people that is the conqueror and ruler of the world, that by its votes it may give or deny whatever privilege it likes to whoever it likes. And it is up to every one of us who sails the stormy seas of popular favour to accept with good grace the verdict of the people, to win them over when their hostility is aroused, to keep them when we have won them, and to calm them down when they are seething. As for high office, if we despise it, we need not join the search for popularity; if we want it, we must not grow weary of that search.

12   Where, then, do the people play their part in all this? Let me explain in their own words rather than mine. Suppose you met them round the conference table and they spoke with just one voice. The discussion might go something like this: 'I did not prefer Plancius to you, Laterensis, since you are both good men of equal standing. But I bestowed my favours on the one who made some **effort to win them** rather than the one who refused to ask me nicely.'

If you replied, as well you might, that you felt that the distinction
and antiquity of your family absolved you from the need to canvass,
the people would refer you to precedent and time-honoured custom,
pointing out that they have always wanted to have their votes
solicited in a civil if not submissive manner. For example, they gave
their votes to Marcus Seius in preference to Marcus Piso; yet Seius,
though a knight of considerable distinction, could not protect himself from conviction in the courts, while Piso was a leading nobleman
of unblemished reputation and egregious eloquence. On another
occasion they did not vote for Quintus Catulus, who was an aristocrat, a scholar, and a truly good man; nor for Gaius Serranus, who
may have been a fool but was certainly a nobleman; nor even for
Gaius Fimbria, who was a 'new man' but at least endowed with
some force of character and common sense – no, it voted of all people
for Gnaeus Mallius, who was distinguished by no family tree, but
only by his total lack of principle or talent, and the sordid and des-
13 picable quality of his private life. In lofty strain the people might go
on: 'Unto thee, Oh Laterensis, I lifted up mine eyes – but you were in
Cyrene! I, rather than my allies, should have had the benefit of your
talents. The greater your value, the greater the loss when I could
not find you. Like a thirsty man in a dry land I longed for your
genius, but you abandoned and deserted me. You did indeed stand
for the tribunate of the people when the times cried out for those
very qualities which you possess of eloquence and courage. But
when you dropped your candidature, what was I to think? That
you felt unable to guide the nation in tumultuous times? If so, I must
perforce have doubts about your courage now. That you were
unwilling to guide it? If so, I must suspect your determination. But
in fact I hope that you were saving yourself for another time. And
if that was so' – the Roman people are still speaking – 'I have called
upon you now; now is the crisis you were waiting for. Stand now for
the office which will give you the best opportunity to be of use.
Whoever the aediles are, my games are much the same. But it is a
matter of profound significance who the tribunes of the people are.
So either fulfil the expectations you once stirred, or else, if you really
prefer it, I will award you the less significant office of aedile that
you are canvassing for so half-heartedly. But if you want the high
offices which your talent so deserves, you must learn, I think, to
solicit my favour with a little more deference and respect.'

(*b*) Noble Birth, and Local Support

Cicero then discusses the claims of noble birth in elections, and shows how, on the other side, 'new men' from the municipal towns of Italy have the advantage of support from their fellow-townsmen, and their neighbours.

Pro Plancio, 14–24:

That is the kind of thing the people would say to you, Laterensis; now listen to what I have to say. It is not the business of this court to investigate the reasons for your defeat, unless it was due to bribery. Otherwise, if we must condemn every man who gets elected over the head of another with a greater claim than he, there is no further point in canvassing, counting votes, or announcing the results, because as soon as I have seen the list of candidates, I can
15 tell you that one, say, is of consular family, another of praetorian, and the rest of equestrian standing. Their records are all clean; they are all equally virtuous and honourable, but, since status is status, praetorian must give way to consular, equestrian must not compete with praetorian. It will be the end of all political followings, campaigning, contested elections, and the right of the people to elect what magistrates they will; the result will be a foregone conclusion lacking any of the usual surprises – just the same dreary routine year after year. As it is now, we are regularly surprised that 'x' was chosen or 'y' rejected; at the elections strong currents of feelings surge, and the assembly, like some vast, deep ocean, bubbles and seethes as the tides of their favour ebb and flow from one candidate to another – how ridiculous to ask for cool logic and rational selection rather than
16 these exciting waves of emotion and impulsive choice! That is why I refuse to let you challenge me to invidious comparisons, Laterensis. The people like this voting system, which shows them men's outward professions but conceals their secret intentions, and makes it possible for voters to be free agents while promising anything they are asked. Why then should you demand that the courts must settle what the elections cannot? Laterensis claims that his status gave him a better right to election than Plancius. If, gentlemen, I object to such a criterion of entitlement to office, he will doubtless ask me for a better. Answer: the present one. The fact that Plancius was elected is to my mind adequate proof of his right to be so elected.

And it is futile for his opponent to ask why Plancius rather than himself. I could offer several answers: that the reasons are obscure; that they are unprintable; that the people made a mistake. I should be extremely reluctant to make that last suggestion, but even if I did, I ought to be free to do so without harming my client in any way, since it would only mean that the electorate had followed inclination rather than logic – and you, Laterensis, have nothing to gain from such an admission.

17   I only wish that, by defending the people's right to choose and by showing that Gnaeus Plancius gained office honourably by the same legitimate route which has always lain open to men of equestrian birth like myself, I could persuade you to eliminate invidious comparisons between the two of you, which are bound to lead to back-biting, and bring you back sooner or later to the real issues that lie behind this prosecution. If Plancius is your inferior by reason of his equestrian birth, the same must apply to all your other fellow-candidates, since they were all sons of equestrians. Comment is clearly superfluous, and I find it remarkable that you have taken issue with the candidate whose tally of votes most greatly differed from your own. Certainly, whenever I am jostled in a crowd – as happens – I do not, for my part, accuse the man at the top end of the Forum when I am at the bottom, but rather the one who actually bumps into me and treads on my foot. Yet you have made no com-plaint against a brave fellow like Quintus Pedius or my own distinguished friend here, Aulus Plotius, but have chosen to regard the man who pushed them out of first place as more responsible than

18   the ones who pushed you out of any place at all. Then, strangely enough, you have also chosen to make the prime issue between you and Plancius one of birth and family status. Here you are un-questionably his superior and I see no harm in admitting the fact. But when I was a candidate for the consulship and other offices, the same could equally well have been said of me in relation to my competitors. And it is perfectly possible that the very thing which you find so despicable was Plancius' greatest asset in the election. Look at it like this: your family is of consular status on both sides. So it is probably reasonable to assume that anyone who supports the nobility and thinks it is the finest institution on earth, and therefore also admires you for your family portraits and distinguished ancestors, is bound to have voted for you as aedile. There is no

doubt about that at all. But if there are just not enough supporters of the nobility, you can hardly blame us for it.

19   I think we can pursue the matter of your origins further still. You, Laterensis, come from the borough of Tusculum. It is of very ancient standing, crowded with more consular families, including the Juventii, than all the other Italian boroughs put together. But Plancius comes from Atina, a town of relatively recent origin, with few distinguished members and situated some way from Rome. All this must have made a great difference to your respective candidatures. Which of the two do you think are more vigorous in their support of their favourite sons? The men of Atina or the men of Tusculum? Those of Atina I know, because I live nearby, were absolutely thrilled when they saw the father of my most distinguished friend, Gnaeus Saturninus here, elected first aedile and then praetor, since he was the first to win the honour of curule office for his town as well as his own family. But the men of Tusculum have never, as far as I know, shown much enthusiasm for the honours of their fellow townsmen, presumably because their consulars are two-a-penny and not, I am sure, because their borough lacks that friendly spirit which I have found so prevalent in my own home

20   town. Certainly, speaking for myself and my brother, I can say that the very fields and hillsides supported us when we gained office. But you would never hear a man of Tusculum boast even that Cato was his fellow-burgess, though he was in every way Rome's greatest citizen, nor Tiberius Coruncanius, nor indeed of all those members of the family of Fulvius; no-one even mentions them. But anyone you meet in Arpinum, whether you like it or not, will insist on talking to you, possibly about me and certainly about Gaius Marius. So that is the first factor we must take into account. Plancius had behind him the burning enthusiasm of his fellow-townsmen, while you, Laterensis, raised about as much support as you could reasonably expect from men who had grown *blasé* about high honours.

21   Then again, your burgesses may perhaps be unmatched in distinction but they are few in number, certainly as compared with those of Atina. For this town is full of excellent fellows; nowhere in Italy has so many. You can see them in their thousands here in court, gentlemen of the jury, in sackcloth and ashes, begging you to spare my client. All these knights of Rome, all these tribunes of the treasury, to say nothing of the common people who do not come to

court but were present at the elections to a man, all of these brought to Plancius' candidature a great body of support and considerable influence, as you may imagine. Not only did they ensure that he got the backing of the Teretina tribe, which I shall discuss later, but they gave him great prestige, made him the focus of all attention, and provided him with a solid, vigorous, and indefatigable following. For of course these boroughs feel a strong bond of loyalty to their

22 neighbours. And I can assure you, gentlemen, that all that I am saying comes from personal experience, since my own Arpinum is close to Atina. Now these bonds of neighbourly feeling deserve our admiration and devotion; they have ever fostered our ancient traditions of concern for one another; they are neither coloured with spite nor characterized by deceit; they are unadulterated and sincere, lacking that veneer of affected emotions so typical of urban and suburban society. Plancius enjoyed the unanimous support of the men of Arpinum, of Sora, of Casinum, of Aquinum. The populous districts round Venafrum, Allifae, and in fact the whole of that rugged hill-country we call home, which supports its sons with simple and undeviating loyalty, felt itself honoured by his election and elevated by his new distinction. And from those same boroughs there have come today delegations of Roman knights to make public testimony for Plancius, with a deep anxiety for his present plight which matches their enthusiasm at his candidature, since to lose one's property on conviction is a worse fate even than failing to win

23 honours. To sum up: you, Laterensis, had the better pedigree; but Plancius had the better local following both in his borough and in the country round about – unless we assume that you were equally helped by Labicum, Gabii, or Bovillae, though they are almost too insignificant even to be able to produce representatives to go to the festival of the Latin League. We might add to my client's advantages, if we may, the fact that his father was a tax-collector. You regard this as a disadvantage, but everyone knows that in the battle for high office it is an enormous help to have the tax-collectors on your side. They include the cream of the equestrian class, the glory of the state, and the bulwark of the *res publica*. And no-one will deny

24 that their enthusiasm for Plancius' candidature was unbounded. No wonder: his father had long been director of one of the collecting syndicates; he was greatly admired by his colleagues; he canvassed painstakingly; he made it clear it was his son for whom he was

asking a favour; Plancius' own services to the order while quaestor and tribune were generally agreed to have been considerable; success for Plancius was felt to mean success for the class and better opportunities for their own children.

(c) A Virtuous Youth, and an Outspoken Father

After mentioning Plancius' public career, and his work in Macedonia, Cicero applauds his private life, and scoffs at the accuser's charges of immorality. He then gives an interesting account of the prejudice that might be aroused by a father who was an *eques* with a reputation for outspokenness.

Pro Plancio, 29–35:

A man's private life is not normally publicized, but when it is, he may derive much credit from it. So too with Plancius. Yet I shall say nothing of this; nothing of his life at home nor of his private relations, with his father first of all, though I believe that all the human virtues stem from close family affections, and Plancius, like most children, almost idolized his father, while also loving him like a companion, brother, and friend; nor shall I mention his relations with his uncle, with all his kith and kin, and with my most distinguished friend, Gnaeus Saturninus, who is here in court today, and you may deduce from this evidence of his deep anxiety about the fate of Plancius how eager he must have been for him to secure the aedileship at the elections. Nor shall I say anything of my own feeling that, when Plancius is in danger, I myself am in the dock beside him; nor anything of the crowds of worthy citizens who throng the court in clothes of mourning. And yet, gentlemen, these are substantial, unequivocal marks and proofs of Plancius' good character; they are not the clichés of law-court language, but actions which bear the authentic stamp of sincerity. It is an easy task to canvass by shaking hands and making flowery speeches; but such superficial appeals will stand no close scrutiny, since distance lends enchantment, and they are subjected to no strict test or examination.

30 But when, Laterensis, you see the support that Plancius commands in court today, are you still surprised he won the aedileship? After all, his public achievements and his private life were equally praiseworthy; he was inferior only in family name; he was your superior in the support he enjoyed from fellow-burgesses, neighbours, and

business partners, and in the credit he gained when men remembered what he had done for me; he was your equal in excellence, honesty, and uprightness.

This is the life whose quality you denigrate by innuendo. You make vague allegations of adultery despite the absence of substance or suspicion in the charge. Not content with inventing charges, you even coin new epithets like 'deuterogamist' with which to blacken his character. You allege that he took a 'friend' with him to Macedonia for immoral purposes; that is not an accusation but a reckless, filthy slander. You say he raped an actress: well, a group of young men are supposed to have done this once in Atina, exercising an ancient privilege at festival-time, and one peculiar to provincial towns. Is that not excellent proof of my client's virtuous youth, gentlemen, that he has to be accused of something which was legal, and even then the accusation is discovered to be groundless? He did, I admit, release a convicted criminal from prison on one occasion in a moment of folly – as indeed you know – but it was as a favour to a young kinsman of excellent character. Anyhow, a warrant was soon out for the man's re-arrest by order of the praetor. And that, gentlemen, is the sum total of the allegations made against my client, on the basis of which you are expected to feel doubts about his honour, his uprightness, and his integrity.

'Nevertheless,' says Laterensis, 'Plancius must pay for what his father did.' What a monstrous claim, totally unworthy of your principles! A man's career is at stake; Plancius stands to lose every penny he possesses; this is an honest jury: you cannot convict the son because of what his father was like. In fact, even if Plancius was the most vile, the most despicable of men, so long as the judges had an ounce of mercy and compassion in their natures, the invocation of the very name of father should count in his favour, since we are all sympathetic to a father's pleas, which naturally arouse our tenderest emotions. In fact, however, Gnaeus Plancius is an *eques*, scion of a long line of Roman *equites*; his father and grandfather, and his grandfather's own father and grandfather before him, were all Roman *equites*, holding pre-eminent status in a highly prosperous community, much respected and very influential. Plancius' own father in his service in the army under Publius Crassus proved outstanding even among Rome's most distinguished *equites* who were his comrades-in-arms. As a result he became a leader whose

31

32

contemporaries referred to him a wide variety of problems, and
respected his judgement implicitly; he founded a number of large
companies, and was head of most of them. Not only has his life been
free from criticism, it has commanded universal admiration. And
this, gentlemen, is the father for whose failings his all too virtuous
son is supposed to have to pay. In fact, with prestige and popularity
like his, he could protect anyone, whether relative or not, and of far
less worthy character into the bargain.

33   'But his criticism of the Senate on one occasion was excessive,'
you say. Outspoken perhaps, but surely not excessive? 'Well,
intolerable anyhow.' No more intolerable, Laterensis, than those
who complain that freedom of speech for Roman *equites* is unaccep
table. What price tradition now? What price our equality before
the law and our ancient right of free speech, due after long oppres-
sion to raise its head again and rise at last like a phoenix from the
flames of civil strife? Need I remind you of the abuse which in the
past the *equites* of Rome have hurled at some of her noblest citizens?
Such as, for example, the cruel, bitter, and unrestrained denunciations of the tax-collectors against Quintus Scaevola, despite his pre-
eminent reputation for ability, fairness, and integrity? You remember how Granius, the auctioneer, met Publius Nasica, the consul,
in the Forum on his way home after he had suspended all public
business? 'Why so sad, Granius?' he asked. 'Nobody to raise the
bidding today?' 'That's not the trouble,' he replied, 'but no visiting
envoys to bid the consul's price.' On another occasion Granius met
one of our most powerful tribunes of the people, Marcus Drusus,
who at the time had a number of political schemes up his sleeve. He
saluted Granius in the usual way with a 'How are you doing,
Granius?' 'I expect *you* are doing plenty anyhow', was the reply. In
fact, Granius found many opportunities to exercise his caustic wit
with impunity, even at the expense of Crassus and Antonius. But
nowadays the quality of political life is so deadened by our petty
self-esteem that, whereas a mere auctioneer like Granius used to be
free to spread derision, now a Roman *eques* is not free even to register

34 his indignation. And it was in indignation that Plancius' father
spoke, not in mere abuse. And he only protested to protect himself
and his associates from victimization and severe financial loss in
Asia. The Senate was being prevented from giving Rome's *equites* an
answer, though such a privilege had never been denied Rome's

enemies. Such manifest injustice roused the fury of every tax-collector; Plancius senior merely paraded his bitterness more openly than most. Others kept quiet about the general resentment; Plancius went further than the rest in his words and gestures, by which he gave vent to all their feelings. Mind you, gentlemen, I know from personal experience that much of what Plancius is supposed to have said he never said at all. I have found that I sometimes let slip a remark that is not the result of preparation but is made in the heat of an argument or in a moment of irritation; as a result, as happens, a wisecrack just slips out – nothing outstandingly witty, but yet not just plain vulgar; and the consequence is that, whoever makes a jest, it gets attributed to me. I am perfectly happy to be credited with some *bon mot* which seems to me to do credit to a scholar and gentlemen, but not to be held responsible for every Tom, Dick, and Harry's second-rate catchphrase.

(d) Bribery and Popularity

Some detailed argument about the *lex Licinia* (of Crassus, in 55) against brotherhoods (*sodalicia*) shows that they were organized in order to secure the votes of one tribe at a time. In consequence, a jury was, by senatorial decree, to be selected from those tribes which the accused was said to have bribed; this the accuser in this case failed to do – or so Cicero alleges. Getting votes by bribery and by popularity are not the same thing; the prosecutor is challenged to name the tribes said to have been bribed by Plancius.

Pro Plancio, 37–48 (abridged):

The general feeling of the Senate when we passed the *lex Licinia* was that a man would be best known to the members of whatever tribe he had either given money to or managed to corrupt by means of that disgraceful form of monetary distribution perpetrated by the associations which are euphemistically known as 'brotherhoods'. We reasoned that, since the tribes nominated for the jury would be the ones most closely attached to the defendant as a result of his bribery, they would play the part of jurymen and witnesses. Certainly it seems singularly hard on the defendant, but since they were bound to be either fellow-tribesmen or particularly closely associated with him, he could hardly raise any objections. But the question we must now

ask, Laterensis, is, what tribes did you nominate for the jury? The
Teretina, of course. That was fair enough, certainly predictable,
and consistent with your sense of principle. Of course you had no
option but to nominate the tribe whose votes you repeatedly
claimed Plancius had sold and bought, and for whom he allegedly
acted as middleman, especially since its members were pillars of
respectability and paragons of principle. But what about the
Voltinia? You enjoyed making vague allegations about them too.
Why did you not nominate them? And what dealings did Plancius
have with the tribes you did nominate, the Lemonia, Oufentina, or
Clustumina, let alone the Maecia which you only put up to provoke
rejection, not as a serious suggestion for the jury at all? Gentlemen,

39 have you any doubt whatever that Laterensis selected you for his
jury because what he wanted was not a legal verdict but one that
was personally and politically motivated? Do you seriously imagine
for one moment that there was any other reason for his failure to
nominate the tribes most closely linked with Plancius than that he
knew they had been honourably canvassed and never bribed at all?
You, Laterensis, have totally ignored the fundamental principle on
which we passed this law – can you deny the suggestion that your
choice is biased and most inequitable? . . .

43 But you argue that, as he had corrupted the Voltinia and bribed
the Teretina tribes, Plancius would not now have a word to say in
front of either of them. But what would *you* have to say in front of
them? Not one of them would be acquiescing in your accusations by
his silence, nor would any be supporting you in the witness-box. If
Plancius had the choice of tribes, he would probably have chosen
the Voltinia since they were close friends and neighbours, certainly
he would have chosen his own, the Teretina. If he had had to
nominate a president for this court, Gaius Alfius, our president,
would have been his first choice; he knows Plancius well; he is a
neighbour, a fellow-Teretine, a most respectable citizen, and the
most just of men. His scrupulous fairness, and indeed his manifest
goodwill towards Plancius, which he makes no effort to conceal and
therefore must dispel all suspicion of ulterior motive, is more than
adequate proof that Plancius had nothing to fear from his fellow-
tribesmen. His first choice for president is one of them.

44 Of course I am not blaming you for failing to select the tribes to
which Plancius was well known; I am merely trying to show you

that you are not acting in accordance with the intentions of the Senate when they passed this law. None of them would be listening to you; you would have nothing to say. If you suggested that Plancius was a professional middleman for bribes, you would be greeted with disbelief, incomprehension, and derision. If you accused him of being popular, they would be listening to you readily enough, but the defence would confidently admit the charge. Do not imagine, Laterensis, that, when the Senate passed these laws to curtail bribery and corruption, they had any intention of outlawing canvassing, sollicitation, or the courting of popularity. There have always been men of complete integrity who have wanted to be popular among

45 their fellow-tribesmen. Even my own order, the Senate, has not been so contemptuous of the people as to refuse to cultivate it by such slender means as are at its disposal. We would certainly not discourage our children from keeping up contacts with their fellow-tribesmen, from cultivating their affections, from canvassing on behalf of their friends, nor from expecting reciprocal services from them in return. This sort of service is as old as the hills and an abundant source of kindness and goodwill. I certainly followed it myself when the pressures of political ambition required it; I have seen our most distinguished citizens do likewise; and, goodness knows, today we need as many popular and influential citizens as we can get. What really would provoke the fury of the Senate and make every decent citizen's blood boil is the professional organization of electoral bribery, which divides the people and tribes into units whose votes are then guaranteed at a price. Prove, Laterensis, by evidence or by any means within your power, that Plancius followed this technique of vote collecting, that he ever acted as middleman, or that he ever made any promises or distributions of bribes. But if you succeed, I can only express surprise at your refusal to employ the weapons which the law afforded you. For if your accusations are true, then Plancius and I must find it not only intolerable to have to endure the stern judgement of his fellow-tribesmen but impossible even to look them in the face . . .

48 So choose for yourself just one tribe, Laterensis – whichever happens to suit you. Demonstrate, since the onus lies on you, who was the middleman that held the cash, and who acted as dis- tribution-manager. And if you prove unable to do so – and I suspect you will not even know how to start – I will tell you how Plancius

did get his votes. Is that fair? Do you agree? Certainly, I doubt if
we can better reduce the issue between us to its barest essentials.
You are silent, Laterensis. But it is no use pretending; you cannot
wriggle out of this. I repeat, I demand, I insist, I require, I adjure
you, I will not take 'no' for an answer: substantiate your accusation.
I repeat, choose any tribe you like whose votes Plancius won and
show the slightest evidence of misdemeanour – if you can. I will then
in my turn show you exactly how he really got their votes. I shall
treat Plancius exactly as I would yourself. If I asked you to account
for the votes of the tribes you won, you could explain whose support
had gained them for you; so, too, I maintain that I can and shall
explain to you in detail, though you are his opponent, exactly how
my client won the votes of each of his tribes.

(e) Electoral Processes: Nobles and 'New Men'

Cicero now rebuts some of Laterensis' assertions. The election had been
held twice; Cicero claims that the first time had been equivalent to winning
the crucial first (*praerogativa*) century in the *comitia centuriata*, and that on
this occasion the election had been a 'snap' vote with the specific object of
eliminating corrupt practices. A defeat in an election for aedileship or
tribunate did not presage an unsuccessful subsequent career, and, as
examples from Roman history showed, did not slight a man's honour,
especially when a defeat was partly due to his having stood on principle.
Cicero then deals with a suggestion of collusion, and goes on to argue that,
while all holders of the same office have the same rank, they are very unequal
in the amount of honour they achieve, and what the Roman people look
for in their magistrates is honesty, and not great talents or technical skills.

Pro Plancio, 49–54, 59–62:

But from the way I am speaking you would think that Plancius
had failed to get elected at the first election-meeting. Quite the
reverse; besides, on that first occasion, corruption was out of the
question, since the election was conducted by a consul whom we all
respect as an authority generally, and who was also personally
responsible for the very laws against bribery which we have been
discussing. Furthermore, he held the election without notice, quite
unexpectedly, so that anyone who might have contemplated bribery
had no chance whatsoever to arrange it. The tribes were summoned,
the votes cast and counted and the result announced – just like that.

Plancius was easily first and there neither was, nor could be, any suspicion of crooked dealing. In the *comitia centuriata*, as you know, one century casts its vote first, and its choice assumes an almost divine significance; whoever wins its vote is bound to be elected consul, even if he does not top the poll. And that is just one century. What then do you find so remarkable in Plancius' election to the aedileship, when not just one century (which is a small section of the populace) but the whole Roman people voted for him? In his case it was not just one century of one tribe casting the vital first vote,
50 it was the whole assembly which cast it. That was the moment for you, Laterensis, if you had felt it consistent with your own self-respect and had wanted to do so; you could have followed the example of so many of your fellow-nobles when they won rather fewer votes than they expected; that was the moment to get an adjournment of the elections and go down on bended knee before the Roman people and, with due humility and self-abasement, to beg them for their votes. Had you done so, I have no doubt that they would have rallied to you, one and all. For it is almost unknown for a nobleman, especially one of unblemished character and reputation, to be rejected by the people when he grovels for their votes. But, very rightly, you thought your own self-respect and personal integrity was worth more than the aedileship; so do not try to have your cake and eat it; you have what you value more highly – stop pining for what you value less. My own order of priorities has always been to strive my utmost first to deserve high office, then to be thought to deserve it, and then, and only then, (though most would put this first) to win it. And when the Roman people do confer high office on a man – as a mark of their esteem and not as a reward for personal solicitation – it is even more satisfying to him.

51 You feel, Laterensis, that you have failed to live up to your ancestry and to the achievements and distinctions of your late-lamented father. How can you face them, you ask. Do not give it a thought – it is far more likely that those same ancestors of yours, in their infinite wisdom, would disapprove of your excessive whining and complaints about your defeat. After all, in your father's life-time one of our leading nobles, Appius Claudius, failed to win the aedileship, despite the support of his brother Gaius, who was one of Rome's most influential and distinguished citizens. But he went on

to win the consulship at the first attempt. Your father was there
when one of his closest friends, the excellent Lucius Volcatius, and
Marcus Piso likewise, suffered some small rebuff in their attempts
to win that aedileship you want so much, but then went on to win
every other high office which the Roman people can bestow. Your
grandfather could have told you how even Publius Scipio Nasica
failed to become aedile, even though he was, I suppose, one of Rome's
greatest heroes; and how Marius, too, was twice defeated for the
aedileship but then became seven times consul. And we all know
that Lucius Caesar, Gnaeus Octavius, and Marcus Tullius all
52 became consuls after being rejected for the aedileship. But never
mind defeats in the aedileship, since, after all, many of those who
failed to win it have thought the Roman people had done them a
favour by saving them the expense. But Lucius Philippus failed to
become military tribune, for all his eloquence and noble birth;
Gaius Caelius failed to become quaestor, despite a distinguished
record at home and in the field; Publius Rutilius Rufus, Gaius
Fimbria, Gaius Cassius, and Gnaeus Orestes were none of them
elected tribunes of the people, but all later became consuls, as we
know. All of this your father and forefathers might very well point
out to you without any wish to comfort you in your defeat or indeed
to mitigate the slight you feel was put upon them, but simply to
encourage you to persevere in the career you have followed from
your early youth. Believe me, Laterensis, you have suffered no loss
of face – indeed, if you consider it dispassionately, your defeat is in
some sense to your credit. People noticed, you know, when you
refused to swear to uphold Caesar's agrarian law, and withdrew
your candidature for the tribunate. You were only a youngster then,
but you made it quite clear where you stood on a major issue of
principle; in fact you made a much more courageous stand than
some who have now held office, a stand perhaps too explicit for one
53 of your limited political experience and high aspirations. So I think
you may safely assume that on an issue in which there was such a
great divergence of opinion you gave some offence by taking such a
bold line, enough offence possibly to have cost you the aedileship on
this occasion, but certainly not enough to cost you any other office
if you are a little more careful and tactful in the future.

Consider your next argument: Laterensis claims, gentlemen, that
there must have been collusion, because Plancius was elected by

almost exactly the same tribes as Plotius. But as they were the two men who were elected, it is hardly surprising that they won roughly the same tribes. You may perhaps argue that this does not account for the fact that in some of the tribes they also got almost identical numbers of votes. But on the contrary, that too was perfectly predictable, since they had both been virtually declared elected at the first meeting. And not even this is a reason to suspect them of collusion; indeed, our ancestors clearly expected that for the aedileship the candidates' votes might be equal on occasion, since otherwise they would not have arranged for such ties to be settled by lot.

54 You also claim that at that first election Plotius promised the votes of the Aniensis tribe to Pedius, and Plancius those of the Teretina to yourself, but that they then stole them back again and kept them for themselves for fear of a close result. What sort of logic is that? Can you seriously argue that, while they were uncertain of how popular opinion stood, these men, allegedly in collusion, were prepared to forfeit the support of their own tribes to help you; but once they realized the extent of their popular support, they wanted to keep everything they could get for fear of a close result – as if by then there was the slightest risk of a close decision or a narrow victory. . . .

59   You also asked me whether I thought that, as the son of a Roman *eques*, it had been easier for me to win high office than it would be for my son who is of consular family. Well, even though my aspirations for him outrun those I have for myself, I have never expected that he will find the path to office easier than I. And moreover, in my efforts to make him feel that I have shown him the way to office rather than won it for him, for all his tender years, my constant advice to him has been the same as that which Atreus, son of Jupiter, gave to his sons:

> 'Be ever on your guard, for plots and snares
> Encompass Virtue's path, while Jealousy
> Scowls down upon you . . .'

you know how the rest of it goes. And of course what that excellent and talented poet wrote was not written for the non-existent children of the mythical King Atreus, but was rather striving to inspire us and our children to noble and honourable deeds.

60   Pursuing this line of argument, you also asked if Plancius could

have got any further had he been the son of Gnaeus Scipio. He could not have gained the aedileship any more effectively, but he would now have the advantage of being much less envied for it. For the various rungs on the ladder of political promotion are no different for the highest or the lowest, but they bring very different degrees of glory to their holders. None of us, for example, would claim to be a match for Manius Curius, Gaius Fabricius, Gaius Duillius, Aulus Atilius Calatinus, Gnaeus and Publius Scipio, Africanus, Marcellus, or Maximus. Yet we have all gone up the same rungs of the ladder as they. But glory is a different thing from rank; its highest degree is won by the greatest merit, and many are the steps on the ladder to it. The highest political honour is the consulship, and so far some eight hundred men have won it. But if you look into it carefully, you will find that barely a tenth of those can be said to have won true glory or renown. Nevertheless, you, Laterensis, are the only one who has ever questioned a man's election to the consulship on the grounds that he could have got no further had he been Lucius Junius Brutus, say, who freed Rome from tyranny. Certainly Brutus could have held no higher office, but he could, and did, achieve a higher, indeed an outstanding, measure of glory. In the same way Plancius is no less a quaestor, or tribune, or aedile for being of less than the noblest lineage; and the same is true of the innumerable others of

61 similar rank who have held these offices. You make great play of the triumphs won by Titus Didius and Gaius Marius, and then enquire what Plancius can show to match them. The men you mention did not win office because of their triumphs; they won triumphs because the offices entrusted to them were those in which success brings triumphs. You deride his lack of military experience; but in fact he served in the ranks in Crete under Quintus Metellus here; he was military tribune in Macedonia, and also quaestor, taking

62 only such time off duty as he felt able to spare for my protection. You ask whether he is a full-blown orator – he does not even think he is, which is the next best thing; and whether he knows his law – anyone would think he was being sued for giving wrong professional advice. You can only criticize a man for being ignorant of technical questions if he lays claim to knowledge and is then found wanting, not if he is only too willing to confess he never studied them. What we want from our candidates for office is not a specious eloquence, specialized know-how, or technical skills, but solid worth, honesty,

and integrity. When any of us buys a slave, if we were buying him as a carpenter or plasterer, however honest he might be, we would naturally be angry if he had none of the skills for which we bought him. But if we were buying a slave to be a steward or shepherd, our sole concern would be that he should be honest, hard-working, and conscientious. So too with the Roman people when they are choosing magistrates to be the stewards of the *res publica*; if such men possess some specialist knowledge, so much the better; if not, they are perfectly satisfied with solid merit and a clean record. Orators and lawyers are few and far between, even if you include every one who claims to practise those professions. If no-one else deserves high office, there is not much future for a large number of the best and most distinguished of our citizens.

The rest of the speech is devoted to Plancius' services to Cicero. Whether he was acquitted or not is uncertain.

64. POMPEY AND THE REVIVAL OF THE NOBLES IN POLITICS

In 54, too, Quintus Cicero went to serve with Caesar in Gaul; Caesar had been delighted at the news that he was coming. *Ad. Q.f.* II, 10, 4: 'Caesar wrote to Balbus that the packet of mail containing Balbus' letter and mine had been delivered to him so completely soaked through that he didn't even know that there was a letter from me. But he had deciphered a few words of Balbus' letter, to which he had replied; "About Cicero, I see you've written something which I have not been able to make out; but as far as I can guess at the meaning, the news is the kind I'd hope for rather than expect to hear".'
After the conference at Luca, Cicero had written to Atticus about the foiling of Domitius' bid for the consulate of 55. *Ad Att.* IV, 8a, 2: 'But if it is true – and I don't know whether it is – that they have lists of future consuls no less long than the list of those who have been elected in the past, what could be more wretched than his plight – unless it be the plight of the *res publica*, in which there isn't even a ray of hope for anything better?' It seems unlikely, however, that this was true; the consuls of 54 and 53 were in fact all aristocrats, who reduced public life to a complete farce by encouraging rioting and bribery. *Ad Att.* IV, 15, 7: 'There's a hot pace being set in bribes – the proof? – The interest-rate rose from 4 per cent to 8 per cent on July 1st . . . Money makes the claims of one candidate as good as those of any of the others'. So Cicero wrote in July, 54, and in the end the consuls of 53 were not elected till July, 53, and those of 52 had not yet been

elected when Clodius was murdered in mid-January, 52. His followers ran wild, cremated his corpse in the forum and, whether by accident or not, burned down the Senate-house. Pompey, the *interrex*, and the tribunes were asked by a *senatus consultum ultimum* to restore order. Pompey acted as promptly as usual, garrisoned the city, and was appointed sole consul by decree of the Senate proposed by Bibulus and Cato, Caesar's most irreconcilable enemies. This commission, which allowed him to bind to himself the whole of the military population of Italy, and did not involve ending his governorship of Spain, won Pompey from Caesar, to whom he was no longer attached by marriage ties, since Julia, Caesar's daughter, had died in 54, as did the child she had borne. Pompey refused a new marriage alliance with Caesar's family, taking instead the daughter of Metellus Scipio to wife, and his new father-in-law as colleague in the consulate for the last part of 52. The consuls of 51, 50, and 49 were all nobles, 3 of them being of the same family, the Claudii Marcelli. Crassus had also died in 53, defeated and treacherously murdered by the Parthians; Pompey's desertion of Caesar in 52 thus seemed to make it certain that political power would polarize around these two great generals and their supporters.

Pompey's sole consulate saw much new legislation, including new laws against rioting and bribery. Under these, Milo was brought to trial for the murder of Clodius, and was condemned despite Cicero's defence; we are told, however, that the literary masterpiece which survives was not the speech actually delivered. There were also laws about provincial governorships, the results of which were, firstly, to remove the bar on tribunician vetoes on the Senate's choice of consular provinces, and, secondly, to compel Cicero to undertake the government of Cilicia, a term which lasted from 31st July, 51 till 30th July, 50. A law passed by the ten tribunes this year, and with the support of Pompey, also granted Caesar in advance the right to stand for a second consulship without personal canvass. This law, known in the contemporary literature as 'Caesar's *ratio*', was to be the real issue on which the civil war was to break out. Caesar maintained that any infringement of his '*ratio*' was an infringement of his honour (*dignitas*), his opponents were determined not to allow him to be consul for a second term unless he went through a period as a private citizen, and thus became liable to prosecution – and they had made it all too clear that such a prosecution would take place. Even this Caesar was in the end ready to concede, if he could be guaranteed a return to a Rome not garrisoned by the troops of Pompey, who had thrown overboard his friendship. However, his enemies would concede nothing, confident that with Pompey, who declared that he could raise an army in Italy by lifting his little finger, they could crush Caesar.

VII. The Provinces in the *Res Publica*

65. ADVICE TO QUINTUS

From the speech *Pro lege Manilia*, spoken in 66, until the *De officiis*, published in 44, Cicero consistently maintained three things:

1. That governing the provinces was an aspect of a public man's life in the *res publica*, and that the provincials are human beings, just as much as the Romans themselves.

2. That a sense of justice, together with competence and incorruptibility are qualities fundamentally necessary for a governor to have.

3. That these are not enough, but they must also be accompanied by humanity and approachability.

These ideas appear sporadically in the forensic speeches, including the Verrines, (published in, or shortly after, 70), but they are treated systematically in the first letter to Quintus (*Ad Q.f.*, I, 1), which was written about 60, and is clearly not a private letter, but a pamphlet addressed to a wider public. 'Controlling the part of the *res publica* now in your hands (i.e. as governor of Asia) is not a question of luck, but mainly an exercise in judgement, and a question of hard work (4). . . . And since fortune plays either no part at all, or only a minute part, in your sphere of duty in the *res publica*, it seems to me that everything rests on your character and self-control. . . . Your province is in a state of complete and unbroken peace, yet it could utterly ruin an idle governor, though it could also delight a wideawake one (5). . . . For what trouble is it to control those over whom you rule if you can control yourself? This may be indeed a serious problem to other people, just as self-control is very difficult for them; but you have never found any problem at all in self-control. Certainly there ought never to have been any problem for you, as you seem to have the gift of self-control naturally, even without any training and education, while in fact the education you have had is good enough to improve a character of even the worst type. You always resist the temptations of money, pleasure, and

possessiveness, and since this is so, I suppose there is some danger
that you won't be able to control some rascal of a business-man, or
grasping tax-contractor' (7). Cicero then goes on to praise his
brother's incorruptibility (8–9), to praise those members of his staff
selected by Quintus himself, and to urge him to keep an eye on
those he got by the luck of the draw from among the junior magistrates, and on all the servants of the governor's court: in 3 years,
however, Quintus had become less unquestioningly trusting of his
staff (10–12). 'See that it is common knowledge that your ears hear
what is actually said, and are not the sort that pick up whispers and
imaginary tales for the sake of a profit. See that your signet ring is
not some mere implement, but, as it were, yourself in person, not
the servant of another's will, but the evidence of yours. Let your
attendant be what our ancestors wished him to be; they thought
that an attendant's post was not intended to be a place of profit, but
a post to which men were promoted for hard work. Therefore they
hesitated to appoint to the post anyone except their own freedmen,
and those they made do their bidding just as if they were slaves.
Let your lictor be the instrument of your mercy, not of his own, and
see that those axes and rods he bears before you are symbols which
signify his rank, and not his power. See that the whole province
knows that the life and family and reputation and fortune of every
man under your government is close to your heart. See that it is
widely known that you will come down heavily not just on those
who have taken any form of bribe, but also on those who have given
one; this will put an end to bribery' (13). It was not that Cicero
wanted to criticize Quintus' existing staff, he said, but he should
watch any provincials on the staff especially carefully – 'men are
not so concerned to protect the reputation of those with whom they
are not going to have to live; and since they know all the roads that
lead to profits, they do everything for money' (15). In dealing with
the slaves, 'there's much advice I could give, but the shortest and
easiest rule to keep is that their behaviour during your progress
through Asia should be the same as if you were travelling the Appian
Way; they should think that it makes no difference whether they
are arriving at Tralles in Asia or at Formiae in Italy. If you have a
notably reliable slave, let him show his reliability in your private
and household affairs, but do not let him have anything to do with
any of your public functions, or any part of the *res publica*. There are

many things which can perfectly well be entrusted to reliable slaves, yet they should not be entrusted to them in the interests of avoiding gossip and criticism' (17). 'So, let these be the foundations of men's opinion of you (your *dignitas*); first your own personal incorruptibility and self-control, next, the integrity of all who are with you; then add an extreme caution in choosing your associates, both natives and Greeks, and a firm, continuous control over your household (*familia*) (18). These principles and rules of life are capable of supporting both your judicial decisions, and all those others you have made, and also the strict honesty which evoked criticisms I was glad to hear in those cases about which I have heard complaints,' (19) . . . since the complaints emanated from rascals. 'You see, without complete incorruptibility on your part, I should not find it easy to get these decisions of yours upheld, nor the others which you have made in the same spirit of strict adherence to the honest course. So, see to it that you remain strict on the bench; don't become slack under pressure; keep your severity the same for all comers. Even so, of course, it does not do a great deal of good if your own legal judgements are conscientiously and impartially given, unless the same is true of those to whom you delegate any part of your responsibility (20). . . . You must also be ready to listen, to be kindly in cross-examination, and to be conscientious both in satisfying the parties to a case and in expounding your decisions. C. Octavius was remarkably good about this; in his court the chief lictor kept quite still, the court-attendant said nothing, every man spoke as often as he wanted, and as long as he wanted. In this respect, perhaps he was too mild, except that his mildness went with strict decisions; Sulla's supporters were forced to restore what they had got by intimidation; those who had made wrongful decisions as magistrates had to submit to the same legal code themselves when they became private citizens. His strictness would seem harsh if it were not sweetened by the sauce of human kindness. But if it is welcome in Rome for a man to have a mild manner, just imagine how welcome it must be in Asia. In Rome, men are proud and independent, their freedom is unfettered and their wilfulness uninhibited; there are innumerable magistrates and means of redress; the people can apply pressure and the Senate its influence. But in Asia, just think of all those citizens and allies, all those cities and other communities, all looking to the verdict of one person. They have no right of appeal, nor means of making a complaint; the governor has no Senate or popular meetings to face. And since this is so, a well-educated man of good natural qualities has a duty, in a position of so much power, to exercise that power with such mildness his subjects want him to be the only person with any power at all (21–22). . . . And in my opinion, the objective of all those who govern others is that all who will be under their jurisdiction should be as happy as possible; this is the touchstone by which everything should be tested. . . . When a man is in charge of anything, whether it is allies and citizens, or even slaves and dumb animals, he must put first the interests of those in his charge (24). Everyone agrees, I hear, that you are putting a great deal of work into this; the local authorities are not incurring any new debts, and you have relieved many of some of the load of their old ones; a number of centres where the buildings were ruinous and almost uninhabited have been given a new lease of life by you . . . You have put an end to civil disorders and party quarrels, and have ensured that the local authorities are run by councils composed of the men of quality (*optimates*). In Mysia, you have put down brigandage . . . and you have established peace throughout the province. . . . You have made the local authorities finance their own expenditures and pay our levies by making equitable demands on all their inhabitants. You have made yourself approachable, you have listened to anybody's complaints; nobody is prevented by lack of resources or lack of supporters from approaching you, and this is true not only when you are sitting on your magisterial bench, in public, but also when you are in your own private room at home. In sum, there is nothing at all harsh or cruel in the whole of your government; everything is pervaded with a spirit of mild and humane mercy (25). . . . Therefore, put all your heart and soul into following the line you have followed hitherto: love those whom the Senate and Roman people have committed to your honour (*fides*) when they put them under you; protect them in every way, and be anxious for them to be as happy as it is possible for them to be' (27). Cicero then discusses the tax-contractors, and argues that the Roman demands are no more severe than those of their previous governments; from there, he passes to the earliest surviving justification of the Roman Empire: 'Besides, the province of Asia should bear this in mind too, that foreign invasion and civil disturbances would never have left it free of every kind of catastrophe, if it were not under the control of this empire of ours. And since our empire cannot possibly be held together without taxation, they ought to be content to contribute some part of their income for a state of permanent peace, and an end to rioting' (34).

An exact parallel to this last claim is put by Tacitus into the mouth of the Roman commander charged with suppressing the revolt on the Rhine in A.D. 70 (*Histories*, IV, 73–4).

66. MORAL ISSUES IN GOVERNMENT

Cicero's next work on the provinces is now lost; it is clear, how-ever, that in *De re publica*, he laid down some precepts for the government of the provinces. This work was published in 51, shortly before he went to Cilicia, and, writing to Atticus from Cilicia, (*Ad Att.* VI, 2, 9) 'If I do that', he says, 'shall I ever dare to read, or to touch those volumes which you praise so much?'; and in another letter, (*Ad Att.* VI, 1, 8) 'I'm in the right, especially as I bound myself to virtue, and gave six books too as security that I would do right, those books that I am delighted to know have your approval'. Cf. *Ad Att.* VI, 3, 3.

Further clues come from *De officiis*, published in 44; Cicero there discusses the virtues of public life as part of the virtue of courage; 'Public life', he declares (I, 72), 'should be the career of all those endowed by nature with the ability for it; they should not hesitate a moment in standing for office and running the *res publica*; this is the only way a state can be governed, and a great spirit be shown'. Peaceful achievements are rated more highly than military ones (Cicero's own, of course above all, (77–78)), and moral courage more highly than physical. In *De officiis*, I, 83ff., he perhaps reflects on his own personal experiences: 'Managing public affairs has its attendant dangers; some of these affect politicians, some the *res publica* itself; some men have to risk their lives, others their reputa-tion and popularity with their fellow-citizens. We must therefore be more ready to face dangers to ourselves than to endanger the state, and to risk our own fame and glory rather than anything else we value'. Cicero then gives examples of people who would not subordinate their own personal position to their country's interests, and adds (84), 'There are also people who don't dare say what they think, even if they are right, because they are afraid of being criticized. In general (85), those who are going to govern the *res publica* should abide by two of Plato's maxims, one that they should keep their eye so determinedly on what benefits the citizens that they forget their own profit, and subordinate all their actions to the service of the citizens; the other, that they should be concerned for the whole of the *res publica*, so as to avoid having an eye to one part and neglecting the others. Managing the business of the *res publica* is like managing that of a ward; the estate must be managed for the advantage of the beneficiary, not for that of the manager. But those who promote the advantage of one sectional interest, and neglect the others, introduce into the state the most vicious possible elements, dissension and party-strife, and when that happens, men become divided into the 'friends of the common people', and the 'servants of all the men of standing', while few pursue the interests of everyone. As a result of party strife (86), the Athenians endured an appalling upheaval, the Romans not merely suffered political quarrels but even the disaster of civil wars. These are things that a responsible and brave man, one who has earned a leading position in the *res publica*, will avoid like poison; he will rather give himself over entirely to the *res publica* and avoid the pursuit of wealth and power, working for the whole *res publica*, and serving the interests of everyone. He will not use false accusations in order to damage any-one's reputation or popularity; he will be so utterly tenacious of honourable and upright principles that he will risk unpopularity and even the danger of death, for their sake, rather than renounce them (87). The most lamentable thing of all though is self-seeking and competition for offices – on which Plato also has a good maxim – 'Those who quarrel among themselves about which of them is to manage the *res publica* behave exactly like sailors quarrelling about who is to steer a ship'; he also advises 'We should consider as enemies only those people who bear arms against us, not those who merely want to manage the *res publica* in the way that they think best'. . . . Nor (88) should we listen to those who think that one should harbour bitter resentment against personal enemies, and that to do this is the mark of a man of spirit and courage; surely there is nothing more commendable, nothing more indicative of a great and distinguished man than to be able to put away resentment, and to be merciful? In a free people, of course, where there is equality before the law, we must also be approachable, and serenely balanced (as it is called); we shall thus avoid losing our tempers if people make ill-timed requests or outrageous demands, and avoid getting into a futile sulk, which merely makes people dislike us. And yet, we can approve of mildness and mercy only in so far as they are united to strictness in applying the letter of the law, for the *res publica* must have that strictness to make satisfactory administration possible at all. Nevertheless, every penalty imposed, and every verbal reproof should avoid humiliating the sufferer, and should have as its object the welfare of the community, and not of the judge passing sentence or castigating the offender. We must see to it (89) that any punishment is proportionate to the offence, and that there is no victimization of some, while others get off scot-free. But the fault most to be avoided in sentencing is acting under the influence of anger. . . . Anger must be renounced in every circumstance; we must cherish the hope that those who govern the *res publica* will be like the laws, which pronounce sentence at the bidding of justice, not of anger'.

Turning to temperance, Cicero comments (99) that 'We should also exercise a sort of respect for all men, upper and lower classes alike; for to neglect a man's opinion of himself shows that a person is not so much arrogant as utterly inconsiderate. Of course, in our relations with other people, there is a difference between justice and consideration for them. Justice demands that we refrain from injuring our fellow men, consideration that we refrain from hurting their feelings; this is where above all we can see the essence of what is proper'. Having then considered men's conduct as being controlled by their talents, career, and age, Cicero turns to the duties of magistrates; 'A magistrate', he says, (124) 'has a particular duty to understand that he represents the state, and therefore he must uphold its honour and dignity; he must uphold the laws, give every man his legal due, and remember that they are entrusted to his honour' (*fides*).

In book II, Cicero's discussion passes on from good deeds done to individuals to services to the *res publica*: 'Some of these', he says (72), 'affect the citizens collectively, other services affect them individually – these are the services which bring the greater measure of popularity. If possible, we should pay attention to serving both community and individuals, but we should be no less concerned to see that, while we serve individuals, our concern for them should serve the interests of the *res publica* too – certainly not be a disservice to it. . . . In the first place, then (73), an administrator will have to see that each man is secured in his own possessions, and that there is no impost on the property of individuals . . . because it was primarily in order that men should be secured in the possession of their property that political organizations of all sorts were established. For even if nature herself led men to form communities, it was in the hope of safeguarding their property that they began to look for the protection provided by civilized life. . . . The leading principle in the conduct of all public business (75) and administration is that it should be impossible to entertain even the slightest suspicion of avarice. . . . There is no vice more repulsive than avarice, (77) especially in the leading citizens, and those who govern the *res publica*. For, to make money out of the *res publica* is not just dishonourable, it is criminal, and wicked. . . . And besides, the ruling classes have no readier means of winning the support of the common people than by employing self-discipline to restrain themselves'. Cicero then goes on to criticize the Roman forms of social relief to the poor, land-allocations and remission of debts.

67. CICERO AS A PROVINCIAL GOVERNOR

Cicero was not anxious to govern a province himself; he was well aware of the pitfalls (*Pro Plancio*, 87), and it would be fair to call him an unwilling victim of Pompey's law of 52. 'Rome, Rome, my dear Rufus', he wrote to Caelius (*Ad fam.* II, 12, 2), 'stay in it and live in its sunshine. All foreign service, as I decided early in my life, is mere eclipse and obscurity for those whose energy is capable of shining at Rome'. His letters from Cilicia contain constant imprecations to Atticus to see that he was not kept in his province for more than one year. *Ad Att.* V, 11, 1 (for example): 'For heaven's sake, while you're in town, take every possible step that can be taken to prevent my term in the province from being extended'. Similar requests appear in letters to both the consuls of 50, when he wrote to congratulate them on their election, and to other leading men such as Cato. But in the provinces he visited he claimed to practise what he preached. *Ad Att.* V, 11, 5: 'So far, we have made our progress through Greece, and I tell you that I have no criticism to make of any of my staff. They seem to understand my attitude, and the terms of their service in my retinue; it is clear that they are bearing my reputation in mind. For the rest, they will remain as they are – if that proverb 'like mistress, like maid' is a true one – for they'll get no example of misconduct to follow from me. . . . But if that is not enough, I will take some stricter measures. Up to now, you see, I have been sweetly reasonable, and, as I expect, am doing some good'. Cicero had not even reached Cilicia; he was still in Athens, where he had spent 10 days.

He travelled to his province unbelievably slowly; he took 6 days to get from Athens to Delos, 11 to reach Ephesus from Delos; he then stayed 5 days at Ephesus before reaching Tralles on July 27th and Laodicea, the first town in his province, on the 31st (*Ad Att.* V, 12, 13, 15). Nevertheless he assured the Senate that he 'could not have arrived earlier than the 31st of July because of the difficulty of the journey, both by land and sea' (*Ad fam.* XV, 2, 1). 'I intend', he wrote from Tralles, 'to make straight for my army' (whose mutiny had just been surpressed), 'and to devote the remaining months of the summer to campaigning, the winter months to legal business' (*Ad Att.* V, 14, 2). These two duties were the essential functions of a provincial governor.

He carried out his intentions. *Ad fam.* XV, 2, 1: 'I thought it most consistent with my duty, and most advantageous to the *res publica*, to attend to the army, and the military situation. . . . I therefore thought I should march through Lycaonia and the lands of the Isaurians, and through Cappadocia. . . . So I proceeded with my army through that part of Cappadocia which adjoins Cilicia, and camped at Cybistra, which is a town in the region of the Taurus mountain.' He still travelled slowly, however; on the way, he wrote to Atticus. *Ad Att.* V, 16: 'Although the tax-contractors' servants are leaving while I am in the middle of a march, and actually on the road, I thought I must snatch a moment to write to you in case you think that I have forgotten your instructions. So here I am sitting right on the road to write you a very brief summary of what needs a longer description. I want you to know that on July 31st I reached this wretched province, which has simply been ruined for good. Everyone was hanging on my arrival; I stayed 3 days in Laodicea, 3 at Apamea, and the same at Synnada. All I heard was about *per capita* taxes that had been demanded, and could not be paid, how the investments of every man jack of them had been sold, how the cities were moaning and groaning at the atrocious behaviour of a creature who is not even human, but some wild and savage animal; they're desperate, as you might guess. However, the pressure on the wretched communities is off, because they are not put to any expense for me, nor for my staff-officers, nor quaestor, nor anyone at all. I'd have you know that I don't merely refuse free hay, and what the law of Caesar allows (this law was passed in 59, and is frequently praised by Cicero, even when opposing Caesar politically) . . . but not even firewood, and none of us ever accepts anything but four beds, and a roof over our heads, and sometimes not even a roof, as we just stay in our tents. The result is that they flock to meet us in an unbelievable way, from the farms and villages and every town; I swear that they are coming to life even on my arrival; the justice, the clean hands, the mercy of your friend Cicero . . . has surpassed the expectations of all'.

Provincial governors wrote to the Senate; these public communications, however, were not as secret as their modern counterparts. *Ad Att.* V, 18, 1: 'I have written to the Senate on the military situation; if you're at Rome, please have a look and see whether you think it should be delivered.' This letter also shows that Cicero hoped that Pompey would be sent out to take over the war against the Parthians which was threatening; his comments on the forces at his disposal show the sort of problem often facing provincial governors. *Ad Att.* V, 18, 2: 'My force is small, but I hope it is fully with me in spirit. Deiotarus (King of Galatia) will double my forces when he comes with his full strength. Our allies are proving much more reliable than anyone else has yet found them; they find my attitude of co-operation and self-control hard to believe. I am conscripting Roman citizens, and having corn-supplies taken in from the farms for storage in defensible places. If the occasion arises, I shall fight, otherwise I shall rely on my position . . . . (3) But I beg of you, please, be in Rome in January if the question of my successor is still unsettled by the first of that month. I know that nothing will go wrong for me if you are there; the consuls are my friends, Furnius, one of the tribunes, is on my side – all the same, we need your persistence and good sense and influence'. It is hard to remember that Atticus was not even in the Senate, and belonged to the class of *equites*, who are often said to have taken no part in politics.

Cicero's letters also reveal facts about the client kings; he had sent his own son and his nephew, the son of Quintus, to stay at the court of Deiotarus: 'I thought it would be best while I'm on summer campaign', he wrote (*Ad Att.* V, 17, 3). King Ariobarzanes of Cappadocia had also been made his special responsibility, as a dispatch shows (*Ad fam.* XV, 2, 4). The reason was perhaps that the king was heavily in debt to Pompey, to whom he paid '30 Attic talents a month, which does not even cover the interest. . . . The king does not pay anyone else anything; he cannot; he has neither treasury nor any revenues, . . . there is no place so stripped bare as that kingdom, nobody on earth so hard-up as the king' (*Ad Att.* VI, 1, 3–4). Appius Claudius had added new tax burdens, but quite in vain; Cicero was being pressed to satisfy M. Brutus, but would do no more than give posts as prefect to two men, M. Scaptius and L. Gavius, though even this was against his principles, and more than he would concede in the province itself – 'yet they are not in business in my province'. A second dispatch to the Senate explains the emergency caused by the Parthians' invasion across the River Euphrates, and recounts Cicero's own advance to Mount Taurus, the division between Cilicia and Syria. *Ad fam.* XV, 1, 3–6: 'Despite the fact that I am aware that our allies are lukewarm, and wavering in anticipation of revolutionary developments, yet I hope that those who have already tasted my policy of mercy and integrity have become better disposed to the Roman people, and that Cilicia too will become more reliable if it also has a taste of my administration. . . . (5) Yet the present situation here is that if you do not send an expeditionary force of the largest normal size, there is a real danger that you will lose all the provinces which provide the Roman people's revenues. This being so, it is no use putting the slightest hope in the present recruiting-drive in the provinces; not many men are available, and those there are run away at the slightest scent of danger. . . . The forces of the allies are no help either; owing to their harsh treatment and the injuries they have suffered at the hands of our empire, they are either so weak that they cannot help us much, or they are so disaffected that we cannot expect anything from them, nor trust them with anything. (6) King Deiotarus, I think, is with us, so are his forces, such as they are; he is well disposed. Cappadocia is helpless. The other kings and petty chiefs are neither strong nor reliable'.

Despite these forebodings, Cicero's campaign, when it took place, was a resounding success. *Ad Att.* V, 20, 3–5: He made a forced march into the Cilician plain on hearing of a Parthian advance, reached Tarsus on 5th October, and launched a sweep against the tribes of Mount Amanus, 'whose watershed divides Syria from Cilicia, a mountain always full of hostile tribes. Here, on 13th October, we killed a large force of enemy troops, captured some very well fortified posts by a night attack under Pomptinus and a dawn attack under my own command. The troops hailed me as their General (*Imperator*). For a few days I camped on the very spot used by Alexander the Great before the Battle of Issus – and he was a better general by a long chalk than either you or I'. Cicero stayed there 5 days, plundered and devastated Mount Amanus, then left, for 'Free Cilicia' where he beseiged and captured, after 57 days, the town of Pindenissum, 'the most strongly fortified town of a tribe who live in a state of perennial warfare'. The town fell on the morning of 17th December, the feast of the Saturnalia, the Roman equivalent of Christmas. The troops 'celebrated in style, since I gave them all the booty of the town except for the prisoners'. These were enslaved, and sold two days later.

The administration of justice engaged Cicero principally after his campaign. *Ad Att.* V, 21, 6–9: 'At the end of our summer campaign, I put Quintus in charge of the troops' winterquarters, and of (Eastern) Cilicia; I sent Q. Volusius, the son-in-law of your kinsman Tiberius, into Cyprus; he's a reliable fellow, and sets a marvellous example of integrity. He is to be there for a few days, to prevent there being any complaints from the handful of Romans in business there that they have never had access to the processes of law – one has to go to Cyprus, because the inhabitants can't be summoned to appear outside the island. (7) I myself set out for the Asian (i.e. western) end of the province. . . . After I crossed Mount Taurus, I was most eagerly expected by the districts of Asia under my rule; in six months of my government they had had no demands by letter, and no demands for billets for anyone. Every year before me the autumn used to be the season for making money on that score; the prosperous cities used to pay large sums to avoid having troops billeted on them for the winter; the Cypriots used to pay 200 Attic talents; I am not taking one penny from the island – it sounds like an exaggeration, but it's the literal truth. So they are dumbfounded at these concessions, but I don't allow them to pay me in anything but speeches. . . . (9) On February 13th, the day I am writing this, I have arranged to hold a court at Laodicea, to hear cases from Cibyra and Apamea; from 15th March, I shall hear cases from Pamphylia, Lycaonia and Isauria at the town of Synnada; from 15th May, I shall move into Cilicia, where I shall spend June (left in peace by the Parthians, I hope); July, if all is well, I must spend in making my way back through the province on my way home.'

These sessions were the formal assizes. Cicero had of course held *ad hoc* courts and given decisions on cases ever since he had arrived in the province, and had been reversing Appius Claudius' rulings - 'healing the wounds inflicted by Appius' (*Ad Att.* V, 17, 6; VI, 1, 2). While he was still in camp at Tarsus, he had been visited by a certain M. Scaptius. *Ad Att.* V, 21, 10–12: 'I had promised him, for Brutus' sake, that I would see that the people of Salamis in Cyprus paid their debts; the fellow thanked me, and asked for the post of prefect. I said that I never gave such posts to businessmen'. We later discover that Appius had made Scaptius prefect of Salamis; he had used his troop of cavalry to beseige the local council in their council-chamber until 5 of them died of starvation; Cicero had heard of it, and had peremptorily ordered them out of the island. 'I told Scaptius that if he wanted to be prefect in order to secure the execution of his contract, I would see to it myself; he thanked me, and left. . . . (11) To keep my promise, when the men of Salamis came to me at Tarsus, and Scaptius with them, I told them to pay up. They started long speeches about the contract, and about their wrongs at Scaptius' hands. I refused to listen. I urged them, begged them, to carry out the contract, and then said I would force them to do so. They not only did not refuse to settle, they even said that they would be paying out of my pocket, since the money they owed to Scaptius was less than the amount they usually gave to the governor, and which I had refused to take. I praised their attitude. "Right", said Scaptius, "let us work out the sum;" before this, I had laid down in my edict that the maximum rate of interest should be 1 per cent per month (12 per cent per year), compound, calculated by the year. Scaptius demanded 4 per cent per month (48 per cent per year), which was what was in the contract. "What?", said I, "can I give a ruling contrary to my own edict?" Scaptius (12) tried unsuccessfully to make Cicero change his mind, then to persuade him that the Cypriots owed him 200 talents, when it was in fact 106, and the Cypriots could prove it. Cicero supported their arithmetic. The only thing that he would agree to was an adjournment without allowing the interest to lapse, though he knew that even this was more than he ought to have conceded. But he acted the way he did in order to try to satisfy M. Brutus, who, a subsequent letter reveals, had deceived Cicero. *Ad Att.* VI, 1, 5: 'I never once heard from Brutus that the money in question was his own; indeed I have his note, in which he says "The men of Salamis owe money to two friends of mine, M. Scaptius and P. Matinius", and commends them to me'. Incidentally, he got no thanks from Brutus for this, nor for other concessions Cicero made him in connection with debts due from the King of Cappadocia, Ariobarzanes.

Cicero was more successful with the tax-contractors. *Ad Att.* VI, 1, 16: 'I name a day, reasonably far off, I proclaim that, if the provincials have paid before it, I shall not allow interest above 1 per cent per month; if they don't pay by that date, it will be the rate of interest in the contract. So, the Greeks pay up at a reasonable rate of interest, and it pleases the contractors greatly, if they also get a full ration of complimentary speeches, and plenty of invitations'.

He was also pleased with the way the assizes went. *Ad Att.* VI, 2, 4–5: 'At my assizes in Laodicea from February 13th to May 1st, for all the districts except Cilicia, I have achieved wonders. Many cities are clear of all debts, many have substantially cut them down, every one has revived under a regime of Home Rule, and using their own customs and laws . . . . (5) The magistrates of the Greek towns themselves had been terribly corrupt too. I personally investigated into those who had held office in the last 10 years; they made a clean breast of it, and so, without my disgracing them, they shouldered the repayment of their public debts themselves. So, the common people had nothing to groan over when the cities paid not only what they owe for this quinquennium, in which they had not paid a penny, but for the last quinquennium as well. So I am the apple of the tax-contractors' eye. . . . The rest of my conduct on the bench too shows my experience, and I combine mercy with complete approachability; I make myself available in a way not at all usual in the provinces; I don't keep a porter on the door (to screen visitors); I stroll about at home before daybreak, just as I used to when standing for office. This is very popular, and a great concession; I don't find it a bore yet, because of my experience long ago'.

Cicero's last letters show his concern about his successor; the political struggle at home prevented the Senate from nominating a successor, but it also refrained from extending his command specifically. So, when a new quaestor was appointed, Cicero was content to hand over to him, despite his youth, and the fact that he was, in Atticus' opinion, 'a mere boy, a silly fellow, lacking both the standing and self-control needed'; but Cicero felt he had no alternative except to stay himself, which he was resolved not to do. *Ad Att.* VI, 6, 3: 'While the Parthian threat hung over us, I had decided to leave Quintus in charge, or even to remain myself for the sake of the *res publica*, and contrary to the Senate's decree'. We must assume from this that the decree had appointed Cicero 'for one year from the day he enters the province', and therefore it was strictly contrary to the decree to remain longer, though the normal rule was that a governor stayed till his successor arrived. 'Apart from Quintus,' he adds, 'there was nobody I could promote above my quaestor without insulting him – especially as he is a man of noble family'.

The close connection of provincial government with the *res publica* is shown by the stream of letters from Cicero which have survived, together with those from his informants in Rome, especially M. Caelius Rufus, whom he had defended, and Appius Claudius, his predecessor, who had evidently written to Cicero complaining of criticism or worse (*Ad fam.* III, 8); Cicero also wrote to neighbouring governors (Minucius Thermus in Asia, P. Silius in Bithynia, and his quaestor, P. Furius Crassipes, *Ad fam.* XIII, 53–57; 61–65; 9, etc.), to solicit favourable consideration for his friends and those of Atticus (*Ad Att.* V, 20, 10). We can hardly doubt that Cicero himself received a great many similar letters, especially as we hear of those from Brutus (*Ad Att.* VI, 1, 7), who 'writes very politely to you about me, but when he writes to me, even when asking a favour, he always writes in an uncivil, arrogant, and tactless way.'

For a very different picture of Roman provincial government, see Cicero's account of the governorship of Verres in Sicily (Sections 9–11 above).

VIII. The End of the *Res Publica*

68. CIVIL WAR AND RECONSTRUCTION

As Cicero left Cilicia, Rome was drifting to war; the circle of
Cato had won the support of Pompey, and gained control of the
political machine in Rome. This they used to force Caesar either to
fight or to submit to a situation in which he could not become consul
again without rendering himself liable to the prosecution which his
enemies had sworn that they would launch. Pompey met Cicero on
December 25th at Formiae, South of Rome. He said that Caesar
hadn't a chance if he decided to fight (*Ad Att.* VII, 8, 4), and certainly his political allies' attitude makes it clear that they too were
convinced that they would win if it came to war. When Caesar
crossed the Rubicon in January, 49, however, they were soon
proved wrong; Italy sided with Caesar, some communities on his
arrival, some anticipating it. Pompey and the consuls, taking the
majority of the Senate with them, retreated ignominiously to
Brundisium, and thence to Epirus in Greece. There they gathered
their forces with a view to returning to Italy when they were strong
enough, and recovering their position by war; they also spoke of
revenge on those who had not supported them, and of conducting
a new Sullan proscription and terror (*Ad Att.* VIII, 11, 2; IX, 10, 6
etc.).

Four years of civil war followed; Caesar established a temporary
government in Rome while he eliminated the forces behind his back
in Spain and in the city of Marseilles. He then crossed to Greece,
and (in 48) defeated the Pompeians in battle at Pharsalus, followed
Pompey to Egypt, but found on his arrival that he had been murdered, and that there was a civil war between the supporters of
Cleopatra and those of her brother (who was also her husband).
In Egypt, he eventually vindicated the claims of Cleopatra, used
her resources to re-equip his forces, and recovered the allegiance of
the client-princes of Asia Minor, who, as Pompey's *clientes*, had

naturally taken his side in the Pharsalus campaign. His campaign against them ended at Zela, in Pontus (the 'veni, vidi, vici' battle), where the aspirations of the son of Mithridates were also destroyed, and late in 47, Caesar returned to Rome.

He had already stated his political position in an open letter, a copy of which was sent to Cicero in March, 49. *Ad Att.* IX, 7C: 'I shall not imitate Sulla; I want to try a new way of conquest, and to fortify my position by mercy and generosity'. Caesar must have hoped that this policy of mercy, and the amnesty granted to all who surrendered after Pharsalus, would cause his opponents' party to break up; had he not done so, it is hard to believe that he would have regarded the recovery of the Eastern provinces, or even his affair with Cleopatra, as more important than following up his victory at Pharsalus.

But if this was so, Caesar was disappointed, since the force which his surviving opponents gathered in Africa was a strong one, and contained many highly-esteemed senators. Caesar crossed to Africa late in 47, and the decisive battle took place at Thapsus in April, 46. Many of the leaders fell in battle, and others committed suicide after it; these latter included Cato. Caesar returned to Rome later that year, and his attitude encouraged Cicero to hope for a time that the *res publica* would be restored. He wrote many letters to his friends still in exile, to encourage them with the hope of recall, and in the Senate he spoke the *Pro Marcello*, which he published, quite certainly during Caesar's lifetime.

(a) Conciliation and Compromise can Save the
Res Publica

M. Marcellus, as consul in 51, had been one of Caesar's bitterest opponents. Cicero wrote to Servius Sulpicius about his recall. *Ad fam.* IV, 4, 3–4: 'In the Senate, Caesar had critized the "acrimony" (his own word) of Marcellus . . . but he suddenly took us all by surprise, and said that, though the omen might be bad, he would not refuse a request of the Senate. The Senate had risen as a man and appealed to Caesar after the name of Marcellus had been mentioned by L. Piso (Caesar's father-in-law), and C. Marcellus had thrown himself at Caesar's feet . . . Everyone who was called upon to speak before me had expressed their thanks to Caesar (except Volcatius Tullus, who said that he would not have done it had he been Caesar). So, when my turn came, I decided to break the resolution I had previously made, which was to remain silent for ever – not from idleness I assure you,

but to show my regret for the position I once had – but Caesar's generosity
and the Senate's sense of loyalty to Marcellus broke my resolution, and I
made quite a long speech of gratitude to Caesar'. This speech is the *Pro
Marcello*.

In the preface, Cicero claims that he will speak in the Senate again
because the *res publica* has been restored by Caesar's clemency. Caesar's
military victories are outstanding, and after his victories the credit he has
won by his generosity to his defeated foes in the *res publica* is also unique.
Caesar has recognised that many who fought against him had honourable
motives, and, as Caesar himself had long sought for some compromise,
many on the other side had tried hard to prevent war.

Pro Marcello, 13–18:

Listen, gentlemen, while I tell you how far Caesar's decision to
be merciful extends. All of us who went to war against him under
the impulse of some wretched, malignant stroke of fate which hit the
res publica have been acquitted of any criminal act, even if we have
been convicted of the frailty of human nature in our judgement.
Caesar has preserved Marcus Marcellus for the *res publica* in response
to your pleas; he has also restored me to my place in the *res publica*,
though nobody pleaded for me, and many other men too, whose
number and quality you can see amongst you, gentlemen. And in
so doing he is not, like an enemy, packing the Senate with supporters,
but rather showing that he really does believe that quite a number
of people went to war against him out of ignorance of the facts, and
unfounded fears, and not because they were motivated by either
14 greed or ferocity. Indeed, during the war I always thought that the
voices speaking for peace should be given a hearing, and I always
regretted that not only was peace itself rejected, but the voices of
those demanding it were repudiated too.

For my part, it was not a civil war that I then took part in – I
have never done that; I have always urged a policy of peace and
civil power, and not war and the rule of the sword. What I followed
was Pompey the man, from a sense of personal obligation not of
public duty. So deep was my debt of gratitude to him that in his
cause I knowingly and in full control of my faculties was willing to
lay down my life for him without expecting or desiring any profit
15 from my actions. I made no bones about it. I often spoke for peace
amongst you before the war began, and even after the fighting
started I repeated it, and at the risk of some danger to myself too.

Nobody will be so unreasonable as to be in any doubt about what Caesar wanted; he has always argued that those who advocated peace should not be persecuted, though he has been more resentful towards the others. This was possibly less surprising when the result of the war was uncertain, and its future hung in the balance, but now, when victory has been won, and the victor favours those who spoke for peace, there can be no doubt that it is true that he would

16 have preferred not to fight than to win. And I can vouch for M. Marcellus in all this, since he and I were always of one mind in peace and war alike. I have often watched his indignation at the language of some men I could name, and his nervousness about the atrocities even a victory would bring; we, therefore, who remember those days should feel the more happy, Caesar, at your generosity of spirit.

Now is not the time to compare the merits of either party's case;

17 we must compare their attitudes to victory. We have seen Caesar's victory, and how it was pressed no further than his successes in battle took it. We have never seen a naked sword unsheathed within the city. We have lost some citizens – indeed we have – but it was the violence of the battles, and not the resentment of the victor which struck them down; we cannot really doubt that Caesar would recall many from the grave, if he could, since he is sparing the lives of as many survivors from the fighting as he can. Of Caesar's opponents, I do no more than make explicit the fear we all shared, that there would have been too vindictive a spirit shown by them if

18 they had won. There were some of them, you know, who kept making all sorts of threats at those who fought against them, and not just at these, but at times against people who did not lift a finger, since they declared a man's loyalty was to be judged not by what he had said and thought, but by where he had been. It even seems that the gods above were punishing the Roman people for some offence or other when they caused a civil war of such calamitous proportions to break out, but that they had either had enough of it, or relented when they turned all our expectations for the future over to a general who is as wise as he is humane.

(b) Caesar's Duty to the *Res Publica*, and to Himself

Cicero goes on to urge Caesar not to take a fatalistic attitude to himself and the threats to his life. The civil war was pointless unless it is followed by restoration of the *res publica*, and only Caesar can do this. Caesar must also bear in mind the reputation he will leave to posterity.

Pro Marcello, 21–34:

Now I come to a most appalling rumour (that Caesar will be assassinated), which arouses our deepest concern about you; you must see about it, not for your own sake so much as for the sake of all the citizens, and of us above all who owe our lives to you. Indeed I hope that the rumour is false, but I shall never underestimate it, since your concern for yourself is our concern too, and if you have to err on the one side or the other, I would prefer you to be over-cautious than not sufficiently wary. But who on earth could be such a lunatic as to plot against you? Surely not one of your own circle? – there cannot be anyone closer to you than those whom you have restored to life when they least expected it. It could hardly be some of your old supporters, since it is incredible that anyone could be so mad as to think more lightly of the life of the man who is the source of all he has than he does of his own. And if your supporters have no criminal designs, you surely need not fear some threat from your political enemies (*inimici*), since all your old *inimici* have either lost their lives through their irreconcilable opposition or now owe them to your mercy. Thus, none of your old *inimici* is still alive, and those
22 who were your *inimici* have become your fervent supporters. Even so, men's minds have many mysterious and secret recesses, and we must therefore increase our concern for you, for this will increase our vigilance too. Surely nobody is so naive and politically unedu-cated, or so reckless and irresponsible, as not to know that his own life depends on yours, and so does that of everyone else? My thoughts turn to you, as they are bound to do, day and night, and I shudder at the changes and chances of fortune which afflict the frailness of our common human condition; I am filled with sorrow as I think how the very existence of the *res publica*, which ought to be immortal,
23 hangs upon the thread of one human life. If treachery, therefore, and criminal conspiracy be added to the hazards of fortune and the problem of survival in health and strength, can we believe there is any power in heaven or earth that can save the *res publica*?

Our whole way of life was destroyed by the shock of war, and, as you are well aware, Caesar, it is in ruins: it could not be helped, but you are the only person who can restore it; you must establish

judicial commissions and restore credit; measures must be taken to curb immorality and to increase the birth-rate; moral standards which have slipped almost out of existence must be tightened up
24 again by stringent legislation. Few have escaped the effects of civil war; we have seen much fighting; feelings have run high; it is no wonder that the *res publica* has been shaken; whatever the result of the war, it was bound to lose many of the features which made it great, and secured its stability, just as both commanders were bound to do many things under arms that they would not have permitted in time of peace.
25   Now, Caesar, you must heal all these wounds of war; nobody but you can do it; I was therefore sorry to hear your remark, worthy of a true and noble philosopher though it was, that you 'have lived long enough alike for nature's claims and for those of glory too'. If you like, you have satisfied the claims of nature; I could even add, if you want, that you have done enough for glory too. But despite the vastness of your achievement, it is not enough for our native land. Give up, I beg of you, that philosopher's wisdom in making light of death; don't pursue your wisdom at our expense. Many a time it has come to my ears that you repeat that same remark that you 'have lived long enough'. I would heed it only if you were living for yourself, as your destiny had intended. But your achievements have involved the future of every citizen, and the whole *res publica*. Your work is not yet done – why, you have hardly yet laid the foundations you have in mind; this is not the point in time at which to judge by your own peace of mind whether you have played your part or not; judge rather by the demands of the *res publica*.
      And what about the claims of glory, have you satisfied them too? You will not deny your appetite for that, I know, philosopher
26 though you may be. I am not suggesting that your achievements fall short of the standard required; you've done enough for many other men; the only thing you still fall short of is yourself. Any container, you know, however large, is not full when there is room for more in it. If the consequence of all your imperishable achievements was going to be that you should overcome all your enemies and then leave the *res publica* in the state it is in now, I think that you should ask yourself whether men will not be astonished at your talents rather than filled with admiration for you personally. Surely the path to glory lies in winning widespread admiration for distinguished

achievements which have brought benefits to fellow-citizens, or the land of one's birth, or the whole human race.

27   This then is the part still waiting for you to play; here the action now waits; now you must labour on to establish a *res publica*, and yourself become one of the principal beneficiaries, enjoying a calm and orderly peace. Then, and only then, will be the time to say, if you wish, that you have lived long enough; when you have paid the debt you owe your country, and, having lived your allotted span, are tired of life. Besides, what is 'long' if it has an end to it? When the end comes, all previous joys turn to ashes because there is no more to come. But that spirit of yours has never been content to be confined within the narrow bounds which nature has given each of us to live in; it has always burned with a passion for imperishable

28   renown. And the fact is that you must not think your life consists of this present period in which you live and breathe – no, I tell you your life is that period when you will live in the memories of all men, when posterity will keep you alive, and every generation will cherish your name. This is the aim you should devote yourself to; this is the audience to which you should show yourself; already it has had many subjects to excite its wonder, now it is also awaiting something to evoke its praise.

There is no doubt about it; future generations will certainly be filled with wonder as they read or hear of all you have done – the commands you have held, the provinces you have subdued, the way you overcame the Rhine, the Ocean, the Nile, your countless battles and astonishing victories and all the trophies, benefactions, and

29   triumphs they have brought. But unless you set this city on a firm and stable basis by devising the institutions we need, your name will spread far and wide, for sure, but it will have no established and settled place at home. Violent quarrels will arise among those yet to be born, as they did amongst us, with some praising and others, perhaps, criticizing your achievements. And unless you quench the flames of civil war by saving your country, far the most serious criticism will be that men will think your achievements were the work of destiny, but your failure to restore the *res publica* that of deliberate policy. Submit therefore to the judgement of posterity, which will pronounce sentence in many hundreds of years time, – and for all I know more impartially than we do; for it will judge without favour or ulterior motives and, on the other hand, without

30 any dislike provoked by envy. For even if this judgement will not concern you (though some are fools enough to think it will), it certainly does concern you now that you should not make yourself liable to have your glory eclipsed by oblivion.

Our citizens' policies have clashed; their arguments have drawn us this way and that; our disputes have not stopped at arguments about party politics; we have taken to settling them by armed might. The issues were not clear; both party-leaders were men of the highest distinction; many men wondered what was best, some what advantage or honour dictated, some even how far they could

31 go; and none knew the answer. The *res publica* met its doom in this wretched, destructive war; the victor was not a man to fan the flames of the enmity he had incurred by his successes, but rather one to put them out by his own qualities. Nor did he think that all who had provoked him deserved the fate of exile or death. Some laid down their weapons, others had them struck from their grasp in battle. But any citizen who persists in his hostility when once his life is guaranteed against danger is as much guilty of ingratitude as he is of unreasonable conduct. In fact he makes the man who poured out his life-blood in battle for the cause a better man than he, since at least the latter's mulish stubbornness can be read as a resolute determination of a kind.

32 But now, our quarrels have been broken up by the clash of arms, and subsequently calmed by the victor's reasonableness; what remains now is that all who have a scrap of sense – never mind wisdom – should all be of one mind. We ourselves cannot survive, Caesar, unless you survive, and remain committed to the same policies as you have followed before, and to which you remain committed today. And therefore, all of us who want the *res publica* to survive beg you, we urge you, to take good care of yourself and to guard your life, and, since you think there may be some undercurrent of ill-will to worry you, let me express on behalf of others also what I think myself: we do not promise you just a bodyguard and an escort, but we promise you our own persons, our own bodies, to guard and protect you.

33 To return to my starting-point; we all thank you to the limit of our capacity, and we have more thanks in store for you. We are all of one mind, as you will have been able to see from the way we have pleaded with you; but since there is no need for everyone to stand

up and say this, they undoubtedly want to hear me saying it, and I am in a way the right person to do so. Before your very eyes is happening what ought to happen on your restoration of M. Marcellus to our order and to the Roman people and the *res publica*. For it seems to me that what we all here are celebrating is not just the rehabilitation of M. Marcellus, but of every one of us. Moreover, for my own part, it is common knowledge how great has always been the fund of goodwill I bear to M. Marcellus, so great indeed that in this I am second only to his excellent and devoted brother Gaius. As long as his recall was in doubt, I devoted long hours of anxiety and effort to his cause; but now, at last, I can claim to be relieved of a great burden of care, and the worries and frustrations that went with it. So, Caesar, you have preserved for me all that I possess, you have heaped honours on me, and now you have done what I thought impossible: you have added the finishing touch to all your benefits, and my thanks to you are expressed in the realization that this is so.

(c) Caesar's *Clementia*

Caesar's mercy (*clementia*) is a theme which frequently appears also in Cicero's letters of this period; for example he wrote to A. Caecina, a friend still in exile, shortly after the *Pro Marcello*.

Ad fam. VI, 6, 8–10:

'Caesar has a temperament naturally mild and merciful, just as it is described in your excellent '*Book of Remonstrances*'. There's also the fact that he is especially well disposed to intellectuals like you, and that he makes concessions to widely-felt views when they are sincere and inspired by true regard, and not hollow or self-interested. So the general sympathy of Etruria for you will certainly make a big impression on him. 'Why, then', you may ask, 'has all this had so little effect so far?'. There are many others whose cases Caesar thinks he cannot reject if once he has made a concession to you, for in your case he has an obviously good reason for resentment. 'All right', you say, 'what can you hope from a man who is nursing his anger?' Well, Caesar will appreciate that he will get an abundant shower of compliments from the same stream that has already given him a bit of a splashing. Besides, he is an intelligent man, and gifted with foresight; he can see that you cannot be kept long out of the life of the *res publica*, when you are easily the leading citizen in a part of Italy that is far from contemptible, and that amongst your contemporaries you are unrivalled in the whole *res publica* for your natural gifts and your influence and your reputation. He will not want you to be restored as a result of the passage of time, but as his gift, and soon.

So much for Caesar. To turn to the general situation; there is no one so bitter towards the cause which Pompey took up so precipitately, and with such inadequate preparation, that he dates to call us traitors or rascals. Here is a point where I always admire Caesar for his dignity and justice and wisdom; he never speaks of Pompey except in the most honourable terms. You may think that his actions against Pompey as a public man were harsh – that's what happens in a war; it was the process of winning, not Caesar's own handiwork. Look how he has welcomed me! Cassius too is his lieutenant, Brutus has been given charge of Gaul, Sulpicius of Greece, Marcellus, who made him furious, has been restored with full honours.'

69. CAESAR AND THE LOST *Res Publica*

(a) Changing Times

Caesar's government was in no way 'republican', however. Even before the *Pro Marcello*, Cicero had written to L. Papirius Paetus, a friend.

Ad fam. IX, 17, 1–3:

'Are you not joking when you ask *me* what *I* think is going to happen about the lands of these boroughs?' (which it was feared Caesar would annex for colonies of veteran soldiers). 'Balbus our friend has been with you; you act as if I'd know anything that he doesn't know, and as if there is anything I do know that did not come from him in the first place. The boot's on the other foot; if you love me, tell me what's going to happen to me – you've been in a position to find out all about it, if not from Balbus sober, then at least from Balbus drunk. But things like that, my dear Paetus, I do not enquire into them; first because I've had a bonus now of 4 years of life – if it is a bonus, or life at all, to be alive still when the *res publica* is dead, secondly, because I think that I too know what is going to happen. What will happen is what *they* want to happen – those who have the power, that is, for conquerors will always have that. So, we should always take what is given us as enough for us; anyone who could not endure this ought to be dead. . . . (2) But if Caesar wants there to be a *res publica* of the sort that maybe he too wants, and we all ought to hope for, he hasn't got the means to do it. He has tied himself up with so many other people. But I go on too long, and it's *you* I'm writing to. (3) But make no mistake about this, it is not merely I who am not in their counsels and do not know what will happen; even our leader himself doesn't know. I do as he tells me; he does as the times dictate; so, Caesar cannot know what the times are going to demand, nor do I know what Caesar thinks.'

In a similar vein, a subsequent letter complains.

Ad fam. IX, 15, 3–4:

'I gathered from your letter, and from this one too, that you thought I could not give up political life; I used to think so myself – or at least not entirely, though perhaps virtually. You talk to me about Catulus, and what happened to him. Where's the resemblance? In his day, I too did not want to be any length of time away from the task of guarding the *res publica*; for then I had my seat at the helm, and my hand on the tiller, but nowadays I can hardly find a place in the scuppers. And do you really think that there will be fewer decrees of the Senate if I am in Naples? Why, when I'm in Rome, and pounding away in the forum, decrees are drafted in Balbus' house – that admirer of yours, my close friend. And as often as it occurs to him to do so, my name is added to the list of sponsors, and I hear that a decree has reached Armenia or Syria, said to have been passed on a motion proposed by me, before I have heard one word about the question at all'.

Resistance to Caesar ended in 45; at Munda in Spain his remaining opponents and their troops were slaughtered at the last and the most savage battle of all, which also cost Caesar many of his veteran troops. Of the leaders, only Sextus Pompeius, Pompey's younger son, escaped. After Caesar's death he tried to take a hand in the power struggle by raising a deet and putting pressure on Octavian (or, as he was later called, Augustus) in Italy. After a series of battles and truces he was eliminated in 36, and is dismissed in a contemptuous reference to 'pirates' in Augustus' *Res gestae*, XXV, 1.

(b) A Woman's Place in the Free *Res Publica*

Cicero's judgement of Caesar's rule was coloured, if not clouded, by personal sorrows. His marriage with Terentia, which had lasted over 25 years, now broke up; an unwise second match, with a much younger woman, Publilia, was a failure; but the blow that shattered his world was the death of his daughter Tullia after giving birth to a child. This was in February, 45. Cicero's old friend, Ser. Sulpicius Rufus, who had been a neutral in the first year of the civil war, was governing Achaea, or Greece; he wrote to Cicero in sympathy. Some of the ideals of the *res publica* as the two men saw them are reflected in their letters.

In *Ad fam.* IV, 5, 1 ff., Servius writes:

'When I heard the news of Tullia's death, I was most deeply moved, and terribly shocked; I had to be, and I thought what a blow it was to both of us. Had I been with you, I should have called round to express my sympathy to you in person. . . . (2) But why does your personal tragedy affect you so much? Just think how fortune has treated us up to now; we have lost everything which men ought to regard with as much affection as their families – our country, our integrity, our standing, all our offices; what could be added to our distress by this single additional tragedy? Or, what spirit that has had experience of these public catastrophes should not now grin and bear it, and think that nothing is such a blow as they are? (3) You are sorry about the *res publica*, I'm sure; you must very often have come to the same conclusion as I have, that in this day and age those people who have been allowed to pass from life to death without suffering have not been harshly treated. What had Tullia now got to inspire her with such a great passion to live? What material things, what expectations, what else to comfort her heart? Did she hope to reach a great age happily married to some young man of good family? I imagine that it was impossible for a man of your standing to choose a son-in-law from among the young fellows of today to whose care (*fides*) you'd think you could safely entrust your daughter. Or did she hope to be a mother of children,

and to enjoy watching them making their way in the world, maintaining the property they had inherited from their fathers, standing
for the public offices in the proper sequence, and enjoying freedom
of action in public life, and in promoting the interests of their
friends? But is there any of these hopes that is not dashed before it
is fulfilled? "Well, it is hard to lose a child", you may say. Yes, it is
hard, only it is harder still to put up with these other things. . . .
(5) You must turn your thoughts away from all that, and prefer to
recall what is worthy of yourself. Tullia lived long enough to satisfy
her; she was a contemporary of the *res publica*; she saw you, her father,
promoted praetor, then consul, then a member of the college of
augurs; she married young men of the best families in the land; she
enjoyed almost all the blessings of life; when the *res publica* perished,
she died. What complaint can you or she have against fortune on
this account? Lastly, do not forget that you are Cicero, one whose
habit it has been to advise, and to discuss problems with others.
Don't be like those bad doctors, who profess a knowledge of the
science of medicine when other people are ill, but cannot look after
themselves; you should rather treat yourself with what you are always
prescribing for other people, and take your own advice to heart.'

Cicero replied; after thanking Servius for his kind letter, he praised his
son for the sympathy he had shown. He then continued, *Ad fam.* IV, 6, 1 ff.:

'Sometimes I am overcome, and can hardly endure my grief, since
I have not got the compensations which other men had, whom I
regard as having been fellow-sufferers of mine. Quintus Fabius
Maximus, for instance, lost his only son when he had been consul,
and was famous for all he had done. Lucius Aemilius Paullus lost
two sons in a week Sulpicius Gallus and Marcus Cato lost excellent
sons who had promised so much, but all these men lived in an age
when the standing they had themselves attained in the *res publica*
compensated for their losses.   (2) My situation though, is that I
have lost the honours of which you speak, and which I obtained by
the most strenuous exertions, and the one consolation left to me was
what death has now torn from me. You see, my thoughts had nothing
to engage them, there was no business to be seen to for my friends,
no affairs of state demanding my attention; I had no stomach for the
forum; I could not endure the sight of the Senate; I thought that I

had lost all that I had won by the hard work that had brought me my success, and this was true. Yet when I reflected that I was in the same boat with you and some others, and when I was getting the better of the mood, and making myself put up with it all, I had some-one to go to, someone to bring me relaxation, someone in whose delightful society I could get rid of all the anguish I felt. But now, this savage blow has made even those scars which seemed to have healed break open again. Now I cannot escape from the sorrow of my home into public affairs, and find any good in them to console me, whereas before I had always a place at home to cheer me up when I came home depressed from the *res publica*. So I'm not at home, and I'm not in the courts, because my home cannot console me for the sorrow I feel for the *res publica*, nor public life for the grief I feel at home.'

Cicero consoled himself by writing a stream of philosophical treatises, a number of which have survived, *De finibus bonorum atque malorum, Tusculan Disputations, De natura deorum* among others.

(*c*) Arbitrary Government

After Caesar's death, when Cicero narrated the events following Caesar's return from the Munda campaign in his attacks on Antony (Marcus Antonius) which we know as the Philippic orations, he recalled the arbitrary character of the rule of Caesar and his circle, as illustrated by their abuse of their priestly offices for electoral reasons.

Philippic II, 78–84:

78 As Caesar returned from the campaign in Spain (after Munda), you (Antony) were the person who went furthest to meet him. You were quick to go and quick to get back, trying to impress him with your energy if you couldn't do so with your courage. By some mysterious means you became intimate with him. I must say that Caesar had this knack; if he found any spendthrift and bankrupt, he was delighted to take him into his circle once he knew that he had no principles and would stick at nothing. When your outstanding
79 talents in this direction brought his approval, by his instructions you were proclaimed as having been elected consul – and with Caesar himself as your colleague. I'm not complaining about how

you treated Dolabella, pushed forward as he was, then led up the garden path and cheated, but surely everyone knows the base treachery of which you were both guilty? Caesar induced him to stand, then took over what had been agreed was his, and you aided and abetted him in his low trick. January 1st (44) came; we were assembled in the Senate-house; Dolabella launched an attack on Caesar much more elaborate and better prepared than my present

80 speech. Ye gods, what a tirade Antony's fury evoked. Caesar made it clear that he would order Dolabella to take over his consulship before he set off for Parthia – yes, he did this, and people still say that Caesar was not a monarch though he was always doing and saying things like that. But despite what Caesar said, Antony claimed he himself had been made an augur for the specific purpose of enabling him to jam the elections or invalidate them afterwards, and added that he would do just that. What a marvellous augur! Yet just look at the man's unbelievable stupidity: in the first place,

81 without being augur at all, as consul he could equally well have done what he said he could do as augur – indeed, he could have done it even more easily. We augurs enjoy only the right of reporting omens when we see them, but consuls and the other magistrates enjoy also the right of looking for them. All right, then, this was inexperience; I suppose we cannot really expect knowledge from a man who is never sober, but just consider the impudence of the course of action he proposed. Many months before the election in question he declared in the Senate that he would either frustrate the election to be held for Dolabella by using the auspices, or that he would do what he actually did. It is impossible to predict what is going to be wrong with the auspices without deciding to watch the sky for omens; now the laws prohibit watching the sky while an election is in progress, and if a magistrate has been watching the skies he must report the fact before the election starts, and not when it is over. So Antony's impudence and inexperience are tied up with one another; he neither knows an augur's rights nor behaves like a man of honour.

82 Let me remind you of the course of Antony's consulate between 1st January and 15th March (the Ides of March, 44); he was the most insignificant and subservient lackey you ever saw; he did nothing of his own initiative; he depended on Caesar for everything; he'd even shove his head into Caesar's litter on the closed side and ask for favours which he could sell, as Caesar's equal colleague.

The day came for Dolabella's election; the first century to vote was determined – not one word from Antony; the result was declared; still silence. The rest of the centuries of the first class were called; their votes were declared; then the second class voted. It was all over in a flash – in less time than it takes me to tell you about it.

83 When it was all over, our paragon of wisdom, like Laelius of old, this augur fellow, proclaims 'Election deferred'. What unparalleled cheek! He'd seen nothing, he'd noticed nothing, he'd heard nothing; he has never said – no, not even to this very day – that he had been watching for omens. All that had frustrated the election was an unfavourable omen which he had prophesied on January 1st would occur, and had seen coming all that time in advance. So you falsified the auspices, Antony; I hope that the powers that be will make you pay for it, and not the *res publica*. You frustrated the Roman people by playing about with our religion; you frustrated yourself as augur and as consul too.

I do not want to say any more now, in case I give the impression that I would render Dollabella's proceedings as consul invalid, because some time or other they will have to be laid before the

84 College of Augurs for approval. But let me call you gentlemen to note Antony's insolent contempt for others. Dolabella had no right to be consul as long as that suited Antony's book, but later, when it suited Antony, his election was perfectly valid. If it is quite irrelevant that an augur used the words that Antony used – 'Election deferred' – then Antony must admit that he was drunk when he used them. But if the words mean anything at all, I ask him as one augur to another just what their significance is.

Cicero then turns to the events of the Lupercalia (Feb. 15th, 44), when Antony offered Caesar a crown, which was thrice refused; the constant harping on this episode in the Philippic speeches shows how important it was felt to be, and how discreditable to Antony.

70. CAESAR'S MURDER, AND THE SEQUEL

(a) The Conspirators' Motives

Caesar was assassinated on the Ides of March, 44. In his attacks on Cicero, it is evident that Antony had asserted that Cicero was party to the plot. In the Second Philippic Cicero replies that the conspirators did not need any inspiration from him, and in any case, everyone who wanted to see Caesar dead was as much involved as he.

Philippic ii, 25–9:

The latest tale is that I was responsible for the plot that killed Caesar. At this point, gentlemen of the Senate, I become frightened of giving the deplorable impression that I have hired a dummy prosecutor, not just to give me credit for what I have done, but to adorn me with the laurels that really belong to others. Nobody has ever heard my name mentioned among those who plotted that glorious feat, but none of the conspirators' names has ever been kept a secret, and, never mind their being no secret, they were in fact widely publicized on the spot. I have less hesitation in saying that there are people who have boasted that they had been in the know when they hadn't, than in saying that there are people who 26 were in the know and wanted to keep quiet about it. Moreover, is it in the least likely that among that large number of conspirators, some of whom were nobodies, and others young men incapable of shielding anyone, that my name would have escaped being noticed?

Moreover, if anyone was needed to add the weight of their influence to a proposal to save our country, bear in mind who was going to do the deed. I was hardly the appropriate person to stimulate men of the name of Brutus; both the Brutuses number L. Brutus (who drove out Tarquin) among the ancestors in their family shrine, and one of them is descended from Servilius Ahala too (who assassinated Sp. Maelius for aspiring to tyranny in 439). Do you think that people with ancestors like these were going to look for inspiration from outsiders rather than from within their own family circle? Cassius' family is one which has never been able to tolerate any political boss, never mind anyone with a monopoly of power; it is incredible that Cassius should have needed me to prompt him. Cassius indeed did not even need his distinguished colleagues; he would have finished this business himself once and for all in Cilicia, at the mouth of the river Cydnus, if Caesar had 27 landed on the bank he had intended, and not on the other. As for Cn. Domitius, do you think it was any inspiration from me that spurred him on to the recovery of liberty, rather than the deaths of

his most distinguished father and uncle and the blows that his own
personal position had suffered? I could never have persuaded C.
Trebonius; I would not have dared even to try. The *res publica* owes
him a debt of gratitude all the greater because he thought the liberty
of the Roman people more precious than the friendship he bore to
Caesar, and preferred to strike off the shackles of tyranny to being a
collaborator with it. Nor did Tillius Cimber follow any lead from me
– in his case it was more a matter of admiring him for having done
the deed at all than expecting him to do it, an admiration based on
the fact that he preferred to remember his duty to his country rather
than the kindnesses he had received at Caesar's hands. As for the
two Servilii, they're Ahalas as much as Cascas; if you think it was
my urging that stimulated them into action rather than the affection
they bore their country, the very idea is ridiculous. It would take
too long to go through the list of the others – indeed the very length
of the list does credit to the *res publica*, and gives the participants
something to be proud of too.

28   Let me remind you how our shrewd detective found me implicated: 'As Caesar fell', he said, 'Brutus raised aloft his dripping
dagger and called on Cicero by name, congratulating him on the
recovery of liberty'. Was it because I was in the know that he picked
on me? Can't you see that the reason he picked on me was that he
had achieved a feat comparable with mine, and called me to witness
29 that here was a man with a claim to glory to rival mine? But
Antony is so unintelligent, he does not understand that if, as he
alleges, it is an offence to have wished Caesar dead, it must also be
an offence to have rejoiced at Caesar's death. It makes no odds
whether support is before or after the event: there is no difference
between a wish for a thing to happen and the celebration of its
occurrence. Apart from those who were happy that Caesar had a
monopoly of power, there was nobody against the plot or criticized
the deed. Everyone, therefore, is equally to blame, for all men of
standing slew Caesar to the best of their ability; some lacked the
ability to plan the deed, some the spirit, some the opportunity to do
it; not one lacked the desire to carry it out.

(b) Antony after the Ides of March

After referring again to the auspices at Dolabella's election (sec. 69(c)
above), Cicero accuses Antony of shameless profiteering.

Philippic II, 88–92:

Let us consider the auspices, which is the subject that Caesar was going to propose for debate on 15th March. What would you have done, Antony, that day? I have heard it said that you had come to the Senate with a speech ready prepared, because you thought that I was going to hold forth about the auspices which you had falsified, but which nevertheless we had to be bound by. Caesar's death put an end to your predicament that day, but you seem to think that the good fortune of the *res publica* in this put an end to your view of the auspices too.

But I have reached the point in time which these events must not anticipate. Antony took to his heels that glorious day; he was scared out of his wits; conspirator as he is, he knew that his life was virtually past hope when he took to his heels and sneaked off and found a refuge at home thanks to the kindness of those who wanted to save his life if he were sane.

89   Alas! my predictions of what was to come were all too true, as usual. When those liberators of ours wanted me to go to Antony and urge him to stand up and fight for the *res publica*, I told them, there on the Capitol, more than once, that he would promise anything so long as he was scared, but as soon as he had got over his fear, he would run true to form. So, though the other ex-consuls went off and came back, I stuck to my viewpoint; I did not set eyes on Antony that day or the next, nor did I believe that it was possible for any sort of alliance between men of the highest standing and a public enemy of the worst type to come to anything.

On 17th March, I attended the Senate in the temple of Tellus; I
90 was not keen to come, as every approach was under armed guard. What a day that was in your life, Antony! Though you have suddenly revealed yourself as my enemy, I am sorry for you because you have been your own worst enemy as well. Heavens above, what a man you might have been, what heights you might have attained had your attitude not changed! We would now be enjoying the state of peace which had been created by M. Bambalio's aristocratic young grandson, when he offered himself as a hostage; but alas it was only your fear that brought you into the ranks of the men of sense, and fear cannot keep a man up to the mark for long. Your characteristic

impudence, which shows whenever you're not scared, soon made you a rascal once again.

Yes, we might have peace now despite your scandalous behaviour at the time when others thought you a very sound man, though I did not. You took charge of the tyrant's funeral, if funeral is the right word for it. That fine eulogy was your work, so was the pity it
91 aroused, and the feelings that it stirred up; it was you, Antony, who set the burning brands afire, both those by which Caesar's body was half burned and those which set L. Bellienus' house ablaze and burned it to the ground. It was you, Antony, who launched the attacks on our houses by gangs of ruffians – mostly slaves – which we had to beat off by might and main. Despite all this, it was you too who seemed to have cleaned yourself up on the other days, when you presided over the Senate's passing of some excellent decrees – 'There shall be no personal tax-exemptions or favours granted after 15th March' for example. You yourself remember the views you then expressed about the exiles, and about personal exemptions from taxes. The best of all those you procured though, was that 'The name of dictator is banished for ever from the state'. By this act it appeared that you had taken such a dislike to monarchical rule that, because our recent master had been called 'Dictator', you were
92 removing all fear of it for the future. Some people thought that a *res publica* had been achieved; I did not. With you at the helm, I was always afraid that the ship would get wrecked. I wondered if I was wrong, or if a man could long suppress his true character. Well, you watched, gentlemen, you saw how proclamations began to be posted all over the Capitol, tax-concessions were sold, not just to individuals, but to whole communities, citizenship was granted, not just to one person at a time, but to whole provinces. And so, if these grants stand ratified, which they cannot if the *res publica* is on its feet, you have lost whole provinces, gentlemen of the Senate. For it is not just revenues, but the whole extent of the Roman people's dominions that has been reduced in this fellow's private market-
93 place. Where are the seven hundred million sesterces listed in the accounts kept in the temple of Ops? It consists, I know, of Caesar's ill-gotten gains, but it is money which could relieve us of taxation, if it is not to go back to its original owners. And I'd like to know just how Antony, who was forty million sesterces in debt on the Ides of March, had managed to get the slate wiped clean by 1st April.

Cicero then passes to further allegations of corruption by Antony. Not all these should be accepted at their face value, but they must have borne a close enough resemblance to the facts for Cicero's audience not to have been certain that he was inventing everything.

(c) The Assassins' Failure

The amnesty above mentioned, however, and the Senate's decrees did not provide a revival of the *res publica*. The common people and Caesar's veteran soldiers bitterly resented Caesar's murder; they rioted at Caesar's funeral; they supported the efforts of a certain Amatius to set up an altar and a cult to Caesar's memory. When Caesar's heir, Octavius, landed in Italy to claim his inheritance, the veterans settled in Campania offered to rise and fight for him. When he reached Rome, his acceptance of that inheritance, his borrowing of money to pay Caesar's legacies (Antony having already spent most of Caesar's capital), and his attempt to become by adoption a full member of Caesar's house were all calculated to win the support which was vociferously expressed at the games he held in July in memory of Caesar's victory at Pharsalus.

Caesar's assassins had acted without a carefully thought-out plan for after the murder. As Cicero wrote on 11 or 12 May (*Ad Att.* XIV, 21, 3): 'The deed was done with the courage of men, but with the planning of children'. Thanks to their divided and vacillating counsels, the assassins were out-manoeuvred by Antony at every point, since, as consul, the initiative lay in his hands. By mid-April he had begun to find his feet; he succeeded in ignoring the Senate's decree about Caesar's edicts, and with the aid of Caesar's secretary, Faberius, he was able to produce papers whose genuineness nobody could dispute effectively, and from the middle of April he began to do so. Cicero wrote to Cassius (*Ad fam.* XII, 1, 1): 'I see no end to the business; decrees are being invented, exemptions granted, enormous sums of money are being squandered, exiles recalled, non-existent decrees of the Senate registered'. On 27th April, he wrote to Atticus, *Ad Att.* XIV, 14, 2–4 (abridged): 'Though the tyrant is dead, I see the tyranny still here. . . . We are now enslaved to the papers of the man to whom we could not be enslaved in person. . . . (3) The Ides of March may have given our friends an entry to the realm of the gods, but they have not given freedom to the Roman people. Do you remember what you said to me, and how you exclaimed that all was lost if Caesar was given a public funeral? How right you were; you can see the consequences of that funeral. (4) You write that Antony is going to propose a motion about the provinces on 1st June; he is to have the Gallic provinces, and both he and Dolabella (the other consul, after Caesar's murder) are to have long terms; shall we be allowed a free vote? If we are, I shall celebrate the recovery of freedom; if we are not, that change of masters will have brought nothing with it but the satisfaction of having watched the deserved end of a tyrant'.

Antony also had the advantage of having one of his brothers as praetor in 44, and the other was tribune. They were thus able to keep a watch on affairs in Rome, and on Dolabella, at a time when Antony himself was visiting the veteran settlements (in May), and Dolabella seemed likely to veer towards the assassins. Antony's intention was to canvass support for his political programme, as Balbus told Cicero (*Ad Att.* XIV, 21, 2).

(d) The View of a Friend of Caesar's

There were also many senators who did not regard Caesar as having been a tyrant, but as a personal friend. They would not support, nor even sympathize with, attempts to blacken his memory in the interests of the assassins. Among these was Matius, whose dignified defence of his position has survived. He had heard that Cicero had spoken ill of him for helping Octavius with his games in July.

Ad fam. XI, 28, 2–5:

'I am well aware of the things said against me since the death of Caesar. People reproach me for my grief at the death of a close friend, and my resentment at the murder of one I loved. They claim that patriotism must come before friendship, as if they had already proved that his death was beneficial to the *res publica*. But I shall not be clever; I frankly admit that I cannot reach their heights of philosophy. To me, fighting for Caesar in the civil war meant fighting, not for a principle, but for a friend. I did not like his actions, but I could not desert him. I did not approve of the civil war, nor even of the cause of the quarrel, but I did my best to strangle it at birth. So,

when my friend won, I was not enthralled by profits or promotion –
I left those things for others who were less close to him than I, and
who have abused them scandalously. Financially, in fact, I have
become worse off by that law of Caesar's which allowed many of
those who are rejoicing at Caesar's death to retain their standing in
the state. I put as much effort into saving the lives of the defeated
party as to saving myself. (3) How can I, who wanted nobody to
be killed, fail to feel resentful at the death of the man who had the
same wish, especially when the same people were responsible for his
unpopularity and his death? "You will catch it", they say, "for
daring to condemn what we have done". Damned insolence for
some men to boast of a crime, while denying others the right even to
criticize with impunity! Why, even slaves have the right to feelings:
to fear, to rejoice, to sorrow when they want to, and not when they
are told. And that is what these self-styled "champions of liberty"
are trying to intimidate us out of doing. (4) But they won't succeed;
I shall never be intimidated into abandoning my duty and the
claims of humanity. I have never thought that an honourable death
should be shirked – no, it should be welcomed. But why should they
be angry with me? All I want is that they should regret what they
have done. I want everyone to be sorry that Caesar is dead. "Ah,
but as a loyal citizen I should be glad to have the *res publica* safe"; so
they say. But the whole of my past career and all my future hopes
are proof that that is my desire too; I don't have to put it into words;
if that's not so I can't prove it. (5) I ask you, then, seriously, to let
actions speak louder than words, and if you think that right actions
count, not to believe that I will have any part with rascals. Am I,
in the evening of my life, to change radically the principles I maintained in my youth, when mistakes are venial? or shall I unravel
my past? That I will not do, nor will I cause wanton offence; all
that I will do is to regret the death of a most distinguished man
who was a great friend of mine. If I were inclined to do otherwise,
I should never deny what I was doing, for I have no wish to be
thought a rascal for doing wrong, and a cowardly hypocrite for my
pretensions.'

This letter shows how difficult it was, if not impossible, to bridge the gap
in thought between the assassins of Caesar, and those who felt as Matius
did.

71. ANTONY'S *Res Publica*

(*a*) Brutus and Cassius Protest

In Rome, the arrival of Caesar's heir had upset Antony's plans. Caesar, as he called himself, (though we usually call him Octavian to prevent confusion with the dead dictator) now presented himself as a candidate for the tribunate vacated by Helvius Cinna when he was lynched in error for one of the assassins. This was a brilliant stroke; Antony had either to admit his candidature, or allow his adoption as Caesar's heir to go through, an adoption he had hitherto obstructed. For, only as a patrician Julius could Octavian be disbarred from election. Octavian thus drove Antony to make conciliatory moves towards the assassins, but these were dropped when the veterans protested, and Antony was then reconciled to Octavian.

Antony next repudiated Brutus and Cassius by an edict, and wrote letters to them which, they told him in a letter dated August 4th (*Ad fam.* XI, 3, 1), were 'like your edict, insulting, intimidating, and quite improper for you to send to us'. The close of their letter was no less threatening; Antony had complained that they were enlisting men, and sending agitators to tamper with the legions in Macedonia, and had attacked them in a speech for the murder of Caesar.

Ad fam. XI, 3, 3–4:

'Just reflect how intolerable it is for praetors to be unable to resign some of their prerogatives in the interest of civil harmony and freedom without being threatened by the consul with military force. As we rely on this, we cannot be intimidated by you. We do not think it right to submit to threats, nor do we agree to do so; nor do we think it is the business of Antony to issue orders to those whose actions have made him a free man. If other circumstances demanded that we should engage in a civil war, your letter would be useless; letters full of threats carry no weight with free men. You know perfectly well that we are not to be driven in any direction; and it may be the case that your threats are designed to make our sensible approach seem to be motivated by fear. (4) These are our feelings; we are anxious that you should have an important and honourable position in a free *res publica*; we shall not provoke you, but we value our own freedom more highly than your friendship. Please review very carefully what you are undertaking, and the means at your disposal; reflect on how long Caesar reigned, not on how long he lived; we pray to the gods that whatever you plan may serve the interests of the *res publica* and yourself; if they do not, we hope that the *res publica* may be preserved, and that you yourself may suffer as little as possible'.

(*b*) Cicero's View

Cicero had decided to leave Italy until the end of Antony's consulate (that is, till December 31, 44). Dolabella, who had been Cicero's son-in-law, had named him as one of his officers, so he had an excuse to go abroad. An urgent summons from Atticus recalled him to Rome after he had in fact sailed for Greece; but, since contrary winds had forced him back, he received Atticus' message. He was too late though; Atticus had summoned him for the first of August, but the letter did not reach him in time, and he missed the breach between Antony and the assassins. On August 31st, he reached Rome, and found that the topic for discussion on September 1st was not the *res publica*, as he had thought, but honours to Caesar, and he therefore did not attend, sending a note to say that he was exhausted by his journey. Antony attacked him in the Senate, and Cicero replied the following day in Antony's absence, in the *First Philippic Oration*.

A letter to Munatius Plancus, who was governing Transalpine Gaul (the area later known as Gallia Narbonensis, and now as Provence and Southern France) illustrates the political atmosphere.

Ad fam. x, 1:

'I was out of the city on the way to Greece; the call of the *res publica* brought me back in the middle of my journey, and ever since I have never been left in peace by Antony. He is not arrogant – you can find that vice anywhere – he is positively brutal, and to such an extent that he cannot even put up with the looks of free men, let alone free speech. So I am deeply concerned, not for my own life, since I have lived long enough, and (if this is relevant) I am famous enough; I am worried about our country. First of all, my dear Plancus, I am anxiously waiting for you to become consul (which was due to be in 42, the next year but one), but it seems such a long time to wait that all we can hope for is to stay alive long enough to see the *res publica* in it; but what can we hope for in a *res publica* as it is now, when everything is under the heel of a man who is incomparably the most violent and intractable we know? Neither Senate nor people has any power at all; we have no laws, no courts, nor any vestige or trace of a constitution'.

Cicero was subjected to another violent attack from Antony on September 19th, to which the *Second Philippic Oration* is ostensibly an answer, though this speech was never spoken but issued as a pamphlet. As invective, it is a brilliant piece of work; as a source for historical information it requires to be used with great caution.

72. OCTAVIAN, AND CICERO'S ATTEMPT TO SAVE THE *Res Publica*

'At the age of 19 I raised an army on my own initiative, and at my own expense, and with it I freed the Roman people from the domination of a faction which held it in its grasp'; so the Emperor Augustus wrote at the start of his '*Acts*' (*Res gestae*). This illegal act was the principal action of the autumn of 44. With this force Octavian (as he then was) marched to Rome and addressed the people. It was not a success. *Ad Att.* XVI, 15, 3: 'What a speech! I had a copy sent me. He prayed, stretching out his arm towards Caesar's statue as if to a god's, that he might attain the position and honours of his father (Caesar)'. But at least, as Atticus had written, 'The boy has got the backing, and at present stands up to Antony'; even so 'the outcome must be awaited, and the *res publica* is in too desperate a state for medicine'.

For his part, Antony concentrated his efforts on building up a strong military power in Cisalpine Gaul (the Po Valley) in anticipation of the end of his consulate on 31 December, 44, when he would have to deal with young Octavian, the military designs of Caesar's assassins who had illegally seized power in the Eastern provinces, and the unfriendly attitude of Hirtius and Pansa, the consuls-elect, both of whom had belonged to Caesar's party, but were opposed to Antony's policies.

In this interest Antony executed a number of officers and men of legions summoned from Macedonia to Italy, when they were at Brundisium, on the grounds that they had been tampered with by Octavian's agents when they refused the donative Antony offered them – Octavian's had been bigger. He then returned to Rome with a strong escort (interpreted by Cicero as an army) and threatened both Octavian, who had retired to Etruria after his unsuccessful address to the people, and Cicero, and demanded a full attendance at the Senate on 24th November. The mutiny of the legion known as the 'Martian', however, caused him to cancel this meeting; when he returned to Rome from an unsuccessful bid to recover their

loyalty, he convened the Senate on the Capitol in the evening of
28th November, and threatened hostile tribunes with death if they
appeared at the meeting. The revolt of another legion, the fourth,
announced at this precise moment, caused Antony again to modify
his proposals, though a number were passed for the purpose of gaining supporters. After this, he left Rome, when it was already dark,
and made for the province of Cisalpine Gaul, which he had been
allotted in June.

(a) December, 44

On December 9th, Cicero arrived in Rome, and wrote to Decimus Brutus
who was still in command in Cisalpine Gaul.

Ad fam. xi, 5, 1–3:

'I thought that the most important thing was for me to have an
immediate meeting with Pansa (consul-elect); he told me what I had
most hoped to hear from you. . . .   (2) I think you ought to know,
in brief, that the Roman people waits for every bit of news from you,
and pins on you every hope it has of recovering its freedom sometime. . . . For if that fellow (sc. Antony) gets a hold of the province
(sc. Cisalpine Gaul), I see no hope of safety left to us. He used always
to be a friend of mine before I found that he was in arms against the
res publica, as he is, quite deliberately, and enthusiastically too.
(3) I beg you therefore, in the same terms as the Senate and the
Roman people do, to free the *res publica* for ever from the tyranny of
a monarch. . . . It is up to you; you have to play your part.'

Decimus played his part. By a happy coincidence a dispatch
arrived from him on 20th December, the day the new tribunes had
chosen for a meeting of the Senate, and Cicero wrote to him.

Ad fam. xi, 6, 2–3:

'The tribunes of the people had given notice that the Senate
would meet on December 20th. They intended to make a proposal
about protecting the consuls-designate. So, although I had decided
not to attend the Senate before the first of January, I heard that
your proclamation had been put down for discussion that very day;

I therefore thought it scandalous that the Senate should be held without discussing your services to the *res publica* – which is what would have happened had I not attended – or that I should not be in my place if by chance there had been any resolution in your favour proposed. So I came to the house first thing in the morning. (3) On my appearance being noticed, a big gathering quickly assembled. I should prefer you to hear from others what I said about you in the Senate, and in a very large public meeting afterwards.'

What Cicero said on these occasions was published as the *Third* and *Fourth Philippic Orations*. The *Third Philippic* is in effect a call to arms to defend the *res publica* against Antony, whose behaviour, Cicero argues, was more that of a public enemy than a consul. The speech opens with a declaration of support for Octavian (referred to as Caesar), whose action in raising an army Cicero says should be endorsed.

Third Philippic, 1–8:

It is somewhat later than the *res publica's* hour of need demanded, gentlemen, yet here we are, assembled at last. Every day I have been insistent that this should happen – after all I have been watching the horrors of a war against our hearths and homes and against our persons and property not just in preparation but actually in progress under the instigation of a profligate desperado. We are waiting for New Year; Antony is not waiting, as he tries to launch a violent military assault upon the province held by that excellent citizen, Decimus Brutus, and keeps threatening that he will return from it
2 fully equipped and prepared for anything. But why are we waiting?, why are we putting things off even for an instant? New Year's Day is almost upon us, but even a short time is too long if men are not ready. Any day, any hour even, often brings disaster crashing down unless foresight has been employed. Government is not like religion; you do not wait for a given date to plan your course of action. If the first day Antony took to his heels in flight from the city had been New Year's Day, or if we had not decided to wait for New Year's Day, we would not now have a war on our hands. We should easily have smashed the reckless madman by using the Senate's position backed by popular support. For my part, I have every confidence that our consuls-elect will do this as soon as they have entered upon their offices; I have never seen a better or shrewder or more har-

monious pair. My reason for pressing the issue urgently is not just a
3 passion for victory, but for a quick victory. Just how long will private
initiative stave off the wicked atrocity of civil war? Why does public
support not reinforce it as quickly as possible? Look at young Gaius
Caesar – he's scarcely more than a lad, but he has raised a devoted
army of those veterans of Caesar's who have never known defeat;
we did not ask him to do it, we did not expect it, we did not even hope
for it because it seemed impossible. His is an astonishing, I might say
superhuman, quality of mind and spirit; he acted, you will remember,
when Antony's mad frenzy was at its height, and we were dreading
the grim threat that his imminent return from Brundisium was
bringing to us all. He has generously poured out all his inherited
resources, or rather I should say that he has invested them in the
4 preservation of the *res publica*. We cannot thank him adequately for
this, but we must do so to the limit of our ability.

There is not one of us so naive, or so ignorant of public affairs as
to be unaware of what would have happened if Antony had been
able to carry out his threats, and had arrived from Brundisium with
the force which he expected that he would have; there's scarcely any
atrocity we should not have witnessed. While a guest under the roof
of a friend at Brundisium he ordered the murder of good men and
true, brave and valiant citizens. As they fell dying at his feet, his
wife's face was spattered with their blood, as everyone knows. When
he had been so inhuman there, how do you think he would have
reacted to all the men of standing here, to whom he bore a much
worse grudge than he did to those he massacred there? There is not
one of us he would have spared, nor any man of any standing at all.
5   This is the menace from which C. Caesar has of his own initiative
liberated the *res publica*; he took the only possible way, and had there
not been such a man as he, we would not now have any *res publica* at
all, thanks to Antony's villainy. For this is how I see it; in my opinion,
had a single young man not put an end to this fellow's mad attacks
and criminal designs, the *res publica* would have utterly collapsed.
Today therefore, gentlemen, which is the first day that we can enjoy
the gift of free speech that Caesar has given us, we must give him our
formal support, so that his defence of the *res publica* may be not just
his own private enterprise but a commission from us.
6   Similarly, we can now speak of the Martian legion; there is no
more valiant force, nor has there ever been one more devoted to the

res publica than the entire Martian legion. When it decided that Antony was an enemy of the Roman people, it declined to become a collaborator in his mad design. It deserted the consul, something it would not have done had it thought that he was really a consul. No, it saw that he was a man whose entire activities and plans were aimed at the slaughter of citizens and the destruction of the state. This legion has occupied Alba, which is the handiest city for participation in events here in Rome, as well as having a loyal population, which

7 is as gallant as it is devoted to the *res publica*. Under the leadership of our quaestor Lucius Egnatuleius, the Fourth legion followed the splendid lead of the Martian. That excellent and valiant officer brought it over to join the forces following Caesar's lead. It is our duty now, gentlemen, to pass a motion approving the initiative of this outstanding young man, and his present activities, and commending the valiant veterans, the Martian and the Fourth legions for their wonderful and united efforts to recover the *res publica*, and undertaking that as soon as our consuls-designate have entered their · office, we shall devote our attention to the question of their living-conditions, promotion and pay.

8   Now what I have said to you about C. Caesar and his army has been familiar enough to you for some time . . . but this recent edict of D. Brutus which has only just been published must certainly receive a mention. He undertakes to hold onto the province of Cisalpine Gaul, and to retain it under the jurisdiction of the Senate and Roman people. Here indeed is a true-born republican, who has not forgotten the ancestors from whom he got his name. Freedom was the watchword, in whose name our ancestors drove out Tarquin, but their anxiety to win their liberty was no more pressing than ours is to retain it by shaking the yoke of Antony from off our necks. Our ancestors had learned from the time the city was founded how to live under the rule of kings; we had forgotten, in all the years since the kings were expelled, what it means to be slaves.

Cicero then goes on to a comparison between Antony and Tarquin, one not favourable to Antony.

(b) Octavian's Family

Octavian's claim to leadership in Caesar's party was based entirely on his position as Caesar's legal heir. Antony had attacked his descent as well as his morals, and Cicero takes up the cudgels on his behalf. It is evident that in 44 it was still possible to use the non-Roman origin of a man's family as a political weapon in the same way that Cicero's opponents had done some 20 years before this time.

Philippic III, 15–17:

Antony's edicts are insulting and uncouth and primitive; take first the one directed against Caesar in which he piled up a stock of insults culled from his recollections of the sink of his own iniquities. In fact though, Caesar's youth has been a perfect model of good, clean living and self-control, and since he came of age he has been a distinguished example of old-fashioned integrity, whereas his detractor has always been the vilest of the vile. Antony has charged Caesar's son with being low-born, though his father would certainly have been consul had he lived long enough. 'His mother came from Aricia', Antony says – well, you'd think he'd said 'from Tralles' or 'from Ephesus'; you see how every one of us who come from the country boroughs are looked down upon – even though that means every single person present here today. After all, there is scarcely anyone who doesn't come from one, and a man who despises the borough of Aricia so much is bound to despise the others as well, since Aricia is one of the first to be founded; it had its own treaty with us, it is right on Rome's doorstep, it has a record of distinguished

16 sons; the authors of the Voconian and Atinian laws came from there, so have many curule magistrates both in our own day and in that of our fathers; its men of property are numerous and very prosperous.

But if you disapprove of having a wife from Aricia, why approve of one from Tusculum? Apart from anything else, the pure and excellent lady Atia's father, M. Atius Balbus, reached the rank of praetor, and the highest rank among men of integrity. But what about your own wife, Mark Antony? She is a good woman and well enough off, I suppose, but her father was a nobody called Bambalio; the name was given him because of his stammer and his innate stupidity, a sort of insult to the poor booby. 'His grandfather was a noble though', you say; I suppose you mean that Sempronius Tuditanus who used to dress like a Greek actor and shower the people with small change from the speakers' rostrum – what a good thing it would have been had he managed to hand on his lack of interest in money to his descendants.

So much then for the aristocratic descent of which he is so proud.
17 But I wonder how Antony thinks that the son of Julia is a low-born
person when he boasts at the same time of his own descent from the
same family on his mother's side? It is crazy in any case for a man
to talk of people marrying below them when his father married
Numitoria of Fregellae, a woman whose father had been a traitor,
and had begotten sons from the daughter of a freedman. But that's
not how real gentlemen have seen it; L. Philippus has a wife from
Aricia, C. Marcellus' mother-in-law is from there, and I know that
they have no cause to blush for their admirable ladies.

(c) The Last Hope of Saving the *Res Publica*

After arguing that Antony is a public enemy rather than a consul, Cicero
concludes his speech with a call to rally to what is the last chance of saving
the *res publica*, and proposes a series of motions calling on the Senate to
approve the actions taken by Octavian, D. Brutus, and the legions which
had abandoned Antony, and to strengthen the hand of Hirtius and Pansa
whose consulship was due to begin on January 1st, 43, some 12 days later.

Philippic III, 28–39:

Today, gentlemen of the Senate, for the first time for a long time
we are setting our feet onto the path that leads to the freedom for
which I fought as long as I could, and managed to preserve for a
time. But when this proved beyond me, I remained silent, and
nursed my resentment at the ending of those good old days, and
managed to retain some standing in the state by avoiding a dishonourable subservience. But nobody can tolerate Antony anyhow;
he's a perfect monster composed of lust and cruelty and ungovern-
able ferocity of temper; these are the whole of his make-up, since
he entirely lacks any sense of what is honest and decent or belongs
29 to a sane and modest sense of honour. Hence, since we have now
reached a critical point at which Antony must be punished for his
crimes against the *res publica*, or we must be slaves, let us, in Heaven's
name, gentlemen, now summon up at long last that fighting spirit
which is our national heritage, that we may recover the liberty
which is the birthright of all who bear the name of Roman, or
perish in the attempt.

We have endured much that is intolerable in a free state, some of us, I suppose, in the hope of recovering our freedom, others through clinging too fondly to life itself, but even if we have endured what necessity, by a sort of blind ordinance of fate, compelled us to tolerate – though in fact we got rid of it – shall we also endure to be ground under the filthy heel of this ferocious and tyrannical brigand?

30 For, if he gets the power, what will he do when he is incensed? So far he has shown himself the enemy of all men of standing when he had no cause for resentment against anyone. What will he stick at in the hour of triumph, whose crimes since Caesar's death are beyond reckoning, even though he has not yet had the licence granted by military victory?

He has emptied Caesar's house of its treasures, plundered his estates, and transferred all his valuables into his own possession; he has used Caesar's funeral as an excuse for provoking murder and arson; after two or three sound, constitutional decrees proposed in the Senate, he has converted public business into a source of plunder for personal enrichment. He has sold exemptions from taxation, he has freed whole cities from their obligations to the Exchequer, and has removed whole provinces from the jurisdiction of the Roman people's government; he has restored exiles, has had false laws and false decrees attributed to Caesar permanently recorded in the state's archives on the Capitol, and has established a private market in all these things. He has imposed laws on the Roman people, and excluded them and their magistrates from the forum by surrounding it with a force of armed guards; he has hedged the Senate round about with troops, and had armed men actually stationed in the temple of Concord while the Senate was in session there. He has run off to Brundisium to meet the troops, and has butchered all the soundest of the centurions; he has tried to march on Rome to

31 slaughter us and destroy the city. He was frustrated in this plan by Caesar and the forces he raised, the support he got from the veterans and the courage of the legions, but not even fortune could break his resolve or diminish his reckless behaviour or stop the onrush of his mad career. He is now leading his crippled army off to Cisalpine Gaul; he has one legion with him whose loyalty is questionable, and he is there waiting for his brother Lucius, who is just a carbon copy of himself. This beast-fighter turned commander, this gladiator turned general takes fire and sword with him wherever he goes. He bursts open the stores, slaughters the herds and flocks and any other

domestic animals that he can get his hands on; the soldiers feast royally, but like his brother, he's incapable with drink himself. The fields I say are being devastated, the country-houses are being plundered, married women, girls, boys of free birth, are all being kidnapped and given to the licentious soldiery, and Antony's army behaved just the same wherever he took it.

32 Will you open the gates of Rome to these brother-monsters? Will you ever allow them into the city? You have an opportunity before you; will you not use it? You have commanders ready to serve you, and troops agog for action. The Roman people is in sympathy with you, the whole of Italy is alive with the hope of recovering its liberty, the gods are with you. If you lose this chance, you will not get another; if Antony reaches Gaul, he will be surrounded, front and rear and on both flanks.

Moreover, we must put pressure on Antony by means of our decrees as well as by military action; when the Senate is of one mind, it has a great deal of power as well as a great moral effect. The forum is full, as you can see, as the Roman people is eagerly looking to recover its liberty; they see the large number of us here present for the first time in months, and they think that this means

33 we are now meeting as free men. This is the day I have been waiting for, for which I avoided the assaults of Antony's illegal forces at the time when he was attacking me behind my back without understanding the moment for which I was holding my hand. If I had been willing to reply to him at the time he opened his campaign to get rid of me, I would not now be able to serve the *res publica*. But now I have this opportunity I shall not let any time go by, either day or night, without considering what plans must be made to defend the liberty of the Roman people and your honour, what steps must be taken, and what we must achieve. This is a task I shall not decline; I shall look for it, and claim it as my own. I have always done this when I could; I stopped doing it only when I was frustrated. But now the opportunity is here; we have an obligation too, unless we prefer to live in slavery rather than put our heart and

34 soul into the battle against it. Heaven has provided us with two weapons, Caesar to defend the city, Brutus, Gaul. If Antony had been able to grab the city, we should have been enslaved then and there, and all men of quality and standing slaughtered, and the same would happen soon after if he is now able to grab (Cisalpine) Gaul.

But now you have this chance offered you, gentlemen of the Senate, grasp it, in heaven's name, and recall in time that you are the leaders of the world's greatest assembly. Show the Roman people that your counsel does not fail the *res publica*, since the people are showing that their courage will not fail it. I have no warnings to offer; none of you is so stupid as not to understand that if we go to sleep on this occasion we must bear with a humiliating tyranny, and one stained with crimes, and not just the normal cruelty and pride

35 of an arbitrary rule. You know Antony's arrogance, you know his friends, and his whole entourage; slavery reaches its summit of misery and shame when the masters are creatures of wanton lust, without any decency or morality, mere gamblers and drunkards.

But if the last hour of the *res publica* should come – which god forbid – and with it a fate I hardly dare describe, let us see that we, the leaders of all nations upon earth, do what proud gladiators do; let us prefer to die with our honour unsullied than to live in humiliat-

36 ing slavery. There is nothing so odious as humiliation, nothing so loathesome as slavery. We were born free, and meant to live in honour, and let us either preserve these things or die with our honour untarnished. Far too long we have concealed our thoughts, but all is in the open again now; every man, of every shade of opinion, openly expresses his opinions and his wishes. There are of course the disloyal – far too many of them when you consider the love we bear our country, but they are only a handful against the mass of patriots, – but the Powers-That-Be have given the *res publica* a remarkable and quite fortuitous opportunity to suppress them. In addition to the forces already at our disposal, we shall soon have a pair of wise and brave consuls, united in their policies, who have now for many months been engaged in thinking of the liberty of the Roman people. They will take the initiative and lead us; heaven will grant its blessing; we shall be vigilant to anticipate coming events; the Roman people will give us their backing – in short we shall soon be free, and the recollection of our past slavery will make the taste of freedom all the sweeter.

37   I therefore give you my verdict: the tribunes of the common people have asked for the Senate to receive protection for its meeting on the First of January (43), and for a promise of freedom of speech for all on all public questions; I therefore propose, firstly, that C. Pansa and A. Hirtius, consuls-designate, should take all steps

necessary to secure this. Secondly, in regard to the edict which D. Brutus, commander in the field, and consul-designate, has issued, I propose that the Senate should declare that Brutus deserves the thanks of the *res publica* for upholding the authority of the Senate, and defending the freedom and the dominions of the Roman people.

38 Thirdly, I propose that, as he is retaining command of the province of Cisalpine Gaul, and of its excellent, valiant, and loyal citizens, and of the army there, and maintaining it under the orders of the Senate, therefore we declare that he, and his army, and the boroughs and other towns of the province of Gaul have acted, and are acting, in a proper fashion, and in the public interest. Fourthly, I propose that the Senate declare that it is in the national interest that D. Brutus and L. Plancus, commanders in the field and consuls-designate, and the others who are governing provinces, should retain control of them under the terms of the Julian law until such time as a successor is appointed to each by decree of the Senate, and that they should take steps to ensure that these provinces and the armies therein remain under the control of the Senate and Roman people for the purpose of the defence of the *res publica*. Since Gaius Caesar (i.e. Octavian) acted for the defence of the *res publica* when he boldly took the initiative in thought and action, and secured the support of the veteran troops who followed his lead, and is now so acting, I propose that we declare that the Roman people has thereby been protected, and is now being protected from imminent disaster.

39 Sixthly, since the Martian legion stationed at Alba, a community as loyal as it is valiant, has joined the forces acting in support of the Senate's authority and the liberty of the Roman people, and since the Fourth legion under the command of L. Egnatuleius, our excellent quaestor and distinguished fellow-citizen, has shown comparable resolution and judgement in its past and present defence of the Senate's authority and the liberty of the Roman people, I propose that the Senate should declare that it is now resolved, and will remain resolved, that they shall be rewarded for their services to the *res publica*, and thanked for them. Finally, I propose that the Senate should resolve that C. Pansa and A. Hirtius, if they think fit, shall bring all these matters before this house for debate at the earliest opportunity in each case, in whatever manner they think most appropriate to their own honour and to the advantage of the *res publica*.

Postscript

This speech, and the *Fourth Philippic* (to the people) were triumphs. Cicero wrote to Trebonius (*Ad fam.* X, 28, 2): 'I embraced the whole *res publica* (in my speech); I spoke very forcefully, and recalled the Senate to its ancient, courageous ways, when it was already drooping in spirits and worn out. . . . This day, and the exertions I made in my speech, has kindled the Roman people's hope of recovering their freedom. After that, I never let up my planning for the *res publica* and acting on my plans as well'. 'That was the day', he wrote to Cornificius (*Ad fam.* XII, 25, 2), 'I first entered upon the hope of freedom, and though others hesitated, I laid the foundations of a real *res publica*'.

Fighting broke out in Cisalpine Gaul when D. Brutus refused to cede the province to Antony. Antony marched North across the Rubicon, and beseiged him in Mutina, while his brother, L. Antonius, marched into the area through Ariminum, according to Cicero (*Philippic* III, 31, above) acting like an enemy invader in the devastation he spread behind him. On January 1st, 43, the customary debate on the *res publica* began; it lasted four days. Cicero spoke the *Fifth Philippic* on the first day, but his attempt to secure a declaration of war against Antony failed. The final decision was to send an embassy to Antony, and in the evening of January 4th, Cicero addressed the *Sixth Philippic* to the people in the forum. He was now convinced that only a war leading to the crushing of Antony could again restore the *res publica*. Towards the end of January he spoke again; this was the *Seventh Philippic*. He recognised that the advocacy of war was a new departure for him, *Philippic* VII, 7–8: 'I am one who have always been an advocate of peace. I have always been among those principally concerned for peace, especially civil peace. Peace has always been the aim of all men of standing; the whole course of my efforts, in the forum, in the Senate house, in my defence of friends against attacks, has been directed to this. This has been the source of my highest honours, of my reasonable

prosperity, of the position I enjoy in men's estimation, such as it is ...
yet I do not want peace with Antony'.

To this end Cicero poured out the rest of his *Philippic* orations,
and a veritable flood of letters to sympathizers in the provinces.
Philippic XIV, 20: 'I have watched over the *res publica* from January
1st to this hour continuously, my house and my ears have been open
day and night to all the counsel and advice available. I have
written, I have sent messages, I have urged everyone, wherever they
may be, to come to the defence of their country'.

Cicero was eventually successful in having Antony declared a
public enemy; he was attacked and defeated by the combined
armies of Hirtius and Pansa (now consuls) and Octavian, to whom
a place in the Senate had been decreed when he was given pro-
praetorian command by a decree of the Senate on December 20th,
44. But this victory did not bring peace; it only brought another
war. Antony retreated across the Alps where he was joined by
Lepidus, and Lepidus too became a public enemy. Hirtius and
Pansa died, and young Octavian demanded one of the vacant
consulates. A refusal by the Senate, and the unwillingness of Caesar's
old soldiers to fight one another, led to the successive *coups d'état*
which produced Octavian's first consulate, and subsequently the
Triumvirate of Antony, Octavian and Lepidus, which was established on November 27th, 43, 'for the reconstruction of the *res
publica*'.

The triumvirs' first action was to murder their opponents, setting
a price upon their heads, and mutilating their corpses by decapita-
tion. This was the ultimate denial of any sort of *res publica*, that men
should die unheard and uncondemned, without charges, evidence
or defence, at the bidding of a military junta.

Many fell, including the elderly Cicero, but it was clear some
months before his death that this last attempt to save the *res publica*
had failed. Arms did not give place to civilians' gowns, as he had
dreamed, nor did wreaths of victory give place to words of praise.

Roman Money

The Romans calculated in very small units, either *sestertii* (notionally 4 *asses*, each of $\frac{1}{2}$ oz. of copper), which were copper coins, though none were minted in the late republic, or *denarii* (*nummi*, notionally 16 copper *asses*, or 4 *sestertii*), which were silver coins. *Denarii* weighed $\frac{1}{84}$ of 1 (Roman) pound, thus each weighed about $\frac{1}{7}$ ounce, so that the value of 1 sestertius is $\frac{1}{28}$ of an ounce of silver in bullion terms (Tenney Frank, Economic Survey of Ancient Rome, I, 47f.). In value for purchasing food, the grain-laws seem to have allowed each recipient 5 *modii* of wheat per month. Wheat cost (unsubsidized) about 3 *sestertii* per *modius* so that the cost of a month's wheat would be 15 *sestertii*, or just under 4 *denarii*; barley cost about $\frac{1}{2}$ to $\frac{2}{3}$ as much as wheat. The subsidized wheat seems to have cost 6 $\frac{1}{3}$ *asses* per *modius* till 58, when it became free.

Suggested Topics for Study

1. Suggest reasons why the *res publica* of Sulla's nobles failed to win the support of the Roman people.
2. Discuss how far Sulla's example influenced the political life of the *res publica* down to 49.
3. Discuss the claims of 'new men' as represented by Cicero; how far were they incompatible with those of the nobles?
4. 'The results of Catiline's conspiracy were more important than the conspiracy itself'. Discuss.
5. Why was '*concordia*' not a successful policy?
6. Discuss Pompey's role in the *res publica* after his return from Asia at the end of 62.
7. Discuss the claims of the noble *populares*, and Cicero's criticisms of them.
8. Discuss Caesar's policy of '*clementia*'; how far did it contribute to his initial success in 49 and subsequent failure?
9. '*Regnum*' and '*dominatio*': how far were these mere slogans in the life of the *res publica*?
10. What part did the Roman people play in the political life of the *res publica*?
11. Give an account of the main factors which determined the outcome of a Roman election.
12. How far was the Senate's method of working an important factor contributing to the weakness of the *res publica*?
13. What part did the courts (*quaestiones perpetuae*) play in the life of the *res publica*?
14. What part did religion play in the public life of the *res publica*?
15. 'Noble women were not treated as persons, but as pawns in the public life of the *res publica*.' Discuss.
16. 'The economic basis of a senator's career was at the root of the malaise from which the *res publica* suffered in Cicero's day.' Discuss.
17. 'The most important mechanisms in Roman politics were

unofficial – *patronatus* and *clientela*, *amicitia* and *inimicitia* and the like.' Discuss.

18. How far did the personal relationships between individual senators and the provincial communities affect the life of the *res publica*?

19. What were the main duties of Roman provincial governors, and what tools were they given for carrying them out?

20. Discuss Cicero's ideals for republican government; how far were they practicable?

21. How far did circumstances compel Cicero to modify his policies? Were such modifications sufficient to suggest that he lacked principle or consistency?

Index

The following does not claim to be a fully comprehensive index. Its main purpose is to pick up the subjects in the suggested essay topics, and the most important names in Cicero's career.

There is no entry under Cicero himself as this would involve every page of the book; the main stages of his career can be found in the 'Table of Contents' at the beginning of the book.

Ahenobarbus, Cn. Domitius, 225, 227

Ambitus, 4–5, 37, 39–40, 43, 51, 80, 95, 139, 156, 159, 161, 169, 177, 254, 258, 265–268, 273, 276

Amicitia/Amici, 5, 12, 73, 85, 107, 120, 146–7, 209, 254, 285, 290

Antonius, Marcus, 303–311, 313, 314–327

Asia, 71–86, 139, 163, 165, 167–171, 275–9

Atticus, T. Pomponius, 13–15, 151–165, 184, 196, 197, 252, 273, 279, 282, 283, 284, 286, 289, 310, 314, 315

Auspicia, 131, 208, 304–5, 308

Brutus, M., 285, 287, 288, 289, 299, 306–7, 313

Caelius Rufus, M., 225, 239–252, 282, 289

Caesar, C. Julius, 15, 87, 95–96, 131, 134, 151, 160–1, 162–165, 176, 199, 205, 225–227, 228–234, 252, 273–274, 290–301, 303–312, 322

Campus Martius, 8, 107, 110, 111, 131, 182, 213

Catilinarian Conspiracy, 115–139, 148, 153, 163, 205

Catiline, 87, 97, 115–139, 165, 172, 176

Cato, M. Porcius, 138, 151, 156,

159, 160, 162, 164, 177, 225, 274, 282, 291

Catulus, Q., 45–46, 83–86, 122–123, 155, 210, 219, 300

Cicero, Quintus, 15, 97, 132, 183, 194, 196, 197, 225, 226, 273, 275–279, 289

Cilicia, 68–69, 79, 85, 174, 274, 279, 282–289

Claudius, Appius, 221–222, 226, 287

Clientes/Clientela, 11, 104, 285, 290–291

Clodia, 165, 217, 225, 239–252

Clodius, P., 72, 151, 152, 153–155, 159, 163, 164–165, 175–176, 177, 178, 185–188, 190–193, 194–202, 205, 210–218, 225–227, 230, 236, 242–244, 252, 274

Comitia Centuriata, 8–9, 13, 107, 182, 268, 269

Concordia Ordinum, 134–138, 157–198, 225

Crassus, M. Licinius, 69–70, 87, 139, 152–153, 157, 162, 197, 226, 239, 252

Curio, C., 38–39, 86, 153, 164

Dignitas, 5, 6, 12, 124, 134, 140, 146, 151, 152, 155, 160, 174, 201, 205, 211, 212, 214, 216, 223, 224, 274, 277

Dominatio; see Regnum

Elections, 253–273

Equites, 3, 8, 13, 44, 84, 90–94, 118, 121, 135, 153, 154, 157–159, 160–161, 163, 164, 167, 173, 176, 214, 225, 257–259, 262–263, 271, 284

Gaul, 68, 78, 126, 160, 163, 174, 225, 227–233, 273, 314, 316–317, 319, 325, 326

Gracchus, Tiberius and Gaius Sempronius, 91, 103, 111–112, 133, 199, 209, 211, 227

Haruspices, 128, 194–196, 198, 201–202

Hortensius, Q., 38, 40, 43–44, 48, 64, 83–86, 113, 141, 153–154, 203

Inimicitia/Inimici, 5, 81–82, 137, 146–147, 166, 173, 225, 227–238, 254, 280, 294

Knights, see *Equites*

Laws/*Leges*, 87–95, 149–150, 206–207, 209, 213; Caesar's *ratio*, 274; Flavius' Agrarian Law, 159–160; law of adoption, 187; *lex Aelia*, 216; *lex Cornelia*, 93; *lex Fabia*, 110; *lex Gabinia*, 71; *lex Licinia*, 265; *lex Manilia*, 86; *lex Porcia*, 110–111; Sulla's proscription law, 26–27 *lex Sempronia*, 91–93; *lex Valeria de provocatione*, 176; *lex Vatinia*, 163

Libertas, 6–8, 60, 62, 93, 103, 105, 112, 135, 185, 202, 302, 310, 313, 319, 321–325, 326

Marius, C., 67, 68, 84, 87, 95, 141, 217, 229, 231, 260, 270, 272

Metellus Nepos, 139, 177, 197, 226

Milo, T. Annius, 177, 197–198, 206–207, 274

'New men', 13, 66–67, 100–103, 223, 257–262, 268–273

Nobiles, 2, 5, 28–29, 32, 37, 65, 66–67, 92, 100, 122, 139, 140–141, 155, 156, 163, 205, 223, 225, 257, 258–262, 268–273, 313

Optimates, 198–200, 207–224, 278

Otium, 98, 102, 106, 136, 176, 205, 208, 209, 211, 224–225, 292, 325–326

Patronatus, 1, 11, 148–149

Pax, 228–229, 233, 278–279

Pompey, Cn., 45–46, 68, 70, 72–86, 97, 139, 151, 152–153, 155–156, 159–165, 171, 176, 177, 179, 197–198, 200, 213, 225–227, 231, 233, 252–253, 273–274, 284, 285, 290–291, 299

Pontifices, 6, 107, 151, 185–193, 195, 230

Populares, 98, 107–115; noble *populares*, 151–184, 198–200, 208–223, 234; *popularis* consul, 102–105, 123, 145

Populus Romanus, and the *Concordia Ordinum*, 135–138; and the law, 93–95; Cicero's first speech as consul to, 100–106; Cicero on return from exile to, 182–184; freedom of, 6–8; in Asia, 73–76; rights of, 61–66; Verres' crimes against, 57–63; other references, 39, 44, 45, 67, 82, 91, 107, 111, 113, 121, 134, 144, 167, 208, 211, 216, 217, 220, 253, 255, 293, 310, 325, 326

Provincial government, 5, 47–51, 163, 227–238, 274, 275–289, 325

Quaestiones perpetuae, 4–5, 17, 44–47, 66, 87–90, 95, 209

Regnum, 2, 16, 92, 124, 139, 140–143

Res Repetundae, 39, 43–47, 56–57

Senate: and a rigged vote, 153–154; and Antony, 307–310; and Catiline, 115–118; and Cicero's recall, 180–182; and judicial scandals, 45–47; and the *Concordia Ordinum*, 135–138; career of a Senator, 90–94; Cicero's speech on the *populares*, 98–100; composition of, 2–4, 9–10; in disturbed times, 178–180; precedents established by, 84–85; quarrels with *Equites*, 157–160; other references, 6, 44, 84–85, 97, 107, 108, 120, 121, 130, 131, 150, 163, 167, 186, 193, 208, 213, 217, 223, 226, 253, 267, 274, 290, 300, 304, 314, 321

Sicily, 33–36, 47–63, 78, 79, 84, 169

Spain, 78, 79, 83, 160, 174, 226, 227, 274, 290, 300

Sulla, Lucius Cornelius, 4, 16–31, 34, 78, 83, 86, 87, 91, 96, 97, 124, 148, 277

Taxation, 3, 71–72, 75–76, 157, 159, 161, 201, 261, 264, 278, 283, 288

Tribunes, 6, 99, 103–105, 150, 154, 163, 177, 178, 186, 190, 204, 206, 216, 225, 268, 270, 274, 311, 313, 316, 324

Verres, C., 4, 33, 34–67, 87

Vestal Virgins, 128, 132, 151, 243

Vis, 4, 197–198, 202–207

Women, 11, 25, 49, 68–69, 214, 243, 263, 301–303